Suzuki Intruder, Marauder, Volusia, C50, M50 & S50

Service and Repair Manual

by Alan Ahlstrand

Models covered

VS700/750/800 Intruder, 1985 thru 2004
VZ800 Marauder, 1997 thru 2004
VL800 Volusia, 2001 thru 2004
Boulevard C50, 2005 thru 2009
Boulevard M50, 2005 thru 2009
Boulevard S50, 2005 thru 2009

ABCDE
FGHIJ
KLMNO

(2618 - 7Q3)

© Haynes North America, Inc. 2006, 2009
With permission from J.H. Haynes & Co. Ltd.

A book in the **Haynes Service and Repair Manual Series**

All rights reserved. No part of this book may be reproduced or transmitted in any form or by any means, electronic or mechanical, including photocopying, recording or by any information storage or retrieval system, without permission in writing from the copyright holder.

ISBN-13: **978-1-56392-779-9**
ISBN-10: **1-56392-779-9**

Library of Congress Control Number: 2009931527
Printed in the USA

Haynes Publishing
Sparkford, Nr Yeovil, Somerset BA22 7JJ, England

Haynes North America, Inc
861 Lawrence Drive, Newbury Park, California 91320, USA

09-248

Contents

LIVING WITH YOUR SUZUKI

Introduction

Suzuki - Every Which Way	Page	0•4
Acknowledgements	Page	0•8
About this manual	Page	0•8
Identification numbers	Page	0•10
Buying spare parts	Page	0•10
Safety first!	Page	0•11

Daily (pre-ride) checks

Engine/transmission oil level check	Page	0•12
Coolant level check	Page	0•13
Brake fluid level checks	Page	0•14
Tire checks	Page	0•15

MAINTENANCE

Routine maintenance and servicing

Specifications	Page	1•1
Recommended lubricants and fluids	Page	1•2
Component locations	Page	1•4
Maintenance schedule	Page	1•6
Maintenance procedures	Page	1•8

Contents

REPAIRS AND OVERHAUL

Engine, transmission and associated systems

Engine, clutch and transmission	Page	**2•1**
Cooling system	Page	**3•1**
Fuel and exhaust systems - carbureted models	Page	**4A•1**
Fuel, engine management and exhaust systems - fuel injected models	Page	**4B•1**
Ignition system	Page	**5•1**

Chassis and bodywork components

Steering	Page	**6•1**
Suspension	Page	**6•11**
Final drive	Page	**6•14**
Brakes	Page	**7•1**
Wheels	Page	**7•11**
Tires	Page	**7•14**
Frame and bodywork	Page	**8•1**

Electrical system

	Page	**9•1**

Wiring diagrams

	Page	**9•23**

REFERENCE

Dimensions and Weights	Page	**REF•1**
Tools and Workshop Tips	Page	**REF•4**
Conversion Factors	Page	**REF•22**
Motorcycle chemicals and lubricants	Page	**REF•23**
Storage	Page	**REF•24**
Troubleshooting	Page	**REF•27**
Troubleshooting equipment	Page	**REF•36**
Technical terms explained	Page	**REF•41**

Index

	Page	**REF•49**

Suzuki Every Which Way

by Julian Ryder

From Textile Machinery to Motorcycles

Suzuki were the second of Japan's Big Four motorcycle manufacturers to enter the business, and like Honda they started by bolting small two-stroke motors to bicycles. Unlike Honda, they had manufactured other products before turning to transportation in the aftermath of World War II. In fact Suzuki has been in business since the first decade of the 20th-Century when Michio Suzuki manufactured textile machinery.

The desperate need for transport in post-war Japan saw Suzuki make their first motorised bicycle in 1952, and the fact that by 1954 the company had changed its name to Suzuki Motor Company shows how quickly the sideline took over the whole company's activities. In their first full manufacturing year, Suzuki made nearly 4500 bikes and rapidly expanded into the world markets with a range of two-strokes.

Suzuki didn't make a four-stroke until 1977 when the GS750 double-overhead-cam across-the-frame four arrived. This was several years after Honda and Kawasaki had established the air-cooled four as the industry standard, but no motorcycle epitomises the era of what came to be known as the Universal

The T500 two-stroke twin

Introduction

One of the later GT750 'kettle' models with front disc brakes

50 cc racer won six of the eight world titles chalked up by Suzuki during the 1960s as well as providing Mitsuo Itoh with the distinction of being the only Japanese rider to win an Isle of Man TT. Mr Itoh still works for Suzuki, he's in charge of their racing program.

Europe got the benefit of Suzuki's two-stroke expertise in a succession of air-cooled twins, the six-speed 250 cc Super Six being the most memorable, but the arrival in 1968 of the first of a series of 500 cc twins which were good looking, robust and versatile marked the start of mainstream success.

So confident were Suzuki of their two-stroke expertise that they even applied it to the burgeoning Superbike sector. The GT750 water-cooled triple arrived in 1972. It was big, fast and comfortable although the handling and stopping power did draw some comment. Whatever the drawbacks of the road bike, the engine was immensely successful in Superbike and Formula 750 racing. The roadster has its devotees, though, and is now a sought-after bike on the classic Japanese scene. Do not refer to it as the Water Buffalo in such company. Joking aside, the later disc-braked versions were quite civilised, but the audacious idea of using a big two-stroke motor in what was essentially a touring bike was a surprising success until the fuel crisis of the mid-'70s effectively killed off big strokers.

The same could be said of Suzuki's only real lemon, the RE5. This is still the only mass-produced bike to use the rotary (or Wankel) engine but never sold well. Fuel consumption in the mid-teens allied to frightening complexity and excess weight meant the RE5 was a non-starter in the sales race.

Japanese motorcycle better than the GS. So well engineered were the original fours that you can clearly see their genes in the GS500 twins that are still going strong in the mid-1990s. Suzuki's ability to prolong the life of their products this way means that they are often thought of as a conservative company. This is hardly fair if you look at some of their landmark designs, most of which have been commercial as well as critical successes.

Two-stroke Success

Early racing efforts were bolstered by the arrival of Ernst Degner who defected from the East German MZ team at the Swedish GP of 1961, bringing with him the rotary-valve secrets of design genius Walter Kaaden. The new Suzuki 50 cc racer won its first GP on the Isle of Man the following year and winning the title easily. Only Honda and Ralph Bryans interrupted Suzuki's run of 50 cc titles from 1962 to 1968.

The arrival of the twin-cylinder 125 racer in 1963 enabled Hugh Anderson to win both 50 and 125 world titles. You may not think 50 cc racing would be exciting - until you learn that the final incarnation of the thing had 14 gears and could do well over 100 mph on fast circuits. Before pulling out of GPs in 1967 the

Suzuki's GT250X7 was an instant hit in the popular 250 cc 'learner' sector

Introduction

The GS400 was the first in a line of four-stroke twins

Development of the Four-stroke range

When Suzuki got round to building a four-stroke they did a very good job of it. The GS fours were built in 550, 650, 750, 850, 1000 and 1100 cc sizes in sports, custom, roadster and even shaft-driven touring forms over many years. The GS1000 was in on the start of Superbike racing in the early 1970s and the GS850 shaft-driven tourer was around nearly 15 years later. The fours spawned a line of 400, 425, 450 and 500 cc GS twins that were essentially the middle half of the four with all their reliability. If there was ever a criticism of the GS models it was that with the exception of the GS1000S of 1980, colloquially known as the ice-cream van, the range was visually uninspiring.

They nearly made the same mistake when they launched the four-valve-head GSX750 in 1979. Fortunately, the original twin-shock version was soon replaced by the 'E'-model with Full-Floater rear suspension and a full set of all the gadgets the Japanese industry was then keen on and has since forgotten about, like 16-inch front wheels and anti-dive forks. The air-cooled GSX was like the GS built in 550, 750 and 1100 cc versions with a variety of half, full and touring fairings, but the GSX that is best remembered is the Katana that first appeared in 1981. The power was provided by an 1000 or 1100 cc GSX motor, but wrapped around it was the most outrageous styling package to come out of Japan. Designed by Hans Muth of Target Design, the Katana looked like nothing seen before or since. At the time there was as much anti feeling as praise, but now it is rightly regarded as a classic, a true milestone in motorcycle design. The factory have even started making 250 and 400 cc fours for the home market with the same styling as the 1981 bike.

Just to remind us that they'd still been building two-strokes for the likes of Barry Sheene, in 1986 Suzuki marketed a road-going version of their RG500 square-four racer which had put an end to the era of the four-stroke in 500 GPs when it appeared in 1974. In 1976 Suzuki not only won their first 500 title with Sheene, they sold RG500s over the counter and won every GP with them - with the exception of the Isle of Man TT which the works riders boycotted. Ten years on, the RG500 Gamma gave road riders the nearest experience they'd ever get to riding a GP bike. The fearsome beast could top 140 mph and only weighed 340 lb - the other alleged GP replicas were pussy cats compared to the Gamma's man-eating tiger.

The RG only lasted a few years and is already firmly in the category of collector's item; its four-stroke equivalent, the GSX-R, is still with us and looks like being so for many years. You have to look back to 1985 and its launch to realise just what a revolutionary step the GSX-R750 was: quite simply it was the first race replica. Not a bike dressed up to look like a race bike, but a genuine racer with lights on, a bike that could be taken straight to the track and win.

The first GSX-R, the 750, had a completely new motor cooled by oil rather than water and an aluminium cradle frame. It was sparse, a little twitchy and very, very fast. This time Suzuki got the looks right, blue and white bodywork based on the factory's racing colours and endurance-racer lookalike twin headlights. And then came the 1100 - the big GSX-R got progressively more brutal as it chased the Yamaha EXUP for the heavyweight championship.

And alongside all these mould-breaking designs, Suzuki were also making the best looking custom bikes to come out of Japan, the Intruders; the first race replica trail bike,

The GS750 led the way for a series of four cylinder models

Introduction 0•7

Later four-stroke models, like this GSX1100, were fitted with 16v engines

the DR350; the sharpest 250 Supersports, the RGV250; and a bargain-basement 600, the Bandit. The Bandit proved so popular they went on to build 1200 and 750 cc versions of it. I suppose that's predictable, a range of four-stroke fours just like the GS and GSXs. It's just like the company really, sometimes predictable, admittedly - but never boring.

It's a V-twin Jim, but not as we know it

The late 1990s was a time when Honda and Suzuki decided it was time to keep up with their Italian neighbours at Ducati and build a V-twin. Both built a softer, road orientated version and a harder-edged model to homologate for Superbike racing. Honda's bike was uncontroversial, and did exactly what it said on the tin. Suzuki's didn't.

Everybody agreed the TL1000S had a great engine that felt just like a big V-twin should and that in the days before the R1 it was as quick as you could want. Then rumours started circulating about some nasty habits. Some reports in specialist magazines said the TL was prone to vicious tank-slappers; others equally vehemently said the rumours were rubbish. It was enough to persuade the British importer to retro-fit steering dampers, and suspicion centred on the rear suspension system and its innovative (or weird, depending on which camp you were in) rotary damper. After some unpleasant accidents and subsequent court cases, things quietened down. The steering damper certainly helped and fuel-injection tweaks that smoothed out the power delivery on later models helped riders keep the bike under control. However, the model's reputation was seriously damaged and a lot of people fought shy of the TL – which means second-hand examples are satisfyingly cheap for those in the know.

The R-model isn't just a modified version of the S, it's a completely different machine. This was the bike that was supposed to take on Ducati on the tracks and take over Suzuki's racing efforts from the ageing and now out-gunned GSX-R750. It didn't happen. The R was still high, long and, at nearly 200 kg dry, heavy. They did turn up on race tracks but never made it to the World Superbike grid. The Alstare Corona organisation that ran the works World Superbike effort secretly developed a race-ready TL1000R with multiple World Superbike winner and World Endurance Champion Stephane Mertens of Belgium as the test rider. However, even the team that kept the old 750 competitive well after its sell-by date couldn't get the big twin competitive.

The motor did win a race though, but in a Bimota chassis.

Aussie wild child Anthony Gobert rode a Bimota SB8 with TL1000 motor for the first part of the 2000 season. He scored points in race two of the opening round of the year in South Africa then with an inspired tyre gamble on a drying Phillip Island track at home in Oz he won the first race of round two and followed it up with ninth place in the second race. Next time out in Japan, it blew up spectacularly, flinging Gobert down the track and following him into the barriers. Even the Go-Show admitted it was a crash that scared him severely as well as giving him a collection of minor fractures and burns. The team folded soon afterwards, citing lack of funds. The whole episode summed up the TL's relationship with the race track.

Nothing daunted, Suzuki took another cue from Honda and put their V-twin in a giant trailbike, and again just like Honda they gave it a very strange name, the V-Strom (that is not a misprint). Pushing peak power down to produce more midrange and bottom end made for a very nice motor which suited the chassis brilliantly. The V-Strom, along with its compatriots in the giant trailbike class, is sadly under-rated by those obsessed with sports bikes, but it's the sort of machine on which you can load two people and their luggage and set off to travel on anything from motorways to dirt tracks and enjoy it.

Suzuki's GSX-R range represented their cutting edge sports bikes

Introduction

The TL1000S-W

The TL1000R-K1

The DL1000-K2 V-Strom

It would be a shame to consign such a great motor to an early grave so unappreciated, so Suzuki went back to the original TL, the S, and re-invented the bike as a budget sportster in the SV range. It may wear a different designation, but the SV has all the DNA of the TL. With the exception of that strange damper.

Suzuki's first major success in the V-twin cruiser market came with the 750 Intruder in 1985. Using a liquid-cooled engine with a 45-degree angle between the cylinders, twin-shock rear suspension and shaft drive, the bike gave Suzuki a credible entry in the category.

Displacement was reduced to 700cc (and the model designation changed to VS700) for US models in 1986 and 1987. This was in response to a tariff on Japanese bikes over 700cc, which was designed to protect Harley-Davidson, at that time in severe financial peril. The tariff was rescinded at HD's request as their business picked up, and displacement on US models was returned to 750cc in 1988.

The VZ800 Marauder added some styling variety to Suzuki's cruiser line, beginning in 1997. The bike was mechanically almost the same as the Intruder, with chain drive being the most important difference.

The VL800 Volusia, added to the line in 2001, was more of a cruiser than a chopper. It used a single carburetor, rather than the dual carbs of the Intruder and Marauder. The fuel tank was wide, the fenders swoopy, and the front forks made to look plump with the addition of trim covers on the upper fork legs.

The Intruder was renamed the Boulevard S50 (as in 50 cubic inches of piston displacement) for 2005. Mechanically, it's almost unchanged from the Intruder.

The Marauder was renamed the Boulevard M50 for 2005. Its carburetors were replaced by a dual-throttle fuel injection system.

The Volusia was renamed the Boulevard C50 for 2005 and equipped with the same fuel injection system as the M50.

Acknowledgements

Our thanks are due to Grand Prix Sports of Santa Clara, California, for supplying the motorcycles used in the photographs throughout this manual; Mark Zueger, service manager, for arranging the facilities and fitting the project into his shop's busy schedule; and Craig Wardner, service technician, for doing the mechanical work and providing valuable technical information. The introduction "Suzuki – Every Which Way" was written by Julian Ryder, with additional information on the models covered in this manual by Alan Ahlstrand.

About this manual

The aim of this manual is to help you get the best value from your motorcycle. It can do so in several ways. It can help you decide what work must be done, even if you choose to have it done by a dealer; it provides information

Identification numbers

and procedures for routine maintenance and servicing; and it offers diagnostic and repair procedures to follow when trouble occurs.

We hope you use the manual to tackle the work yourself. For many simpler jobs, doing it yourself may be quicker than arranging an appointment to get the motorcycle into a dealer and making the trips to leave it and pick it up. More importantly, a lot of money can be saved by avoiding the expense the shop must pass on to you to cover its labor and overhead costs. An added benefit is the sense of satisfaction and accomplishment that you feel after doing the job yourself.

References to the left or right side of the motorcycle assume you are sitting on the seat, facing forward.

We take great pride in the accuracy of information given in this manual, but motorcycle manufacturers make alterations and design changes during the production run of a particular motorcycle of which they do not inform us. No liability can be accepted by the authors or publishers for loss, damage or injury caused by any errors in, or omissions from, the information given.

Engine and frame numbers

The frame serial number is stamped into the right side of the steering head. The engine number is stamped into the top rear of the crankcase and is visible from the right side of the machine. Both of these numbers should be recorded and kept in a safe place so they can be given to law enforcement officials in the event of a theft.

The frame serial number and engine serial number should also be kept in a handy place (such as with your driver's license) so they are always available when purchasing or ordering parts for your machine.

Identification numbers

Buying spare parts

Once you have found all the identification numbers, record them for reference when buying parts. Since the manufacturers change specifications, parts and vendors (companies that manufacture various components on the machine), providing the ID numbers is the only way to be reasonably sure that you are buying the correct parts.

Whenever possible, take the worn part to the dealer so direct comparison with the new component can be made. Along the trail from the manufacturer to the parts shelf, there are numerous places that the part can end up with the wrong number or be listed incorrectly.

The two places to purchase new parts for your motorcycle – the accessory store and the franchised dealer – differ in the type of parts they carry. While dealers can obtain virtually every part for your motorcycle, the accessory dealer is usually limited to normal high wear items such as shock absorbers, tune-up parts, various engine gaskets, cables, chains, brake parts, etc. Rarely will an accessory outlet have major suspension components, cylinders, transmission gears, or cases.

Used parts can be obtained for considerably less than new ones, but you can't always be sure of what you're getting. Once again, take your worn part to the salvage yard for direct comparison.

Whether buying new, used or rebuilt parts, the best course is to deal directly with someone who specializes in parts for your particular make.

The engine number is stamped into the back of the crankcase

The frame serial number is stamped into the right side of the steering head

Safety first!

Professional mechanics are trained in safe working procedures. However enthusiastic you may be about getting on with the job at hand, take the time to ensure that your safety is not put at risk. A moment's lack of attention can result in an accident, as can failure to observe simple precautions.

There will always be new ways of having accidents, and the following is not a comprehensive list of all dangers; it is intended rather to make you aware of the risks and to encourage a safe approach to all work you carry out on your bike.

Asbestos

● Certain friction, insulating, sealing and other products - such as brake pads, clutch linings, gaskets, etc. - contain asbestos. Extreme care must be taken to avoid inhalation of dust from such products since it is hazardous to health. If in doubt, assume that they do contain asbestos.

Fire

● Remember at all times that gasoline is highly flammable. Never smoke or have any kind of naked flame around, when working on the vehicle. But the risk does not end there - a spark caused by an electrical short-circuit, by two metal surfaces contacting each other, by careless use of tools, or even by static electricity built up in your body under certain conditions, can ignite gasoline vapor, which in a confined space is highly explosive. Never use gasoline as a cleaning solvent. Use an approved safety solvent.

● Always disconnect the battery ground terminal before working on any part of the fuel or electrical system, and never risk spilling fuel on to a hot engine or exhaust.

● It is recommended that a fire extinguisher of a type suitable for fuel and electrical fires is kept handy in the garage or workplace at all times. Never try to extinguish a fuel or electrical fire with water.

Fumes

● Certain fumes are highly toxic and can quickly cause unconsciousness and even death if inhaled to any extent. Gasoline vapor comes into this category, as do the vapors from certain solvents such as trichloro-ethylene. Any draining or pouring of such volatile fluids should be done in a well ventilated area.

● When using cleaning fluids and solvents, read the instructions carefully. Never use materials from unmarked containers - they may give off poisonous vapors.

● Never run the engine of a motor vehicle in an enclosed space such as a garage. Exhaust fumes contain carbon monoxide which is extremely poisonous; if you need to run the engine, always do so in the open air or at least have the rear of the vehicle outside the workplace.

The battery

● Never cause a spark, or allow a naked light near the vehicle's battery. It will normally be giving off a certain amount of hydrogen gas, which is highly explosive.

● Always disconnect the battery ground terminal before working on the fuel or electrical systems (except where noted).

● If possible, loosen the filler plugs or cover when charging the battery from an external source. Do not charge at an excessive rate or the battery may burst.

● Take care when topping up, cleaning or carrying the battery. The acid electrolyte, even when diluted, is very corrosive and should not be allowed to contact the eyes or skin. Always wear rubber gloves and goggles or a face shield. If you ever need to prepare electrolyte yourself, always add the acid slowly to the water; never add the water to the acid.

Electricity

● When using an electric power tool, inspection light etc., always ensure that the appliance is correctly connected to its plug and that, where necessary, it is properly grounded. Do not use such appliances in damp conditions and, again, beware of creating a spark or applying excessive heat in the vicinity of fuel or fuel vapor. Also ensure that the appliances meet national safety standards.

● A severe electric shock can result from touching certain parts of the electrical system, such as the spark plug wires (HT leads), when the engine is running or being cranked, particularly if components are damp or the insulation is defective. Where an electronic ignition system is used, the secondary (HT) voltage is much higher and could prove fatal.

Remember...

✗ **Don't** start the engine without first ascertaining that the transmission is in neutral.

✗ **Don't** suddenly remove the pressure cap from a hot cooling system - cover it with a cloth and release the pressure gradually first, or you may get scalded by escaping coolant.

✗ **Don't** attempt to drain oil until you are sure it has cooled sufficiently to avoid scalding you.

✗ **Don't** grasp any part of the engine or exhaust system without first ascertaining that it is cool enough not to burn you.

✗ **Don't** allow brake fluid or antifreeze to contact the machine's paintwork or plastic components.

✗ **Don't** siphon toxic liquids such as fuel, hydraulic fluid or antifreeze by mouth, or allow them to remain on your skin.

✗ **Don't** inhale dust - it may be injurious to health (see Asbestos heading).

✗ **Don't** allow any spilled oil or grease to remain on the floor - wipe it up right away, before someone slips on it.

✗ **Don't** use ill-fitting wrenches or other tools which may slip and cause injury.

✗ **Don't** lift a heavy component which may be beyond your capability - get assistance.

✗ **Don't** rush to finish a job or take unverified short cuts.

✗ **Don't** allow children or animals in or around an unattended vehicle.

✗ **Don't** inflate a tire above the recommended pressure. Apart from overstressing the carcass, in extreme cases the tire may blow off forcibly.

✔ **Do** ensure that the machine is supported securely at all times. This is especially important when the machine is blocked up to aid wheel or fork removal.

✔ **Do** take care when attempting to loosen a stubborn nut or bolt. It is generally better to pull on a wrench, rather than push, so that if you slip, you fall away from the machine rather than onto it.

✔ **Do** wear eye protection when using power tools such as drill, sander, bench grinder etc.

✔ **Do** use a barrier cream on your hands prior to undertaking dirty jobs - it will protect your skin from infection as well as making the dirt easier to remove afterwards; but make sure your hands aren't left slippery. Note that long-term contact with used engine oil can be a health hazard.

✔ **Do** keep loose clothing (cuffs, ties etc. and long hair) well out of the way of moving mechanical parts.

✔ **Do** remove rings, wristwatch etc., before working on the vehicle - especially the electrical system.

✔ **Do** keep your work area tidy - it is only too easy to fall over articles left lying around.

✔ **Do** exercise caution when compressing springs for removal or installation. Ensure that the tension is applied and released in a controlled manner, using suitable tools which preclude the possibility of the spring escaping violently.

✔ **Do** ensure that any lifting tackle used has a safe working load rating adequate for the job.

✔ **Do** get someone to check periodically that all is well, when working alone on the vehicle.

✔ **Do** carry out work in a logical sequence and check that everything is correctly assembled and tightened afterwards.

✔ **Do** remember that your vehicle's safety affects that of yourself and others. If in doubt on any point, get professional advice.

● If in spite of following these precautions, you are unfortunate enough to injure yourself, seek medical attention as soon as possible.

Daily (pre-ride) checks

1 Engine/transmission oil level check

Before you start:
✔ Start the engine and allow it to reach normal operating temperature.

Caution: Do not run the engine in an enclosed space such as a garage or workshop.

✔ Stop the engine and support the motorcycle on its sidestand. Allow it to stand undisturbed for a few minutes to allow the oil level to stabilize. Make sure the motorcycle is on level ground.

✔ The oil level is viewed through the window in the clutch cover on the right-hand side of the engine. Wipe the glass clean before inspection to make the check easier.

Bike care:
● If you have to add oil frequently, you should check whether you have any oil leaks. If there is no sign of oil leakage from the joints and gaskets the engine could be burning oil (see *Troubleshooting*).

The correct oil
● Modern, high-revving engines place great demands on their oil. It is very important that the correct oil for your bike is used.
● Always top up with a good quality oil of the specified type and viscosity and do not overfill the engine.

Oil type
SAE 10W-40, API grade SF/SG or SH/SJ meeting JASO standard MA - the MA standard is required to prevent clutch slippage.

The oil filler cap is located at the top of the right crankcase cover. Unscrew the cap to add oil. Add the specified oil to bring the level to the upper mark on the inspection window, but don't overfill.

Daily (pre-ride) checks 0•13

2 Coolant level check

> ⚠ **Warning: DO NOT remove the filler neck pressure cap to add coolant. Topping up is done via the coolant reservoir tank filler. DO NOT leave open containers of coolant about, as it is poisonous.**

Before you start:

✔ Make sure you have a supply of coolant available (a mixture of 50% distilled water and 50% corrosion inhibited ethylene glycol anti-freeze is needed).
✔ Always check the coolant level when the engine is cold.

Caution: Do not run the engine in an enclosed space such as a garage or workshop.
✔ Ensure the motorcycle is held vertical while checking the coolant level. Make sure the motorcycle is on level ground.

Bike care:

● Use only the specified coolant mixture. It is important that anti-freeze is used in the system all year round, and not just in the winter. Do not top the system up using only water, as the system will become too diluted.
● Do not overfill the reservoir tank. If the coolant is significantly above the F (full) level line at any time, the surplus should be siphoned or drained off to prevent the possibility of it being expelled out of the overflow hose.
● If the coolant level falls steadily, check the system for leaks (see Chapter 1). If no leaks are found and the level continues to fall, it is recommended that the machine is taken to a Suzuki dealer for a pressure test.
● **NOTE:** *These procedures apply only to C50 and M50 models. Intruder, S50, Volusia and Marauder models do not have a coolant reservoir system. Coolant level on these models is check and adjusted as described in Chapter 1.*

1 The coolant reservoir is located on the left side of the bike. The coolant level lines on the side of the reservoir are visible through a window in the side cover.

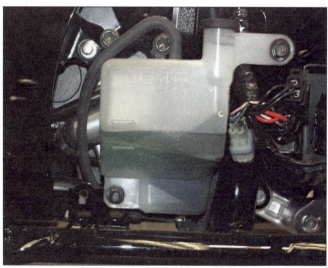

2 Pull off the cap, add coolant to bring the level to the upper line, then tighten the cap securely.

3 Brake and clutch fluid level check

The rear brake fluid level check only applies to Vulcan 800 Drifter models.

> ⚠ **Warning:** Hydraulic fluid can harm your eyes and damage painted surfaces, so use extreme caution when handling and pouring it and cover surrounding surfaces with rag. Do not use fluid that has been standing open for some time, as it absorbs moisture from the air which can cause a dangerous loss of braking effectiveness.

Before you start:

✔ Ensure the motorcycle is held vertical while checking the levels. Make sure the motorcycle is on level ground.

✔ Make sure you have the correct hydraulic fluid. DOT 4 is recommended. Never reuse old fluid.

✔ Wrap a rag around the reservoir being worked on to ensure that any spillage does not come into contact with painted surfaces.

Bike care:

● The fluid in the front and rear brake master cylinder reservoirs will drop slightly as the brake pads wear down.

● If any fluid reservoir requires repeated topping-up this is an indication of a hydraulic leak somewhere in the system, which should be investigated immediately.

● Check for signs of fluid leakage from the hydraulic hoses and components – if found, rectify immediately.

● Check the operation of both brakes before taking the machine on the road; if there is evidence of air in the system (spongy feel to lever or pedal), it must be bled as described in Chapter 7.

1 With the front brake fluid reservoir as level as possible, check that the fluid level is above the LOWER level line on the inspection window. If the level is below the LOWER level line, remove the cover screws (arrows) and lift off the cover and diaphragm. Top up fluid to the upper level line; don't overfill the reservoir, and take care to avoid spills (see WARNING above). Compress the diaphragm, reinstall the diaphragm and cover and tighten the screws securely.

2 If the motorcycle has a hydraulic clutch (Intruder and S50 models), check the clutch fluid level in the same manner as the brake fluid level. Use the same fluid for clutch and brakes.

3 Check rear brake lining wear. Press the brake pedal and note the position of the wear indicator pointer. If it's past the BRAKE LINING WEAR LIMIT area cast on the brake drum, it's time for new brake shoes (see Chapter 7).

Daily (pre-ride) checks 0•15

4 Tire checks

The correct pressures:
- The tires must be checked when **cold**, not immediately after riding. Note that low tire pressures may cause the tire to slip on the rim or come off. High tire pressures will cause abnormal tread wear and unsafe handling.
- Use an accurate pressure gauge.
- Proper air pressure will increase tire life and provide maximum stability and ride comfort.

Tire care:
- Check the tires carefully for cuts, tears, embedded nails or other sharp objects and excessive wear. Operation of the motorcycle with excessively worn tires is extremely hazardous, as traction and handling are directly affected.
- Check the condition of the tire valve and ensure the dust cap is in place.
- Pick out any stones or nails which may have become embedded in the tire tread. If left, they will eventually penetrate through the casing and cause a puncture.
- If tire damage is apparent, or unexplained loss of pressure is experienced, seek the advice of a tire fitting specialist without delay.

Tire tread depth:
- Suzuki recommends a minimum of 1.6 mm on the front tire. The minimum on the rear tire is 2 mm.
- Many tires now incorporate wear indicators in the tread. Identify the triangular pointer or 'TWI' mark on the tire sidewall to locate the indicator bar and replace the tire if the tread has worn down to the bar.

Final drive checks:
- On chain drive models, check the drive chain slack isn't excessive and adjust it if necessary (see Chapter 1).
- On chain drive models, lubricate the chain if it looks dry (see Chapter 1).
- On shaft drive models, inspect the differential for oil leakage and check the oil level if leaks can be seen (see Chapter 1).

Tire pressures

Intruder and S50	
Solo rider	
Front	29 psi (200 kPa)
Rear	33 psi (225 kPa)
Rider and passenger	
Front	33 psi (225 kPa)
Rear	36 psi (250 kPa)
Marauder	
Front	29 psi (200 kPa)
Rear	33 psi (225 kPa)
Volusia and M50	
Front	29 psi (200 kPa)
Rear	36 psi (250 kPa)
C50	
Front	33 psi (225 kPa)
Rear	36 psi (250 kPa)

1 Check the tire pressures when the tires are **cold** and keep them properly inflated.

2 Measure tread depth at the center of the tire using a tread depth gauge.

3 Tire tread wear indicator bar and its location marking (usually either an arrow, a triangle or the letters TWI) on the sidewall (arrowed).

Daily (pre-ride) checks

Notes

Chapter 1
Tune-up and routine maintenance

Contents

Air filter element - servicing	18
Battery electrolyte level/specific gravity - check	12
Brake pads and linings - wear check	5
Brake pedal position and play - check and adjustment	7
Brake system - general check	6
Carburetor synchronization (twin carburetor models) - check and adjustment	17
Clutch - check and adjustment	10
Cooling system - check	20
Cooling system - draining, flushing and refilling	27
Drive chain and sprockets (Marauder) - check, adjustment and lubrication	3
Engine oil and filter - change	26
Evaporative emission control system (California models only) - check	22
Exhaust system - check	23
Fasteners - check	19
Fluid levels - check	4
Fuel system - check and filter cleaning	24
Idle speed - check and adjustment	16
Introduction to tune-up and routine maintenance	2
Intruder, Marauder, Volusia and Boulevard Routine maintenance intervals	1
Lubrication - general	9
PAIR system - check	21
Spark plugs - replacement	13
Steering head bearings - check and adjustment	11
Suspension - check	25
Throttle and choke operation/grip freeplay - check and adjustment	15
Tires/wheels - general check	8
Valve clearances - check and adjustment	14

Degrees of difficulty

| **Easy,** suitable for novice with little experience | | **Fairly easy,** suitable for beginner with some experience | | **Fairly difficult,** suitable for competent DIY mechanic | 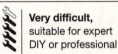 | **Difficult,** suitable for experienced DIY mechanic | 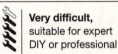 | **Very difficult,** suitable for expert DIY or professional | |

Specifications

Engine

Spark plugs (Intruder, S50 and Marauder)
Type... NGK DPR8EA-9 or ND X24EPR-U9
Gap.. 0.8 to 0.9 mm (0.031 to 0.035 inch)

Spark plugs (Volusia, C50 and M50)
All except 2009 and later C50 and M50 UK, Europe, Australia and Canada models
Type... NGK DPR7EA-9 or ND X22EPR-U9
Gap.. 0.8 to 0.9 mm (0.031 to 0.035 inch)
2009 and later C50 and M50 UK, Europe, Australia and Canada models
Type... NGK DR7EA-9 or ND X22ESR-U
Gap.. 0.6 to 0.7 mm (0.024 to 0.028 inch)

Tune-up and routine maintenance

Engine idle speed

Intruder and S50
   1985 through 1991 .... 1000 +/- 100 rpm
   1992
      Switzerland .... 1100 +/- 100 rpm
      All others .... 1200 +/- 100 rpm
   1993 through 1995 .... 1100 +/- 100 rpm
      US except California .... 1200 +/- 50 rpm
      California .... Not specified
      Europe except Switzerland .... 1100 +/- 100 rpm
      Switzerland and Canada .... 1200 +/- 50 rpm
   1996
      US .... 1200 +/- 50 rpm
      Europe except Switzerland .... 1100 +/- 100 rpm
      Switzerland .... 1200 +/- 50 rpm
      Canada .... 1200 +/- 100 rpm
   1997 and later
      US .... 1200 +/- 50 rpm
      Europe except Switzerland .... 1100 +/- 100 rpm
      Switzerland .... 1200 +/- 50 rpm
      Canada .... 1200 +/- 100 rpm
      Brazil .... 1100 +/- 1- rpm
Marauder
   1997 .... 1200 +/- 100 rpm
   1998 through 2004
      Switzerland .... 1200 + 100, -50 rpm
      All others .... 1200 +/- 100 rpm
Volusia, C50, M50 .... 1100 +/- 100 rpm

Fast idle rpm (fuel injection)

C50, M50 (engine cold) .... 2100 rpm

Valve clearances (COLD engine)

Intruder, S50, Marauder .... 0.08 to 0.13 mm (0.003 to 0.005 inch)
C50, M50
   Intake .... 0.08 to 0.13 mm (0.003 to 0.005 inch)
   Exhaust .... 0.17 to 0.22 mm (0.007 to 0.009 inch)

Cylinder numbering

Front .... No. 2
Rear .... No. 1

Chassis

Brake pad minimum thickness .... To limit line on pads
Rear brake lining minimum thickness .... To end of wear indicator
Brake pedal position
   Intruder and S50 .... 40 mm (1.6 inch) above top of footrest
   Marauder .... 60 mm (2.4 inches) above top of footrest
   Volusia, C50 and M50
      All except 2009 and later C50 .... 75 to 85 mm (3.0 to 3.3 inches) above top of footrest
      2009 and later C50 .... 95 to 105 mm (3.7 to 4.1 inches) above top of footrest
Brake pedal freeplay (all models) .... 20 to 30 mm (0.8 to 1.2 inches)
Throttle grip freeplay
   Intruder
      1985 through 1995 .... 0.5 to 1.0 mm (0.002 to 0.04 inch)
      1996 through 2003 .... 3.0 to 6.0 mm (0.12 to 0.24 inch)
      2004 and later .... 2.0 to 4.0 mm (0.08 to 0.16 inch)
Clutch lever freeplay at lever tip (cable clutch) .... 10 to 15 mm (0.4 to 0.6 inch)
Choke lever freeplay .... 0.5 to 1.0 mm (0.002 to 0.04 inch)
Drive chain slack (Marauder) .... 15 to 25 mm (0.6 to 1.0 inch)

Torque specifications

Oil drain plug .... 18 to 23 Nm (13.0 to 16.5 ft-lbs)
Oil filter
   Step 1 .... Until gasket just touches engine
   Step 2 .... An additional 5/6 turn
Oil screen cover .... 10 Nm (84 inch-lbs)
Coolant drain and bleed bolts (Intruder and S50) .... Not specified
Spark plugs .... 18 Nm (144 inch-lbs)
Valve adjuster cover bolts .... Not specified

Recommended lubricants and fluids

Engine/transmission oil
Type.. API grade SF or SG or API grade SH or SJ meeting JASO standard MA*
Viscosity... SAE 10W40
Capacity (Intruder and S50)
   With filter change.. 2.8 liters (3.0 US qt, 5.0 Imp pt)
   Oil change only... 2.4 liters (2.5 US qt, 4.2 Imp pt)
Capacity (Marauder)
   With filter change.. 2.8 liters (3.0 US qt, 5.0 Imp pt)
   Oil change only... 2.1 liters (2.2 US qt, 3.6 Imp pt)
Capacity (Volusia, C50, M50)
   With filter change.. 3.4 liters (3.6 US qt, 6.0 Imp pt)
   Oil change only... 3.0 liters (3.2 US qt, 5.2 Imp pt)

Coolant
  Type... 50/50 mixture of ethylene glycol based antifreeze and soft water
  Capacity
   Intruder and S50.. 1.7 liters (1.8 US qt, 3.0 Imp pt)
   Marauder Volusia, C50, M50... 1.5 liters (1.6 US qt, 2.7 Imp pt)

Final drive oil
  Type... SAE 90, API GL-5
  Capacity.. 200 to 220 cc (6.8 to 7.0 US fl oz, 7.4 to 7.7 Imp fl oz)

Brake and clutch fluid .... DOT 4

Miscellaneous
  Wheel bearings .... Medium weight, lithium-based multi-purpose grease
  Swingarm pivot bearings .... Medium weight, lithium-based multi-purpose grease
  Cables and lever pivots.. Chain and cable lubricant or 10W30 motor oil
  Sidestand/centerstand pivots... Medium-weight, lithium-based multi-purpose grease
  Brake pedal/shift lever pivots .... Chain and cable lubricant or 10W30 motor oil
  Throttle grip.. Multi-purpose grease or dry film lubricant

* JASO standard MA is required for SH and SJ oils to prevent clutch slippage.

1•4 Tune-up and routine maintenance

Component locations - Intruder and S50 models

1. Front brake fluid reservoir
2. Steering head bearing adjuster
3. Oil level window
4. Coolant drain plug (on left side)
5. Battery
6. Final drive oil drain plug (on left side)
7. Rear brake pedal adjuster
8. Final drive oil filler hole (on left side)
9. Rear brake wear indicator
10. Engine oil filler cap
11. Air filters (under tank)
12. Clutch fluid reservoir

Tune-up and routine maintenance 1•5

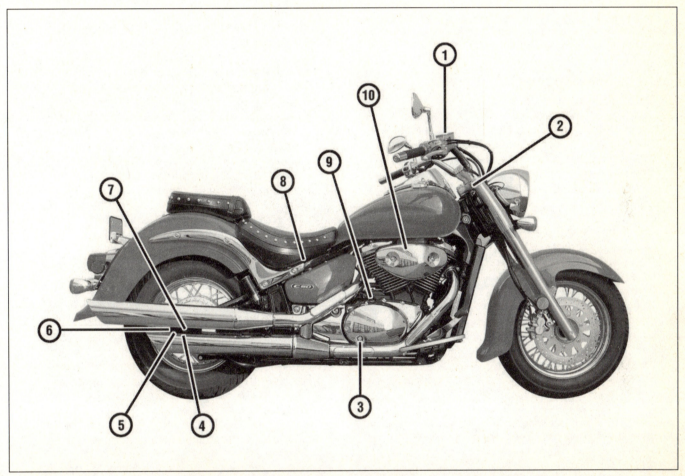

Component locations - Boulevard C50 models (Volusia and M50 similar)

1 Front brake fluid reservoir
2 Steering head bearing adjuster
3 Oil level window
4 Final drive oil drain plug (on left side)
5 Rear brake pedal adjuster
6 Final drive oil filler hole (on left side)
7 Rear brake wear indicator
8 Battery (under seat)
9 Engine oil filler cap
10 Air filter

Intruder, Marauder, Volusia and Boulevard Routine maintenance intervals

Note: *The pre-ride inspection outlined in the owner's manual covers checks and maintenance that should be carried out on a daily basis. It's condensed and included here to remind you of its importance. Always perform the pre-ride inspection at every maintenance interval (in addition to the procedures listed). The intervals listed below are the shortest intervals recommended by the manufacturer for each particular operation during the model years covered in this manual. Your owner's manual may have different intervals for your model.*

Daily or before riding
- [ ] Check the engine oil level
- [ ] Check the fuel level and inspect for leaks
- [ ] Check the engine coolant level and look for leaks
- [ ] Check the operation of both brakes - also check the fluid level and look for leakage (disc brakes)
- [ ] Check the tires for damage, the presence of foreign objects and correct air pressure
- [ ] Check the throttle for smooth operation and correct freeplay
- [ ] Check the operation of the clutch - make sure the freeplay is correct
- [ ] Make sure the steering operates smoothly, without looseness and without binding
- [ ] Check for proper operation of the headlight, taillight, brake light, turn signals, indicator lights, speedometer and horn
- [ ] Make sure the sidestand and centerstand (if equipped) return to their fully up positions and stay there under spring pressure
- [ ] Make sure the engine STOP switch works properly

After the initial 600 miles (1000 km)
This service is usually performed by a dealer service department, since the bike is still under warranty. It consists of all of the daily checks plus:
- [ ] Engine oil and filter change
- [ ] Air filter element cleaning
- [ ] Valve clearance adjustment
- [ ] Idle speed adjustment
- [ ] Throttle freeplay adjustment
- [ ] Drive chain slack adjustment (chain drive models)
- [ ] Final drive oil change (shaft drive models)
- [ ] Exhaust system and chassis fastener tightness check

Every 600 miles (1000 km)
- [ ] Lubricate the drive chain and check play (chain drive models) (Section 3)

Every 4000 miles (6000 km)
- [ ] Check the brake fluid level (Section 4)
- [ ] Check the brake disc(s), pads, drum and shoes (Section 5)
- [ ] Check/adjust the brake pedal position (Section 6)
- [ ] Check the operation of the brake light (Section 7)
- [ ] Check the tires and wheels (Section 8)
- [ ] Lubricate all cables (Section 9)
- [ ] Lubricate the clutch and brake lever pivots (Section 9)
- [ ] Lubricate the shift/brake lever pivots and the sidestand pivots (Section 9)
- [ ] Adjust the clutch freeplay (cable clutch) (Section 10)
- [ ] Check the steering (Section 11)
- [ ] Check the battery electrolyte level (Section 12)
- [ ] Clean and gap the spark plugs (Section 13)
- [ ] Check and adjust valve clearance (Section 14)
- [ ] Check/adjust the throttle and choke operation and freeplay (carburetor models) (Section 15)
- [ ] Check/adjust the idle speed (Section 16)
- [ ] Check/adjust the carburetor synchronization (twin carburetors) (Section 17)
- [ ] Inspect/clean the air filter element (Section 18)
- [ ] Check fastener tightness (Section 19)
- [ ] Inspect the cooling system (Section 20)
- [ ] Change the engine oil (Section 26)

Every 7500 miles (12,000 km)
All of the items above plus:
- [ ] Check the operation of the PAIR system (if equipped) (Section 21)
- [ ] Check the evaporative emission control system (California models) (Section 22)
- [ ] Replace the spark plugs (Section 13)
- [ ] Replace the air filter element (Section 18)
- [ ] Check the exhaust system for leaks and check the tightness of the fasteners (Section 23)
- [ ] Check the cleanliness of the fuel system and the condition of the fuel and vacuum hoses (Section 24)
- [ ] Inspect the rear suspension and swingarm (Chapter 6)
- [ ] Check the front forks (Section 25)
- [ ] Check the differential oil (shaft drive models) (Section 4)
- [ ] Change the engine oil and oil filter (Section 26)

Every two years
- [ ] Check the cooling system and replace the coolant (Sections 20 and 27)
- [ ] Change the brake fluid (Chapter 7)
- [ ] Change the clutch fluid (Intruder and S50) (Chapter 2)

Every four years
- [ ] Replace the fuel hoses (Chapter 4)
- [ ] Replace the clutch hoses (hydraulic clutch models) (Chapter 2)
- [ ] Replace the brake hose(s) (Chapter 7)

2 Introduction to tune-up and routine maintenance

1 This Chapter covers in detail the checks and procedures necessary for the tune-up and routine maintenance of your motorcycle. Section 1 includes the routine maintenance schedule, which is designed to keep the machine in proper running condition and prevent possible problems. The remaining Sections contain detailed procedures for carrying out the items listed on the maintenance schedule, as well as additional maintenance information designed to increase reliability.

2 Since routine maintenance plays such an important role in the safe and efficient operation of your motorcycle, it is presented here as a comprehensive check list. For the rider who does all of the bike's maintenance, these lists outline the procedures and checks that should be done on a routine basis.

3 Maintenance information is printed on decals in various locations on the motorcycle. If the information on the decals differs from that included here, use the information on the decal.

4 Deciding where to start or plug into the routine maintenance schedule depends on several factors. If you have a motorcycle whose warranty has recently expired, and if it has been maintained according to the warranty standards, you may want to pick up routine maintenance as it coincides with the next mileage or calendar interval. If you have owned the machine for some time but have never performed any maintenance on it, then you may want to start at the nearest interval and include some additional procedures to ensure that nothing important is overlooked. If you have just had a major engine overhaul, then you may want to start the maintenance routine from the beginning. If you have a used machine and have no knowledge of its history or maintenance record, you may desire to combine all the checks into one large service initially and then settle into the maintenance schedule prescribed.

5 The Sections which outline the inspection and maintenance procedures are written as step-by-step comprehensive guides to the performance of the work. They explain in detail each of the routine inspections and maintenance procedures on the check list. References to additional information in applicable Chapters are also included and should not be overlooked.

6 Before beginning any maintenance or repair, the machine should be cleaned thoroughly, especially around the oil filter, spark plugs, cylinder head covers, side covers, carburetor(s), etc. Cleaning will help ensure that dirt does not contaminate the engine and will allow you to detect wear and damage that could otherwise easily go unnoticed.

7 The motorcycle comes from the factory with a tool kit that's useful for some of the maintenance procedures, as well as for emergency repairs. If the factory tool kit is missing or incomplete, you can put together your own or order the factory tool kit from a Suzuki dealer.

3.3 Check drive chain play halfway along the bottom run of the chain

3 Drive chain and sprockets (Marauder) - check, adjustment and lubrication

Check

1 A neglected drive chain won't last long and can quickly damage the sprockets. Routine chain adjustment and inspection isn't difficult and will ensure maximum chain and sprocket life.

2 To check the chain, place the bike on its stand and shift the transmission into Neutral. Make sure the ignition switch is off.

3 Push up on the bottom run of the chain and measure the slack midway between the two sprockets **(see illustration)**, then compare your measurements to the value listed in this Chapter's Specifications. As the chain stretches with wear, adjustment will periodically be necessary. Since the chain will rarely wear evenly, rotate the rear wheel so that another section of chain can be checked; do this several times to check the entire chain.

4 In some cases where lubrication has been neglected, corrosion and galling may cause the links to bind and kink, which effectively shortens the chain's length. Such links should be thoroughly cleaned and worked free. If the chain is tight between the sprockets, rusty or kinked, it's time to replace it with a new one. If you find a tight area, mark it with felt pen or paint, and repeat the measurement after the bike has been ridden. If the chain's still tight in the same area, it may be damaged or worn. Because a tight or kinked chain can damage the transmission bearings, it's a good idea to replace it with a new one.

5 Remove the chain guard. Check the entire length of the chain for damaged rollers, loose links and pins, and missing O-rings and replace it if damage is found. **Note:** *Never install a new chain on old sprockets, and never install a used chain on new sprockets - replace the chain and sprockets as a set.*

6 Remove the front sprocket cover from the engine. Check the teeth on the front sprocket and the rear sprocket for wear **(see illustration)**.

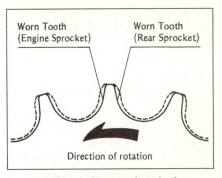

3.6 Check the sprockets in the areas indicated to see if they're worn excessively

Adjustment

7 Support the bike with the rear wheel off the ground and rotate the rear wheel until the chain is positioned with the tightest point at the center of its bottom run.

8 Once you have the tightest point of the chain positioned correctly, lower the bike and place it on its sidestand. The adjustment should be made with the bike on its sidestand.

9 Loosen the rear brake adjusting nut (see Section 7).

10 Remove the cotter pin (if equipped) from the rear axle nut, then loosen the axle nut (see Chapter 7 if necessary).

11 Loosen the locknuts on the adjuster bolts **(see illustration)**.

12 Turn the chain adjusting bolts on both sides of the swingarm until the proper chain tension is obtained (get the adjuster on the chain side close, then set the adjuster on the opposite side). Be sure to turn the adjusting

3.11 On chain drive models, loosen the chain adjuster bolt locknuts (left arrow), then turn the adjusting bolts (right arrow); turn both adjusters evenly

4.6 Here are the final drive filler plug (upper arrow) and drain plug (lower arrow)

5.2 Look into the front of the caliper to check the brake pads for wear (arrows)

bolts evenly to keep the rear wheel in alignment. If the adjusting bolts reach the end of their travel, the chain is excessively worn and should be replaced with a new one (see Chapter 6).

13 When the chain has the correct amount of slack, make sure the marks on the adjusters correspond to the same relative marks on each side of the swingarm **(see illustration 3.11)**.

14 Tighten the axle nut snugly, then apply the rear brake firmly to center the shoes. Recheck drive chain slack and readjust if necessary, then tighten the axle nut to the torque listed in the Chapter 7 Specifications and install a new cotter pin (if equipped). If necessary, turn the nut an additional amount to line up the cotter pin hole with the castellations in the nut - don't loosen the nut to do this.

15 Tighten the adjuster locknuts and adjust the rear brake (see Section 7).

4 Fluid levels - check

Engine oil

1 Engine oil level should be checked before every ride as described in *Daily (pre-ride) checks* at the beginning of this manual, as well as at the specified maintenance intervals.

Brake and clutch fluid

2 Fluid level in the front brake master cylinder (and clutch fluid level on Intruder and S50 models) should be checked before every ride as described in *Daily (pre-ride) checks* at the beginning of this manual, as well as at the specified maintenance intervals.

Coolant

3 Coolant level in the reservoir tank (if equipped) should be checked before every ride as described in *Daily (pre-ride) checks* at the beginning of this manual, as well as at the specified maintenance intervals. **Note:** *Intruder, S50 and Marauder models do not have a reservoir tank.*

Final drive oil (shaft drive models)

4 Final drive oil should be checked at the specified maintenance interval; before every ride, take a quick look for signs of leakage around the differential housing.

5 Support the bike securely in a level position.

⚠ *Warning: When the bike is operated, the final drive unit gets hot enough to cause burns. If the machine has been ridden recently, make sure the final drive unit is cool to the touch before checking the level.*

6 Remove the filler plug from the final drive housing **(see illustration)**.

7 Look inside the hole and check the oil level. It should be even with the top of the hole. If it's low, add oil of the type listed in this Chapter's Specifications with a funnel or hose, then reinstall the filler plug and tighten to the torque listed in this Chapter's Specifications.

5 Brake pads and linings - wear check

1 Disc brake pads and drum brake linings should be checked at the recommended intervals and replaced with new ones when worn beyond the limit listed in this Chapter's Specifications (disc brakes) or Chapter 7 (drum brakes).

2 To check disc brake pads, remove the caliper (without disconnecting the brake hose) so you can see clearly into the front of the brake caliper (see Chapter 7). The brake pads should have at least the specified minimum amount of lining material remaining on the metal backing plate **(see illustration)**.

3 If the pads are worn excessively, they must be replaced with new ones (see Chapter 7).

4 To check drum brake linings, press the brake pedal firmly and look at the indicator on the brake drum as described in *Daily (pre-ride) checks* at the beginning of this manual. If the pointer is beyond the wear limit scale, replace the brake shoes (see Chapter 7).

6 Brake system - general check

1 A routine general check of the brakes will ensure that any problems are discovered and remedied before the rider's safety is jeopardized.

2 Check the brake lever and pedal for loose connections, excessive play, bends, and other damage. Replace any damaged parts with new ones (see Chapter 7).

3 Make sure all brake fasteners are tight. Check the brake pads and linings for wear (see Section 5) and make sure the fluid level in the reservoir is correct (see *Daily (pre-ride) checks* at the beginning of this manual). Look for leaks at the hose connections and check for cracks in the hoses. If the lever is spongy, bleed the brakes as described in Chapter 7.

4 Make sure the brake light operates when the brake lever is depressed.

5 Make sure the brake light is activated when the rear brake pedal is depressed approximately 15 mm (0.6 inch).

6 If adjustment is necessary, hold the switch and turn the adjusting nut on the switch body **(see illustration)** until the brake light is activated when required. Turning the

Tune-up and routine maintenance

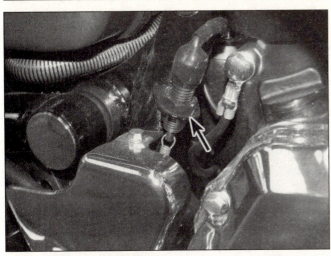

6.6 To adjust the rear brake light switch, hold the switch body and turn the locknut (arrow)

7.2a To adjust the brake pedal position, loosen the locknut (upper arrow) and turn the adjusting bolt (lower arrow) (this is an Intruder/S50) . . .

switch out will cause the brake light to come on sooner, while turning it in will cause it to come on later. If the switch doesn't operate the brake lights, check it as described in Chapter 9.

7 The front brake light switch is not adjustable. If it fails to operate properly, replace it with a new one (see Chapter 9).

7 Brake pedal position and play - check and adjustment

1 Rear brake pedal position is largely a matter of personal preference. Locate the pedal so that the rear brake can be engaged quickly and easily without excessive foot movement. The recommended factory setting is listed in this Chapter's Specifications.
2 To adjust the position of the pedal, loosen the locknut on the adjusting bolt, turn the bolt to set the pedal position and tighten the locknut **(see illustrations)**.
3 If necessary, adjust the brake light switch (see Section 6).

4 With the pedal position adjusted correctly, check freeplay. Apply the rear brake and compare the pedal travel with that listed in this Chapter's Specifications.
5 To adjust the freeplay, turn the adjuster at the rear end of the brake rod **(see illustration 12.9 in Chapter 7)**.

8 Tires/wheels - general check

1 Routine tire and wheel checks should be made with the realization that your safety depends to a great extent on their condition.
2 Check the tires carefully for cuts, tears, embedded nails or other sharp objects and excessive wear. Operation of the motorcycle with excessively worn tires is extremely hazardous, as traction and handling are directly affected. Measure the tread depth at the center of the tire and replace worn tires with new ones when the tread depth is less than specified. **Note:** *In the UK, tread depth must be at least 1 mm over 3/4 of the tread breadth all the way around the tire, with no bald patches.*
3 Repair or replace punctured tires as soon as damage is noted. Do not try to patch a torn tire, as wheel balance and tire reliability may be impaired.
4 Check the tire pressures when the tires are cold and keep them properly inflated **(see illustration)**. Proper air pressure will increase tire life and provide maximum stability and ride comfort. Keep in mind that low tire pressures may cause the tire to slip on the rim or come off, while high tire pressures will cause abnormal tread wear and unsafe handling.

Cast wheels

5 The cast wheels used on some models are virtually maintenance free, but they should be kept clean and checked periodically for cracks and other damage. Never attempt to repair damaged cast wheels; they must be replaced with new ones.
6 Check the valve stem locknuts to make sure they are tight. Also, make sure the valve stem cap is in place and tight. If it is missing, install a new one made of metal or hard plastic.

7.2b . . . this is an M50 . . .

7.2c . . . and this is a C50

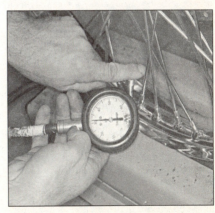

8.4 Use an accurate gauge to check the air pressure in the tires

1•10 Tune-up and routine maintenance

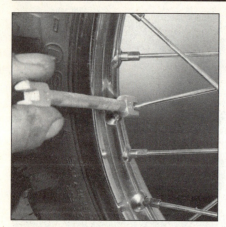

8.7 Check the tension of the spokes periodically, but don't over-tighten them

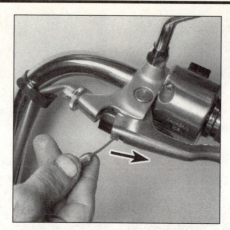

9.3a Line up the slots in the bracket, locknut and adjuster, then rotate the cable in the direction of the arrow, slide it through the slots and lower it out of the lever

9.3b Lubricating a cable with a pressure lube adapter (make sure the tool seats around the inner cable)

Wire wheels

7 The wire wheels used on some models should be checked periodically for cracks, bending, loose spokes and corrosion. Never attempt to repair damaged wheels; they must be replaced with new ones. Loose spokes can be tightened with a spoke wrench (see illustration), but be careful not to overtighten and distort the wheel rim.

9 Lubrication - general

1 Since the controls, cables and various other components of a motorcycle are exposed to the elements, they should be lubricated periodically to ensure safe and trouble-free operation.
2 The footpegs, clutch and brake lever, brake pedal, shift lever and side and centerstand (if equipped) pivots should be lubricated frequently. In order for the lubricant to be applied where it will do the most good, the component should be disassembled. However, if chain and cable lubricant is being used, it can be applied to the pivot joint gaps and will usually work its way into the areas where friction occurs. If motor oil or light grease is being used, apply it sparingly as it may attract dirt (which could cause the controls to bind or wear at an accelerated rate). **Note**: *One of the best lubricants for the control lever pivots is a dry-film lubricant (available from many sources by different names).*
3 The clutch cable should be separated from the handlebar lever and bracket before it is lubricated (see illustration). This is a convenient time to inspect the Teflon bushing at the end of the cable. The cable should be treated with motor oil or a commercially available cable lubricant which is specially formulated for use on motorcycle control cables. Small adapters for pressure lubricating the cables with spray can lubricants are available and ensure that the cable is lubricated along its entire length (see illustration). If motor oil is being used, tape a funnel-shaped piece of heavy paper or plastic to the end of the cable, then pour oil into the funnel and suspend the end of the cable upright. Leave it until the oil runs down into the cable and out the other end. When attaching the cable to the lever, be sure to lubricate the barrel-shaped fitting at the end with high-temperature grease. **Note**: *While you're lubricating, check the barrel end of the cable for fraying. Replace frayed cables.*
4 To lubricate the throttle cables (and choke cable on carbureted models), disconnect the cable(s) at the lower end, then lubricate the cable with a pressure lube adapter (see illustration 9.3b). See Chapter 4 for the choke cable removal procedure.
5 The speedometer cable should be removed from its housing and lubricated with motor oil or cable lubricant.
6 Refer to Chapter 6 for the swingarm needle bearing lubrication procedure.

10 Clutch - check and adjustment

Cable clutch

1 Correct clutch freeplay is necessary to ensure proper clutch operation and reasonable clutch service life. Freeplay normally changes because of cable stretch and clutch wear, so it should be checked and adjusted periodically. If the clutch lever play can't be adjusted within the specified range, the cable should be replaced.
2 Clutch cable freeplay is checked at the lever on the handlebar. Slowly pull in on the lever until resistance is felt, then note how far the lever has moved away from its bracket at the pivot end (see illustration). Compare this distance with the value listed in this Chapter's Specifications. Too little freeplay may result in the clutch not engaging completely. If there is too much freeplay, the clutch might not release fully.

Volusia, C50 and M50

3 Remove the left side cover (see Chapter 8). Remove the secondary gearcase cover and clutch release cover (see Chapter 2).
4 Loosen the locknut on the cable adjuster at the handlebar. Turn the adjuster all the way in against the lever.
5 Loosen the locknut on the cable adjuster at the left side of the engine (see illustration). Back out the adjusting screw two or three turns, then turn it back in just until you feel resistance. From this point, back it out 1/4 turn, then tighten the locknut.
6 Loosen the locknut on the cable adjuster at the top of the engine (see illustration). Turn the adjusting nut to adjust play at the clutch lever so it's within the range listed in this Chapter's Specifications, then tighten the locknut.
7 Turn the locknut at the clutch lever against the adjuster to secure it.

Marauder models

8 Loosen the locknut on the cable adjuster at the handlebar. Turn the adjuster all the way in against the lever.
9 Loosen the mid-line cable adjuster on the side of the engine as far as possible, so

10.5 Loosen the locknut (right arrow) and turn the screw (left arrow) . . .

Tune-up and routine maintenance 1•11

10.6 . . . complete the adjustment with the cable nuts (arrow)

12.1 Check the battery electrolyte level through the window (Intruder and S50)

there is slack in the clutch cable.
10 Loosen the locknut on the cable adjuster at the top of the engine. Turn the adjusting nut to adjust play at the clutch lever so it's within the range listed in this Chapter's Specifications, then tighten the locknut.
11 Turn the locknut at the clutch lever against the adjuster to secure it.

Hydraulic clutch
12 The hydraulic clutch used on Intruder and S50 models is self-adjusting. If the clutch doesn't disengage when the lever is pulled all the way to the handlebar, refer to Chapter 2 and bleed air from the clutch hydraulic system. If that doesn't work, the master and slave cylinders should be overhauled or replaced.

11 Steering head bearings - check

1 These motorcycles are equipped with tapered roller or caged ball steering head bearings which can become dented, rough or loose during normal use of the machine. In extreme cases, worn or loose steering head bearings can cause steering wobble that is potentially dangerous.

Check
2 To check the bearings, place the motorcycle on the centerstand (if equipped). If not, prop it securely upright. Block the machine so the front wheel is raised off the ground.
3 Point the wheel straight ahead and slowly move the handlebars from side-to-side. Dents or roughness in the bearing races will be felt and the bars will not move smoothly.
4 Next, grasp the fork legs and try to move the wheel forward and backward. Any looseness in the steering head bearings will be felt. If play is felt in the bearings, adjust the steering head as described in Chapter 6.
5 Refer to Chapter 6 for steering head

bearing lubrication and replacement procedures.

12 Battery electrolyte level/ specific gravity - check

 Warning: *Be extremely careful when handling or working around the battery. The electrolyte is very caustic and an explosive gas (hydrogen) is given off when the battery is charging.*

Note: *This procedure applies to fillable batteries, installed as original equipment on Intruder and S50 models. The maintenance-free batteries used on other models do not require periodic checks of the electrolyte level.*

1 The electrolyte level is visible through a window on the right side of the bike, above the muffler **(see illustration)**. It should be between the Upper and Lower level lines.
2 If the electrolyte level is low, refer to Chapter 9 and remove the battery to top up the electrolyte and check specific gravity.

13 Spark plugs - replacement

TOOL TiP *This motorcycle is equipped with spark plugs that have an 18 mm wrench hex. Make sure your spark plug socket is the correct size before attempting to remove the plugs.*

1 If you're working on a Volusia, C50 or M50, remove the seat and fuel tank (see Chapters 8 and 4). If you're working on the front cylinder of a 2009 or later M50 equipped with dual spark plugs (UK, Europe, Australia and California models), unbolt the cylinder head cover cap at the front corner and swing it rearward. Unscrew the spark plug with a spark plug socket, universal joint and extension.
2 Disconnect the spark plug caps from the spark plugs **(see illustration)**. If available, use compressed air to blow any accumulated debris from around the spark plugs. Remove the plugs **(see illustration)**.

13.2a Work the plug boot loose from each spark plug . . .

13.2b . . . and unscrew the plug with the correct size spark plug socket and a swivel extension where necessary

1•12 Tune-up and routine maintenance

13.6a Spark plug manufacturers recommend using a wire type gauge when checking the gap - if the wire doesn't slide between the electrodes with a slight drag, adjustment is required

13.6b To change the gap, bend the side electrode only, as indicated by the arrows, and be very careful not to crack or chip the ceramic insulator surrounding the center electrode

a wrench to tighten them an additional 1/4 turn. Regardless of the method used, do not over-tighten them.
9 Reconnect the spark plug caps.

14 Valve clearances - check and adjustment

1 The engine must be completely cool for this maintenance procedure, so let the machine sit overnight before beginning.
2 Remove the seat and fuel tank (see Chapters 8 and 4). Remove the spark plugs (see Section 13).

Intruder and S50
3 Remove the front carburetor and air intake tube (see Chapter 4A).

Marauder
4 Remove the front air cleaner and disconnect the choke plunger from the front carburetor (see Chapter 4A). Unbolt the frame crosspiece that's mounted directly behind the front carburetor.
5 Loosen the clamp that secures the rear carburetor to its air intake pipe. Pull the carburetor out of the air intake pipe and let it sit loosely on the pipe.

C50 and M50
6 Remove the right side cover (see Chapter 8). If you're working on a 2009 or later M50, remove the right frame head cover (see Chapter 8), air cleaner and outlet tube (see Chapter 4).
7 Loosen the clamps that secure the air intake pipe and remove the PAIR pipe (see Chapter 4B).

All models
8 Remove the cylinder head trim covers and the rubber pads beneath them **(see illustrations)**.

3 Inspect the electrodes for wear. Both the center and side electrodes should have square edges and the side electrode should be of uniform thickness. Look for excessive deposits and evidence of a cracked or chipped insulator around the center electrode. Compare your spark plugs to the color spark plug reading chart. Check the threads, the washer and the ceramic insulator body for cracks and other damage.
4 If the electrodes are not excessively worn, and if the deposits can be easily removed with a wire brush, the plugs can be regapped and reused (if no cracks or chips are visible in the insulator). If in doubt concerning the condition of the plugs, replace them with new ones, as the expense is minimal.
5 Cleaning spark plugs by sandblasting is permitted, provided you clean the plugs with a high flash-point solvent afterwards.
6 Before installing new plugs, make sure they are the correct type and heat range. Check the gap between the electrodes, as they are not preset. For best results, use a wire-type gauge rather than a flat gauge to check the gap **(see illustration)**. If the gap must be adjusted, bend the side electrode only and be very careful not to chip or crack the insulator nose **(see illustration)**. Make sure the washer is in place before installing each plug.
7 Since the cylinder heads are made of aluminum, which is soft and easily damaged, thread the plugs into the heads by hand. Since the plugs are quite recessed, slip a short length of hose over the end of the plug to use as a tool to thread it into place **(see illustration)**. The hose will grip the plug well enough to turn it, but will start to slip if the plug begins to cross-thread in the hole - this will prevent damaged threads and the accompanying repair costs.
8 Once the plugs are finger tight, the job can be finished with a socket. If a torque wrench is available, tighten the spark plugs to the torque listed in this Chapter's Specifications. If you do not have a torque wrench, tighten the plugs finger tight (until the washers bottom on the cylinder head) then use

13.7 A length of rubber hose will save time and prevent damaged threads when installing the spark plugs

14.8a Remove the cylinder head trim covers . . .

Tune-up and routine maintenance 1•13

14.8b ... and the rubber pads underneath them

14.9a Remove the nuts and bolts that secure the valve adjuster covers (arrows) (engine removed for clarity)

14.9b Slip the covers out between the engine and frame

14.9c Replace the cover O-rings if they're damaged or deteriorated

9 Remove the valve adjusting hole covers **(see illustrations)**.
10 Remove the cover from the crankshaft rotation bolt and timing window **(see illustration)**.
11 Position the front cylinder's piston at Top Dead Center (TDC) on the compression stroke. Do this by turning the crankshaft, with a socket placed on the crankshaft bolt, until the R/T mark on the rotor is centered in the timing window **(see illustration)**. Wiggle the rocker arms - if they're loose, the rear cylinder is at TDC on the compression stroke. If they can't be wiggled, and one of the rocker arms is lower than the other, the piston is at TDC on the exhaust stroke. Rotate the crankshaft one full turn to bring the cylinder to TDC compression. Wiggle the rocker arms to confirm it. With the engine in this position, all of the valves for cylinder no. 1 (the rear cylinder) can be checked.

 This procedure will be much easier if you use offset feeler gauges and bend them slightly as described in Step 12.

12 Obtain a set of offset feeler gauges of the thickness listed in this Chapter's Specifications from a Suzuki dealer or aftermar-

14.10 Unscrew the plugs from the timing hole (left arrow) and crankshaft bolt (right arrow)

14.11 Rear cylinder TDC is indicated by an R/T mark next to a paint mark inside the hole (arrow); front cylinder TDC is indicated by an F/T mark

1•14 Tune-up and routine maintenance

14.12a These offset feeler gauges will make measuring valve clearance much easier...

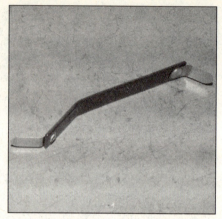

14.12b ...especially if you bend the gauge slightly as shown (arrow)

14.13a Slip the feeler gauge between the rocker arm and valve stem...

ket tool supplier **(see illustration)**. Bend the gauge handle slightly with pliers **(see illustration)**.

13 Insert the feeler gauge between each rocker arm and valve adjusting screw **(see illustrations)**. Pull the feeler gauge out slowly - you should feel a slight drag. If there's no drag, the clearance is too loose. If there's a heavy drag, the clearance is too tight.

14 If the clearance is incorrect, write it down.

15 Repeat the clearance measurement for the other valves on the front cylinder, writing the measurements down.

 Suzuki makes a special tool for valve adjustment, but you can use a box wrench and pliers instead.

16 Loosen the locknut on any valves that need to be adjusted. Hold the locknut with a wrench and turn the adjusting screw with pliers **(see illustration)**.

17 Once the clearance is set correctly, hold the adjusting screw so it won't turn and tighten the locknut securely.

18 Adjust the remaining valve on that side of the cylinder. Get the setting as close as possible to the valve you just adjusted.

19 Adjust the remaining two valve for the cylinder. Again, get the settings for the pair of valves as close as possible to each other.

20 Turn the crankshaft to place the front cylinder at TDC compression. When this occurs, the F/T mark inside the timing hole will be centered in the hole and it will be possible to wiggle the rocker arms with fingers.

21 Repeat Steps 13 through 19 to adjust any other valves that need it.

22 Once all of the valves are correctly adjusted, install the valve adjusting hole covers and all of the components that had to be removed for access. Install the covers over the crankshaft rotation bolt and timing window.

15 Throttle and choke operation/grip freeplay - check and adjustment

Throttle check

1 With the engine stopped, make sure the throttle grip rotates easily from fully closed to fully open with the front wheel turned at various angles. The grip should return automatically from fully open to fully closed when released. If the throttle sticks, check the throttle cables for cracks or kinks in the housings. Also, make sure the inner cables are clean and well-lubricated.

2 Check for a small amount of freeplay at the grip and compare the freeplay to the value listed in this Chapter's Specifications.

⚠️ **Warning: With the engine idling, idle speed should not change as the handlebars are moved through their travel. If idle speed does change, find and fix the problem before riding the bike.**

Throttle adjustment

Note: *Some models use two throttle cables - a pull cable and a return cable.*

Single cable

3 Freeplay adjustments are made at the handlebar end of the cable. Loosen the locknut on the cable where it leaves the handlebar **(see illustration)**. Turn the adjuster until the desired freeplay is obtained, then retighten the locknut.

14.13b ...there are two intake valve adjusters and two exhaust valve adjusters per cylinder (arrows)

14.16 Hold the lock-nut and turn the adjusting screw

Tune-up and routine maintenance 1•15

Dual cables, dual carburetors

4 Loosen the return cable locknut **(see illustrations)**. Turn the adjuster to obtain the return cable freeplay listed in this Chapter's Specifications. Hold the adjuster so it won't turn and tighten the locknut.

5 Adjust the pull cable in the same manner as the return cable.

Dual cables, single carburetor or fuel injection

6 Minor adjustments are made at the handlebar end of the cable. Major adjustments are made at the carburetor or throttle body.

Minor adjustment

7 Loosen the return cable locknut and thread the adjuster all the way in **(see illustration 15.4a or 15.4b)**. Leave the locknut loose for now.

8 Loosen the pull cable locknut. Turn the adjuster to achieve the amount of throttle freeplay listed in this Chapter's Specifications. Hold the adjuster so it won't turn and tighten the locknut.

9 Hold the throttle grip in the closed position and turn the return cable adjuster just until you feel resistance. Hold the adjuster at this point and tighten the locknut.

10 If the throttle cable can't be adjusted at the throttle grip, make major adjustments as described below.

Major adjustment

11 Remove the seat and fuel tank. See Chapters 8 and 4.

12 Loosen the return cable locknut. On carbureted models, it's the cable toward the right side of the motorcycle. On fuel injected models, it's the lower cable at the throttle body pulley **(see illustration)**. Turn the adjuster to create slack in the cable.

13 Loosen the pull cable locknut. Turn the adjuster to set freeplay at the throttle grip to the value listed in this Chapter's Specifications. Hold the adjuster at this point and tighten the locknut.

14 Hold the throttle grip in the closed position and turn the return cable adjuster to produce side-to-side slack of 1 mm (0.04 inch). Hold the adjuster in this position and tighten the locknut.

Choke check (carbureted models)

15 Inspect the choke knob and cable. The choke should pull out easily and stay out by itself. If it doesn't, adjust the knob's tension with the plastic nut behind the knob. If this

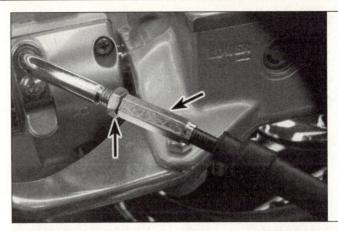

15.3 Here is the locknut (left arrow) and adjuster (right arrow) on a single throttle cable

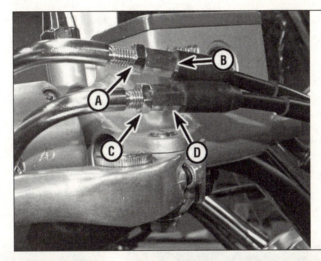

15.4a Throttle cable adjuster details (Volusia and C50)

A Pull cable locknut
B Pull cable adjusting nut
C Return cable locknut
D Return cable adjusting nut

15.4b Throttle cable adjuster details (M50)

A Pull cable locknut
B Pull cable adjusting nut
C Return cable locknut
D Return cable adjusting nut

15.12 Throttle cable pulley details (fuel injected models)

A Pull cable locknut
B Pull cable adjusting nut
C Return cable locknut
D Return cable adjusting nut

1•16 Tune-up and routine maintenance

16.3 Throttle stop screw (arrow) (S50 shown, others similar)

doesn't help, check the plunger bushing for wear or damage and replace as necessary.
16 If the choke movement is rough or the cable sticks, remove the cables and lubricate them (see Chapter 4A and Section 9).

16 Idle speed - check and adjustment

1 The idle speed should be checked and adjusted at the specified maintenance intervals and when it is obviously too high or too low. On twin-carburetor models, the carburetors should be synchronized as described in Section 17 as part of the procedure. Before adjusting the idle speed, make sure the valve clearances and spark plug gaps are correct. Also, turn the handlebars back-and-forth and see if the idle speed changes as this is done. If it does, the accelerator cable may not be adjusted correctly, or it may be worn out. Be sure to correct this problem before proceeding.
2 The engine should be at normal operating temperature, which is usually reached after 10 to 15 minutes of stop and go riding. Place the motorcycle on the centerstand (if equipped). If not, prop it securely upright. Make sure the transmission is in Neutral.

3 Turn the throttle stop screw **(see illustration)**, until the idle speed listed in this Chapter's Specifications is obtained.
4 Snap the throttle open and shut a few times, then recheck the idle speed. If necessary, repeat the adjustment procedure.
5 If a smooth, steady idle can't be achieved, the fuel/air mixture may be incorrect. Refer to Chapter 4 for additional information.

17 Carburetor synchronization (twin carburetor models) - check and adjustment

Warning: *Gasoline (petrol) is extremely flammable, so take extra precautions when you work on any part of the fuel system. Don't smoke or allow open flames or bare light bulbs near the work area, and don't work in a garage where a gas-type appliance (such as a water heater or clothes dryer) is present. If you spill any fuel on your skin, rinse it off immediately with soap and water. When you perform any kind of work on the fuel system, wear safety glasses and have a fire extinguisher suitable for a class B type fire (flammable liquids) on hand.*

1 Carburetor synchronization is simply the process of adjusting the carburetors so they pass the same amount of fuel/air mixture to each cylinder. This is done by measuring the vacuum produced in each cylinder. Carburetors that are out of synchronization will result in decreased fuel mileage, increased engine temperature, less than ideal throttle response and higher vibration levels.
2 To properly synchronize the carburetors, you will need some sort of vacuum gauge setup, preferably with a gauge for each cylinder, or a mercury manometer, which is a

17.12a Cable arrangement (dual carburetors)

1 Front carburetor
2 Rear carburetor
3 Synchronizing cable
4 Throttle cable
5 Throttle cable
6 Choke cable
7 Synchronizing cable adjuster
8 Throttle stop screw

17.12b Synchronizing cable adjuster (front carburetor)

A Adjuster
B Locknut
C Do not turn this screw

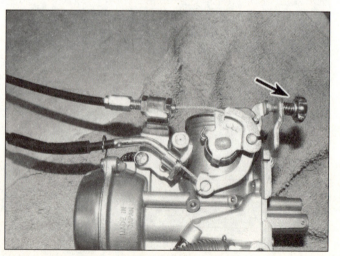

17.12c Here's a close-up of the throttle stop screw on the rear carburetor

Tune-up and routine maintenance 1•17

18.3 Remove the screws and pull the filter element out (Intruder/S50 front air cleaner)

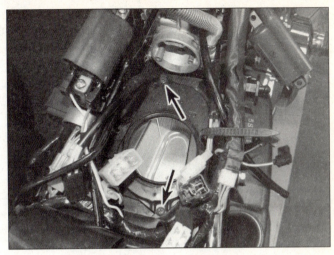

18.4a Remove the screws (arrows) . . .

calibrated tube arrangement that utilizes columns of mercury to indicate engine vacuum.

3 A manometer can be purchased from a motorcycle dealer or accessory shop and should have the necessary rubber hoses supplied with it for hooking into the vacuum hose fittings on the carburetors.

4 A vacuum gauge setup can also be purchased from a dealer or fabricated from commonly available hardware and automotive vacuum gauges.

5 The manometer is the more reliable and accurate instrument, and for that reason is preferred over the vacuum gauge setup; however, since the mercury used in the manometer is a liquid, and extremely toxic, extra precautions must be taken during use and storage of the instrument.

6 Because of the nature of the synchronization procedure and the need for special instruments, most owners leave the task to a dealer service department or a reputable motorcycle repair shop.

7 Start the engine and let it run until it reaches normal operating temperature, then shut it off.

8 Detach the vacuum hoses from the fittings on the carburetors.

9 Hook up the vacuum gauge set or the manometer according to the manufacturer's instructions. Make sure there are no leaks in the setup, as false readings will result.

10 Start the engine and make sure the idle speed is correct.

11 The vacuum readings for both of the cylinders should be the same. If the vacuum readings vary, adjust as necessary.

12 To perform the adjustment, synchronize the carburetors. To do this, loosen the locknut on the front carburetor's synchronizing cable adjuster **(see illustrations)**. Turn the synchronizing adjuster on the rear carburetor and the throttle stop screw on the front carburetor, until the vacuum is identical or nearly identical for both cylinders and the engine runs at the idle speed listed in this Chapter's Specifications.

13 When the adjustment is complete, recheck the vacuum readings and idle speed, then stop the engine. Remove the vacuum gauge or manometer and attach the hoses to the fittings on the carburetors.

18 Air filter element - servicing

Intruder and S50

1 Remove the seat (see Chapter 8).
2 Remove the fuel tank and air intake pipes (see Chapter 4A).
3 Remove the screws that secure the front air cleaner and pull it rearward out of its housing **(see illustration)**.
4 Remove the screws that secure the rear air filter and pull it upward out of its housing **(see illustrations)**.
5 Wipe out the housing with a clean rag, then stuff a rag into each opening to keep out foreign material.
6 Check the element and its foam gasket for tears or other damage. Replace the element if it's damaged.
7 If compressed air is available, use it to clean the element by blowing from the inside out (from the mesh side toward the foam side). You can blow it out with a shop vacuum set up to blow air if you don't have a compressor. If the element is extremely dirty or torn, replace it with a new one. It should be replaced at alternate serviced intervals, regardless of how it looks.
8 Check the air cleaner drain tube for accumulated water and clean it is necessary **(see illustration)**.

Marauder

9 Remove the seat, side covers and steering head covers (see Chapter 8).
10 Remove the fuel tank (see Chapter 4).
11 Remove the screws and detach the rear cylinder's air cleaner from the right side of the bike. Note that the arrow on the air cleaner housing faces upward.
12 Loosen the clamp that secures the air intake tube to the rear carburetor.
13 Remove the front air cleaner housing mounting bolts (one on each side of the bike, just behind the fuel tank mounting dampers).

18.4b . . . and lift the filter element out of the rear air cleaner (Intruder/S50)

18.8 Check the air cleaner drain tube for accumulated water

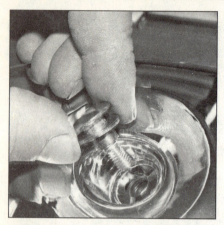

18.17a Remove the screws (three on Intruder/S50, two on other models) ...

18.17b ... and remove the filter element

18.19a Check the grommet ...

14 Remove the screw that secures the throttle cable housing to the left side of the front air cleaner housing. Take the air cleaner housing out of the bike. Note that the arrow on the air cleaner housing faces downward.

15 Remove the screws that secure the air cleaner element and lift it out of the housing.

16 Clean the housing and inspect the element as described in Steps 5 through 7 above.

Volusia, C50 and M50

17 Remove the cover screws (two for Volusia and C50, three for M50), lift off the air filter cover and remove the air filter element **(see illustrations)**.

18 Clean the element by blowing compressed air from the inside of the element to the outside.

19 Inspect the rubber grommet and edge seal and replace as necessary **(see illustration)**.

20 Clean any accumulated water from the air cleaner drain tube.

All models

21 Reinstall the filter by reversing the removal procedure. Make sure the element is seated properly in the filter housing before installing the cover.

18.19b ... and edge seal for damage or deterioration

19 Fasteners - check

1 Since vibration of the machine tends to loosen fasteners, all nuts, bolts, screws, etc. should be periodically checked for proper tightness.

2 Pay particular attention to the following:
   Spark plugs
   Engine oil drain plug
   Oil filter
   Oil screen cover bolt
   Gearshift lever
   Footpegs and sidestand
   Engine mount bolts
   Shock absorber mount bolts
   Front axle and clamp bolt
   Rear axle nut

3 If a torque wrench is available, use it along with the torque specifications at the beginning of this, or other, Chapters.

20 Cooling system - check

⚠ *Warning: The engine must be cool before beginning this procedure.*

Note: *If you're working on a C50 or M50, refer to Daily (preride) checks at the beginning of this manual and check the coolant level before performing this check.*

1 The entire cooling system should be checked carefully at the recommended intervals. Look for evidence of leaks, check the condition of the coolant, check the radiator for clogged fins and damage and make sure the fan operates when required.

2 Examine each of the rubber coolant hoses along its entire length. Look for cracks, abrasions and other damage. Squeeze each hose at various points. They should feel firm, yet pliable, and return to their original shape when released. If they are dried out or hard, replace them with new ones.

3 Check for evidence of leaks at each cooling system joint. Tighten the hose clamps carefully to prevent future leaks.

4 Check the radiator for evidence of leaks and other damage. Leaks in the radiator leave telltale scale deposits or coolant stains on the outside of the core below the leak. If leaks are noted, remove the radiator (refer to Chapter 3) and have it repaired at a radiator shop or replace it with a new one.

Caution: Do not use a liquid leak stopping compound to try to repair leaks.

5 Check the radiator fins for mud, dirt and insects, which may impede the flow of air through the radiator. If the fins are dirty, force water or low pressure compressed air through the fins from the backside. If the fins are bent or distorted, straighten them carefully with a screwdriver.

6 For access to the cooling system pressure cap on Intruder, S50 and Marauder models, remove the fuel tank and steering head covers (see Chapters 4 and 8). Remove the pressure cap by turning it counterclockwise until it reaches a stop. If you hear a hissing sound (indicating there is still pressure in the system), wait until it stops. Now, press down on the cap with the palm of your hand and continue turning the cap counterclockwise until it can be removed **(see illustration 27.2a or 27.4)**. Check the condition of the coolant in the system. If it is rust colored or if accumulations of scale are visible, drain, flush and refill the system with new coolant. Check the cap gaskets for cracks and other damage. Have the cap tested by a dealer service department or replace it with a new one. Install the cap by turning it clockwise until it reaches the first stop, then push down on the cap and continue turning until it can turn no further.

7 Check the antifreeze content of the coolant with an antifreeze hydrometer. Sometimes coolant may look like it's in good condition, but might be too weak to offer adequate protection. If the hydrometer indicates a weak mixture, drain, flush and refill

Tune-up and routine maintenance 1•19

the cooling system (see Section 27).

8 Start the engine and let it reach normal operating temperature, then check for leaks again. As the coolant temperature increases, the fan should come on automatically and the temperature should begin to drop. If it does not, refer to Chapter 3 and check the fan and fan circuit carefully.

9 If the coolant level is consistently low, and no evidence of leaks can be found, have the entire system pressure checked by a Kawasaki dealer service department, motorcycle repair shop or service station.

21 PAIR system - check

1 This system, installed on some models, uses one-way check valves that allow fresh air to flow into the exhaust ports. The suction developed by the exhaust pulses pulls the air from the air filter, through a hose to the air switching valve, through a pair of hoses and a pair of reed valves, and finally into the exhaust ports. The introduction of fresh air helps ignite any fuel that may not have been burned by the normal combustion process.

2 Inspection and testing of the PAIR valves, and the solenoid that controls them on some models is described in Chapter 4A (carbureted models) or Chapter 4B (fuel injected models).

22 Evaporative emission control system (California models only) - check

1 This system, installed on California models to conform to stringent emission control standards, routes fuel vapors from the fuel system into the engine to be burned, instead of letting them evaporate into the atmosphere. When the engine isn't running, vapors are stored in a carbon canister.

Hoses

2 To begin the inspection of the system, remove the seat and side covers (see Chapters 8 and 4 if necessary). Inspect the hoses from the fuel tank, carburetors and liquid/vapor separator to the canister for cracking, kinks or other signs of deterioration.

Component inspection

3 Label and disconnect the hoses, then remove the separator and canister from the machine (see Chapter 4).

4 Check the separator closely for cracks or other signs of damage. If these are found, replace it.

5 Inspect the canister for cracks or other signs of damage. Tip the canister so the nozzles point down. If fuel runs out of the canister, the liquid/vapor separator is probably

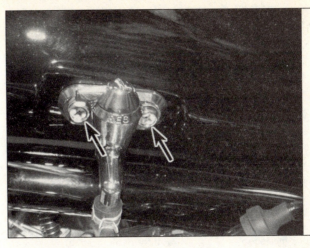

24.9 Remove the screws (arrows) and detach the fuel tap from the tank

bad. The fuel inside the canister has probably caused damage, so it would be a good idea to replace it also.

23 Exhaust system - check

1 Periodically check all of the exhaust system joints for leaks and loose fasteners. If tightening the clamp bolts fails to stop any leaks, replace the gaskets with new ones (a procedure which requires disassembly of the system).

2 The exhaust pipe flange nuts at the cylinder heads are especially prone to loosening, which could cause damage to the head. Check them frequently and keep them tight.

24 Fuel system - check and filter cleaning

 Warning: Gasoline (petrol) is extremely flammable, so take extra precautions when you work on any part of the fuel system. Don't smoke or allow open flames or bare light bulbs near the work area, and don't work in a garage where a gas-type appliance (such as a water heater or clothes dryer) is present. If you spill any fuel on your skin, rinse it off immediately with soap and water. When you perform any kind of work on the fuel system, wear safety glasses and have a fire extinguisher suitable for a class B type fire (flammable liquids) on hand.

1 Check the fuel tank, the fuel tap, the lines and the carburetor(s) or throttle body for leaks and evidence of damage.

2 If carburetor gaskets are leaking, the carburetor(s) should be disassembled and rebuilt by referring to Chapter 4.

3 If the fuel tap is leaking on carbureted models, tightening the screws may help. If leakage persists, the tap should be disassembled and repaired or replaced with a new one.

4 If the fuel lines are cracked or otherwise deteriorated, replace them with new ones.

5 On carbureted models, check the vacuum hose connected to the fuel tap. If it is cracked or otherwise damaged, replace it with a new one.

6 The fuel filter on carbureted models, which is attached to the fuel tap, may become clogged and should be removed and cleaned periodically. In order to clean the filter, the fuel tank must be drained and the fuel tap removed.

7 The fuel strainer and fuel filter on fuel injected models may become clogged. They are mounted on the fuel pump unit, which is inside the fuel tank. They should only be removed for inspection if troubleshooting procedures indicate lack of fuel pressure. See Chapter 4B for details.

8 To check the filter on carbureted models, remove the fuel tank (see Chapter 4). Drain the fuel into an approved fuel container.

9 Once the tank is emptied, loosen and remove the screws that attach the fuel tap to the tank (see illustration). Remove the tap and filter.

10 Clean the filter with solvent and blow it dry with compressed air. If the filter is torn or otherwise damaged, replace the entire fuel tap with a new one. Check the mounting flange O-ring and the gaskets on the screws. If they are damaged, replace them with new ones.

11 Install the O-ring, filter and fuel tap on the tank, then install the tank. Refill the tank and check carefully for leaks around the mounting flange and screws.

25 Suspension - check

1 The suspension components must be maintained in top operating condition to ensure rider safety. Loose, worn or damaged

1•20 Tune-up and routine maintenance

25.3 Check the area around the fork seals for oil leakage and check the tubes for scratches or other damage

26.4 Unscrew the drain plug from the bottom of the crankcase

26.5 The oil filter is mounted on the front of the engine between the frame rails

suspension parts decrease the vehicle's stability and control.
2 While standing alongside the motorcycle, lock the front brake and push on the handlebars to compress the forks several times. See if they move up-and-down smoothly without binding. If binding is felt, the forks should be disassembled and inspected as described in Chapter 6.
3 Carefully inspect the area around the fork seals for any signs of fork oil leakage **(see illustration)**. If leakage is evident, the seals must be replaced as described in Chapter 6.
4 Check the tightness of all suspension nuts and bolts to be sure none have worked loose.
5 Inspect the rear shock absorber(s) for fluid leakage and tightness of the mounting nuts. If leakage is found, the shock(s) should be replaced. Replace both shocks as a pair on twin-shock models.
6 Prop the bike securely upright. Grab the swingarm on each side, just ahead of the axle. Rock the swingarm from side to side - there should be no discernible movement at the rear. If there's a little movement or a slight clicking can be heard, make sure the pivot shaft fasteners are tight. If the pivot

nuts are tight but movement is still noticeable, the swingarm will have to be removed and the bearings replaced as described in Chapter 6.

26 Engine oil and filter - change

1 Consistent routine oil and filter changes are the single most important maintenance procedure you can perform on a motorcycle. The oil not only lubricates the internal parts of the engine, transmission and clutch, but it also acts as a coolant, a cleaner, a sealant, and a protectant. Because of these demands, the oil takes a terrific amount of abuse and should be replaced often with new oil of the recommended grade and type. Saving a little money on the difference in cost between a good oil and a cheap oil won't pay off if the engine is damaged.
2 Before changing the oil and filter, warm up the engine so the oil will drain easily. Be careful when draining the oil, as the exhaust pipes, the engine, and the oil itself can cause severe burns.
3 Prop the motorcycle upright over a

clean drain pan. Remove the oil filler cap to vent the crankcase and act as a reminder that there is no oil in the engine. If the bike is equipped with a skid plate under the engine, remove it.
4 Remove the drain plug from the bottom of the crankcase **(see illustration)** and allow the oil to drain into the pan. Discard the sealing washer on the drain plug; it should be replaced whenever the plug is removed.
5 As the oil is draining, remove the oil filter **(see illustration)**. If additional maintenance is planned for this time period, check or service another component while the oil is allowed to drain completely.
6 Wipe any remaining oil off the filter sealing area of the crankcase.
7 Check the condition of the drain plug threads.
8 Coat the gasket on a new filter with clean engine oil. Install the filter and tighten it to the amount listed in this Chapter's Specifications.
9 Slip a new sealing washer over the drain plug, then install and tighten the plug. Tighten the drain plug to the torque listed in this Chapter's Specifications. Avoid overtightening, as damage to the engine case will result.
10 Before refilling the engine, check the old oil carefully. If the oil was drained into a clean pan, small pieces of metal or other material can be easily detected. If the oil is very metallic colored, then the engine is experiencing wear from break-in (new engine) or from insufficient lubrication. If there are flakes or chips of metal in the oil, then something is drastically wrong internally and the engine will have to be disassembled for inspection and repair.
11 If there are pieces of fiber-like material in the oil, the clutch is experiencing excessive wear and should be checked.
12 Regular inspection of the oil screen in the bottom of the crankcase is not required. However, if the contaminants in Steps 10 and 11 are found, the screen should be removed for inspection and cleaning. Remove the oil screen cover bolts **(see illustration)**. Remove the oil screen and its

26.12a Unbolt the oil screen cover and inspect its O-ring

26.12b Remove the oil screen screws with an impact driver

Tune-up and routine maintenance 1•21

27.1 The coolant drain bolt on Intruder and S50 models is in the left frame rail below the muffler

27.2a The pressure cap on Intruder and S50 models is on top of the radiator - DO NOT unscrew it while the engine is hot!

O-ring from the engine **(see illustration)**. Clean the screen in solvent and inspect it for damage, then reinstall it in the engine using a new O-ring. Install the cover and tighten its bolts securely.

13 If the inspection of the oil turns up nothing unusual, refill the crankcase to the proper level with the recommended oil and install the filler cap. Start the engine and let it run for two or three minutes. Shut it off, wait a few minutes, then check the oil level. If necessary, add more oil to bring the level up to the Maximum mark, but do not overfill. Check around the drain plug and filter housing for leaks.

14 The old oil drained from the engine cannot be reused in its present state and should be disposed of. Check with your local refuse disposal company, disposal facility or environmental agency to see whether they will accept the oil for recycling. Don't pour used oil into drains or onto the ground. After the oil has cooled, it can be drained into a suitable container (capped plastic jugs, topped bottles, milk cartons, etc.) for transport to one of these disposal sites.

27 Cooling system - draining, flushing and refilling

Warning: Allow the engine to cool completely before performing this maintenance operation. Also, don't allow antifreeze to come into contact with your skin or painted surfaces of the motorcycle. Rinse off spills immediately with plenty of water. Antifreeze is highly toxic if ingested. Never leave antifreeze lying around in an open container or in puddles on the floor; children and pets are attracted by its sweet smell and may drink it. Check with local authorities about disposing of used antifreeze. Many communities have collection centers which will see that antifreeze is disposed of safely. Antifreeze is also combustible, so don't store or use it near open flames.

Draining

Intruder and S50

1 Place a drain beneath the drain bolt, which is threaded into the lower left frame member **(see illustration)**. The frame member acts as a coolant passage.

2 Unscrew the drain bolt. If the cooling system is airtight, coolant should only dribble out at this point. Make sure the drain pan is positioned correctly, then unscrew the radiator cap **(see illustration)**. Coolant should now flow freely **(see illustration)**.

Marauder, Volusia, C50 and M50

3 Remove the seat and fuel tank (see Chapters 8 and 4).

4 Unscrew the cooling system pressure cap **(see illustration)**.

5 Place a drain pan in position, then dis-

27.2b Coolant will flow forcefully once the cap is removed, so be sure to have a drain pan ready

27.4 The pressure cap on Volusia, C50 and M5 models is beneath the fuel tank - DO NOT unscrew it while the engine is hot!

connect the lower radiator hose from the radiator or water pump, whichever is more convenient.

6   Drain the coolant catch bottle or reservoir. Refer to Chapter 3 for the catch bottle or reservoir removal procedure. Wash the reservoir out with water.

Flushing

7   Flush the system with clean tap water by inserting a garden hose in the radiator filler neck. Allow the water to run through the system until it is clear when it exits the drain bolt hole. If the radiator is extremely corroded, remove it by referring to Chapter 3 and have it cleaned at a radiator shop.

8   On Intruder and S50 models, check the drain bolt gasket. Replace it with a new one if necessary. Clean the hole, then install the drain bolt and tighten it to the torque listed in this Chapter's Specifications.

9   Fill the cooling system with clean water mixed with a flushing compound. Make sure the flushing compound is compatible with aluminum components, and follow the manufacturer's instructions carefully.

10   Start the engine and allow it to reach normal operating temperature. Let it run for about ten minutes.

11   Stop the engine. Let the machine cool for a while, then cover the pressure cap with a heavy rag and turn it counterclockwise (anti-clockwise) to the first stop, releasing any pressure that may be present in the system. Once the hissing stops, push down on the cap and remove it completely.

12   Drain the system once again.

13   Fill the system with clean water, then repeat Steps 8, 9 and 10.

Refilling
Intruder and S50

14   Unscrew the bleed valve bolt from the upper left frame member.

15   Fill the radiator with the proper coolant mixture (see this Chapter's Specifications). Note that Suzuki specifies adding two packages of Bars Leaks anti-leak material to the coolant. Keep filling until it flows from the bleed valve, then install the radiator cap and bleed valve bolt.

16   Start the engine. Allow the engine to reach normal operating temperature, then shut it off.

17   Let the engine cool off for awhile, cover the radiator cap with a heavy rag and loosen it to the first stop to allow any pressure in the system to bleed off before the cap is removed completely. Once this is done, remove the cap and bleed valve bolt again. Recheck the coolant level in the radiator filler neck. If it's low, add more coolant until it reaches the top of the filler neck. Reinstall the cap and bleed valve bolt.

18   Repeat Steps 16 and 17 until the coolant level stays at the top of the filler neck. You may need to warm up and cool down the engine several times to accomplish this.

Marauder

19   Fill the radiator with the proper coolant mixture (see this Chapter's Specifications).

20   Start the engine. Allow the engine to reach normal operating temperature, then shut it off.

21   Let the engine cool off for awhile, cover the radiator cap with a heavy rag and loosen it to the first stop to allow any pressure in the system to bleed off before the cap is removed completely. Once this is done, remove the cap. Recheck the coolant level in the radiator filler neck. If it's low, add more coolant until it reaches the top of the filler neck. Reinstall the cap.

22   Repeat Steps 20 and 21 until the coolant level stays at the top of the filler neck. You may need to warm up and cool down the engine several times to accomplish this.

Volusia, C50 and M50

23   Fill the radiator with the proper coolant mixture (see this Chapter's Specifications). Straddle the bike and slowly lean it to left and right several times to bleed air out of the cooling system. Top up the radiator with coolant.

24   Start the engine. While it's running, check the coolant level and top it up as the level drops (this means that air is being bled out of the system).

25   Once the coolant level has stabilized, install the radiator cap. Fill the coolant reservoir to the Full mark with coolant (see *Daily (pre-ride) checks* at the beginning of this manual).

26   Warm up and cool down the engine several times, each time checking the coolant level in the reservoir tank. Top it up as needed. Continue this until the level stabilizes.

All models

27   Check the system for leaks.

28   Do not dispose of the old coolant by pouring it down a drain. Instead, pour it into a heavy plastic container, cap it tightly and take it to an authorized disposal site or a service station.

Chapter 2
Engine, clutch and transmission

Contents

Cam chain tensioners - locking, removal and installation	11
Camshaft chains and guides - removal, inspection and installation	23
Camshafts - removal, inspection and installation	9
Clutch – removal, inspection and installation	20
Clutch cable (except Intruder and S50) - replacement	18
Clutch hydraulic system (Intruder and S50) - bleeding, removal, inspection and installation	17
Clutch release mechanism (cable clutch) - removal, inspection and installation	19
Connecting rod bearings - general note	26
Connecting rods and bearings - removal, inspection, bearing selection and installation	28
Crankcase - disassembly and reassembly	24
Crankcase components - inspection and servicing	25
Crankshaft and main bearings - removal, inspection and installation	27
Cylinder compression - check	2
Cylinder head and valves - disassembly, inspection and reassembly	13
Cylinder heads and cylinders - removal, separation and installation	10
Cylinders - inspection	14
Engine - removal and installation	6
Engine disassembly and reassembly - general information	7
External shift mechanism - removal, inspection and installation	21
General information	1
Initial start-up after overhaul	34
Major engine repair - general note	5
Oil pump - removal, inspection and installation	29
Operations possible with the engine in the frame	3
Operations requiring engine removal	4
Piston rings - installation	16
Pistons - removal, inspection and installation	15
Primary drive gear	22
Recommended break-in procedure	35
Rocker assemblies - removal and installation	8
Secondary drive gear (shaft drive models) - removal, inspection and installation	33
Shift drum and forks - removal, inspection and installation	30
Transmission shafts - disassembly, inspection and reassembly	32
Transmission shafts - removal and installation	31
Valves/valve seats/valve guides - servicing	12

Degrees of difficulty

Easy, suitable for novice with little experience	**Fairly easy,** suitable for beginner with some experience	**Fairly difficult,** suitable for competent DIY mechanic	**Difficult,** suitable for experienced DIY mechanic 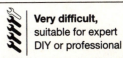	**Very difficult,** suitable for expert DIY or professional

Specifications

General
Bore
- VS700, VS750 .... 80.0 mm (3.2 inches)
- VS800 .... 83.0 mm (3.268 inches)

Stroke
- VS700 .... 69.6 m (2.7 inches)
- VS750, VS800 .... 74.4 mm (2.9 inches)

Displacement
- VS700 .... 699 cc (43 cubic inches)
- VS750 .... 747 cc (45.6 cubic inches)
- VS800 .... 805 cc (49.1 cubic inches)

Compression ratio .... 10.0 to 1

Compression pressure
- Intruder, S50, Marauder, Volusia
  - Standard .... 1300 to 1700 kPa (185 to 242 psi)
  - Limit .... 1100 kPa (156 psi)
- C50 and M50
  - Standard .... 1300 to 1700 kPa (185 to 242 psi)
  - Limit .... 1100 kPa (156 psi)

Camshaft and rocker arms

Rocker arm bore diameter... 12.000 to 12.018 mm (0.4724 to 0.4731 inch)
Rocker pivot bolt diameter.. 11.966 to 11.984mm (0.4711 to 0.4718 inch)
Lobe height (intake)
   VS750 (1985)
      Standard.. 35.925 to 35.965 mm (1.4144 to 1.4159 inch)
      Minimum.. 35.62 mm (1.401 inch)
   VS750 and VS800 (1986 on)
      Standard.. 35.954 to 35.994 mm (1.4155 to 1.4171 inch)
      Minimum.. 35.65 mm (1.404 inch)
   VZ800 Marauder (Switzerland)
      Standard.. 35.950 to 35.998 mm (1.4154 to 1.4172 inch)
      Limit.. 35.660 mm (1.4039 inch)
   VZ800 Marauder (except Switzerland)
      Standard.. 35.954 to 36.002 mm (1.4155 to 1.4174 inch)
      Limit.. 35.620 mm (1.4417 inch)
   VL800 front cylinder
      Standard.. 35.95 to 35.99 mm (1.415 to 1.417 inch)
      Limit.. 35.65 mm (1.404 inch)
   VL800 rear cylinder
      Standard.. 35.50 to 35.54 mm (1.398 to 1.399 inch)
      Limit.. 35.20 mm (1.386 inch)
Lobe height (exhaust)
   VS700/800
      Standard.. 36.919 to 36.959 mm (1.4535 to 1.4551 inch)
      Minimum.. 36.61 mm (1.441 inch)
   VZ800 Marauder
      Standard.. 36.919 to 36.967 mm (1.4535 to 1.4554 inch)
      Limit.. 36.620 mm (1.4417 inch)
   VL800 front cylinder
      Standard.. 36.92 to 36.96 m (1.454 to1.455 inch)
      Limit.. 36.62 mm (1.42 inch)
   VL800 rear cylinder
      Standard
         Carbureted models .... 36.58 to 36.62 mm (1.440 to1.442 inch)
         Fuel injected models .... 36.52 to 36.62 mm (1.438 to 1.442 inch)
      Limit.. 36.28 mm (1.428 inch)
Camshaft bearing inside diameter
   Rear cylinder right side, front cylinder left side.............. 20.012 to 20.025 mm (0.7879 to 0.7884 inch)
   Rear cylinder left side, front cylinder right side.............. 25.012 to 25.025 mm (0.9847 to 0.9852 inch)
Journal diameter
   Rear cylinder right side, front cylinder left side.............. 19.959 to 19.980 mm (0.7858 to 0.7866 inch)
   Rear cylinder left side, front cylinder right side.............. 24.959 to 24.980 mm (0.9826 to 0.9835 inch)
Bearing clearance
   Standard .... 0.032 to 0.066 mm (0.0013 to 0.0026 inch)
   Limit .... 0.15 mm (0.006 inch)
Camshaft runout limit .... 0.10 mm (0.004 inch)
Camshaft chain 20-link length limit................................... 128.9 mm (5.07 inch)

Cylinder head, valves and valve springs

Cylinder head warpage limit... 0.05 mm (0.002 inch)
Valve stem bend limit (total indicator reading) .... 0.05 mm (0.002 inch)
Valve stem diameter
   1995 and earlier
      Intake... 5.465 to 5.480 mm (0.2152 to 0.2157 inch)
      Exhaust.. 5.450 to 5.465 mm (0.2146 to 0.2152 inch)
   1996 and later
      Intake... 5.475 to 5.490 mm (0.2156 to 0.2161 inch)
      Exhaust.. 5.455 to 5.470 mm (0.2148 to 0.2154 inch)
Valve head thickness limit .... 0.5 mm (0.020 inch)
Valve guide inside diameter (intake and exhaust)
   Standard .... 5.50 to 5.512 mm (0.2165 to 0.2170 inch)
   Maximum .... 5.58 mm (0.2196 inch)
Valve stem to guide clearance (1995 and earlier)
   Intake
      Standard.. 0.020 to 0.047 mm (0.0008 to 0.0019 inch)
      Limit.. 0.35 mm (0.014 inch)

Exhaust
  Standard .... 0.035 to 0.062 mm (0.0014 to 0.0024 inch)
  Limit .... 0.35 mm (0.014 inch)
Valve stem to guide clearance (1996 and later)
  Intake .... 0.010 to 0.037 mm (0.0004 to 0.0015 inch)
  Exhaust .... 0.035 to 0.062 mm (0.0014 to 0.0024 inch)
  Limit .... 0.35 mm (0.014 inch)
Valve seat width (intake and exhaust) .... 0.9 to 1.1 mm (0.035 to 0.043 inch)
Valve spring free length limit
  Inner .... 38.3 mm (1.51 inch)
  Outer .... 40.1 mm (1.58 inch)

Cylinders
Bore diameter
  VS700, VS750
    Standard .... 80.000 to 80.015 mm (3.1496 to 3.1502 inches)
    Limit .... 80.085 mm (3.1529 inches)
  VS800, VZ800, VL800
    Standard .... 83.000 to 83.015 mm (3.2677 to 3.2683 inches)
    Limit .... 83.085 mm (3.2711 inches)
Taper limit .... 0.05 mm (0.002 inch)
Out-of-round limit .... 0.05 mm (0.002 inch)

Pistons and rings
Piston diameter (VS700)
  Standard .... 79.950 to 79.965 mm (3.1476 to 3.1482 inches)
  Limit .... 79.880 mm (3.1449 inches)
Piston diameter (VS750)
  1985
    Standard .... 79.945 to 79.960 mm (3.1474 to 3.1480 inches)
    Limit .... 79.880 mm (3.1449 inches)
  1986
    Standard .... 79.950 to 79.965 mm (3.1476 to 3.1482 inches)
    Limit .... 79.880 mm (3.1449 inches)
Piston diameter (VS800, VZ800, VL800)
  Standard .... 82.950 to 82.965 mm (3.2657 to 3.2663 inches)
  Limit .... 82.880 mm (3.2630 inches)
Piston-to-cylinder clearance
  1985
    Standard .... 0.05 to 0.06 mm (0.0020 to 0.0024 inch)
    Limit .... 0.120 mm (0.0047 inch)
  1986 and later
    Standard .... 0.045 to 0.055 mm (0.0018 to 0.0022 inch)
    Limit .... 0.120 mm (0.0047 inch)
Pin bore in piston
  Standard .... 20.003 to 20.008 mm (0.7875 to 0.7877 inch)
  Limit .... 20.030 mm (0.7886 inch)
Piston pin diameter
  Standard .... 19.996 to 20.000 mm (0.7872 to 0.7874 inch)
  Limit .... 19.980 mm (0.7866 inch)
Ring side clearance limit
  Top ring... 0.180 mm (0.007 inch)
  Second ring .... 0.150 mm (0.006 inch)
Ring groove width
  Top.. 1.01 to 1.03 mm (0.0398 to 0.0406 inch)
  Second .... 1.21 to 1.23 mm (0.0476 to 0.0484 inch)
  Oil .... 2.51 to 2.53 mm (0.0988 to 0.0996 inch)
Ring thickness
  Top.. 0.975 to 0.990 mm (0.0384 to 0.0390 inch)
  Second .... 1.170 to 1.190 mm (0.0461 to 0.0469 inch)
Ring end gap (top and second)
  Standard .... 0.20 to 0.35 mm (0.008 to 0.014 inch)
  Limit .... 0.70 mm (0.028 inch)

Crankshaft and bearings
Main bearing journal diameter... 47.965 to 47.980 mm (1.8884 to 1.8890 inch)
Main bearing oil clearance
  Standard .... 0.020 to 0.050 mm (0.0008 to 0.0020 inch)
  Limit .... 43.09 mm (1.696 inch)

2•4 Engine, clutch and transmission

Crankshaft and bearings (continued)
Crankshaft runout limit .... 0.05 mm (0.002 inch)
Crankshaft endplay
  1985 through 1991 .... 0.040 to 0.120 mm (0.0016 to 0.0047 inch)
  1992 and later .... 0.05 to 0.10 mm (0.002 to 0.004 inch)
Connecting rod side clearance
  Standard .... 0.10 to 0.20 mm (0.004 to 0.008 inch)
  Maximum .... 0.30 mm (0.012 inch)
Connecting rod bearing oil clearance
  Standard .... 0.024 to 0.042 mm (0.0009 to 0.0017 inch)
  Maximum .... 0.080 mm (0.0031 inch)

Clutch
Spring free length limit .... 34.0 mm (1.34 inch)
Friction plate thickness
  All except last plate
    Standard .... 2.9 to 3.08 mm (0.115 to 0.121 inch)
    Minimum .... 2.62 mm (0.103 inch)
  Last plate
    Standard .... 3.45 to 3.5 mm (0.136 to 0.140 mm)
    Limit .... 3.15 mm (0.124 inch)
Steel plate warpage limit .... 0.10 mm (0.004 inch)
Master cylinder bore diameter .... 14.000 to 14.003 mm (0.5512 to 0.5529 inch)
Master cylinder piston diameter .... 13.957 to 13.984 mm (0.5495 to 0.5506 inch)

Transmission
Shift fork groove to groove clearance
  Standard .... 0.10 to 0.30 mm (0.004 to 0.012 inch)
  Limit .... 0.5 mm (0.020 inch)
Shift fork finger thickness
  No. 1 forks .... 5.30 to 5.40 mm (0.209 to 0.213 inch)
  No. 2 fork .... 4.30 to 4.40 mm (0.169 to 0.173 inch)

Torque specifications

Intruder and S50
Engine mounting bolts .... 70 to 88 Nm (51 to 63 ft-lbs)
Engine mounting bracket bolts
  M6 .... 8 to 12 Nm (72 to 102 inch-lbs)
  M8 .... 18 to 28 Nm (13 to 20 ft-lbs)
Frame section mounting bolts .... 40 to 60 Nm (29 to 43 ft-lbs)
Rocker assembly bolts
  M6 .... 9 to 11 Nm (78 to 96 inch-lbs)
  M8 .... 21 to 25 Nm (15 to 18 ft-lbs)
Cylinder head/cylinder bolts and nuts
  M6 .... 9 to 11 Nm (78 to 96 inch-lbs)
  M8 .... 8 to 12 Nm (72 to 102 inch-lbs)
  M10 .... 35 to 40 Nm (26 to 29 ft-lbs)
Camshaft sprocket bolts .... 14 to 16 Nm (120 to 129 inch-lbs)
Rocker arm pivot bolts .... 25 to 30 Nm (18 to 21 ft-lbs)
Cam chain tensioner bolts .... 8 to 12 Nm (72 to 102 inch-lbs)
Clutch center nut .... 50 to 70 Nm (36 to 50 ft-lbs)
Primary drive gear bolt .... 80 to 110 Nm (58 to 79 ft-lbs)
Oil pump bolts .... 7 to 9 Nm (60 to 78 inch-lbs)
Secondary gearcase bolts .... 20 to 24 Nm (15 to 17 ft-lbs)
Crankcase bolts
  M6 .... 9 to 13 Nm (78 to 14 inch-lbs)
  M8 .... 20 to 24 Nm (15 to 17 ft-lbs)
Connecting rod nuts .... 49 to 53 Nm (36 to 38 ft-lbs)
Oil pressure relief valve .... 25 to 30 Nm (18 to 21 ft-lbs)
Oil pipe retainer bolts .... 8 to 12 Nm (72 to 102 inch-lbs)
Secondary drive gear nut .... 80 to 110 Nm (58 to 79 ft-lbs)
Transmission shaft bolt .... 60 to 70 Nm (44 to 50 ft-lbs)
Secondary drive gear Allen bolts .... 18 to 28 Nm (13 to 20 ft-lbs)
Crankcase oil passage plugs
  M6 .... 4 to 7 Nm (36 to 60 inch-lbs)
  M8 .... 15 to 20 Nm (11 to 14 ft-lbs)
  M10 .... 12 to 18 Nm (102 to 156 inch-lbs)
  M14, M16 .... 20 to 25 Nm (15 to 18 ft-lbs)

Engine, clutch and transmission 2•5

VZ800 (Marauder)
Engine mounting bolts	88 Nm (63 ft-lbs)
Engine mounting bracket bolts	50 Nm (36 ft-lbs)
Engine sprocket nut	115 Nm (83 ft-lbs)
Frame section mounting bolts	
M8	25 Nm (18 ft-lbs)
M10	50 Nm (36 ft-lbs)
Rocker assembly bolts	
M6	11 Nm (96 inch-lbs)
M8	23 Nm (16 ft-lbs)
Cylinder head/cylinder bolts and nuts	
M6	11 Nm (96 inch-lbs)
M8	25 Nm (18 ft-lbs)
M10	38 Nm (27 ft-lbs)
Camshaft sprocket bolts	11 Nm (123 inch-lbs)
Rocker arm pivot bolts	28 Nm (20 ft-lbs)
Cam chain tensioner bolts	10 Nm (84 inch-lbs)
Clutch center nut	95 Nm (68 ft-lbs)
Primary drive gear bolt	95 Nm (68 ft-lbs)
Oil pump bolts	8 Nm (72 inch-lbs)
Crankcase bolts	22 Nm (17 ft-lbs)
Connecting rod nuts	51 Nm (37 ft-lbs)
Oil pressure relief valve	28 Nm (20 ft-lbs)
Oil pipe retainer bolts	8 to 12 Nm (72 to 102 inch-lbs)
Crankcase oil passage plugs	Not specified

VL800 (Volusia and C50)
Engine mounting bolts	79 Nm (57 ft-lbs)
Engine mounting bracket bolts	23 Nm (16 ft-lbs)
Frame section mounting bolts	
M8	23 Nm (16 ft-lbs)
M10	50 Nm (36 ft-lbs)
Rocker assembly bolts	
M6	10 Nm (84 inch-lbs)
M8	25 Nm (18 ft-lbs)
Cylinder head/cylinder bolts and nuts	
M8	
Initial setting	10 Nm (84 inch-lbs)
Final setting	25 Nm (18 ft-lbs)
M10	
Initial setting	25 Nm (18 ft-lbs)
Final setting	38 Nm (27 ft-lbs)
Camshaft sprocket bolts	15 Nm (156 inch-lbs)
Rocker arm pivot bolts	27 Nm (19 ft-lbs)
Cam chain tensioner bolts	10 Nm (84 inch-lbs)
Clutch center nut	60 Nm (47 ft-lbs)
Primary drive gear bolt	95 Nm (68 ft-lbs)
Oil pump bolts	11 Nm (96 inch-lbs)
Secondary gearcase bolts	
Hex bolts	22 Nm (16 ft-lbs)
Allen bolts	23 Nm (16.5 ft-lbs)
Crankcase bolts	
M6	11 Nm (96 inch-lbs)
M8	
Initial setting	15 Nm (123 inch-lbs)
Final setting	22 Nm (16 ft-lbs)
Connecting rod nuts	
Initial setting	25 Nm (18 ft-lbs)
Final setting	51 Nm (37 ft-lbs)
Oil pressure relief valve	28 Nm (20 ft-lbs)
Secondary drive gear Allen bolts	
Initial setting	15 Nm (123 inch-lbs)
Final setting	22 Nm (16 ft-lbs)
Oil pipe retainer bolts	Not specified
Crankcase oil passage plugs	
M6	6 Nm (52 inch-lbs)
M8	18 Nm (156 inch-lbs)
M10	15 Nm (123 inch-lbs)
M14	23 Nm (16 ft-lbs)
M16	25 Nm (25 ft-lbs)

2•6 Engine, clutch and transmission

1 General information

The engine/transmission unit on all models is a liquid-cooled V-twin. The valves are operated by single overhead camshafts which are chain driven off the crankshaft. The engine/transmission assembly is constructed from aluminum alloy. The crankcase is divided horizontally.

The crankcase incorporates a wet sump, pressure-fed lubrication system which uses a chain-driven oil pump, oil filter, mesh oil screen, relief valve and oil pressure switch. The transmission gears are contained in the crankcase. Power from the crankshaft is routed to the transmission via the clutch, which is of the wet, multi-plate type and is gear-driven off the crankshaft. The transmission is a five-speed, constant-mesh unit. On shaft drive models, a bevel gear unit transmits power from the transmission to the driveshaft.

2 Cylinder compression - check

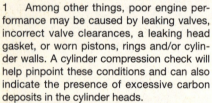

2.5 A compression gauge with a threaded fitting for the spark plug hole is preferred over the type that requires hand pressure to retain the seal

1 Among other things, poor engine performance may be caused by leaking valves, incorrect valve clearances, a leaking head gasket, or worn pistons, rings and/or cylinder walls. A cylinder compression check will help pinpoint these conditions and can also indicate the presence of excessive carbon deposits in the cylinder heads.
2 The only tools required are a compression gauge and a spark plug wrench. Depending on the outcome of the initial test, a squirt-type oil can may also be needed.
3 Run the engine until it reaches normal operating temperature. Place the motorcycle on the centerstand (if equipped). If not, prop it securely upright. Remove the fuel tank, then remove the spark plugs (see Chapter 1, if necessary). Work carefully - don't strip the spark plug hole threads and don't burn your hands. If you're working on a dual-plug model (2009 and later M50, UK, Europe, Australia and Canada), remove only one spark plug from each cylinder.
4 Disable the ignition by unplugging the primary wires from the coils (see Chapter 5). Be sure to mark the locations of the wires before detaching them.
5 Install the compression gauge in one of the spark plug holes **(see illustration)**. Hold or block the throttle wide open.
6 Crank the engine over a minimum of four or five revolutions (or until the gauge reading stops increasing) and observe the initial movement of the compression gauge needle as well as the final total gauge reading. Repeat the procedure for the other cylinder and compare the results to the value listed in this Chapter's Specifications.
7 If the compression in both cylinders built up quickly and evenly to the specified amount, you can assume the engine upper end is in reasonably good mechanical condition. Worn or sticking piston rings and worn cylinders will produce very little initial movement of the gauge needle, but compression will tend to build up gradually as the engine spins over. Valve and valve seat leakage, or head gasket leakage, is indicated by low initial compression which does not tend to build up.
8 To further confirm your findings, add a small amount of engine oil to each cylinder by inserting the nozzle of a squirt-type oil can through the spark plug holes. The oil will tend to seal the piston rings if they are leaking. Repeat the test for the other cylinder.
9 If the compression increases significantly after the addition of the oil, the piston rings and/or cylinders are definitely worn. If the compression does not increase, the pressure is leaking past the valves or the head gasket. Leakage past the valves may be due to insufficient valve clearances, burned, warped or cracked valves or valve seats, or valves that are hanging up in the guides.
10 If compression readings are considerably higher than specified, the combustion chambers are probably coated with excessive carbon deposits. It is possible (but not very likely) for carbon deposits to raise the compression enough to compensate for the effects of leakage past rings or valves. Remove the cylinder heads and carefully decarbonize the combustion chambers (see Chapter 2).

3 Operations possible with the engine in the frame

The components and assemblies listed below can be removed without having to remove the engine from the frame. If, however, a number of areas require attention at the same time, removal of the engine is recommended. **Note:** *The engine is a tight fit in the frame, so the engine must be removed for most major procedures.*

Intruder, Volusia, S50, C50, M50

Gearshift mechanism external components
Water pump
Starter motor
Clutch plates and discs
Oil pump
Primary driven gear
Secondary bevel driven gear
Alternator
Starter clutch and reduction gears

Marauder

Gearshift mechanism external components
Water pump
Starter motor
Clutch plates and discs
Oil pump
Primary drive and driven gears
Alternator
Starter clutch and reduction gears

4 Operations requiring engine removal

It is necessary to remove the engine from the motorcycle to gain access to the following components:
Rocker assembly and camshafts
Cylinder heads
Cam chain tensioner
Cylinders and pistons
Crankshaft, connecting rods and bearings
Transmission shafts
Secondary drive gear (shaft drive models)
Shift drum and forks
Cam chains

5 Major engine repair - general note

1 It is not always easy to determine when

Engine, clutch and transmission

6.17a Engine lower rear mount and lower frame bolts (M50 shown; others similar)

6.17b Remove the frame section from the right front part of the frame

or if an engine should be completely overhauled, as a number of factors must be considered.

2 High mileage is not necessarily an indication that an overhaul is needed, while low mileage, on the other hand, does not preclude the need for an overhaul. Frequency of servicing is probably the single most important consideration. An engine that has regular and frequent oil and filter changes, as well as other required maintenance, will most likely give many miles of reliable service. Conversely, a neglected engine, or one which has not been broken in properly, may require an overhaul very early in its life.

3 Exhaust smoke and excessive oil consumption are both indications that piston rings and/or valve guides are in need of attention. Make sure oil leaks are not responsible before deciding that the rings and guides are bad. Refer to Section 3 and perform a cylinder compression check to determine for certain the nature and extent of the work required.

4 If the engine is making obvious knocking or rumbling noises, the connecting rod and/or main bearings are probably at fault.

5 Loss of power, rough running, excessive valve train noise and high fuel consumption rates may also point to the need for an overhaul, especially if they are all present at the same time. If a complete tune-up does not remedy the situation, major mechanical work is the only solution.

6 An engine overhaul generally involves restoring the internal parts to the specifications of a new engine. During an overhaul the piston rings are replaced and the cylinder walls are bored and/or honed. If a rebore is done, then new pistons are also required. The main and connecting rod bearings are generally replaced with new ones and, if necessary, the crankshaft is also replaced. Generally the valves are serviced as well, since they are usually in less than perfect condition at this point. While the engine is being overhauled, other components such as the carburetors and the starter motor can be rebuilt also. The end result should be a like-new engine that will give as many trouble free miles as the original.

7 Before beginning the engine overhaul, read through all of the related procedures to familiarize yourself with the scope and requirements of the job. Overhauling an engine is not all that difficult, but it is time consuming. Plan on the motorcycle being tied up for a minimum of two weeks. Check on the availability of parts and make sure that any necessary special tools, equipment and supplies are obtained in advance.

8 Most work can be done with typical shop hand tools, although a number of precision measuring tools are required for inspecting parts to determine if they must be replaced. Often a dealer service department or motorcycle repair shop will handle the inspection of parts and offer advice concerning reconditioning and replacement. As a general rule, time is the primary cost of an overhaul so it doesn't pay to install worn or substandard parts.

9 As a final note, to ensure maximum life and minimum trouble from a rebuilt engine, everything must be assembled with care in a spotlessly clean environment.

6 Engine - removal and installation

Note: *Engine removal and installation should be done with the aid of an assistant to avoid damage or injury that could occur if the engine is dropped. A hydraulic floor jack should be used to support and lower the engine if possible (they can be rented at low cost).*

Removal

1 Support the bike securely upright and disconnect the battery (negative cable first). Refer to Chapter 9 and remove the battery from the bike.

2 Remove the seat (see Chapter 8) and the fuel tank (see Chapter 4).

3 Remove the side covers and steering head covers (see Chapter 8).

4 Drain the coolant and the engine oil and remove the oil filter (see Chapter 1).

5 Remove the air filter housing (see Chapter 4).

6 Remove the PAIR system air cover and solenoid (if equipped) (see Chapter 4).

7 Remove the carburetor(s) or throttle body (see Chapter 4) and plug the intake openings with rags. If you're working on an Intruder or S50, remove the choke cable bracket.

8 Remove the radiator, radiator hoses, cooling fan and water pump hoses (see Chapter 3). If you're working on a Volusia, C50 or M50, remove the coolant reservoir tank. If you're working on an Intruder or S50, remove the water pump.

9 Remove the ignition coils and brackets (see Chapter 5).

10 Remove the exhaust system (see Chapter 4).

11 Remove the shift pedal (see Section 21).

12 If you're working on a shaft drive model, remove the front bevel gearcase cover from the engine (see Chapter 6).

13 If you're working on a chain drive model, remove the engine sprocket cover, detach the engine sprocket and separate the sprocket and drive chain from the engine (see Chapter 6).

14 If the motorcycle has a cable clutch, disconnect the lower end of the clutch cable from the lever and remove the cable from the lower bracket (see Chapter 1). If it has a hydraulic clutch, remove the slave cylinder.

15 Mark and disconnect the wires from the oil pressure switch, neutral switch, coolant temperature sender, starter relay and starter motor. Unplug the brake light switch, alternator, sidestand and pick-up coil electrical connectors (see Chapters 5 and 9). Disconnect the engine ground cable and spark plug wires. If you're working on an Intruder or S50, remove the ignition switch (see Chapter 9).

16 Disconnect the rear brake link (see Chapter 7).

17 Remove the frame downtube from the right side of the frame **(see illustrations)**.

2•8 Engine, clutch and transmission

6.19a Upper rear engine mount and ground cable (M50 shown; others similar)

6.19b Front engine mount (S50 shown; others similar)

6.21 Be sure to have enough help to remove the engine; we used two strong people to lift it out and a third person to operate the jack

7.2a A selection of brushes is required for cleaning holes and passages in the engine components

18 Support the engine with a floor jack and a wood block.
19 With the engine supported, remove the mounting bolts **(see illustrations)**.
20 Make sure no wires or hoses are still attached to the engine.
21 With the help of at least one assistant, slowly and carefully guide the engine out the right side, away from the bike **(see illustration)**.

Installation

22 Installation is the reverse of removal. Note the following points:
 a) *Don't tighten any of the engine mounting bolts until they all have been installed.*
 b) *Use new gaskets at all exhaust pipe connections.*
 c) *Tighten the engine mounting bolts and frame downtube bolts securely.*
 d) *Adjust the drive chain (if equipped), rear brake, throttle cables, choke cable (if equipped) and clutch cable (if equipped) following the procedures in Chapter 1.*

7 Engine disassembly and reassembly - general information

1 Before disassembling the engine, clean the exterior with a degreaser and rinse it with water. A clean engine will make the job easier and prevent the possibility of getting dirt into the internal areas of the engine.
2 In addition to the precision measuring tools mentioned earlier, you will need a torque wrench, a valve spring compressor, oil gallery brushes, a piston ring removal and installation tool, a piston ring compressor, a pin-type spanner wrench and a clutch holder tool (which is described in Section 20). Some new, clean engine oil of the correct grade and type, some engine assembly lube (or moly-based grease), a tube of Suzuki Bond liquid gasket or equivalent, and a tube of RTV (silicone) sealant will also be required. Although it may not be considered a tool, some Plastigage (type HPG-1) should also be obtained to use for checking bearing oil clearances **(see illustrations)**.

7.2b Type HPG-1 Plastigage is needed to check bearing oil clearances

3 An engine support stand made from short lengths of 2 x 4's bolted together will facilitate the disassembly and reassembly

Engine, clutch and transmission

7.3 An engine stand can be made from short lengths of 2 x 4 lumber and lag bolts or nails

8.3 Rocker assembly bolts (S50 shown; others similar)

procedures **(see illustration)**. The perimeter of the mount should be just big enough to accommodate the engine oil pan. If you have an automotive-type engine stand, an adapter plate can be made from a piece of plate, some angle iron and some nuts and bolts.

4 When disassembling the engine, keep "mated" parts together (including gears, cylinders, pistons, etc. that have been in contact with each other during engine operation). These "mated" parts must be reused or replaced as an assembly.

5 Engine/transmission disassembly should be done in the following general order with reference to the appropriate Sections.

Remove the rocker assemblies
Remove the camshafts
Remove and separate the cylinder heads and cylinders
Remove the timing chain tensioners
Remove the pistons
Remove the clutch
Remove the external shift mechanism
Remove the alternator rotor/stator coils and starter clutch (see Chapter 9)
Separate the crankcase halves
Remove the crankshaft and connecting rods
Remove the transmission shafts/gears
Remove the shift drum/forks
Remove the secondary drive gear (shaft drive models)

6 Reassembly is accomplished by reversing the general disassembly sequence.

8 Rocker assemblies - removal and installation

Removal

1 Remove the engine from the motorcycle (see Section 6).
2 Remove the trim covers and valve adjusting hole covers (see Chapter 1).
3 Remove the rocker assembly bolts **(see illustration)**.
4 Lift the rocker assembly off the cylinder **(see illustration)**.

Inspection

5 Turn the rocker assembly over and check for wear and damage on the valve and camshaft contact surfaces **(see illustrations)**. If

8.4 Lift the rocker assembly off the cylinder head; locate the dowels and the front cylinder's O-ring (arrows)

the camshaft contact surfaces in the cover are damaged, the cover should be replaced with a new one. If the rocker arms are worn or damaged, remove them as described below.

8.5a Check the contact surfaces for wear (arrows); replace the O-ring with a new one

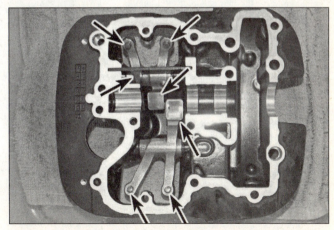

8.5b Inspect the rear rocker assembly in the same way as the front; check the rubber baffle (arrow) for damage or deterioration

2•10 Engine, clutch and transmission

8.6a Pry out the trim plugs from the pivot bolts . . .

8.6b . . . unscrew the pivot bolts with an Allen wrench . . .

8.6c . . . and remove the rocker arm, noting the wave washer location (arrow)

6 Pry the trim plugs out of the rocker shafts **(see illustration)**. Unscrew the rocker shafts with an Allen wrench and take them out of the cover. Note the location of the wave washer that fits between the rocker shaft and the cover **(see illustrations)**.

7 Remove the O-ring from the underside of the front cover if you haven't already done so. Use a new one on installation.

8 Check the rubber oil baffle in the rear cover for damage or deterioration and install a new one if its condition is in doubt **(see illustration 8.5b)**.

Installation

9 Remove all traces of sealant from the cylinder head and cover mating surfaces. Clean the mating surfaces with lacquer thinner, acetone or brake system cleaner. Apply a thin film of RTV sealant to the outer perimeter surface, but be sure not to get any on the camshaft bearing surfaces or the center mating surfaces along the camshaft.

10 Make sure the dowels and O-ring or rubber oil baffle are in position **(see illustrations 8.5a or 8.5b)**. Install the rubber camshaft plug in its recess **(see illustration)**.

11 Position the cover on the cylinder head, making sure the O-ring (front cover) doesn't slip out of place.

12 Install the bolts, tightening them slightly in a criss-cross pattern. Finish by tightening, again in a criss-cross pattern, to the torque listed in this Chapter's Specifications.

13 The remainder of installation is the reverse of removal.

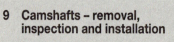

9 Camshafts – removal, inspection and installation

Removal

1 Remove the engine (see Section 5). Remove the rocker assembly from the cylinder you're working on (see Section 8).

2 Remove the rubber plug if it didn't come off with the cover **(see illustration 8.10)**.

3 Bend back the lockwasher tabs **(see illustration)**.

8.10 Don't forget to install the rubber plug

4 Turn the crankshaft to place the cylinder you're working on at TDC on the compression stroke (see the valve adjustment procedure in Chapter 1). Check the camshaft alignment marks to make sure they're in the correct position **(see illustrations)**.

9.3 Bend back the lockwasher tabs

9.4a The front cylinder is at TDC when the arrow and line (arrows) are parallel with the cylinder head surface and the dowel is positioned as shown

9.4b The rear cylinder is at TDC when the arrow and line (arrows) are parallel with the cylinder head surface and the dowel is positioned as shown

Engine, clutch and transmission 2•11

9.5a Unbolt the sprocket and pull it off the camshaft, then disengage it from the chain

9.5b Support the chain so it doesn't drop into the engine

5 Remove the camshaft sprocket bolts and pull the sprocket off the camshaft **(see illustration)**. Disengage the sprocket from the chain, lift the camshaft out of the engine and support the chain **(see illustration)**.

Inspection

Note: *Before replacing camshafts or the cylinder head and bearing caps because of damage, check with local machine shops specializing in motorcycle engine work. In the case of the camshafts, it may be possible for cam lobes to be welded, reground and hardened, at a cost far lower than that of a new camshaft. If the bearing surfaces in the cylinder head are damaged, it may be possible for them to be bored out to accept bearing inserts. Due to the cost of a new cylinder head it is recommended that all options be explored before condemning it as trash!*

6 Inspect the cam bearing surfaces of the head and the rocker assembly. Look for score marks, deep scratches and evidence of spalling (a pitted appearance).
7 Check the camshaft lobes for heat discoloration (blue appearance), score marks, chipped areas, flat spots and spalling **(see illustration)**. Measure the height of each lobe with a micrometer **(see illustration)** and compare the results to the minimum lobe height listed in this Chapter's Specifications. If damage is noted or wear is excessive, the camshaft must be replaced. Also, be sure to check the condition of the rocker arms, as described later in this Section.
8 Next, check the camshaft bearing oil clearances. Clean the camshafts, the bearing surfaces in the cylinder head and the bearing caps with a clean, lint-free cloth, then lay the cams in place in the cylinder head, with the punch marks on the sprockets facing away from each other and level with the valve cover gasket surface of the cylinder head **(see illustrations 9.4a and 9.4b)**. Engage the cam chain with the cam sprockets, so the camshafts don't turn as the bearing caps are tightened.
9 Cut two strips of Plastigage (type HPG-1) and lay one piece on each bearing journal, parallel with the camshaft centerline.
10 Make sure the rocker assembly dowels are installed. Install the assembly as descried in Section 8. While doing this, DO NOT let the camshafts rotate!
11 Now unscrew the bolts, a little at a time, and carefully lift off the rocker assembly.
12 To determine the oil clearance, compare the crushed Plastigage (at its widest point) on each journal to the scale printed on the Plastigage container (refer to *Tools and Workshop Tips* at the end of this manual for details). Compare the results to this Chapter's Specifications. If the oil clearance is greater than specified, measure the diameter of the cam bearing journal with a micrometer. If the journal diameter is less than the specified limit, replace the camshaft with a new one and recheck the clearance. If the clearance is still too great, replace the cylinder head and bearing caps with new parts (see the Note that precedes Step 6). Remove all traces of Plastigage from the components without scratching their surfaces.
13 Except in cases of oil starvation, the camshaft chain wears very little. If the chain has stretched excessively, which makes it difficult to maintain proper tension, replace it with a new one (see Section 23).

9.7a Check the lobes of the camshaft for wear - here's a good example of damage which will require replacement (or repair) of the camshaft

9.7b Measure the height of the camshaft lobes with a micrometer

2•12 Engine, clutch and transmission

9.16 The front camshaft has an F mark (arrow) and the rear camshaft has an R mark in the same place; don't mix them up

9.17 Install the camshaft in the head with the lobes downward

14 Check the sprockets for wear, cracks and other damage, replacing them if necessary. If the sprockets are worn, the chain is also worn. If wear this severe is apparent, the entire engine should be disassembled for inspection.

15 Check the chain guides for wear or damage. If they are worn or damaged, the chain is worn out or improperly adjusted. Replacement of the guide requires removal of the cylinder head and cylinder.

Installation

16 If both camshafts have been removed at once, look for the F (front) and R (rear) marks that indicate which cylinder the camshaft belongs in (see illustration). The camshafts are not interchangeable, so don't install them in the wrong cylinder.

17 Place the piston for the cylinder you're working on at top dead center (see the valve adjustment procedure in Chapter 1). Coat the camshaft journals and lobes with assembly lube and lay it in the cylinder head with the lobes downward (see illustration).

18 Install the sprocket in the chain and place the sprocket on the camshaft. Make sure the camshaft timing marks are correctly positioned (see illustration 9.4a or 9.4b).

19 Place a new lockwasher on the sprocket. Install the camshaft bolts, tighten them to the torque listed in this Chapter's Specifications and bend the lockwasher tabs against the bolt heads.

20 Install the other camshaft as described above if it was removed.

21 The remainder of installation is the reverse of the removal steps.

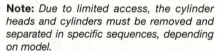

10 Cylinder heads and cylinders - removal, separation and installation

Note: *Due to limited access, the cylinder heads and cylinders must be removed and separated in specific sequences, depending on model.*

1 Remove the engine from the motorcycle (see Section 6).

2 Remove the rocker assemblies and camshafts (see Sections 8 and 9).

Intruder and S50

3 Remove the cylinder head/cylinder bolts from both cylinders (see illustration).

4 Unbolt the coolant fitting from the rear cylinder and loosen the hose clamps on the fitting that connects the front and rear cylinders (see illustration).

5 Remove the intake manifold (see Chapter 4).

6 Remove the coolant hose and pipe from the rear cylinder (see Chapter 3. **Note:** *The next step will be easier with two people.*

7 Lift the cylinders and heads off together (see illustration). This is necessary because there isn't enough room to remove the head-to-cylinder fasteners between the cylinders, or to completely remove the coolant fittings between the cylinders, when the cylinders are installed on the engine. As the cylinders are lifted off, they will spread apart from each other, causing the coolant fitting and connecting hose between the cylinders to separate.

8 Locate the cylinder base gaskets and dowels (see illustrations). They may stay on the crankcase or come off with the cylinders.

10.3 Loosen the cylinder head/cylinder bolts (arrows) in several stages, in a criss-cross pattern

10.4 Loosen the hose clamps and remove the fitting bolts (arrows)

10.7 On Intruder and S50 models, both cylinders must be lifted off at once; the base gaskets (arrows) may come off with the cylinders

Engine, clutch and transmission 2•13

10.8a Be sure to install the base gaskets (arrow); take great care not to tear them

10.8b Locate the dowels (arrows); they may stay in the cylinders or crankcase

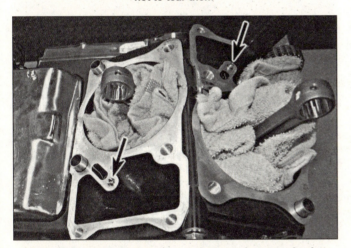

10.8c Stuff clean rags into the crankcase to keep out foreign material and carefully pull out the oil jets (arrows) . . .

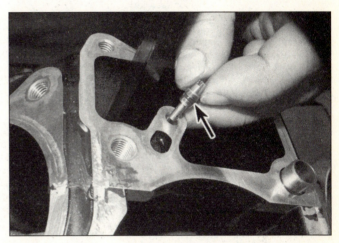

10.9 . . . use new O-rings on installation

Stuff rags into the crankcase around the connecting rods to keep foreign material out of the crankcase.

9 Remove the oil jets and store them where they won't be lost **(see illustration 10.8c and the accompanying illustration)**.

10 Compress and lock the timing chain tensioners (see Section 11).

11 Remove the nuts and bolts that secure the undersides of the cylinder heads to the cylinders **(see illustrations)**.

12 Separate the heads from the cylinders by tapping with a rubber mallet. If the heads won't come off easily, check to make sure all the fasteners have been removed (there are nuts and bolts on both sides of the cylinder that secure the underside of the head).

13 Remove the head gasket and locate the dowels **(see illustration)**. They may stay in the cylinder or come off with the head.

10.11a Unscrew the nut(s) arrow) . . .

10.11b . . . that secure the underside of the cylinder head (S50 shown)

10.13 Lift the cylinder head off the cylinder and locate the dowels (arrows)

2•14 Engine, clutch and transmission

10.38 If you're experienced and very careful, you can install the cylinder without using a ring compressor, but a compressor is recommended

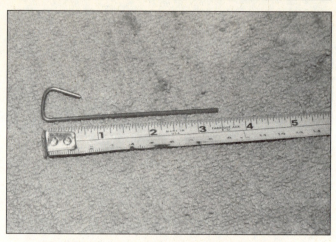

11.1 The tensioner locking tool should be about 3-1/2 inches (89 mm) long

Marauder

14 Perform Steps 4 through 6 above.
15 Remove the cylinder head/cylinder bolts from the rear cylinder **(see illustration 10.3)**.
16 Remove the nuts (on the front and rear side of the rear cylinder) that secure the underside of the rear cylinder head to the rear cylinder.
17 Compress and lock the rear cylinder's timing chain tensioner (see Section 11).
18 Remove the rear cylinder head from the cylinder as described above.
19 If you're planning to remove the chain tensioner, do it now (see Section 11). Remove the cam chain guide that's closest to the center of the engine.
20 Remove the rear cylinder as described above.
21 Remove the front cylinder head, then the front cylinder, as described above.

Volusia, M50 and C50

22 Perform Steps 3 through 6 above. Loosen the hose clamps on both hoses that connect the cylinders.
23 Remove the cylinder head/cylinder bolts from the front cylinder **(see illustration 10.3)**.
24 Compress and lock the rear cylinder's timing chain tensioner (see Section 11).
25 Remove the front cylinder head and cylinder together, then separate them, as described above.
26 Remove the cylinder head/cylinder bolts from the rear cylinder **(see illustration 10.3)**.
27 Remove the nuts (on the front and rear side of the rear cylinder) that secure the underside of the rear cylinder head to the rear cylinder.
28 Remove the cylinder head/cylinder bolts from the rear cylinder **(see illustration 10.3)**.
29 Remove the rear cylinder head, then the cylinder, as described above.

Installation

Note: *On Intruder and S50 models, you'll need to install both cylinders at once. Be sure the coolant hoses between the cylinder are in position with the hose clamps loosely installed, so that they can connect properly when the cylinders slide into position.*
30 Be sure the cylinder oil jets are in position. Use new O-rings on the oil jets.
31 Install new cylinder base gaskets.

HAYNES HINT *Since the coolant hoses and fitting O-rings between the cylinders can't be replaced without removing the cylinders from the engine, which requires removing the engine from the bike, they should be replaced now - while it's convenient - even if they appear to be in good condition.*

32 Reverse the disassembly sequences above to install the cylinder heads on the cylinders. Note that this occurs at different points on the sequence, depending on model. On Intruder and S50 models, install the rear cylinder first, leaving it about an inch (25 mm) above the crankcase, then install the rear cylinder, then lower both of them all the way. **Note:** *During the following steps, use a piece of wire to pull the cam chain up through the guides. The chain will catch partway up, so you'll need to grab it with a magnet and pull it up to where you can use your fingers on it. Keep the chain taut at all times or the slack will bunch up and prevent cylinder installation.*

Caution: *It is extremely easy to tear the cylinder base gaskets, especially on the front cylinder front side at the center, while installing the cylinders. It is also very difficult to guide the cylinders on while pulling the cam chain up between the guides. This procedure requires two people, one to keep the cam chain taut and stabilize the cylinder, and one to lower the cylinder over the piston.*

33 Lubricate the cylinder bores with plenty of clean engine oil.
34 Apply a thin film of moly-based grease to the piston skirts.
35 Install the dowel pins, then place a new cylinder base gasket on the crankcase.
36 Slowly rotate the crankshaft until the piston is at top dead center.
37 Attach a piston ring compressor to the piston and compress the piston rings. A large hose clamp can be used instead - just make sure it doesn't scratch the piston, and don't tighten it too much.
38 Install the cylinder over the piston and carefully lower it down until the piston crown fits into the cylinder liner **(see illustration)**. While doing this, pull the camshaft chain up, using a hooked tool or a piece of coat hanger. Push down on the cylinder, making sure the piston doesn't get cocked sideways, until the bottom of the cylinder liner slides down past the piston rings. A wood or plastic hammer handle can be used to gently tap the cylinder down, but don't use too much force or the piston will be damaged.
39 Remove the piston ring compressor or hose clamp, being careful not to scratch the piston.
40 The remainder of installation is the reverse of the removal steps. Tighten the cylinder head/cylinder bolts to the torque listed in this Chapter's Specifications.

11 Cam chain tensioners - locking, removal and installation

TOOL TIP *The tensioner must be locked in the compressed position to remove it or to separate the cylinder head from the cylinder. There's a special Suzuki tool available for this, but you can make a substitute from stiff wire as described below.*

1 Cut a piece of stiff wire (such as a coat hanger) and bend one end into a loop **(see illustration)**. The length of the tool after it's formed should be about 3-1/2 inches. If it's

Engine, clutch and transmission 2•15

11.4a Here's the tensioner piston in the extended position

11.4b Catch the snap-ring with a pointed tool (arrow) and turn it . . .

11.4c . . . so its gap is up like this; otherwise the snap-ring will catch on the engine when you compress the piston

11.5a Release the latch and compress the piston . . .

longer than this, it will be in the way when you separate the cylinder head from the cylinder.

2 Remove the engine from the motorcycle (see Section 6). Remove the rocker assembly and camshaft from the cylinder you're working on.

Locking

3 Locking the tensioner in the compressed position is necessary to remove the tensioner, as well as to separate the cylinder head from the cylinder.
4 The tensioner piston will be extended **(see illustration)**. To compress it, start by turning the circlip straight up with a pointed tool **(see illustrations)**. This is necessary to prevent the circlip from catching on the cylinder head when you try to compress the piston.
5 Compress the piston with a finger and lock it by inserting the special tool **(see illustrations)**. The tool needs to be off to one side of the gap as shown.

Removal

6 Lock the tensioner as described above.
7 Separate the cylinder head from the cylinder (see Section 10).
8 Remove the tensioner mounting bolts and take it off the cylinder **(see illustration 11.5b)**. Note the F and R marks indicating front and rear cylinder. The tensioners are not interchangeable.
9 Check the tensioner for wear on the piston contact surface and for damage, such as a broken spring. Release the latch and compress the piston several times to make sure it slides smoothly. Make sure the latch locks securely. Replace it as a unit if any problems are found.

Installation

10 Installation is the reverse of the removal steps. If both tensioners have been removed, refer to the F and R marks to make sure they're installed on the correct cylinder **(see illustration 11.5b)**. Tighten the tensioner mounting bolts to the torque listed in this Chapter's Specifications.

11 Once the cylinder and head have been reassembled, remove the locking tool and let the tensioner piston extend.

11.5b . . . place the locking tool at one side of the gap to secure it and remove the mounting bolts (upper arrows); the F or R mark (lower arrow) identifies the cylinder

2•16 Engine, clutch and transmission

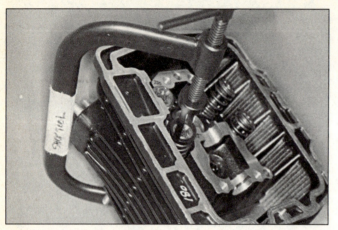

13.7a Compressing the valve springs with a valve spring compressor

13.7b Remove the valve keepers with needle-nose pliers or tweezers

12 Valves/valve seats/valve guides - servicing

1 Because of the complex nature of this job and the special tools and equipment required, servicing of the valves, the valve seats and the valve guides (commonly known as a valve job) is best left to a professional.
2 The home mechanic can, however, remove and disassemble the head, do the initial cleaning and inspection, then reassemble and deliver the head to a dealer service department or properly equipped motorcycle repair shop for the actual valve servicing. Refer to Section 15 for those procedures.
3 The dealer service department will remove the valves and springs, recondition or replace the valves and valve seats, replace the valve guides, check and replace the valve springs, spring retainers and keepers (as necessary), replace the valve seals with new ones and reassemble the valve components.
4 After the valve job has been performed, the head will be in like-new condition. When the head is returned, be sure to clean it again very thoroughly before installation on the engine to remove any metal particles or abrasive grit that may still be present from the valve service operations. Use compressed air, if available, to blow out all the holes and passages.

13 Cylinder head and valves - disassembly, inspection and reassembly

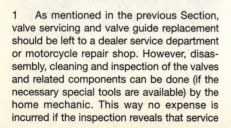

1 As mentioned in the previous Section, valve servicing and valve guide replacement should be left to a dealer service department or motorcycle repair shop. However, disassembly, cleaning and inspection of the valves and related components can be done (if the necessary special tools are available) by the home mechanic. This way no expense is incurred if the inspection reveals that service

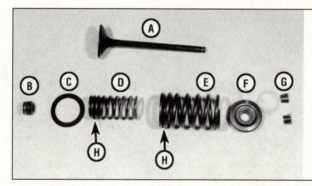

13.7c Valve components - exploded view

A Valve
B Oil seal
C Spring seat
D Inner valve spring
E Outer valve spring
F Valve spring retainer
G Keepers
H Tightly wound coils

work is not required at this time.
2 To properly disassemble the valve components without the risk of damaging them, a valve spring compressor is absolutely necessary. This special tool can usually be rented, but if it's not available, have a dealer service department or motorcycle repair shop handle the entire process of disassembly, inspection, service or repair (if required) and reassembly of the valves.

Disassembly

3 Remove the cylinder head from the engine (see Sections 10 and 11).
4 Before the valves are removed, scrape away any traces of gasket material from the head gasket sealing surface. Work slowly and do not nick or gouge the soft aluminum of the head. Gasket removing solvents, which work very well, are available at most motorcycle shops and auto parts stores.
5 Carefully scrape all carbon deposits out of the combustion chamber area. A hand held wire brush or a piece of fine emery cloth can be used once the majority of deposits have been scraped away. Do not use a wire brush mounted in a drill motor, or one with extremely stiff bristles, as the head material is soft and may be eroded away or scratched by the wire brush.
6 Before proceeding, arrange to label and store the valves along with their related components so they can be kept separate and reinstalled in the same valve guides they are

removed from (again, plastic bags work well for this).
7 Compress the valve spring on the first valve with a spring compressor, then remove the keepers (see illustrations) and the retainer from the valve assembly. Do not compress the springs any more than is absolutely necessary. Carefully release the valve spring compressor and remove the springs and the valve from the head (see illustration). If the valve binds in the guide (won't pull through), push it back into the head and deburr the area around the keeper groove with a very fine file or whetstone (see illustration).
8 Repeat the procedure for the remaining valves. Remember to keep the parts for each

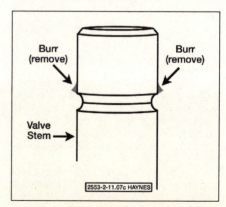

13.7d If the valve binds in the guide, deburr the area above the keeper groove

Engine, clutch and transmission 2•17

13.15 Measuring the valve seat width

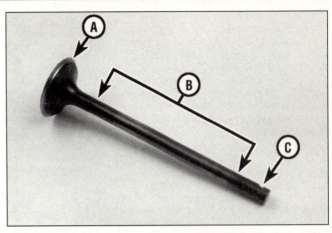

13.17 Check the valve face (A), stem (B) and keeper groove (C) for signs of wear and damage

valve together so they can be reinstalled in the same location.

9 Once the valves have been removed and labeled, pull off the valve stem seals with pliers and discard them (the old seals should never be reused), then remove the spring seats.

10 Next, clean the cylinder head with solvent and dry it thoroughly. Compressed air will speed the drying process and ensure that all holes and recessed areas are clean.

11 Clean all of the valve springs, keepers, retainers and spring seats with solvent and dry them thoroughly. Do the parts from one valve at a time so that no mixing of parts between valves occurs.

12 Scrape off any deposits that may have formed on the valve, then use a motorized wire brush to remove deposits from the valve heads and stems. Again, make sure the valves do not get mixed up.

Inspection

13 Inspect the head very carefully for cracks and other damage. If cracks are found, a new head will be required. Check the cam bearing surfaces for wear and evidence of seizure. Check the camshaft and rocker arms for wear as well (see Sections 8 and 9).

14 Using a precision straightedge and a feeler gauge, check the head gasket mating surface for warpage, referring to *Tools and Workshop Tips* at the end of this manual. If the feeler gauge can be inserted between the head and the straightedge, the head is warped and must either be machined or, if warpage is excessive, replaced with a new one.

15 Examine the valve seats **(see illustration)**. If they are pitted, cracked or burned, the head will require valve service that is beyond the scope of the home mechanic. Measure the valve seat width and compare it to this Chapter's Specifications. If it is not within the specified range, or if it varies around its circumference, valve service work is required. **Note:** *Suzuki recommends against lapping valves and seats after they have been machined.*

16 Clean the valve guides to remove any carbon buildup, then measure the inside diameters of the guides, referring to *Tools and Workshop Tips* at the end of the manual. If the guides exceed the maximum value given in the Chapter's Specifications, they must be replaced. The guides are measured at the ends and at the center to determine if they are worn in a bell-mouth pattern (more wear at the ends). If they are, guide replacement is an absolute must.

17 Carefully inspect each valve face for cracks, pits and burned spots. Check the valve stem and the keeper groove area for cracks **(see illustration)**. Rotate the valve and check for any obvious indication that it is bent. Check the end of the stem for pitting and excessive wear. The presence of any of the above conditions indicates the need for valve servicing.

18 Measure the valve stem diameter and replace if it exceeds the minimum value listed in this Chapter's Specifications **(see illustration)**. Also check the valve stem for bending. Set the valve in a V-block with a dial indicator touching the middle of the stem. Rotate the valve and note the reading on the gauge. If the stem runout exceeds the value listed in this Chapter's Specifications, replace the valve.

19 Check the end of each valve spring for wear and pitting. Measure the free length **(see illustration)** and compare it to this Chapter's Specifications. Any springs that are shorter than specified have sagged and should not be reused. Stand the spring on a flat surface and check it for squareness **(see illustration)**.

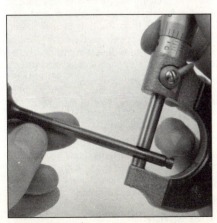

13.18 Measure the valve stem diameter with a micrometer

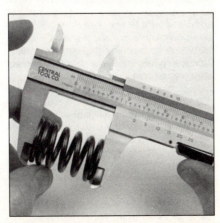

13.19a Measure the free length of the valve springs

13.19b Check the valve springs for squareness

20 Check the spring retainers and keepers for obvious wear and cracks. Any questionable parts should not be reused, as extensive damage will occur in the event of failure during engine operation.
21 If the inspection indicates that no service work is required, the valve components can be reinstalled in the head.

Reassembly

22 Lay the spring seats in place in the cylinder head, then install new valve stem seals on each of the guides. Use an appropriate size deep socket to push the seals into place until they are properly seated. Don't twist or cock them, or they will not seal properly against the valve stems. Also, don't remove them again or they will be damaged.
23 Coat the valve stems with assembly lube or moly-based grease, then install one of them into its guide. Next, install the spring seats, springs and retainers, compress the springs and install the keepers. **Note:** *Install the inner and outer springs with the tightly wound coils at the bottom (next to the spring seat). When compressing the springs with the valve spring compressor, depress them only as far as is absolutely necessary to slip the keepers into place. Apply a small amount of grease to the keepers* **(see illustration)** *to help hold them in place as the pressure is released from the springs. Make certain that the keepers are securely locked in their retaining grooves.*
24 Support the cylinder head on blocks so the valves can't contact the workbench top, then very gently tap each of the valve stems with a soft-faced hammer. This will help seat the keepers in their grooves.
25 Once all of the valves have been installed in the head, check for proper valve sealing by pouring a small amount of solvent into each of the valve ports. If the solvent leaks past the valve(s) into the combustion chamber area, valve service is required.

14 Cylinders - inspection

1 Remove the engine from the motorcycle, remove the cylinders and heads and separate them (see Sections 6, 10 and 11).
Caution: Don't attempt to separate the liners from the cylinder block.
2 Check the cylinder walls carefully for scratches and score marks.
3 Using the appropriate precision measuring tools, check each cylinder's diameter 10 mm down from the top, 60 mm down from the top, and 20 mm up from the bottom of the cylinder bore, parallel to the crankshaft axis. Next, measure each cylinder's diameter at the same three locations across the crankshaft axis. Compare the results to this Chapter's Specifications. If the cylinder walls are tapered, out-of-round, worn beyond the specified limits, or badly scuffed or scored, have them rebored and honed by a dealer service department or a motorcycle repair shop. If a rebore is done, oversize pistons and rings will be required as well.
4 As an alternative, if the precision measuring tools are not available, a dealer service department or motorcycle repair shop will make the measurements and offer advice concerning servicing of the cylinders.
5 If they are in reasonably good condition and not worn to the outside of the limits, and if the piston-to-cylinder clearances can be maintained properly (see Section 17), then the cylinders do not have to be rebored; honing is all that is necessary.
6 To perform the honing operation you will need the proper size flexible hone with fine stones, or a "bottle brush" type hone, plenty of light oil or honing oil, some shop towels and an electric drill motor. Hold the cylinder block in a vise (cushioned with soft jaws or wood blocks) when performing the honing operation. Mount the hone in the drill motor, compress the stones and slip the hone into the cylinder. Lubricate the cylinder thoroughly, turn on the drill and move the hone up and down in the cylinder at a pace which will produce a fine crosshatch pattern on the cylinder wall with the crosshatch lines intersecting at approximately a 60-degree angle. Be sure to use plenty of lubricant and do not take off any more material than is absolutely necessary to produce the desired effect. Do not withdraw the hone from the cylinder while it is running. Instead, shut off the drill and continue moving the hone up and down in the cylinder until it comes to a complete stop, then compress the stones and withdraw the hone. Wipe the oil out of the cylinder and repeat the procedure on the remaining cylinder. Remember, do not remove too much material from the cylinder wall. If you do not have the tools, or do not desire to perform the honing operation, a dealer service department or motorcycle repair shop will generally do it for a reasonable fee.
7 Next, the cylinders must be thoroughly washed with warm soapy water to remove all

13.23 A small dab of grease will help hold the keepers in place on the valve spring while the valve is released

15.3a Mark the piston F or R for front or rear cylinder and make sure there's an arrow mark (arrows)

traces of the abrasive grit produced during the honing operation. Be sure to run a brush through the bolt holes and flush them with running water. After rinsing, dry the cylinders thoroughly and apply a coat of light, rust-preventative oil to all machined surfaces.

15 Pistons - removal, inspection and installation

1 The pistons are attached to the connecting rods with piston pins that are a slip fit in the pistons and rods.
2 Before removing the pistons from the rods, stuff a clean shop towel into each crankcase hole, around the connecting rod **(see illustration 10.8)**. This will prevent the circlips from falling into the crankcase if they are inadvertently dropped.

Removal

3 Using a sharp scribe, scratch the position of each piston (front or rear cylinder) into its crown. Each piston should also have an arrow pointing toward the front of the engine **(see illustration)**. If not, scribe an arrow into the piston crown before removal. Be sure to label the pistons according to which cylinder they came from. Support the piston and remove the circlip with needle-nose pliers or a pointed tool **(see illustration)**. Push the piston pin out with fingers **(see illustration)**. If the pin won't come out, fabricate a piston pin removal tool (drawbolt) as described in *Tools and Workshop Tips* at the end of this manual.
4 Push the piston pin out from the opposite end to free the piston from the rod. You may have to deburr the area around the groove to enable the pin to slide out (use a triangular file for this procedure). Repeat the procedure for the other piston.

Inspection

5 Before the inspection process can be carried out, the pistons must be cleaned and

Engine, clutch and transmission 2•19

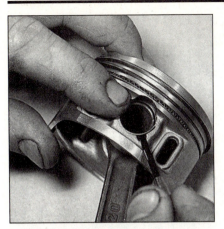

15.3b Wear eye protection and pry the circlip out of the groove with a pointed tool

15.3c Push the piston pin part-way out, then pull it the rest of the way

15.6 Remove the piston rings with a ring removal and installation tool

the old piston rings removed.

6 Using a piston ring installation tool, carefully remove the rings from the pistons **(see illustration)**. Do not nick or gouge the pistons in the process.

7 Scrape all traces of carbon from the tops of the pistons. A hand-held wire brush or a piece of fine emery cloth can be used once most of the deposits have been scraped away. Do not, under any circumstances, use a wire brush mounted in a drill motor to remove deposits from the pistons; the piston material is soft and will be eroded away by the wire brush.

8 Use a piston ring groove cleaning tool to remove any carbon deposits from the ring grooves. If a tool is not available, a piece broken off the old ring will do the job. Be very careful to remove only the carbon deposits. Do not remove any metal and do not nick or gouge the sides of the ring grooves.

9 Once the deposits have been removed, clean the pistons with solvent and dry them thoroughly. Make sure the oil return holes below the oil ring grooves are clear.

10 If the pistons are not damaged or worn excessively and if the cylinders are not rebored, new pistons will not be necessary. Normal piston wear appears as even, vertical wear on the thrust surfaces of the piston and slight looseness of the top ring in its groove. New piston rings, on the other hand, should always be used when an engine is rebuilt.

11 Carefully inspect each piston for cracks around the skirt, at the pin bosses and at the ring lands **(see illustration)**.

12 Look for scoring and scuffing on the thrust faces of the skirt, holes in the piston crown and burned areas at the edge of the crown. If the skirt is scored or scuffed, the engine may have been suffering from overheating and/or abnormal combustion, which caused excessively high operating temperatures. The oil pump and cooling system should be checked thoroughly. A hole in the piston crown, an extreme to be sure, is an indication that abnormal combustion (pre-ignition) was occurring. Burned areas at the edge of the piston crown are usually evidence of spark knock (detonation). If any of the above problems exist, the causes must be corrected or the damage will occur again.

13 Measure the piston ring-to-groove clearance by laying a new piston ring in the ring groove and slipping a feeler gauge in beside it **(see illustration)**. Check the clearance at three or four locations around the groove. Be sure to use the correct ring for each groove; they are different. If the clearance is greater than specified, new pistons will have to be used when the engine is reassembled.

14 Check the piston-to-bore clearance by measuring the bore (see Section 16) and the piston diameter. Make sure that the pistons and cylinders are correctly matched. Measure the piston across the skirt on the thrust faces at a 90-degree angle to the piston pin, 15 mm (0.6 inch) up from the bottom of the skirt **(see illustration)**. Subtract the piston diameter from the bore diameter to obtain the clearance. If it is greater than specified, the cylinders will have to be rebored and new oversized pistons and rings installed. If the appropriate precision measuring tools are not available, the piston-to-cylinder clearances can be obtained, though not quite as accurately, using feeler gauge stock. Feeler gauge stock comes in 12-inch lengths and various thicknesses and is generally available at auto parts stores. To check the clearance, select a piece of feeler gauge stock the

15.11 Check the piston pin bore and the piston skirt for wear, and make sure the internal holes are clear

15.13 Measure the piston ring-to-groove clearance with a feeler gauge

15.14 Measure the piston diameter with a micrometer

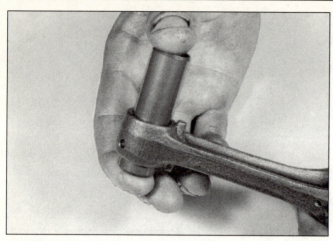

15.16 Slip the pin into the piston and try to wiggle it back-and-forth; if it's loose, replace the piston and pin

15.18 Make sure both piston pin circlips are securely seated in the piston grooves

same thickness as the recommended piston clearance listed in this Chapter's Specifications. Slip the gauge into the cylinder alongside of the piston. The cylinder should be upside down and the piston must be positioned exactly as it normally would be. Place the feeler gauge between the piston and cylinder on one of the thrust faces (90-degrees to the piston pin bore). The piston should slip through the cylinder (with the feeler gauge in place) with moderate pressure. If it falls through, or slides through easily, the clearance is excessive and a new piston will be required. If the piston binds at the lower end of the cylinder and is loose toward the top, the cylinder is tapered, and if tight spots are encountered as the feeler gauge is placed at different points around the cylinder, the cylinder is out-of-round. Repeat the procedure for the remaining piston and cylinder. Be sure to have the cylinders and pistons checked by a dealer service department or a motorcycle repair shop to confirm your findings before purchasing new parts.

15 Apply clean engine oil to the pin, insert it into the piston and check for freeplay by rocking the pin back-and-forth. If the pin is loose, new pistons and pins must be installed.

16 Repeat Step 15, this time inserting the pin into the connecting rod **(see illustration)**. If the pin is loose, measure the pin diameter and the pin bore in the connecting rod (or have this done by a dealer service department or machine shop). Replace the piston and pin if the pin is worn; replace the connecting rod if the pin bore is worn.

17 Refer to Section 16 and install the rings on the pistons.

Installation

18 Install the piston in its original location (front or rear cylinder) with the arrow pointing to the exhaust side of the cylinder. Lubricate the pin and the rod bore with clean engine oil. Install a new circlip in the piston groove on one side of the piston (don't reuse the old circlips). Push the pin into position from the opposite side and install a new circlip. Compress the circlips only enough for them to fit in the piston. Make sure the circlips are properly seated in the grooves **(see illustration)**.

19 Repeat the procedure to install the other piston.

16 Piston rings - installation

1 Before installing the new piston rings, the ring end gaps must be checked.
2 Lay out the pistons and the new ring sets so the rings will be matched with the same piston and cylinder during the end gap measurement procedure and engine assembly.
3 Insert the top (No. 1) ring into the bottom of the cylinder and square it up with the cylinder walls by pushing it in with the top of the piston **(see illustration 3.1 in Tools and Workshop Tips at the end of this manual)**. The ring should be about one inch above the bottom edge of the cylinder. To measure the end gap, slip a feeler gauge between the ends of the ring and compare the measurement to the Specifications.
4 If the gap is larger or smaller than specified, double check to make sure that you have the correct rings before proceeding.
5 If the gap is too small, it must be enlarged or the ring ends may come in contact with each other during engine operation, which can cause serious damage. The end gap can be increased by filing the ring ends very carefully with a fine file **(see illustration)**. When performing this operation, file only from the outside in.
6 Excess end gap is not critical unless it is greater than 0.040 in (1 mm). Again, double check to make sure you have the correct rings for your engine.
7 Repeat the procedure for each ring that will be installed in the first cylinder and for each ring in the remaining cylinder. Remember to keep the rings, pistons and cylinders matched up.
8 Once the ring end gaps have been checked/corrected, the rings can be installed on the pistons.
9 The oil control ring (lowest on the pis-

16.5 If the end gap is too small, clamp a file in a vise and file the ring ends (from the outside in only) to enlarge the gap slightly

Engine, clutch and transmission 2•21

16.9a Installing the oil ring expander - make sure the ends don't overlap

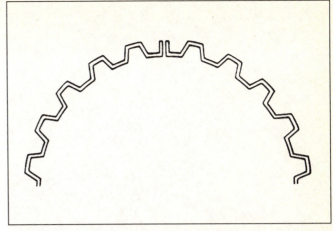

16.9b Butt the ends of the oil ring expander together like this - don't overlap them

ton) is installed first. It is composed of three separate components. Slip the expander into the groove, then install the upper side rail **(see illustrations)**. Do not use a piston ring installation tool on the oil ring side rails as they may be damaged. Instead, place one end of the side rail into the groove between the spacer expander and the ring land. Hold it firmly in place and slide a finger around the piston while pushing the rail into the groove. Next, install the lower side rail in the same manner.

10 After the three oil ring components have been installed, check to make sure that both the upper and lower side rails can be turned smoothly in the ring groove.

11 Install the second compression ring (middle ring) next. It can be readily distinguished from the top compression ring by its cross-section shape **(see illustration)**. Do not mix the top and middle rings.

12 To avoid breaking the ring, use a piston ring installation tool and make sure that the identification mark is facing up. Fit the ring into the middle groove on the piston. Do not expand the ring any more than is necessary to slide it into place.

13 Finally, install the top compression ring in the same manner. Make sure the identifying mark is facing up.

14 Repeat the procedure for the remaining piston and rings. Be very careful not to confuse the middle and top rings.

15 Once the rings have been properly installed, stagger the end gaps, including those of the oil ring side rails **(see illustrations)**.

17 Clutch hydraulic system (Intruder and S50) – bleeding, removal, inspection and installation

1 These models use a hydraulic clutch release system consisting of a lever-operated master cylinder on the left handlebar and a slave (release cylinder) on the left side of the engine.

Bleeding the system

2 Air in the system will compress, rather than transmitting hydraulic pressure through

16.9c Installing an oil ring side rail - don't use a ring installation tool to do this

the lines, so it needs to bled out whenever it enters the system. This can happen if the fluid level drops too low or when a hydraulic line is disconnected.

3 Turn the handlebar so the clutch master cylinder is as level as possible.

4 Remove the reservoir cover and top

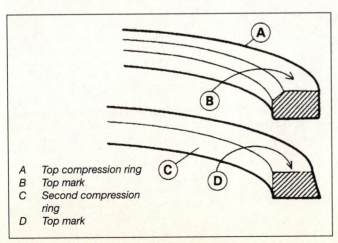

A Top compression ring
B Top mark
C Second compression ring
D Top mark

16.11 Piston ring profiles

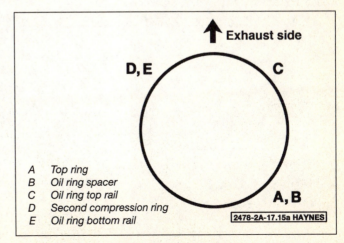

A Top ring
B Oil ring spacer
C Oil ring top rail
D Second compression ring
E Oil ring bottom rail

16.15 Ring gap locations

2•22 Engine, clutch and transmission

17.5 Remove the left rear engine cover bolts for access to the slave cylinder (Intruder and S50)

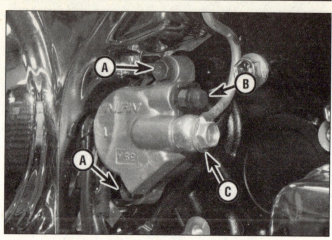

17.6 Slave cylinder details (Intruder and S50)

- A Mounting bolts
- B Bleed valve
- C Banjo fitting

up the master cylinder as described in *Daily (Pre-ride) Checks* at the beginning of this manual.

5 Remove the left rear engine cover **(see illustration)**.

6 Remove the cap from the bleeder valve on the clutch slave cylinder **(see illustration)**, place a box wrench on the bleeder valve nut and connect a clear vinyl bleeder hose to the bleeder valve. Immerse the other end of the bleeder hose in a container of clean clutch fluid.

7 Pump the clutch lever several times and watch the bubbles rising from the bleed holes in the bottom of the master cylinder reservoir. When the bubbles stop, hold in the clutch lever and tap on the master cylinder body several times to free any air bubbles that might be stuck to the sides of the fluid line or the master cylinder bore.

8 Pump the lever several times and hold it in, then crack the bleeder valve nut open just enough to allow fluid and any air bubbles in the system to escape, then tighten the bleeder valve nut. Slowly release the clutch lever, wait several seconds, then repeat:

Pump the lever several times, hold it in, crack the bleeder valve, etc. Continue this process until no more air bubbles come out at the bleeder valve. Keep an eye on the fluid level in the master cylinder reservoir and top it up as necessary.

9 When you're done, remove the bleeder hose, tighten the bleeder valve to the torque listed in this Chapter's Specifications, install the crankcase left rear cover, top up the master cylinder reservoir, install the diaphragm, set plate and cover and tighten the cover screws securely.

Master cylinder

Removal

10 Unscrew the rear view mirror from the master cylinder.

11 Disconnect the electrical lead from the clutch switch underneath the master cylinder.

12 Drain the hydraulic release system: Turn the handlebar so that the clutch master cylinder reservoir is as level as possible. Remove the reservoir cover screws, then remove the cover, set plate and diaphragm from the

reservoir. Remove the left rear engine cover **(see illustration 17.5)** and connect a bleeder hose to the bleeder valve on the clutch slave cylinder. Loosen the bleeder valve and pump the clutch lever. Continue doing so until no more fluid comes out of the bleeder valve. The system is now essentially empty.

13 Unscrew the banjo fitting from the master cylinder and disconnect the clutch hydraulic fluid hose from the master cylinder. Discard the old banjo bolt sealing washers.

14 Remove the master cylinder clamp bolt trim plugs **(see illustration)**, unscrew the bolts, remove the clamp and remove the master cylinder from the handlebar.

Overhaul

15 Remove the clutch switch (see Chapter 9).

16 Remove the nut from the clutch lever pivot bolt, pull out the pivot bolt and remove the clutch lever.

17 Remove the pushrod and dust boot **(see illustration)**.

18 Remove the snap-ring **(see illustration)**.

17.14 Pry the trim plugs from the screw holes (arrows)

17.17 Pull out the rubber dust boot and remove the pushrod

17.18 Remove the snap-ring from its groove in the bore

17.32a Remove the slave cylinder and its dowels; pull out the pushrod (arrow) for inspection

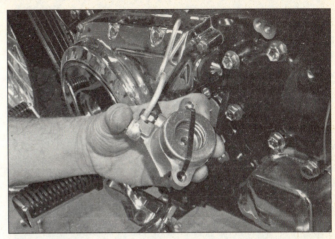
17.32b If you're not planning to disassemble the slave cylinder, tie it with a zip tie so the piston won't pop out

19 Remove the washer, secondary cup/master piston, primary cup and spring. If a part sticks in the bore, blow low-pressure compressed air through the fluid line hole.

⚠ **Warning: Do NOT point the open bore of the master cylinder at yourself when using compressed air to dislodge a stuck piston, which can shoot out with enough force to cause serious injury. Instead, point the piston bore toward a pile of shop rags inside a box and apply pressure sparingly.**

20 Thoroughly clean all the components in clean brake fluid. Do NOT use a petroleum-based solvent.
21 Inspect the piston and master cylinder bore for corrosion, rust, scratches and any other damage. If the piston shows signs of any type of wear or damage, replace it, and both rubber cups, as a set. If the master cylinder bore has similar damage or wear, replace the master cylinder. Do NOT try to hone out an aluminum master cylinder bore!
22 Even if there is no obvious damage or wear, measure the inside diameter of the master cylinder piston bore with a small hole gauge and a one-inch micrometer and measure the outside diameter of the master piston. Compare your measurements to the dimensions listed in this Chapter's Specifications. If either part is outside the specified limit, replace it.
23 Reassembly is the reverse of disassembly. Dip all the parts in clean brake fluid, then install the spring (big end first), primary cup, master piston/secondary cup and washer.
24 Depress the piston/spring assembly and install the snap-ring. Make sure it's correctly seated in its groove inside the master cylinder bore. Install the rubber boot and pushrod.
25 Grease the clutch lever pivot bolt. Align the hole in the clutch lever with the holes in the clutch lever bracket and insert the pivot bolt. Install the pivot bolt nut and tighten it securely.
26 Install the clutch switch (see Chapter 9).

Installation

27 Installation is the reverse of removal. Be sure to use new sealing washers when installing the clutch hose banjo bolt and tighten the banjo bolt to the torque listed in this Chapter's Specifications.
28 Before installing the left rear engine cover, bleed the hydraulic release system (see Steps 2 through 8).

Slave cylinder
Removal

29 Remove the left rear engine cover (see illustration 17.5).
30 If you're planning to disassemble, inspect and/or replace the slave cylinder, drain the hydraulic release system as described above. If you're simply detaching the slave cylinder from the engine to remove the engine or service something else, don't bleed the system.
31 If you're going to disconnect the fluid hose, put some shop rags and a container under the slave cylinder to catch spilled fluid. Remove the fluid hose banjo bolt (see illustration 17.6). Discard the old sealing washers. Put the end of the fluid hose in the container to catch any fluid still in the system.
32 Remove the slave cylinder mounting bolts and detach the slave cylinder from the engine (see illustration). If you're not planning to disassemble it, run a tie wrap through the bolt holes and around the cylinder to keep the piston from popping out (see illustration).

Inspection

33 Remove the end cap from the slave cylinder (see illustration). Check for fluid leakage from the cylinder and for corrosion or damage to the piston. If problems are found, or if bleeding the system and overhauling the master cylinder don't solve disengagement problems, replace the slave cylinder as a unit.

Installation

34 Installation is the reverse of removal. Be sure to use new sealing washers when installing the fluid hose banjo bolt. Tighten the banjo bolt to the torque listed in this Chapter's Specifications.
35 Before installing the crankcase left rear cover, bleed the hydraulic system (see Steps 2 through 8).

17.33 Remove the end cap for inspection

18.3 On cable clutch models, remove the left rear engine cover for access to the cable (C50 shown)

18.4 Loosen the locknuts (arrows) and slip the cable out of the engine slot

18 Clutch cable (except Intruder and S50) - replacement

1 Loosen the cable adjuster at the engine and the handlebar cable adjuster to provide as much slack as possible in the cable (see Chapter 1).
2 Disconnect the upper end of the clutch cable from the lever (see Chapter 1).

Volusia, C50 and M50
3 Remove the left rear engine cover (see illustration).
4 Loosen the locknut and adjuster at the left side of the engine (see illustration). Lift the cable up and slip it out of the slot in the crankcase.
5 Turn the cable to align it with the slot on the release mechanism, then slip it out of the slot.
6 Installation is the reverse of the removal steps. Adjust the cable as described in Chapter 1.

 Before removing the cable from the bike, tape the lower end of the new cable to the upper end of the old cable. Slowly pull the lower end of the old cable out, guiding the new cable down into position. Using this method will ensure the cable is routed correctly.

7 Lubricate the cable (see Chapter 1). Reconnect the ends of the cable by reversing the removal procedure, then adjust the cable following the procedure given in Chapter 1.

Marauder
8 Loosen the locknuts that secure the cable to the bracket on the left side of the engine above the clutch cover. Free the cable from the bracket.
9 Turn the cable to align it with the slot in the release lever on the left side of the engine, then free it from the slot.
10 Remove the old cable and install the new one, referring to the Haynes Hint above.
11 Lubricate the cable (see Chapter 1). Reconnect the ends of the cable by reversing the removal procedure, then adjust the cable following the procedure given in Chapter 1.

19 Clutch release mechanism (cable clutch) - removal, inspection and installation

Volusia, C50 and M50
1 Remove the left rear engine cover and disconnect the clutch cable as described in Section 18.
2 Remove the release mechanism mounting bolts and take it off the engine (see illustration).
3 Check the mechanism for wear and damage. Check the spring for stretching or breakage. Replace the mechanism if problems are found.
4 Installation is the reverse of the removal steps. Tighten the release mechanism bolts to the torque listed in this Chapter's Specifications. Adjust the clutch cable (see Chapter 1).

Marauder
5 Disconnect the clutch cable from the release lever (see Section 18).
6 Make alignment marks on the release shaft and lever (the lever the cable was detached from at the engine). Remove the pinch bolt and slip the lever off the shaft.
7 Remove the clutch cover from the engine (see Section 20).
8 Detach the release shaft and pull the shaft, oil seal and bearing out of the cover.

19.2 Disconnect the cable from the release mechanism, then remove its mounting bolts (arrows)

9 Pull the push piece, thrust bearing and thrust washer out of the clutch pressure plate.
10 Check all parts for wear and damage and replace as needed. The shaft seal should be replaced whenever it's removed.
11 Installation is the reverse of the removal steps. Lubricate the push piece and thrust bearing with molybdenum disulfide grease. Lubricate and adjust the cable as described in Chapter 1.

20 Clutch - removal, inspection and installation

Clutch removal
1 Support the bike securely upright.
2 Drain the engine oil (see Chapter 1).

Engine, clutch and transmission 2•25

20.4a Remove the clutch cover (S50 shown) . . .

20.4b . . . and locate the dowels (arrows); unscrew the pressure plate bolts . . .

20.5a . . . remove the springs . . .

20.5b . . . take off the pressure plate and remove the push piece, thrust bearing and thrust washer (arrows)

20.6a The friction plate with the thicker tab goes in first (arrow)

3   Disconnect the clutch cable (if equipped) (see Section 18).
4   Remove the clutch cover bolts and take the cover off (together with the release lever on Marauder models) (see illustrations). If the cover is stuck, tap around its perimeter with a soft-face hammer.
5   Loosen the clutch pressure plate bolts in a criss-cross pattern (see illustration). Remove the clutch springs, pressure plate, push piece, thrust bearing and thrust washer (see illustration).
6   Remove the friction plates, metal plates, damper spring and spring seat from the clutch housing (see illustrations).

20.6b Pull off the friction and metal plates, then remove the damper spring (right arrow) and spring seat (left arrow)

20.6c The spring seat and damper spring fit inside the last plate like this (arrow) . . .

20.6d . . . and the concave side of the damper spring faces away from the engine (arrow)

2•26 Engine, clutch and transmission

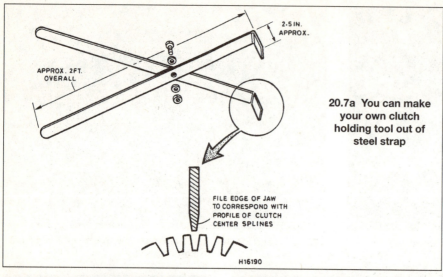

20.7a You can make your own clutch holding tool out of steel strap

20.7b Unscrew the center nut . . .

20.7c . . . and remove the lockwasher

20.10 On all except Marauder models, remove the snap-ring from the oil pump sprocket (arrow); remove the clutch housing together with the oil pump chain

7 Remove the clutch center nut, using a strap wrench or clutch holding tool **(see illustration)**. You can make your own tool out of steel strap. Hold the clutch center so it won't turn, unscrew the nut and remove the lockwasher **(see illustrations)**.

8 If you're working on a Marauder, remove the two clutch cams from behind the thrust washer.

9 Slide the clutch center off **(see illustration 20.7c)**.

10 On all except Marauder models, remove the snap-ring from the oil pump driven sprocket **(see illustration)**. Slide the clutch housing off, together with the oil pump drive chain and driven sprocket.

Caution: Do not lose the oil pump drive pin, which fits in the sprocket, or the thrust washer, which goes behind the sprocket.

On Marauders, the oil pump is gear-driven, so there is no chain to remove. The oil pump drive gear is on the back of the clutch housing and will come off with it.

11 Remove the needle roller bearing, collar, thrust washer and spacer from the transmission shaft **(see illustrations)**.

20.11a Remove the needle roller bearing and bushing . . .

20.11b . . . and the thrust washer and spacer

Engine, clutch and transmission 2•27

20.12 Pull the pushrod out of the transmission shaft

20.13 Check the clutch center splines (arrows) for wear and distortion

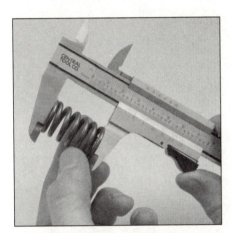

20.14 Measure the clutch spring free length

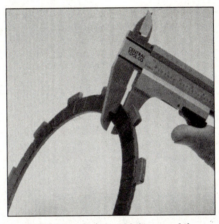

20.15 Measure the thickness of the friction plates

20.16 Check all plates for warpage

12 On all except Marauders, remove the clutch pushrod from the transmission shaft **(see illustration)**.

Clutch inspection

13 Examine the splines on both the inside and the outside of the clutch center **(see illustration)**. If any wear is evident, replace the hub with a new one.

14 Measure the free length of the clutch springs **(see illustration)** and compare the results to this Chapter's Specifications. If the springs have sagged, or if cracks are noted, replace them with new ones as a set.

15 If the lining material of the friction plates smells burnt or if it is glazed, new parts are required. If the metal clutch plates are scored or discolored, they must be replaced with new ones. Measure the thickness of each friction plate **(see illustration)** and compare the results to this Chapter's Specifications. Replace the friction plates as a set if they are near the wear limit.

16 Lay all metal and friction plates, one at a time, on a perfectly flat surface (such as a piece of plate glass) and check for warpage by trying to slip a 0.012-inch (0.3 mm) feeler gauge between the flat surface and the plate **(see illustration)**. Do this at several places around the plate's circumference. If the feeler gauge can be slipped under the plate, it is warped and should be replaced with a new one.

17 Check the tabs on the friction plates for excessive wear and mushroomed edges. They can be cleaned up with a file if the deformation is not severe.

18 Check the edges of the slots in the clutch housing for indentations made by the friction plate tabs **(see illustration)**. If the indentations are deep they can prevent clutch release, so the housing should be replaced with a new one. If the indentations can be removed easily with a file, the life of the housing can be prolonged to an extent.

19 Make sure the pushrod is not bent (roll it on a perfectly flat surface or use V-blocks and a dial indicator).

20 Clean all traces of old gasket material from the right crankcase cover.

Clutch installation

21 Installation is the reverse of the removal steps, with the following additions:

a) On all except Marauder models, lubricate the pushrod and install it in the output shaft.
b) Lubricate the needle roller bearing with clean engine oil.

20.18 Check the slots on the clutch housing for indentations - if they're worn, replace the clutch housing

2•28 Engine, clutch and transmission

21.3a On Volusia and C50 models, remove the pedal bolt and nut . . .

21.3b . . . on M50 models, remove the pedal snap-ring

21.4a . . . mark the lever and shift shaft for alignment, remove the pinch bolt (arrow) and slip the lever off the shift shaft; this is a C50

21.4b . . . and this is an M50

c) If you're working on a Marauder, make sure the oil pump drive gear is in position on the back of the clutch housing. On all other models, make sure the oil pump thrust washer is installed behind the sprocket and the drive pin is installed in the sprocket.

d) Install the clutch center thrust washer with its concave side toward the clutch center.

e) Tighten the clutch center nut to the torque listed in this Chapter's Specifications. Use the technique described in Step 8 to prevent the hub from turning.

f) Coat the clutch friction plates with engine oil. Install the clutch plates, starting with the plate that has the thickest tab. Position its spring seat and damper spring within the circumference of the first friction plate **(see illustrations 20.6d and 20.6c)**.

g) Use a new gasket on the clutch cover and tighten the bolts evenly to the torque listed in this Chapter's Specifications.

21 External shift mechanism - removal, inspection and installation

Shift pedal

Removal

1 Prop the bike securely upright.
2 On Intruder and S50 models, mark the shift pedal or lever shaft next to the split in the pedal, then remove the shift pedal bolt. Take the shift pedal off the shaft.
3 On Volusia and C50 models, remove the pedal pivot bolt and nut **(see illustration)**. On M50 models, remove the pedal snap-ring **(see illustration)**. Take the pedal off.
4 On Volusia, C50 and M50 models, disconnect the link rod and remove the shift pedal from the motorcycle **(see illustrations)**.

Installation

5 Installation is the reverse of removal, plus the following additions:

a) On all except for Volusia and C50 models, align the match marks and slip the pedal onto the shaft. Install the bolt and tighten it securely.
b) On Volusia and C50 models, install the pivot bolt, washer and nut.
c) If necessary, adjust pedal position as described below.

Adjustment

6 To raise or lower the pedal to suit your personal taste, loosen the locknuts on the linkage rod, rotate the rod to shorten or lengthen it, then tighten the locknuts.

Shift mechanism

Removal

7 Remove the clutch (see Section 20).
8 Pull the shift shaft out of the engine **(see illustration)**.
9 Remove the retainer screws with an impact driver **(see illustration)**.
10 Remove the nuts and take off the shift pawl retainer.

Engine, clutch and transmission 2•29

21.8 Pull the shift shaft out of the engine

21.9 Loosen the strainer screws with an impact driver - secure them with thread locking agent on installation

21.11a Unscrew the pawl assembly bolt . . .

21.11b . . . hold the pawls in with fingers and take the assembly off

21.12 Remove the drum shifter and locate the dowels

11 Remove the bolt and take the pawls and ratchet off of the shift drum **(see illustrations)**.
12 Remove the drum shifter from the shift drum **(see illustration)**.
13 Remove the shift drum retainers **(see illustration)**. Removal of the shift drum from the engine requires splitting the crankcase (see Section 24).

Inspection

14 Check the shift shaft for bends and damage to the splines or spring **(see illustration)**. If either condition is found it will have to be replaced.
15 Check the condition of the gear positioning lever, spring and shift drum cam. Replace them if they are cracked or distorted.
16 Check the shift mechanism arm for cracks, distortion and wear. Pay special attention to the tips of the pawl where they engage the shift drum cam. If any of these conditions are found, replace the shift mechanism.
17 Make sure the return spring pin on the engine isn't loose. If it is, unscrew it, apply a non-permanent locking compound to the threads, then reinstall the pin and tighten it securely.

18 Check the condition of the seal in the cover. If it has been leaking, drive it out with a hammer and punch. Drive a new seal in with a socket.

21.13 Remove the shift drum bearing retainers (arrows)

21.14 The return spring fits on the shaft like this - the ends fit over the return spring pin on the crankcase

2•30 Engine, clutch and transmission

21.19 Pawl assembly details - the flat ends of the pins face the springs and the rounded ends face away

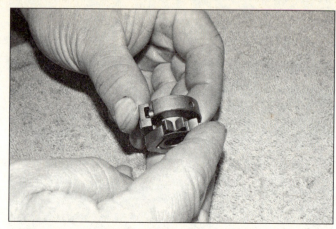

21.20a The pin slots are offset as shown - be sure to position them correctly

21.20b The external linkage should look like this when assembled (S50 shown; others similar)

22.2a Unscrew the primary drive gear bolt clockwise - the L mark indicates left-hand threads

19 Check the pawls, ratchet, springs and pins for wear or damage and replace as needed **(see illustration)**.

Installation

20 Installation is the reverse of the removal steps, with the following additions:

a) *If you removed the drum shifter, be sure to install its dowel pins and use non-permanent thread locking agent on the threads of the bolt. Tighten the bolt securely.*

b) *Assemble the pawl assembly with the flat ends of the pins toward the springs and the rounded ends toward the pawls **(see illustration 21.19)**. Be sure the pawl offsets are facing the right way **(see illustration)**.*

c) *Check to make sure the linkage is installed correctly before installing the components removed for access **(see illustration)**.*

22 Primary drive gear

Removal

1 Remove the right crankcase cover (see Section 20).
2 Slip a copper washer or penny between the primary gear and the gear on the clutch housing to keep the primary gear from turning **(see illustration)**. Unscrew the primary gear bolt and take the gear off **(see illustration)**.
3 Pull off the gear.

Inspection

4 Check the gear for worn or damaged teeth and replace it if necessary. If the primary gear is worn or damaged, also check the clutch housing gear. You may need to replace the clutch housing as well.

Installation

5 Installation is the reverse of the removal steps. Tighten the bolt to the torque listed in this Chapter's Specifications.

22.2b Remove the bolt and take the gear off the crankshaft - the thrust washer (arrow) is used to determine crankshaft end play

Engine, clutch and transmission 2•31

23.2 Pull the chain guide out, noting how its pins fit their slots (arrow)

23.3a Chain guide bolt (left); sprocket alignment marks (center) and chain guide slot (right)

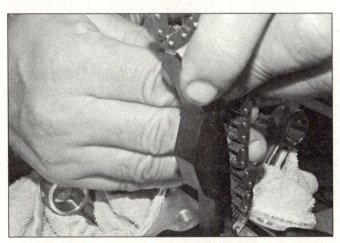

23.3b Unbolt the chain guide and lift it out of the cylinder

23.4 Slip the sprocket off and disengage the chain

23 Camshaft chains and guides - removal, inspection and installation

Removal

1 Remove the engine from the motorcycle. Remove the cylinder heads and cylinder and separate them (see Sections 6 and 10).
2 Lift the unbolted guide out of its pocket and remove it from the cylinder (see illustration).
3 Unbolt the lower end of the bolted guide and lift it out of the crankcase (see illustrations).
4 Note the alignment marks on the sprocket and crankshaft (see illustration 23.3a). If they aren't visible, make our own. Slip the sprocket off the crankshaft and disengage the chain from it (see illustration).

Inspection

5 Pull the chain tight to eliminate all slack and measure the length of twenty links, pin-to-pin (see illustration). Compare your findings to this Chapter's Specifications. The measurement is the same for upper and lower chains.
6 Also check the chain for binding and obvious damage.
7 If the twenty-link length is not as specified, or there is visible damage, replace the chain.
8 Check the chain guides for deep grooves, cracking and other obvious damage, replacing them if necessary.
9 Check the sprocket for worn or damaged teeth and replace it if problems are found. If the sprocket needs to be replaced, the timing chain should also be replaced.

Installation

10 Installation is the reverse of the removal steps. Be sure to align the marks on sprocket and crankshaft.

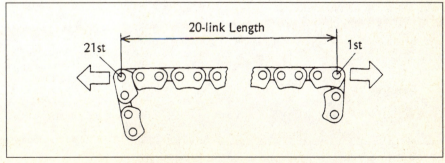

23.5 Stretch the chain and measure the length of 20 links

24.4a Right side crankcase bolts (S50 shown; others similar)

24.4b Left side crankcase bolts (S50 shown; others similar)

24 Crankcase - disassembly and reassembly

1 To examine and repair or replace the crankshaft, connecting rods, bearings, transmission components and secondary drive gear (shaft drive models), the crankcase must be split into two parts.
2 Remove the engine from the motorcycle. Remove the secondary driven gear, cylinders and heads (see Sections 6 and 10).
3 Remove the clutch, primary drive gear and oil pump (see Sections 20, 22 and 29).
4 Remove the crankcase bolts from both sides of the crankcase **(see illustrations)**. Loosen the bolts evenly, in several stages. Some of the bolts have copper washers **(see illustration)**. The bolts are different lengths, so label them so they can be returned to the correct locations.
5 Separate the crankcase halves **(see illustration)**. Locate the dowel pins and the O-ring that fits between the crankcase halves **(see illustration)**.
6 Refer to Sections 25 through 33 for information on the internal components of the crankcase.

24.4c Note that some of the bolts have copper washers (arrows)

24.5a Tap gently on the end of the transmission shaft to separate the case halves

Reassembly

7 Remove all traces of sealant from the crankcase mating surfaces. Be careful not to let any fall into the case as this is done.

24.5b Separate the case halves and locate the O-ring (arrow) - use a new O-ring on assembly . . .

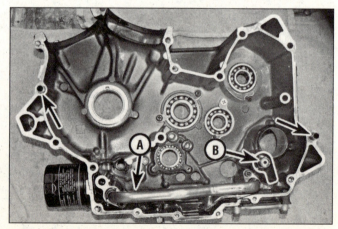

24.5c . . . locate the dowels as well (arrows) - they may stay in either case half

A Oil pipe   B Oil pressure relief valve

Engine, clutch and transmission 2•33

24.9 Crankcase internal components (typical) - the secondary drive gear is not used on chain drive models

25.2a Unbolt the retainers at each end of the oil pipe . . .

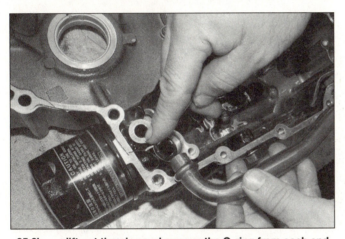

25.2b . . . lift out the pipe and remove the O-ring from each end - use new ones on assembly

25.2c Check for oil passage plugs (arrows) - remove them to clean the passages

8 Check to make sure the two dowel pins and the O-ring are in place in the mating surfaces of the crankcase half **(see illustrations 24.5b and 24.5c)**.
9 Make sure all components are in place inside the crankcase **(see illustration)**.
10 Pour some engine oil over the transmission gears, the crankshaft main bearings and the shift drum. Don't get any oil on the crankcase mating surface.
11 Apply a thin, even bead of silicone sealant to the crankcase mating surface.

Caution: Don't apply an excessive amount of sealant, as it will ooze out when the case halves are assembled.

12 Check the position of the shift drum, shift forks and transmission shafts - make sure they're in the neutral position.
13 Carefully assemble the crankcase halves.
14 Install the crankcase bolts and tighten them so they are just snug.
15 In several stages, tighten them to the torque listed in this Chapter's Specifications **(see illustrations 24.4a and 24.4b)**.
16 Turn the transmission shaft (and the secondary drive shaft on shaft drive models),

to make sure they turn freely. Also make sure the crankshaft turns freely.
17 The remainder of installation is the reverse of removal, with the following additions:
a) *Once the external shift linkage is installed, shift the transmission through all the gear positions and back to Neutral.*
b) *Be sure to refill the engine oil and coolant.*

25 Crankcase components - inspection and servicing

1 After the crankcases have been separated and the crankshaft, shift drum and forks, balancer shaft, oil pump and transmission components removed, the crankcases should be cleaned thoroughly with new solvent and dried with compressed air.
2 Remove the internal oil pipe **(see illustration 24.5c and the accompanying illustrations)**. All oil passages and lines should be blown out with compressed air **(see illustra-

tion)**. Use new O-rings, lubricated with clean engine oil, when installing the oil pipe. Apply non-permanent thread locking agent to the threads of the oil pipe bolts and tighten them to the torque listed in this Chapter's Specifications.
3 Unscrew the oil pressure relief valve **(see illustration)**. Check the valve for free movement and for any visible wear or damage. Replace it if problems are found.

25.3 Unscrew the oil pressure relief valve

2•34 Engine, clutch and transmission

27.3a Lift the crankshaft out of the crankcase

27.3b The thrust washer is used to adjust crankshaft end play

4 All traces of old gasket sealant should be removed from the crankcase mating surfaces as described in *Tools and Workshop Tips* at the end of this manual. Minor damage to the surfaces can be cleaned up with a fine sharpening stone.

Caution: Be very careful not to nick or gouge the crankcase mating surfaces or leaks will result. Check both crankcase sections very carefully for cracks and other damage.

5 If any damage is found that can't be repaired, replace the crankcase halves as a set.

6 Check the crankcase bearings for wear or damage **(see illustrations 24.5b and 24.5c)**. Unbolt the bearing retainer from bearings so equipped. Inspection of the crankshaft main bearings is described in Section 27. Rotate the other bearings with fingers and check for roughness, looseness or noise. Replace bearings that are in doubtful condition as described in *Tools and Workshop Tips* at the end of this manual.

7 Check and clean all threaded holes as described in *Tools and Workshop Tips* at the end of this manual.

26 Connecting rod bearings - general note

1 Even though connecting rod bearings are generally replaced with new ones during the engine overhaul, the old bearings should be retained for close examination as they may reveal valuable information about the condition of the engine.

2 Bearing failure occurs mainly because of lack of lubrication, the presence of dirt or other foreign particles, overloading the engine and/or corrosion. Regardless of the cause of bearing failure, it must be corrected before the engine is reassembled to prevent it from happening again.

3 When examining the bearings, remove them from the connecting rods and caps and lay them out on a clean surface in the same general position as their location on the crankshaft journals. This will enable you to match any noted bearing problems with the corresponding side of the crankshaft journal.

4 Dirt and other foreign particles get into the engine in a variety of ways. It may be left in the engine during assembly or it may pass through filters or breathers. It may get into the oil and from there into the bearings. Metal chips from machining operations and normal engine wear are often present. Abrasives are sometimes left in engine components after reconditioning operations such as cylinder honing, especially when parts are not thoroughly cleaned using the proper cleaning methods. Whatever the source, these foreign objects often end up imbedded in the soft bearing material and are easily recognized. Large particles will not imbed in the bearing and will score or gouge the bearing and journal. The best prevention for this cause of bearing failure is to clean all parts thoroughly and keep everything spotlessly clean during engine reassembly. Frequent and regular oil and filter changes are also recommended.

5 Lack of lubrication or lubrication breakdown has a number of interrelated causes. Excessive heat (which thins the oil), overloading (which squeezes the oil from the bearing face) and oil leakage or throw off (from excessive bearing clearances, worn oil pump or high engine speeds) all contribute to lubrication breakdown. Blocked oil passages will also starve a bearing and destroy it. When lack of lubrication is the cause of bearing failure, the bearing material is wiped or extruded from the steel backing of the bearing. Temperatures may increase to the point where the steel backing and the journal turn blue from overheating.

6 Riding habits can have a definite effect on bearing life. Full throttle low speed operation, or lugging the engine, puts very high loads on bearings, which tend to squeeze out the oil film. These loads cause the bearings to flex, which produces fine cracks in the bearing face (fatigue failure). Eventually the bearing material will loosen in pieces and tear away from the steel backing. Short trip riding leads to corrosion of bearings, as insufficient engine heat is produced to drive off the condensed water and corrosive gases produced. These products collect in the engine oil, forming acid and sludge. As the oil is carried to the engine bearings, the acid attacks and corrodes the bearing material.

7 Incorrect bearing installation during engine assembly will lead to bearing failure as well. Tight fitting bearings which leave insufficient bearing oil clearances result in oil starvation. Dirt or foreign particles trapped behind a bearing insert result in high spots on the bearing which lead to failure.

8 To avoid bearing problems, clean all parts thoroughly before reassembly, double check all bearing clearance measurements and lubricate the new bearings with engine assembly lube or moly-based grease during installation.

27 Crankshaft and main bearings - removal, inspection and installation

Crankshaft removal

1 Separate the crankcase halves.

2 Before removing the crankshaft check the side clearance. Install the thrust washer, cam chain sprocket and primary drive gear on the end of the crankshaft. Tighten the primary drive gear bolt to the torque listed in this Chapter's Specifications. Insert a feeler gauge between the thrust washer (on the outside of the crankcase) and the crankcase thrust surface. Compare your findings with this Chapter's Specifications. If the clearance is excessive, it can be reduced by using a thicker thrust washer. Thrust washers are available in several thicknesses.

3 Lift the crankshaft out and set it on a clean surface **(see illustration)**. Remove the thrust washer from the crankshaft **(see illustration)**.

Engine, clutch and transmission 2•35

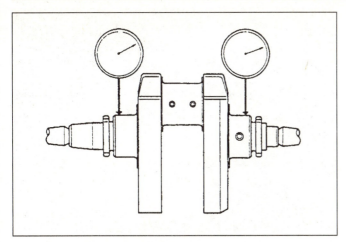

27.7 Measure crankshaft journal runout with a pair of dial indicators

27.8 Measure main journal diameter with a micrometer

Inspection

4 If you haven't already done so, mark and remove the connecting rods from the crankshaft (see Section 28).

5 Clean the crankshaft with solvent, using a rifle-cleaning brush to scrub out the oil passages. If available, blow the crank dry with compressed air. Check the main and connecting rod journals for uneven wear, scoring and pits. Rub a copper coin across the journal several times - if a journal picks up copper from the coin, it's too rough. Replace the crankshaft.

6 Check the camshaft chain sprockets on the crankshaft for chipped teeth and other wear. If any undesirable conditions are found, replace the crankshaft. Check the chains as described in Section 24. Check the rest of the crankshaft for cracks and other damage. It should be magnafluxed to reveal hidden cracks - a dealer service department or motorcycle machine shop will handle the procedure.

7 Set the crankshaft on V-blocks and check the runout with a dial indicator touching each of the main journals (see illustration). Compare your findings with this Chapter's Specifications. If the runout exceeds the limit, replace the crank.

8 Measure the diameter of the crankshaft journals with a micrometer (see illustration) and compare your findings with this Chapter's Specifications. Also, by measuring the diameter at a number of points around each journal's circumference, you'll be able to determine whether or not the journal is out-of-round. Take the measurement at each end of the journal to determine if the journal is tapered.

9 If any crank journal has worn down past the service limit, replace the crankshaft.

10 Using a telescoping gauge and a micrometer, measure the diameters of the main bearing bores, then compare the measurements with those listed in this Chapter's Specifications (see illustration). If the measurements are beyond the specified limit, the crankcase halves must be replaced as a set.

Crankshaft installation

11 Lubricate the bearings with engine assembly lube or moly-based grease.

12 Carefully lower the crankshaft into place.

13 Assemble the case halves (see Section 25) and check to make sure the crankshaft and the transmission shafts turn freely.

28 Connecting rods and bearings - removal, inspection, bearing selection and installation

Removal

1 Before removing the connecting rods from the crankshaft, measure the side clearance of the rods with a feeler gauge (see illustration). If the clearance on either rod is greater than that listed in this Chapter's Specifications, the rods will have to be replaced with new ones.

2 Mark the connecting rods with the cylinder identification (front or rear) (see illustration).

3 Look for numbers stamped across the connecting rods and caps (see illustra-

27.10 Measure main bearing diameter with a hole gauge

28.1 Measure side clearance at the gap (right arrow) – the number marks (center and left arrows) are used for bearing selection

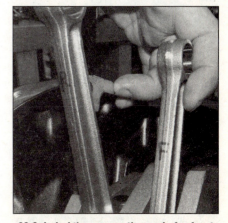

28.2 Label the connecting rods for front and rear cylinders

2•36 Engine, clutch and transmission

28.4a Remove the connecting rod cap nuts (arrows) . . .

28.4b . . . and remove the caps, together with the bearing inserts

tion 28.1). The numbers (1 through 3) indicate different inside diameter sizes of the connecting rod big end. The numbers can also be used to determine which cap goes on which rod, since the numbers are stamped across the parting line of rod and cap. If the halves of the number don't line up perfectly, the cap is on the wrong rod.

4 Unscrew the bearing cap nuts, separate the cap from the rod, then detach the rod from the crankshaft (see illustrations). If the cap is stuck, tap on the ends of the rod bolts with a soft face hammer to free them.

Caution: Do not dislodge the rod bolts from the connecting rods.

5 Separate the bearing inserts from the rods and caps, keeping them in order so they can be reinstalled in their original locations. Wash the parts in solvent and dry them with compressed air, if available.

Inspection

6 Check the connecting rods for cracks and other obvious damage. Lubricate the piston pin for each rod, install it in the proper rod and check for play (see Section 15). If it is loose, replace the connecting rod and/or the pin.

7 Refer to Tools and Workshop Tips at the end of this manual and examine the connecting rod bearing inserts. If they are scored, badly scuffed or appear to have been seized, new bearings must be installed. Bearings come in five different thicknesses, identified by color code (see illustration). Always replace the bearings in the connecting rods as a set. If they are badly damaged, check the corresponding crankshaft journal. Evidence of extreme heat, such as discoloration, indicates that lubrication failure has occurred. Be sure to thoroughly check the oil pump and pressure relief valve as well as all oil holes and passages before reassembling the engine.

8 Have the rods checked for twist and bending at a dealer service department or other motorcycle repair shop.

Bearing selection

9 If the bearings and journals appear to be in good condition, check the oil clearances with Plastigage as described in Tools and Workshop Tips at the end of this manual.

10 If the clearance is within the range listed in this Chapter's Specifications and the bearings are in perfect condition, they can be reused. If the clearance is beyond the standard range, but within the service limit, replace the bearing inserts with inserts that have blue paint marks, then check the oil clearance once again (these are the thickest bearing inserts, and may be thick enough to bring bearing clearance with the specified range). Always replace all of the inserts at the same time.

11 The clearance might be slightly greater than the standard clearance, but that doesn't matter, as long as it isn't greater than the maximum clearance or less than the minimum clearance.

12 If the clearance is greater than the service limit listed in this Chapter's Specifications, measure the diameter of the connecting rod journal with a micrometer and compare your findings with this Chapter's Specifications. Also, by measuring the diameter at a number of points around the journal's circumference, you'll be able to determine whether or not the journal is out-of-round. Take the measurement at each end of the journal to determine if the journal is tapered.

13 If any journal has worn down past the service limit, replace the crankshaft.

14 If the bearings need to be replaced, refer to the numbers on the connecting rods and on the crankshaft (see illustration 28.1 and the accompanying illustration). Select new bearings according to color code as follows:

Connecting rod code 1:
    With crankpin code 1, green
    With crankpin code 2, black
    With crankpin code 3, brown
Connecting rod code 2:
    With crankpin code 1, black
    With crankpin code 2, brown
    With crankpin code 3, yellow
Connecting rod code 3:
    With crankpin code 1, brown
    With crankpin code 2, yellow
    With crankpin code 3, blue

15 Repeat the bearing selection procedure for the remaining connecting rod.

28.7 Each bearing set has a color code to indicate its thickness (arrow)

28.14 The number marks on the crankshaft (arrow) are used in conjunction with the connecting rod number marks to select bearings

Engine, clutch and transmission 2•37

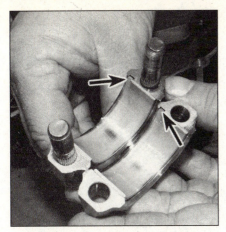

28.16 On assembly, make sure the bearing tabs (arrows) fit securely in the notches

29.1 Remove the snap-ring (arrow) from the oil pump sprocket . . .

29.3 . . . then remove the sprocket, drive pin and thrust washer (arrow)

29.4 Unbolt the oil pump and pull it out of the engine

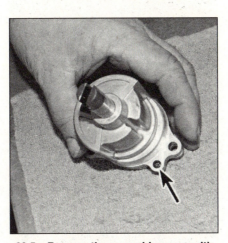

29.5a Remove the assembly screw with an impact driver . . .

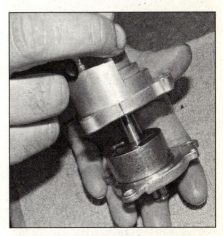

29.5b . . . and separate the pump body

Installation

16 Wipe off the bearing inserts, connecting rods and caps. Install the inserts into the rods and caps, using your hands only, making sure the tabs on the inserts engage with the notches in the rods and caps (see illustration). When all the inserts are installed, lubricate them with engine assembly lube or moly-based grease. Don't get any lubricant on the mating surfaces of the rod or cap.
17 Assemble each connecting rod to its proper journal, making sure the number marks on the rods match perfectly and face the rear of the engine (see illustration 28.1).
18 When you're sure the rods are positioned correctly, tighten the nuts to the torque listed in this Chapter's Specifications.
19 Turn the rods on the crankshaft. If either of them feels tight, tap on the bottom of the connecting rod caps with a hammer - this should relieve stress and free them up. If it doesn't, recheck the bearing clearance.
20 As a final step, recheck the connecting rod side clearances (see Step 1). If the clearances aren't correct, find out why before proceeding with engine assembly.

29 Oil pump - removal, inspection and installation

Removal

1 On all except Marauder models, remove the snap-ring that secures the oil pump drive sprocket (see illustration).
2 If you're working on a Marauder, remove the clutch (see Section 20). Remove the snap-ring that secures the oil pump drive gear.
3 Remove the sprocket or gear, then remove the drive pin and thrust washer (see illustration).
4 Unbolt the oil pump body from the crankcase and pull it out (see illustration).

Inspection

5 Remove the pump assembly screw (see illustration). Separate the rotors and shaft from the pump body (see illustration).
6 Wash all the components in solvent, then dry them off. Check the pump body, the rotors and the shaft for scoring and wear.

29.5c Check the rotors and shaft for wear or damage - DO NOT forget to reinstall the drive pin!

7 Also check the sprocket and chain (except Marauder) or gear (Marauder) for wear or damage and replace them if problems are found.

2•38 Engine, clutch and transmission

30.2a Pull out the shift fork shaft . . .

30.2b . . . and remove the fourth drive gear fork, noting which direction it faces . . .

Installation

8 Installation is the reverse of removal, with the following additions:
  a) Reassemble the pump by reversing the disassembly steps, but before installing the pump body, prime it by pouring oil between the rotors while turning the shaft by hand - this will ensure that it begins to pump oil quickly.
  b) Use non-permanent thread locking agent on the pump mounting bolts and tighten them to the torque listed in this Chapter's Specifications.
  c) Make sure the thrust washer and sprocket or gear drive pin are in place.
  d) Use a new snap-ring and place it securely in the groove.

30 Shift drum and forks - removal, inspection and installation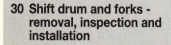

Removal

1 Remove the engine and separate the crankcase halves (see Sections 6 and 24).
2 Support the fork shaft for the fourth and fifth driven gear shift forks and pull the shift forks out **(see illustrations)**.
3 Remove the fork shaft for the third drive gear fork and pull the fork out **(see illustration)**.
4 Lift the shift drum out of the crankcase and remove the pin and spring from the bottom end **(see illustrations)**.
5 It's a good idea to reassemble the forks on the shaft and engage them with the shift drum grooves so you won't forget how they're installed.

Inspection

6 Check the edges of the grooves in the drum for signs of excessive wear. Measure the widths of the grooves and compare your findings to this Chapter's Specifications. Check the cam and bearing on the end of the

30.3 . . . and remove the fifth drive gear fork, also noting which way it faces, then remove the remaining fork shaft and fork

shift drum for wear and damage. If undesirable conditions are found, replace the cam or bearing.
7 Check the pin plate, retainer and snap-ring on the other end of the shift drum for wear or damage. Replace worn or damaged parts.
8 Check the shift forks for distortion and wear, especially at the fork ears. Measure the thickness of the fork fingers and compare your findings with this Chapter's Specifications. If they are discolored or severely worn they are probably bent. If damage or wear is evident, check the shift fork groove in the corresponding gear as well. Inspect the guide pins and the shaft bore for excessive wear and distortion and replace any defective parts with new ones.
9 Check the shift fork rod for evidence of wear, galling and other damage. Make sure the shift forks move smoothly on the rod. If the rod is worn or bent, replace it with a new one.

Installation

10 Installation is the reverse of removal,

30.4a Lift the shift drum out of its bore . . .

noting the following points:
  a) Lubricate all parts with engine oil before installing them.
  b) Don't forget to install the spring and pin in the bottom of the shift drum.
  c) Make sure the shift forks are engaged correctly with the gear grooves.

30.4b . . . and remove the pin and spring from the hole in the shift drum

Engine, clutch and transmission 2•39

31.2a Unscrew the transmission shaft bolt and nut (arrows) (the L mark on the bolt head indicates left-hand threads) . . .

31.2b . . . there's a thrust washer behind the bolt head

31.3a Note how the transmission gears mesh . . .

31.3b . . . then lift them out of the case together

31 Transmission shafts – removal and installation

Removal

1 Remove the engine and separate the case halves (see Sections 6 and 24).
2 Remove the transmission shaft bolt from the outside of the crankcase **(see illustrations)**.
3 Note how the gears fit together, then lift both shafts out of the transmission together **(see illustrations)**.
4 Refer to Section 32 for information pertaining to transmission shaft service and Section 30 for information pertaining to the shift drum and forks.

Installation

5 Carefully lower each shaft into place and make sure the gears engage each other correctly.
6 The remainder of installation is the reverse of removal.

32 Transmission shafts – disassembly, inspection and reassembly

Note: *When disassembling the transmission shafts, place the parts on a long rod or thread a wire through them to keep them in order and facing the proper direction.*
1 Remove the shafts from the crankcase (see Section 31).

Disassembly

2 All of the countershaft parts are held on the shaft by snap-rings, except first gear, which is integral with the shaft **(see illustration)**.

32.2 Transmission countershaft shaft components

2•40 Engine, clutch and transmission

32.3 Transmission input shaft components

32.10 On internally splined bushings, make sure the oil holes in bushings and shaft align

3 All of the input shaft parts are held on the shaft by snap-rings (see illustration).

Caution: *There are several sizes of snap-ring, with only a small difference between them. Be sure to keep the snap rings in their original locations and to replace them with ones of the same size.*

4 To disassemble the shafts, refer to the appropriate illustrations (see illustrations 32.2 and 32.3).

Inspection

5 Wash all of the components in clean solvent and dry them off.
6 Measure the shift fork grooves in the gears. If the groove width exceeds the figure listed in this Chapter's Specifications, replace the gear assembly, and also check the shift fork (see Section 34).
7 Check the gear teeth for cracking and other obvious damage. Check the gear bushings for scoring or heat discoloration. If a gear or bushing is damaged, replace the gear. Also give a close look to its corresponding gear on the other shaft.
8 Inspect the dogs and the dog holes in the gears for excessive wear. Replace the paired gears as a set if necessary.

Reassembly

9 During reassembly, always use new snap-rings and align the opening of the ring with a spline groove. The snap-rings have sharp sides and rounded sides. The rounded sides face toward the direction of thrust (the gear that's pushing against the snap-ring).
10 Make sure that when you install bushings with internal splines and oil holes, the oil hole lines up with the oil hole in the shaft (see illustration).
11 To reassemble the shafts, refer to the exploded views (see illustrations 32.2 and 32.3). Make sure the snap-rings and thrust washers are in the correct positions. Lubricate the components with engine oil before assembling them.
12 Check the assembled shafts to make sure all parts are installed correctly and the gears mesh correctly with each other (see illustration).
13 Lubricate the components with engine oil before assembling them.

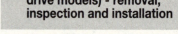

33 Secondary drive gear (shaft drive models) - removal, inspection and installation

Removal

1 Remove the engine and separate the crankcase (see Sections 6 and 24).
2 Remove the gear from the secondary drive shaft (see illustration).
3 Remove the Allen bolts that secure the gear to the crankcase and lift it out together with its shim (see illustrations).

Inspection

4 Check all parts for wear and damage. Disassembly of the gear unit requires special tools and should be done by a dealer service department or other qualified shop.

Installation

5 Installation is the reverse of the removal steps. Tighten the Allen bolts to the torque listed in this Chapter's Specifications.

32.12 The gears should mesh like this when the shafts are assembled

33.2 Lift the gear off the secondary drive shaft

33.3a Unscrew the mounting bolts (arrows) . . .

33.3b . . . and lift the shaft out of the crankcase, together with its shim

34 Initial start-up after overhaul

Note: *Make sure the cooling system is checked carefully (especially the coolant level) before starting and running the engine.*

1 Make sure the engine oil level is correct, then remove the spark plugs from the engine. Place the engine STOP switch in the Off position and unplug the primary (low tension) wires from the coil.
2 Turn on the key switch and crank the engine over with the starter until the oil pressure indicator light goes off (which indicates that oil pressure exists). Reinstall the spark plugs, connect the wires and turn the switch to On. **Note:** *If the oil pressure light won't go out, remove the oil filter (see Chapter 1). Hold the filter with the open end upright and pour oil into the center hole until the filter is full. Let the oil settle, then top it off again (you may need to do this twice). Reinstall the filter (a small amount of oil may leak out when you install it).*
3 Make sure there is fuel in the tank, then turn the fuel tap (carbureted models) to the On position and operate the choke.
4 Start the engine and allow it to run at a moderately fast idle until it reaches operating temperature.

Caution: *If the oil pressure indicator light doesn't go off, or it comes on while the engine is running, stop the engine immediately.*

5 Check carefully for oil leaks and make sure the transmission and controls, especially the brakes, function properly before road testing the machine. Refer to Section 35 for the recommended break-in procedure.
6 Upon completion of the road test, and after the engine has cooled down completely, recheck the valve clearances (see Chapter 1).

35 Recommended break-in procedure

1 Any rebuilt engine needs time to break-in, even if parts have been installed in their original locations. For this reason, treat the machine gently for the first few miles to make sure oil has circulated throughout the engine and any new parts installed have started to seat.
2 Even greater care is necessary if the engine has been rebored or a new crankshaft has been installed. In the case of a rebore, the engine will have to be broken in as if the machine were new. This means greater use of the transmission and a restraining hand on the throttle until at least 500 miles (800 km) have been covered. There's no point in keeping to any set speed limit - the main idea is to keep from lugging the engine and to gradually increase performance until the 500 mile (800 km) mark is reached. These recommendations can be lessened to an extent when only a new crankshaft is installed. Experience is the best guide, since it's easy to tell when an engine is running freely.
3 If a lubrication failure is suspected, stop the engine immediately and try to find the cause. If an engine is run without oil, even for a short period of time, severe damage will occur.

Notes

Chapter 3
Cooling system

Contents

Coolant level check .... See Chapter 1	Cooling system draining, flushing and refilling .... See Chapter 1
Coolant reservoir - removal and installation 4	General information 2
Coolant temperature gauge/light and sender unit - check	Radiator - removal and installation... 7
and replacement 3	Radiator cap - check 3
Coolant tubes - removal and installation...................................... 9	Specifications 1
Cooling fan and thermostatic switch - check and replacement ... 5	Thermostat - removal, check and installation 6
Cooling system check .... See Chapter 1	Water pump - check, removal, inspection and installation 8

Degrees of difficulty

Easy, suitable for novice with little experience	**Fairly easy,** suitable for beginner with some experience	**Fairly difficult,** suitable for competent DIY mechanic	**Difficult,** suitable for experienced DIY mechanic	**Very difficult,** suitable for expert DIY or professional

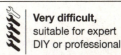

Specifications

General
Coolant type and mixture ratio...	See Chapter 1
Coolant capacity	See Chapter 1
Radiator cap pressure rating..	90 +/- 15 kPa (12.8 +/- 2.1 psi)
Thermostat rating	
Opening temperature...	75 +/- 1.5-degrees C (167 +/- 2.7-degrees F)
Valve travel (when fully open)...	Not less than 8 mm (5/16-inch) at 90-degrees C (194-degrees F)

Torque specifications
Thermostatic fan switch	10 to 15 Nm (84 to 132 inch-lbs)
Coolant temperature sender unit	
Carbureted models	10 to 15 Nm (84 to 132 inch-lbs)
Fuel injected models	18 Nm (13 ft-lbs)
Water pump mounting bolts (Marauder)	10 Nm (84 inch-lbs)
Water pump cover screws (Marauder)	10 Nm (84 inch-lbs)
Water pump impeller bolt (Marauder)...	8 Nm (72 inch-lbs)

1 General information

1 The models covered by this manual are equipped with a liquid cooling system, which utilizes a water/antifreeze mixture to carry away excess heat produced during the combustion process. The cylinders are surrounded by water jackets, through which the coolant is circulated by the water pump. The pump is mounted to the left side of the crankcase and is driven by a shaft connected through the engine to the oil pump. When the engine is warm, the coolant passes up through a hose and coolant pipe, which distributes water around the cylinders. It flows through the water passages in the cylinder heads into the radiator. The hot coolant then flows down through into the radiator (which is mounted on the frame downtubes to take advantage of maximum air flow), where it is cooled by the passing air, through another hose and back to the water pump, where the cycle is repeated. When the engine is cold, the thermostat closes and the coolant circulates through the engine but doesn't pass through the radiator.

2 An electric fan, mounted behind the radiator and automatically controlled by a thermostatic switch, provides a flow of cooling air through the radiator when the motorcycle is not moving. Under certain conditions, the fan may come on even after the engine is stopped, and the ignition switch is off, and may run for several minutes.

3 The coolant temperature sending unit senses the temperature of the coolant and controls the coolant temperature gauge or light on the instrument cluster.

4 The entire system is sealed and pressurized. The pressure is controlled by a valve which is part of the radiator cap. Pressurizing the coolant raises the boiling point, which prevents premature boiling of the coolant. An overflow hose, connected between the radiator and reservoir tank, directs coolant to the tank when the radiator cap valve is opened by excessive pressure. The coolant is automatically siphoned back to the radiator as the engine cools.

5 Many cooling system inspection and service procedures are considered part of routine maintenance and are included in Chapter 1.

Warning: Do not allow antifreeze to come in contact with your skin or painted surfaces of the motorcycle. Rinse off spills immediately with plenty of water. Antifreeze is highly toxic if ingested. Never leave antifreeze lying around in an open container or in puddles on the floor; children and pets are attracted by its sweet smell and may drink it. Check with local authorities about disposing of used antifreeze. Many communities have collection centers which will see that antifreeze is disposed of safely.

Warning: Do not remove the pressure cap from the thermostat housing when the engine and radiator are hot. Scalding hot coolant and steam may be blown out under pressure, which could cause serious injury. To open the pressure cap, wait until the engine has cooled. When the engine has cooled, place a thick rag, like a towel, over the radiator cap; slowly rotate the cap counterclockwise to the first stop. This procedure allows any residual pressure to escape. When the steam has stopped escaping, press down on the cap while turning counterclockwise and remove it.

2 Radiator cap - check

If problems such as overheating and loss of coolant occur, check the entire system as described in Chapter 1. The radiator cap opening pressure should be checked by a dealer service department or service station equipped with the special tester required to do the job. If the cap is defective, replace it with a new one.

3 Coolant reservoir or catch bottle - removal and installation

1 If you're working on an Intruder, S50 or Marauder, remove the frame head covers (see Chapter 8). Where necessary for access, remove the fuel tank (see Chapter 4).

2 If you're working on a C50 or M50, remove the frame cover from the lower left side of the motorcycle (see Chapter 8).

3 Unscrew the tank mounting bolt(s) and remove the tank (see illustrations). Pour the coolant into a suitable container, then disconnect the hoses and remove the tank from the motorcycle.

4 Installation is the reverse of the removal steps. Fill the tank with the specified coolant (see Chapter 1).

3.3a The coolant catch bottle on Intruder and S50 models is mounted above the radiator

4 Cooling fan and thermostatic switch - check and replacement

Check

1 If the engine is overheating and the cooling fan isn't coming on, first check the fuses (see Chapter 9). If the fuse is blown, check the fan circuit for a short to ground (see the *Wiring diagrams* at the end of this book). If the fuses are all good, disconnect the fan electrical connector. Using two jumper wires, apply battery voltage to the terminals in the fan motor side of the electrical connector. If the fan doesn't work, replace the motor.

2 If the fan does come on, the problem lies in the thermostatic fan switch or the wiring that connects the components. Remove the jumper wires and reconnect the electrical connector to the fan.

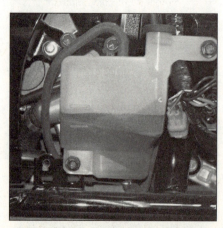

3.3b The reservoir tank on models so equipped is mounted on the left side of the bike

Cooling system

4.3 The fan switch is mounted in the radiator (exact location varies by model)

4.5 Remove the fan bracket bolts (arrows) (left side shown)

4.6a Remove the fan screws . . .

3 The fan switch is mounted in the radiator **(see illustration)**. Disconnect the electrical connector from the fan switch, attach a jumper wire to the harness side of the connector and ground the other end of the jumper wire to the engine. If the fan comes on, the circuit to the motor is good, and the thermostatic fan switch is defective.

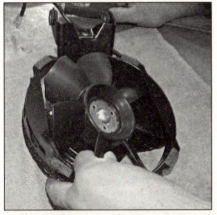

4.6b . . . and rotate the fan so it can be removed from the housing

4.7 Remove the screws (arrows) to separate the fan motor from the bracket

Replacement

Fan motor

 Warning: The engine must be completely cool before beginning this procedure.

4 Disconnect the cable from the negative terminal of the battery and remove the radiator (see Section 7).
5 Unbolt the fan bracket from the radiator **(see illustration)**. Separate the fan and bracket from the radiator.
6 Remove the screws that retain the blades to the fan motor **(see illustration)** and remove the fan blade assembly from the motor **(see illustration)**.
7 Remove the screws that attach the fan motor to the bracket and detach the motor from the bracket **(see illustration)**.
8 Installation is the reverse of the removal steps.

Thermostatic fan switch

 Warning: The engine must be completely cool before beginning this procedure.

9 Remove the radiator.
10 Unscrew the switch from the radiator **(see illustration 4.3)**.
11 Install the new switch, using a new O-ring. Tighten it to the torque listed in this Chapter's Specifications.
12 Connect the electrical connector to the switch. Check, and if necessary, add coolant to the system (see Chapter 1).

5 Coolant temperature sender - check and replacement

Check

1 These motorcycles may be equipped with a coolant temperature gauge or a warning light.
2 If the engine has been overheating but the coolant temperature gauge hasn't been indicating a hotter than normal condition (or the warning light hasn't been coming on), begin with a check of the coolant level (see Chapter 1). If it's low, add the recommended type of coolant and be sure to locate the source of the leak.
3 If you're working on an Intruder or S50, remove the seat and the fuel tank (see Chapters 8 and 4).
4 Locate the coolant temperature sender unit, which is screwed into the cylinder head (Intruder, S50 and fuel injected models) or the radiator (all other models) **(see illustration)**. Disconnect the electrical connector from the sender unit and turn the ignition key to the Run position (don't crank the engine over). If you're working on a model with a temperature gauge, the gauge should read Cold. If you're working on a model with a warning light, the light should stay out.
5 With the ignition key still in the Run position, connect one end of a jumper wire to the sender unit wire. If the bike has a gauge, connect a 17 ohm resistor to the other end of the wire, ten connect another length of wire to the resistor. Connect the free end of the jumper wire to ground. The needle on the

5.4 The coolant temperature sender is mounted on the front cylinder head (shown) or on the radiator

3•4 Cooling system

5.9 If the sender fitting has been leaking, remove it and replace its O-ring

6.3a Remove the water pump cover (arrow) . . .

6.3b . . . and unbolt the water pump housing . . .

temperature gauge should swing over to the Hot mark or the warning light should come on.

Caution: *If the motorcycle has a gauge, don't ground the wire any longer than necessary or the gauge may be damaged.*

6 If the gauge or light passes both of these tests but doesn't operate correctly under normal riding conditions, the temperature sender unit is defective and must be replaced.

7 If the gauge or light didn't respond to the tests properly, either the wire to the gauge is bad, the gauge itself is defective or the bulb is burned out.

Replacement

Sender unit

 Warning: *The engine must be completely cool before beginning this procedure.*

8 Unscrew the sender unit from the cylinder head or radiator and quickly install the new unit, tightening to the torque listed in this Chapter's Specifications.

9 If you're working on an Intruder or S50,

check the sender unit fitting for signs of coolant leakage. If there are any, unbolt the fitting from the head and install a new O-ring **(see illustration)**. Install the fitting and tighten the bolts securely.

10 Connect the electrical connector to the sender unit. Check, and if necessary, add coolant to the system (see Chapter 1).

Coolant temperature gauge or bulb

11 Refer to Chapter 9 for the coolant temperature gauge or bulb replacement procedure.

6 Thermostat - removal, check and installation

 Warning: *The engine must be completely cool before beginning this procedure.*

Removal

1 If the thermostat is functioning properly, the coolant temperature gauge should rise to the normal operating temperature quickly and

then stay there, only rising above the normal position occasionally when the engine gets abnormally hot. If the engine does not reach normal operating temperature quickly, or if it overheats, the thermostat should be removed and checked, or replaced with a new one.

2 Refer to Chapter 1 and drain the cooling system.

3 Remove the water pump cover and housing **(see illustrations)**. Disconnect the radiator hose from the water pump housing and take it out.

4 Remove the screws and take off the thermostat housing **(see illustration)**. Remove the thermostat from the housing **(see illustration)**.

5 Check the thermostat O-ring for leakage and replace the thermostat if its condition is in doubt.

Check

6 Remove any coolant deposits, then visually check the thermostat for corrosion, cracks and other damage. If it was open when it was removed, the thermostat is defective.

7 To check the thermostat operation, submerge it in a container of the specified coolant (50/50 antifreeze and water) along with a

6.3c . . . the O-ring should be replaced whenever the cover is removed

6.4a Remove the thermostat screws (arrows) . . .

6.4b . . . and take the thermostat out of the housing

Cooling system

thermometer. The thermostat should be suspended so it does not touch the sides of the container.

 Warning: Antifreeze is poisonous. Do not use a cooking pan to test the thermostat.

8   Gradually heat the water in the container with a hot plate or stove and check the temperature when the thermostat first starts to open.
9   Compare the opening temperature to the values listed in this Chapter's Specifications.
10   Continue heating the water until the valve is fully open.
11   Measure how far the thermostat valve has opened and compare to the value listed in this Chapter's Specifications.
12   If these specifications are not met, or if the thermostat doesn't open while the water is heated, replace it with a new one.

Installation

13   Install the thermostat into the housing.
14   Install a new O-ring in the groove in the thermostat cover.
15   Place the cover on the housing and install the bolts, tightening them securely.
16   The remainder of installation is the reverse of the removal steps. Fill the cooling system with the recommended coolant (see Chapter 1).

7 Radiator - removal and installation

 Warning: The engine must be completely cool before beginning this procedure.

1   Set the bike on its centerstand (if equipped). Remove the fan (see Section 4).

7.5a On Intruder and S50 models, unscrew the nut through-bolt (arrow) . . .

Drain the cooling system (see Chapter 1).
2   Disconnect the fan motor connector. Disconnect the electrical connector from the fan switch. On models with a temperature sender in the bottom of the radiator, disconnect the sender wire.
3   Remove the seat, frame head cover(s) and fuel tank (see Chapters 8 and 4).
4   Loosen the radiator hose clamps. Work the hoses free from the fittings, taking care not to damage the fittings in the process.
5   Remove the radiator mounting bolts **(see illustrations)**. Intruder and S50 models have a through-bolt at the top and a single bolt at the bottom. All other models have two bolts at the top and single bolt at the bottom. Take the radiator out.
6   Inspect the mounting bushings. Replace them if they're cracked or deteriorated.
7   Installation is the reverse of the removal steps, with the following additions:
a) Don't forget to connect the electrical connector(s).
b) On all models, fill the cooling system with the recommended coolant (see Chapter 1).

8 Water pump - check, removal, inspection and installation

 Warning: The engine must be completely cool before beginning this procedure.

Check

1   Visually check the area around the water pump for coolant leaks. Try to determine if the leak is simply the result of a loose hose clamp or deteriorated hose.
2   Set the bike on its centerstand (if equipped).
3   Drain the engine oil and coolant following the procedure in Chapter 1.
4   On all except Marauders, remove the water pump cover and housing (see Section 6). Try to wiggle the pump impeller back-and-forth and in-and-out. If you can feel movement, the water pump must be overhauled.
5   If you're working on a Marauder, you'll need to remove the water pump from the engine to check it as described below.
6   Check the impeller blades for corrosion. If they are heavily corroded, replace the impeller and flush the system thoroughly (it would also be a good idea to check the internal condition of the radiator).
7   If the cause of the leak was just a defective cover gasket, remove the old gasket and install a new one.

Removal and overhaul

All except Marauder

8   Remove the three screws that secure the water pump to the engine **(see illustration)**. Locate the removal hole(s) **(see illustration)**. Some models have three holes; others have only one. Thread one of the screws you just removed into the hole(s). Tighten the

7.5b . . . on all other models, remove the two bolts at the top of the radiator . . .

7.5c . . . the bottom of the radiator is secured by a single bolt (arrow)

8.8a Remove the water pump screws with an impact driver

8.8b Rotate the impeller to expose the removal screw hole or holes (arrow), then thread the water pump screw into the hole and tighten it to push the water pump out

8.8c Pull the water pump the rest of the way out of the engine; use a new O-ring and gasket (arrows) on installation

screw or screws to push the water pump out. Once it has separated from the engine, pull it the rest of the way out (see illustration).

9 Remove the circlip and pull the impeller shaft out of the water pump (see illustration).

10 Spin the bearing and check for rough or noisy movement. If problems are found, pull the bearing with a slide hammer and internal puller jaws. If the oil seal was leaking, remove it using the same tools used to remove the bearing.

11 Check the mechanical seal for wear and damage. If problems are found, drive it out using a socket or bearing driver the same diameter as the seal. Drive in a new seal, taking care not to damage it.

12 Drive in a new oil seal and bearing. Use a new O-ring on the bearing.

13 The remainder of assembly is the reverse of the disassembly steps. Use new O-rings and a new circlip.

Marauder

14 Remove the gearshift linkage rod (see Chapter 2).

15 Remove the swingarm pivot cover and left front footpeg bracket (see Chapter 8).

16 Remove the engine sprocket cover (see Chapter 6).

17 Remove the rear cylinder's exhaust pipe (see Chapter 4).

18 Disconnect the pipes and hose from the pump.

19 Unbolt the water pump and remove it from the engine.

20 Remove the two Phillips screws that secure the water pump cover. Separate the cover from the pump body and impeller.

21 Unscrew the impeller bolt and remove it, together with the washer and gasket.

22 Pry the mechanical seal ring out of the back of the impeller.

23 Take the impeller shaft out of the pump body.

24 Inspect the bearing and mechanical seal and replace them if necessary as described in Steps 10 and 11.

25 Drive in a new oil seal and bearing. Use a new O-ring on the bearing.

26 The remainder of assembly is the reverse of the disassembly steps. Tighten the impeller bolt and water pump cover screws and water pump mounting bolts to the torques listed in this Chapter's Specifications. Use new O-rings. Lubricate the cover O-ring with grease. Coat the outside of the mechanical seal with non-hardening sealant (Suzuki Bond 1207B or equivalent).

Installation

27 Make sure the weep hole is clear (see illustration).

28 Installation is the reverse of the removal steps. Use a new O-ring and gasket (see illustration 8.8c).

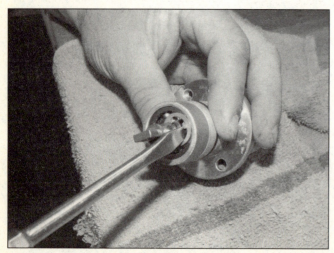

8.9 Remove the impeller circlip – you'll need to pull up on the shaft to provide removal clearance

8.27 Make sure the weep hole (arrow) is clear

Chapter 4 Part A
Fuel and exhaust systems - carbureted models

Contents

Air filter housing - removal and installation	12
Carburetor overhaul - general information	5
Carburetors - disassembly, cleaning and inspection	9
Carburetors - reassembly and fuel level adjustment	10
Choke cable - check and adjustment	See Chapter 1
Evaporative emission control system (California models) - removal and installation	15
Exhaust system - removal and installation	13
Fuel pump - testing and replacement	16
Fuel system - check and filter cleaning	See Chapter 1
Fuel tank - cleaning and repair	3
Fuel tank - removal and installation	2
Fuel tap - removal and installation	See Chapter 1
General information	1
Idle fuel/air mixture adjustment - general information	4
Idle speed - check and adjustment	See Chapter 1
PAIR system - operational test	14
Single carburetor - removal and installation	8
Throttle and choke cables - removal and installation	11
Twin carburetors - removal and installation	6
Twin carburetors - separation and reconnection	7

Degrees of difficulty

| Easy, suitable for novice with little experience | Fairly easy, suitable for beginner with some experience | Fairly difficult, suitable for competent DIY mechanic | Difficult, suitable for experienced DIY mechanic | Very difficult, suitable for expert DIY or professional |

Specifications

General
Fuel tank capacity .... See *Dimensions and Weights* at the end of the manual
Fuel grade .... Unleaded or low-lead (subject to local regulations), minimum octane rating 91 RON

Carburetor type
  VS700/750 Intruder
    Front cylinder .... Mikuni BDS34SS
    Rear cylinder .... Mikuni BS34SS
  VS800 Intruder, S50 and VZ800
    Front cylinder .... Mikuni BDS36SS
    Rear cylinder .... Mikuni BS36SS
  VZ800 .... Mikuni BDSR34
Idle speed .... See Chapter 1

Jet sizes

VS700
Main jet 132.5
Jet needle
  Front carburetor 5D21/1
  Rear carburetor 5D23/1
Needle jet
  Front carburetor P-0
  Rear carburetor P-1
Pilot jet 38
  Front carburetor 32.5
  Rear carburetor 40
Pilot screw (turns out) .... Not specified
Starter (choke) jet
  Front carburetor
    1986 .... 32.5
    1987 .... 37.5
  Rear carburetor 40

Jet sizes (continued)

VS700
Jet needle/clip position
    Front carburetor 5D21/1
    Rear carburetor 5D23/1
Needle jet
    Front carburetor P-0
    Rear carburetor P-1
Pilot jet... 38
    Front carburetor 32.5
    Rear carburetor 40
Pilot screw (turns out).. Not specified

VS750
Main jet
  1985 .... 132.5
  1986 and 1987
    Canada 132.5
    All others... 110
  1988 and 1989
    US and Canada 132.5
    All others
        Front carburetor 100
        Rear carburetor 110
  1990 and 1991
    US and Canada 132.5
    Switzerland 100
    All others
        Front carburetor 100
        Rear carburetor 110
Jet needle/clip position
  1985 .... 5D22/3
  1986 and 1987
    Switzerland 5D27/3
    All others... 5D22/3
  1988 and 1989
    US and Canada 5D22-3
    Switzerland
        Front carburetor 5D32/3
        Rear carburetor 5D33/3
    All others... 5D27/3
  1990
    US
        Front carburetor 5D21/1
        Rear carburetor 5D23/1
    Canada 5D22/3
    Switzerland
        Front carburetor 5D32/3
        Rear carburetor 5D33/3
    All others... 5D27/3
  1991
    US
        Front carburetor 5D21/1
        Rear carburetor 5D23/1
    Canada 5D22/3
    All others... 5D27/3
Needle jet
  1985
    Front carburetor.. P-3
    Rear carburetor P-4
  1986 and 1987
    Switzerland
        Front carburetor P-2
        Rear carburetor P-4
    All others
        Front carburetor P-3
        Rear carburetor P-4

VS750
   1988 and 1989
      US and Canada
         Front carburetor P-3
         Rear carburetor P-4
      Switzerland
         Front carburetor P-2
         Rear carburetor P-1
      All others
         Front carburetor P-2
         Rear carburetor P-4
   1990
      US
         Front carburetor P-4
         Rear carburetor P-1
      Canada
         Front carburetor P-3
         Rear carburetor P-4
      Switzerland
         Front carburetor P-2
         Rear carburetor P-1
      All others
         Front carburetor P-2
         Rear carburetor P-4
   1991
      US
         Front carburetor P-4
         Rear carburetor P-1
      Canada
         Front carburetor P-3
         Rear carburetor P-4
      All others
         Front carburetor P-2
         Rear carburetor P-4
Pilot jet
   1985
      Front carburetor 32.5
      Rear carburetor 40
   1986 and 1987
      Switzerland
         Front carburetor 32.5
         Rear carburetor 40
      All others
         Front carburetor 32.5
         Rear carburetor 37.5
   1988
      US
         Front carburetor 25
         Rear carburetor 40
      Canada
         Front carburetor 32.5
         Rear carburetor 40
      Switzerland
         Front carburetor 25
         Rear carburetor 35
      All others
         Front carburetor 32.5
         Rear carburetor 37.5
   1989
      US
         Front carburetor 25
         Rear carburetor 40
      Canada
         Front carburetor 32.5
         Rear carburetor 40
      Switzerland
         Front carburetor 25
         Rear carburetor 35

4A•4 Fuel and exhaust systems - carbureted models

VS750 (continued)
- All others
  - Front carburetor 32.5
  - Rear carburetor 37.5
- 1990
  - US
    - Front carburetor 25
    - Rear carburetor 40
  - Canada
    - Front carburetor 32.5
    - Rear carburetor 40
  - Switzerland
    - Front carburetor 37.5
    - Rear carburetor 40
  - All others
    - Front carburetor 32.5
    - Rear carburetor 40
- 1991
  - US
    - Front carburetor 25
    - Rear carburetor 40
  - Canada
    - Front carburetor 32.5
    - Rear carburetor 40
  - All others
    - Front carburetor 32.5
    - Rear carburetor 40

Pilot screw (turns out)
- 1985 .... 3-1/2
- 1986 and 1987
  - Switzerland .... Not specified
  - All others 3-1/2
- 1988 through 1990
  - US .... Not specified
  - Switzerland
    - Front carburetor 3-7/8
    - Rear carburetor 3-5/8
  - All others 3-1/2
- 1991
  - US .... Not specified
  - All others 3-1/2

Starter (choke) jet
- Front carburetor
  - Front carburetor 37.5
  - Rear carburetor 40

VS800

Main jet
- 1992 through 2000
  - US and Canada
    - Front carburetor 127.5
    - Rear carburetor 132.5
  - Europe except Switzerland, Germany and Scandinavia
    - Front carburetor 95
    - Rear carburetor 107.5
  - Switzerland
    - Front carburetor 97.5
    - Rear carburetor 107.5
  - Germany and Scandinavia
    - Front carburetor 100
    - Rear carburetor 107.5
  - Brazil
    - Front carburetor 95
    - Rear carburetor 107.5
- 2001 and later
  - US and Canada
    - Front carburetor 127.5
    - Rear carburetor 132.5

Main jet (continued)
    Netherlands, Italy, Belgium, Spain
        Front carburetor 95
        Rear carburetor 107.5
    Scandinavia and Germany
        Front carburetor 100
        Rear carburetor 107.5

Jet needle/clip position
    US
        Front carburetor 5D47-1
        Rear carburetor 5D35-1
    Canada
        Front carburetor 5D48-3
        Rear carburetor 5D61-3
    Switzerland
        Front carburetor 5D48-3
        Rear carburetor 5D107-3
    All others
        Front carburetor 5C29-3
        Rear carburetor 5F109-3

Needle jet
    1992 and later
        US and Canada
            Front carburetor P-2
            Rear carburetor P-7
        Switzerland
            Front carburetor P-1
            Rear carburetor P-5
        Germany and Scandinavia
            Front carburetor P-4
            Rear carburetor P-3
    1996 through 2000
        US and Canada
            Front carburetor P-2
            Rear carburetor P-7
        Switzerland
            Front carburetor P-1
            Rear carburetor P-5
        All others
            Front carburetor P-4
            Rear carburetor P-3

Pilot jet
    1992 and later
        US and Canada
            Front carburetor 40
            Rear carburetor 45
        Switzerland
            Front carburetor 40
            Rear carburetor 42.5
        Germany and Scandinavia
            Front carburetor 40
            Rear carburetor 45
        All others
            Front carburetor 40
            Rear carburetor 42.5

Pilot screw (turns out)
    1992
        US .... Not specified
        Canada
            Front carburetor 1-1/4
            Rear carburetor 1-1/8
        Switzerland
            Front carburetor 1-1/4
            Rear carburetor 1-1/8
        Germany and Scandinavia
            Front carburetor 1
            Rear carburetor 1-3/8
        All others
            Front carburetor 1-1/2
            Rear carburetor 2

4A•6 Fuel and exhaust systems - carbureted models

VS800 (continued)
1993 through 1995
    US .... Not specified
    Canada
        Front carburetor 1-1/4
        Rear carburetor 1-1/8
    Switzerland
        Front carburetor 1-3/4
        Rear carburetor 1-1/4
    Germany and Scandinavia
        Front carburetor 1
        Rear carburetor 1-3/8
    All others
        Front carburetor 1-1/2
        Rear carburetor 2
1996 and later
    US .... Not specified
    Canada
        Front carburetor 1-1/4
        Rear carburetor 1-1/8
    Switzerland
        Front carburetor 1-3/4
        Rear carburetor 1-1/4
    Germany and Scandinavia
        Front carburetor 1-5/8
        Rear carburetor 1-1/2
    All others
        Front carburetor 1-1/4
        Rear carburetor 1-3/4
Starter (choke) jet .... Not specified

VZ800
Main jet
    Front carburetor 90
    Rear carburetor 100
Jet needle
    Front carburetor 5C43
    Rear carburetor 5D83
Needle jet
    Front carburetor P-4M
    Rear carburetor P-3M
Pilot jet 40
    Front carburetor 45
    Rear carburetor 40
Pilot screw (turns out)
    1997 and 1998 .... Not specified
    1999 and later
        US .... Not specified
        Canada 1-1/2
        Switzerland
            Front carburetor 1-1/4
            Rear carburetor 2
        All others... 1-1/2
Starter (choke) jet .... Not specified

VL800
Main jet.. 132.5
Jet needle
    US and Canada.. 5E23
    All others 5E22/3
Needle jet P-0M
Pilot jet 27.50
Pilot screw (turns out)
    US and Canada.. Not specified
    All others 3.0
Starter (choke) jet .... Not specified

Fuel and exhaust systems - carbureted models

Fuel level

VS700
1986
- Front carburetor .... 17.5 +/- 0.5 mm (0.69 +/- 0.02 inch)
- Rear carburetor .... 9.5 +/- 0.5 mm (0.37 +/- 0.02 inch)

1987
- Front carburetor .... 17.0 +/- 0.5 mm (0.67 +/- 0.02 inch)
- Rear carburetor .... 7.0 +/- 0.5 mm (0.28 +/- 0.02 inch)

VS750
1985
- Front carburetor .... 17.5 +/- 0.5 mm (0.69 +/- 0.02 inch)
- Rear carburetor .... 9.5 +/- 0.5 mm (0.37 +/- 0.02 inch)

1986 through 1991
- Front carburetor .... 17.5 +/- 0.5 mm (0.69 +/- 0.02 inch)
- Rear carburetor .... 7.0 +/- 0.5 mm (0.28 +/- 0.02 inch)

VS800
All years .... Not specified

VZ800
- Front carburetor .... 15.0 +/- 0.5 mm (0.59 +/- 0.02 inch)
- Rear carburetor .... 7.3 +/- 0.5 mm (0.29 +/- 0.02 inch)

VL800
All years .... Not specified

Float level

VS700 and VS750
- Front carburetor .... 11.5 +/- 1.0 mm (0.45 +/- 0.04 inch)
- Rear carburetor .... 27.7 +/- 1.0 mm (1.09 +/- 0.04 inch)

VS800
- Front carburetor .... 9.1 +/- 1.0 mm (0.36 +/- 0.04 inch)
- Rear carburetor .... 27.7 +/- 1.0 mm (1.09 +/- 0.04 inch)

VZ800
- Front carburetor .... 9.1 +/- 1.0 mm (0.36 +/- 0.04 inch)
- Rear carburetor .... 27.7 +/- 1.0 mm (1.09 +/- 0.04 inch)

VL800
All models .... 7.0 +/- 0.5 mm (0.28 +/- 0.04 inch)

1 General information

The fuel system consists of the fuel tank, fuel pump, fuel tap and filter, carburetor(s) and connecting lines, hoses and control cables.

The carburetors used on Intruder, S50 and Marauder models are two constant vacuum Mikunis with butterfly-type throttle valves. The 2001 through 2004 Volusia uses a single constant vacuum Mikuni. For cold starting, an enrichment circuit is actuated either by a cable and the choke lever mounted on the left handlebar.

The exhaust system uses separate pipes for each cylinder.

Many of the fuel system service procedures are considered routine maintenance items and for that reason are included in Chapter 1.

2 Fuel tank - removal and installation

Warning: *Gasoline is extremely flammable, so take extra precautions when you work on any part of the fuel system. Don't smoke or allow open flames or bare light bulbs near the work area, and don't work in a garage where a gas-type appliance (such as a water heater or clothes dryer) is present. Since gasoline is carcinogenic, wear fuel-resistant gloves when there's a possibility of being exposed to fuel, and, if you spill any fuel on your skin, rinse it off immediately with soap and water. Mop up any spills immediately and do not store fuel-soaked rags where they could ignite. When you perform any kind of work on the fuel system, wear safety glasses and have a fire extinguisher suitable for a Class B type fire (flammable liquids) on hand.*

1 The fuel tank on all models is held in place at the forward end by a mounting bracket and at the rear by one or two bolts.

2 Remove the seat (see Chapter 8) and disconnect the cable from the negative terminal of the battery. If you're working on a Volusia, remove the speedometer from the top of the tank (see Chapter 9).

3 Disconnect the fuel line from the fitting on the fuel tap (see Chapter 1).

4 Disconnect the fuel gauge connector and fuel tap vacuum hose (Volusia models).

4A•8 Fuel and exhaust systems - carbureted models

2.5a Remove the fuel tank mounting bolt(s) (arrow) (S50 shown) . . .

2.5b . . . and remove the grommets and collar

2.6 The mount at the front of the tank slips into this bracket (arrows)

5 Remove the bolt(s) securing the rear of the tank to the bracket **(see illustrations)**.
6 Slide the tank to the rear to disengage the rubber dampers from the cups, then carefully lift the tank away from the machine **(see illustration)**.
7 If necessary, remove the tank bracket screws and bolt and take the bracket off **(see illustrations)**.
8 Before installing the tank, check the condition of the rubber mounting dampers and grommets and the hoses on the underside of the tank - if they're hardened, cracked, or show any other signs of deterioration, replace them.
9 When installing the tank, reverse the above procedure. Make sure the tank seats properly and does not pinch any control cables or wires. If difficulty is encountered when trying to slide the tank dampers into the cups, a small amount of light oil should be used to lubricate them.

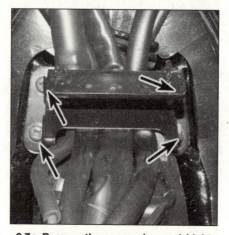

2.7a Remove the screws (arrows) (right screws hidden) . . .

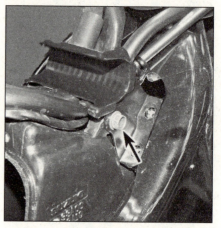

2.7b . . . and the bolt that secures the bracket to the front air cleaner housing (arrow)

3 Fuel tank - cleaning and repair

1 All repairs to the fuel tank should be carried out by a professional who has experience in this critical and potentially dangerous work. Even after cleaning and flushing of the fuel system, explosive fumes can remain and ignite during repair of the tank.
2 If the fuel tank is removed from the vehicle, it should not be placed in an area where sparks or open flames could ignite the fumes coming out of the tank. Be especially careful inside garages where a gas-type appliance is located, because it could cause an explosion.

4 Idle fuel/air mixture adjustment - general information

1 Due to the increased emphasis on controlling motorcycle exhaust emissions, certain governmental regulations have been formulated which directly affect the carburetion of this machine. In order to comply with the regulations, the carburetors on some models have a metal sealing plug pressed into the hole over the pilot screw (which controls the idle fuel/air mixture) on each carburetor, so they can't be tampered with. These should only be removed in the event of a complete carburetor overhaul (described in Section 8), and even then the screws should be returned to their original settings. The pilot screws on other models are accessible, but the use of an exhaust gas analyzer is the only accurate way to adjust the idle fuel/air mixture and be sure the machine doesn't exceed the emissions regulations.
2 If the engine runs extremely rough at idle or continually stalls, and if a carburetor overhaul does not cure the problem, take the motorcycle to a Suzuki dealer service department or other repair shop equipped with an exhaust gas analyzer. They will be able to properly adjust the idle fuel/air mixture to achieve a smooth idle and restore low speed performance.

5 Carburetor overhaul - general information

1 Poor engine performance, hesitation, hard starting, stalling, flooding and backfiring are all signs that major carburetor maintenance may be required.
2 Keep in mind that many so-called carburetor problems are really not carburetor problems at all, but mechanical problems within the engine or malfunctions within the ignition system. Try to establish for certain that the carburetors are in need of a major overhaul before beginning.
3 Check the fuel tap filter, the fuel lines, the tank cap vent, the intake manifold hose clamps, the vacuum hoses, the air filter element, the cylinder compression, the spark plugs, the PAIR system (if equipped) and the carburetor synchronization before assuming that a carburetor overhaul is required.
4 Most carburetor problems are caused by dirt particles, varnish and other deposits which build up in and block the fuel and air

Fuel and exhaust systems - carbureted models 4A•9

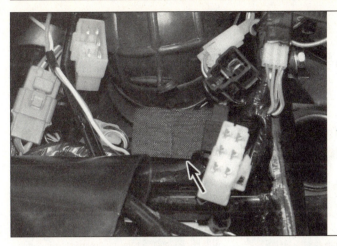

6.3 Remove the cover (arrow) from the clamp screw . . .

6.4a . . . loosen the clamps at top and bottom . . .

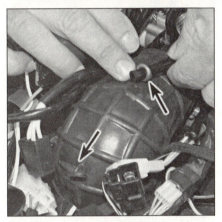

6.4b . . . and free the hose from the retainers on top of the intake tube

6.5a Disconnect the front carburetor's fuel hose . . .

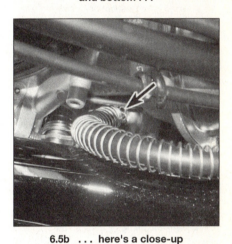

6.5b . . . here's a close-up

passages. Also, in time, gaskets and O-rings shrink or deteriorate and cause fuel and air leaks which lead to poor performance.

5 When the carburetor is overhauled, it is generally disassembled completely and the parts are cleaned thoroughly with a carburetor cleaning solvent and dried with filtered, unlubricated compressed air. The fuel and air passages are also blown through with compressed air to force out any dirt that may have been loosened but not removed by the solvent. Once the cleaning process is complete, the carburetor is reassembled using new gaskets, O-rings and, generally, a new inlet needle valve and seat.

6 Before disassembling the carburetor(s), make sure you have a carburetor rebuild kit (which will include all necessary O-rings and other parts), some carburetor cleaner, a supply of rags, some means of blowing out the carburetor passages and a clean place to work. It is recommended that only one carburetor be overhauled at a time to avoid mixing up parts.

6 Twin carburetors - removal and installation

Warning: *Gasoline is extremely flammable, so take extra precautions when you work on any part of the fuel system (see the Warning in Section 2).*

Removal

Intruder and S50

1 Remove the seat, frame cover(s) and frame head cover (see Chapter 8).

2 Remove the fuel tank and its mounting bracket (see Section 2).

3 Remove the cover from the lower clamp that secures the rear carburetor's air intake tube **(see illustration)**.

4 Loosen the clamps that secure the rear carburetor's air intake tube, pull the hose out of the retainers on top of the tube and remove the tube **(see illustrations)**.

5 Disconnect the fuel hose from the front carburetor **(see illustrations)**. Plug the end of the hose or place it in a plastic bag secured with a rubber band to minimize fuel loss.

6 Remove the choke knob's bracket screw **(see illustration)**.

6.6 Front carburetor mounting details (Intruder and S50)

A Throttle cable splitter
B Front throttle cable
C Rear throttle cable
D Intake tube clamp (large)
E Intake tube clamp (small)
F Carburetor to manifold clamp (hidden)
G Throttle cable retainer
H Choke knob bracket screw

4A•10 Fuel and exhaust systems - carbureted models

6.8 Disconnect the rear carburetor's fuel hose

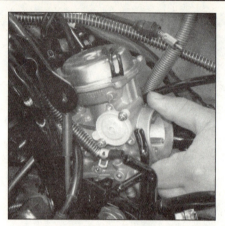

6.13 Lift the carburetor out of the motorcycle

7   Remove the ignition coils (see Chapter 5).
8   Disconnect the fuel hose from the rear carburetor **(see illustration)**. Plug the end of the hose or place it in a plastic bag secured with a rubber band to minimize fuel loss.
9   Loosen the front carburetor's clamp **(see illustration 6.6)**.
10   Disconnect the choke cable from the rear carburetor (see Section 11).
11   Unbolt the air cleaner and slide it rearward to provide removal access for the carburetors (see Section 9).
12   Disconnect the front throttle cable from the rear throttle cables (see Section 11).
13   Free the carburetors from the intake manifolds and lift them out of the motorcycle, together with the throttle cables and synchronizing cable **(see illustration 17.12a in Chapter 1 and the accompanying illustration)**.
14   Don't remove the synchronizing cable unless you have to. The carburetors can be disassembled and cleaned without removing it, and if it's removed the carburetors will have to be synchronized (see Chapter 1).

Marauder

15   Remove the seat, both frame covers and the toolbox (see Chapter 8).
16   Remove the fuel tank (see Section 2). Remove the fuel tank mounting bracket and the plate attached to the top of the frame. Disconnect the electrical connector above the right frame member.
17   Remove the battery (see Chapter 9).
18   Detach the throttle cable connector from the front air box, then remove the air box mounting bolts. Loosen the clamp that secures the carburetor to the air box and remove the air box from the motorcycle.
19   Disconnect the throttle cables at the handlebar and at the connector on top of the front air box (see Section 11).
20   With a rag handy to catch dripping fuel, disconnect the outlet hose at the fuel pump.
21   Loosen the clamps that secure both carburetors to the engine.
22   Detach the push cable from the front carburetor (see Section 11).
23   Lift both carburetors off the engine, together with the hoses and cables. **Note:** *Don't disconnect the synchronizing cable unless absolutely necessary. The carburetors can be overhauled without disconnecting the cable. If the cable is disconnected, you'll need to synchronize the carburetors (see Chapter 1).*

Installation

24   Position the carburetor assembly on the engine. Check to make sure the intake manifolds and their clamping band screws are positioned correctly, then tighten their screws.
25   Lightly lubricate the ends of the throttle cables with multi-purpose grease and attach them to the throttle pulley. Make sure the accelerator and decelerator cables (if equipped) are in their proper positions.
26   The remainder of installation is the reverse of the removal steps, with the following additions:
a) *Be sure the hoses and cables are routed correctly.*
b) *Adjust the throttle grip freeplay and choke freeplay (see Chapter 1).*
c) *Check for fuel leaks.*
d) *Check and, if necessary, adjust the idle speed and carburetor synchronization (see Chapter 1).*

7   Twin carburetors - separation and reconnection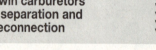

1   Unscrew the choke plunger from the front carburetor (see Section 11).
2   Label the throttle cables (front accelerator, front decelerator, rear accelerator, rear decelerator), then disconnect the throttle cables from the carburetors **(see illustration 17.12a in Chapter 1)**.
3   If necessary, mark the synchronizing cable adjuster with paint so you can return it to its original position, then disconnect it from both carburetors **(see illustration 17.12a in Chapter 1)**.
4   Disconnect the fuel line that runs between the carburetors.
5   Reconnection is the reverse of the disconnection procedure. Synchronize the carburetors (see Chapter 1).

8   Single carburetor - removal and installation

1   A single carburetor is used on Volusia models.
2   Loosen the clamps on the air intake pipe and disconnect its breather hose. Pull the pipe off the carburetor and move it out of the way.
3   Disconnect the throttle cables (see Section10).
4   Disconnect the wiring connectors for the carburetor heater and throttle position sensor.
5   Disconnect the vent hose form the carburetor.
6   Loosen the intake manifold clamp. Separate the carburetor from the intake manifold and lift it up far enough to gain access to the choke plunder. Unscrew the choke plunger from the carburetor body and pull it out.
7   Installation is the reverse of the removal steps. Check the throttle cable free play and adjust if necessary (see Chapter 1).

9   Carburetors - disassembly, cleaning and inspection

⚠ **Warning:** *Gasoline is extremely flammable, so take extra precautions when you work on any part of the fuel system (see the Warning in Section 2).*

Disassembly

1   Remove the carburetors from the machine as described in Section 6. Set the

9.2a Remove the cover screws and lift it off - note the location of the diaphragm tab (arrow) and remove the diaphragm

Fuel and exhaust systems - carbureted models 4A•11

9.2b Remove the jet needle holder screws and remove the holder . . .

9.2c . . . then remove the jet needle, clip, washer and spring

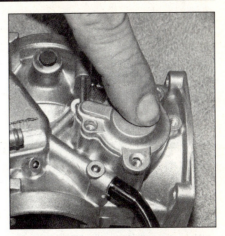

9.2d Hold down the coasting valve cover and remove its screws . . .

9.2e . . . release the spring pressure, lift off the cover and remove the spring and coasting valve

9.2f Remove the float chamber cover screws (arrows) . . .

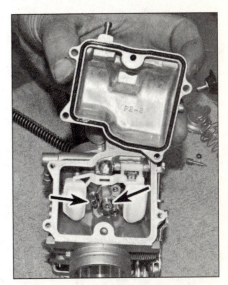

9.2g . . . lift off the cover and O-ring; unscrew the pilot jet (left arrow) and the main jet and holder (right arrow)

assembly on a clean working surface. If you haven't removed the synchronizing cable, don't do so unless there's a specific reason. The carburetors can be disassembled and cleaned with the cable in place.

2   If you're working on twin carburetors, refer to the accompanying illustrations **(see illustrations)** to disassemble the front carburetor and note the following:

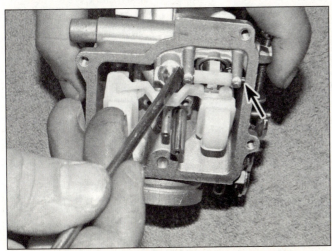

9.2h Push the float pivot pin partway out, then pull on the exposed end (arrow) with pliers to remove it

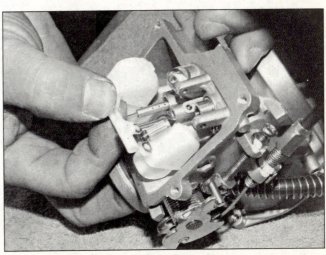

9.2i Remove the floats together with the needle valve

4A•12 Fuel and exhaust systems - carbureted models

9.2j Remove the screw that secures the needle valve seat . . .

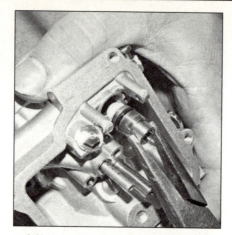

9.2k . . . and pull it out, together with its O-ring

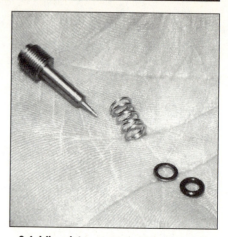

9.4 Idle mixture screw, spring, washer and O-ring

3 Make sure the screwdrivers fit their slots.

4 The pilot (idle mixture) screw is located in a passage in the carburetor body. On US models, this screw is hidden behind a plug which will have to be removed if the screw is to be taken out. The usual way to do this is to drill a hole in the plug, then pry it out. Be careful not to drill into the screw. Turn the pilot screw in, counting the number of turns until it bottoms lightly. Record that number for use when installing the screw. Now remove the pilot screw along with its spring, washer and O-ring (see illustration).

5 If you're working on twin carburetors, refer to the accompanying illustrations (see illustrations) to disassemble the rear carburetor and note the following:

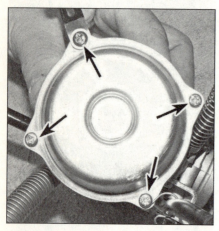

9.5a Remove the cover screws (arrows), noting the locations of the cable retainers

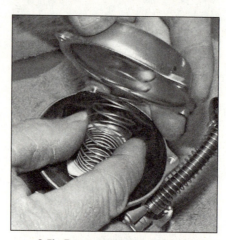

9.5b Remove the cover, spring and diaphragm

9.5c Remove the coasting valve cover, spring and valve

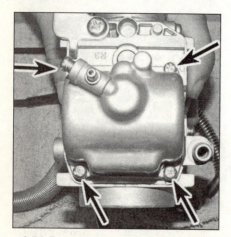

9.5d Remove the float chamber cover screws (arrows) . . .

9.5e . . . and remove the cover and gasket; make sure the float bowl passage (arrow) is clear

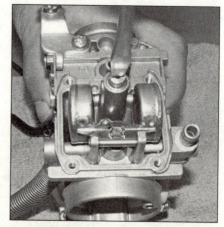

9.5f Unscrew the main jet . . .

Fuel and exhaust systems - carbureted models   4A•13

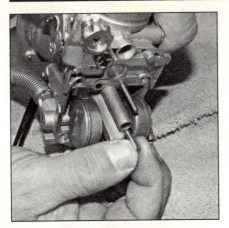

9.5g ... and the pilot jet

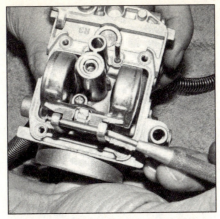

9.5h Tap out the float pivot pin with a spring-loaded punch (it will only come out in the direction shown) ...

9.5i ... and remove the floats together with the needle valve; remove the screw (arrow) ...

6 The single carburetor used on Volusia models is basically the same as the front carburetor used on dual-carburetor models. Refer to **illustrations 9.2a through 9.2k** above and note the instructions in Steps 3 and 4. The needle jet holder is not secured by screws; simply pull it out with needle-nosed pliers.

Cleaning

Caution: Use only a carburetor cleaning solution that is safe for use with plastic parts (be sure to read the label on the container).

7 Submerge the metal components in the carburetor cleaner for approximately thirty minutes (or longer, if the directions recommend it).

8 After the carburetor has soaked long enough for the cleaner to loosen and dissolve most of the varnish and other deposits, use a brush to remove the stubborn deposits. Rinse it again, then dry it with compressed air. Blow out all of the fuel and air passages in the main and upper body.

Caution: Never clean the jets or passages with a piece of wire or a drill bit, as they will be enlarged, causing the fuel and air metering rates to be upset.

9.5j ... and pull out the needle valve seat and O-ring

Inspection

9 Check the operation of the choke plunger. If it doesn't move smoothly, replace it, along with the return spring. Check the tapered end of the plunger for wear and replace if it's worn.

10 Check the tapered portion of the pilot screw for wear or damage **(see illustra-**

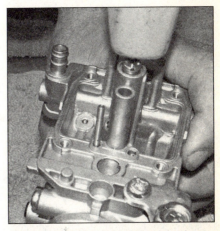

9.5k Thread the main jet back in about one turn and tap on it with a screwdriver to free the needle jet ...

tion 9.4). Replace the pilot screw if necessary.

11 Check the carburetor body, float bowl and top cover for cracks, distorted sealing surfaces and other damage. If any defects are found, replace the faulty component,

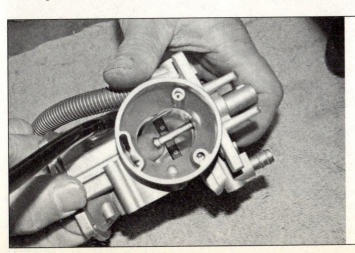

9.5l ... and pull the needle jet out ...

9.5m ... make sure its flat aligns with the pin (arrows) on assembly

10.7 Float chamber drain screw (arrow)

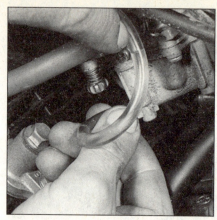

10.8 Rotate the cable out of the groove and slip the end plug out of the pulley

10.9 The front carburetor's fuel level should be even with the index line (arrow)

although replacement of the entire carburetor will probably be necessary (check with your parts supplier for the availability of separate components).

12 Check the diaphragms for splits, holes and general deterioration. Holding it up to a light will help to reveal problems of this nature.

13 Insert the vacuum piston in the carburetor body and see that it moves up-and-down smoothly. Check the surface of the piston for wear. If it's worn excessively or doesn't move smoothly in the bore, replace the carburetor.

14 Check the jet needle for straightness by rolling it on a flat surface (such as a piece of glass). Replace it if it's bent or if the tip is worn.

15 Check the tip of the fuel inlet valve needle. If it has grooves or scratches in it, it must be replaced. Push in on the rod in the other end of the needle, then release it - if it doesn't spring back, replace the valve needle.

16 Check the O-rings. Replace them if they're damaged.

17 Operate the throttle shaft to make sure the throttle butterfly valve opens and closes smoothly. If it doesn't, replace the carburetor.

18 Check the floats for damage. This will usually be apparent by the presence of fuel inside one of the floats. If the floats are damaged, they must be replaced.

10 Carburetors - reassembly and fuel level adjustment

Caution: *When installing the jets, be careful not to over-tighten them - they're made of soft material and can strip or shear easily.*

Note: *When reassembling the carburetors, be sure to use the new O-rings, gaskets and other parts supplied in the rebuild kit.*

Reassembly

1 Reassembly is the reverse of the disassembly procedure, noting the following:

2 Install the pilot screw (if removed) along with its spring, washer and O-ring, turning it in until it seats lightly. Now, turn the screw out the number of turns that was previously recorded. If the pilot screw was covered by a metal plug, install a new one in the hole over the screw. Apply a little bonding agent around the circumference of the plug after it has been seated.

3 To check the float height, hold the carburetor body upside down and measure the height of the float above the float chamber gasket surface. If it's not within the range listed in this Chapter's Specifications, bend the float tang in small increments to adjust it.

Fuel level adjustment

Note: *This procedure applies to twin carburetors only. If you're working on a single carburetor, adjust the float level.*

 Warning: *Gasoline is extremely flammable, so take extra precautions when you work on any part of the fuel system (see the Warning in Section 2).*

4 The carburetors must be installed on the engine for this procedure.

5 If you're working on a Marauder, remove the seat, side cover and toolbox (see Chapter 8).

6 If you're working on a Marauder, remove the air box, PAIR system (including the hoses and bracket), and fuel tank (see Chapter 4). Connect a fuel source (the tank or a container of fuel) to the carburetors.

7 Attach Suzuki service tool no. 09913-10730 to the drain fitting on the bottom of the rear carburetor assembly (both will be checked) **(see illustration).** This is a clear plastic tube graduated in millimeters. An alternative is to use a length of clear plastic tubing and an accurate ruler. Hold the graduated tube (or the free end of the clear plastic tube) against the carburetor body, as shown in the accompanying illustration. If the Suzuki tool is being used, raise the zero mark to a point several millimeters above the parting line between the float chamber and the carburetor (the zero point). If a piece of clear plastic tubing is being used, make a mark on the tubing at this point.

8 Unscrew the drain screw at the bottom of the float bowl a couple of turns, then let fuel flow into the tube **(see illustration).** Wait for the fuel level to stabilize, then slowly lower the tube until the zero mark is level with the upper edge of the coasting enricher diaphragm screw (the zero point). **Note:** *Don't lower the zero mark below the zero point, then bring it back up - the reading won't be accurate. If this happens accidentally, dump the fuel out of the hose and start over.*

9 Measure the distance between the mark and the top of the fuel in the tube or gauge. This distance is the fuel level - write it down on a piece of paper, screw in the drain screw, close off the fuel supply, then move on to the front carburetor and check it the same way. The zero point of the front carburetor is indicated by a line on the carburetor **(see illustration).**

10 Compare your fuel level readings to the value listed in this Chapter's Specifications. If the fuel level in either carburetor is not correct, remove the float bowl and bend the tang up or down, as necessary, then recheck the fuel level. **Note:** *Bending the tang up increases the float height and lowers the fuel level - bending it down decreases the float height and raises the fuel level.*

11 Throttle and choke cables - removal and installation

Throttle cable removal

1 Remove the fuel tank (see Section 2).

2 Loosen the locknuts on the accelerator cable and decelerator cable, if equipped) at the handlebar and screw the cable adjusters in to create as much slack as possible (see Chapter 1).

3 Remove the screws and separate the

Fuel and exhaust systems - carbureted models 4A•15

11.3 Remove the screws (arrows)

11.4a Rotate the cable out of the groove (arrow) . . .

11.4b . . . and slip the end plug (arrow) out of the pulley

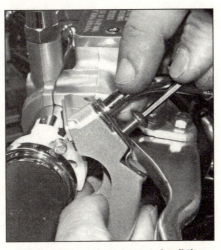

11.4c Remove the screw and pull the cable out of the housing

11.5a Detach the cable retainer from the top of the air cleaner housing (arrow) . . .

throttle housing halves **(see illustration)**.
4 Lift each cable out of its grooves in the throttle grip pulley, align the cables with the pulley slots and slip the cable ends out of the throttle pulley **(see illustrations)**.

Dual carburetors
5 Free the throttle cable from its retainers **(see illustrations)**.
6 Pull back the throttle cable connector cover and disconnect the front throttle cable(s) from the rear cables **(see illustration)**.
7 Label the throttle cables at the carburetor - accelerator (and decelerator if equipped), and if you're working on a dual-

11.5b . . . and from the side (arrow)

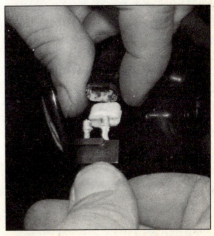

11.6 Separate the cables at the splitter

11.7 Loosen the locknuts (arrows) and slip the cable out of the bracket

11.8 Rotate the cable to align it with the slot, then slip the end plug out of the pulley

11.22a Pull the choke knob out, then unscrew the plunger (arrow) from the rear carburetor . . .

carburetor model, front and rear. Loosen the locknut on each cable housing and slip the cable out of the bracket at the carburetor **(see illustration 17.12a in Chapter 1 and the accompanying illustration).**

8   Rotate each cable so it aligns with the slot in the pulley, then slide the end plug out of the pulley **(see illustration).**
9   Remove the cables, noting how they are routed.

Single carburetor

10   Disconnecting the cables at the carburetor is basically the same as for dual carburetors, but there is only one set of cables.

Throttle cable installation

11   Route the cables into place. Make sure they don't interfere with any other components and aren't kinked or bent sharply.
12   Lubricate the end of the rear accelerator cable with multi-purpose grease and connect it to the throttle pulley at the carburetor. Pass the inner cable through the slot in the bracket, then seat the cable housing in the bracket.
13   Repeat the previous step to connect the decelerator cable, then connect both front carburetor cables in the same manner.
14   Connect the cables to the throttle grip pulley and position them in their slots.
15   Install the cable/switch housing and tighten its screws securely.
16   Follow the procedure outlined in Chapter 1, Throttle operation/grip freeplay - check and adjustment, to adjust the cables.
17   Turn the handlebars back and forth to make sure the cables don't cause the steering to bind.
18   Operate the throttle and check the cable action. The cables should move freely and the throttle pulley at the carburetor should move back and forth in response to both acceleration and deceleration. If the cables don't operate properly, find and fix the problem before you put the fuel tank back on.
19   Install the fuel tank (see Section 2).
20   Start the engine. With the engine idling, turn the handlebars all the way to left and right while listening for changes in idle speed. If idle speed increases as the handlebars turn, the cables are improperly routed. This is dangerous. Find the problem and fix it before riding the bike.

Choke cable removal

21   Pull on the choke cable to create tension on the plunger so it doesn't fall off the cable.
22   Unscrew the choke plunger from the carburetor(s) **(see illustrations).**
23   If necessary, separate the choke plunger from the cable end.
24   Installation is the reverse of the removal steps.

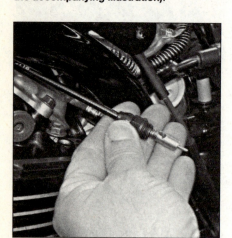

11.22b . . . pull the plunger out and separate it from the cable

11.22c Pull the choke knob out, then unscrew the plunger (arrow) from the front carburetor . . .

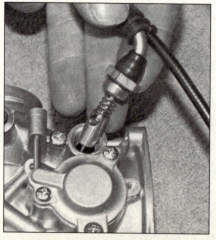

11.22d . . . pull the plunger out and separate it from the cable

12 Air filter housing - removal and installation

Intruder and S50

1   Remove the air intake tubes as described in Section 6.

Fuel and exhaust systems - carbureted models 4A•17

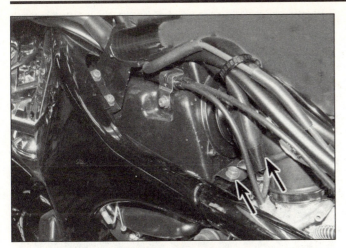

12.2 Two bolts (one hidden, arrows) secure the rear edge of the front air cleaner housing

12.3a The rear air cleaner housing is secured by two screws on the left side (arrows) . . .

2 To remove the front air filter housing, remove the fuel tank bracket (see Section 2). Unbolt the housing from the frame and take it out **(see illustration)**.

3 To remove the rear air filter housing, remove its mounting screws **(see illustrations)**. Free the drain tube from its retainer **(see illustration)** and lift the housing out of the frame.

4 Installation is the reverse of the removal steps.

Volusia models

5 Unbolt the air cleaner housing from its mounting bracket. Disconnect it from the carburetor air duct and remove it.

6 Installation is the reverse of removal.

Marauder models

7 Perform Steps 15 through 18 of Carburetor removal above to remove the front airbox.

8 Remove the toolbox and battery (see Chapter 9).

9 Loosen the clamp that secures the rear airbox to the carburetor. Remove the airbox mounting bolts (one on top and one on the side). Move the airbox to the rear to detach it from the carburetor and lift it out of the motorcycle.

10 Installation is the reverse of the removal steps.

13 Exhaust system - removal and installation

⚠ **Warning: Let the exhaust system cool before starting this procedure.**

1 Remove the nuts or bolts that secure the exhaust pipes to the cylinder head.

2 If you're planning to separate the mufflers for the pipes, loosen the clamps now (this will be easier while the exhaust system is attached to the bike).

3 Remove the muffler mounting bolts and move the exhaust pipes forward to separate them from the engine and remove the exhaust system from the bike.

4 Installation is the reverse of the removal steps, with the following additions:

a) Use new gaskets at the cylinder head **(see illustration)**. Also use new gaskets at the pipe-to-muffler connections if they were separated.
b) Tighten all of the nuts and bolts until they're snug, but don't torque them yet.
c) Tighten the exhaust pipe holder nuts at the cylinder heads evenly.
d) Tighten the remaining nuts and bolts securely.
e) Warm up the engine to normal operating temperature, let it cool, then retighten all of the nuts and bolts.

14 PAIR system - operational test

General information

1 To reduce the amount of unburned hydrocarbons released in the exhaust gases,

12.3b . . . and one screw on the right (arrow)

12.3c Free the drain tube from its retainer (arrow)

13.4 Use a new exhaust gasket (arrow) in each port

15.5 The canister (left arrow) is secured by bolts under and behind it; to disconnect the hoses, remove the trim cover (right arrow)

16.2 The fuel pump (arrow) is on the left side of the bike

a pulse secondary air (PAIR) system is fitted on some models. The system consists of the control valve, the reed valves and the hoses. The control valve is actuated by engine vacuum. Intruder and S50 models have an air switching valve separate from the control valve. On Volusias and Marauders, the control valve is incorporated in the same unit as the reed valves.

2 Under certain operating conditions, the PAIR control valve allows filtered air to be drawn through it, the reed valves and cylinder head passages and into the exhaust ports. The air mixes with the exhaust gases, causing any unburned particles of the fuel in the mixture to be burned in the exhaust port/pipes. This process changes a considerable amount of hydrocarbons and carbon monoxide into relatively harmless carbon dioxide and water. The reed valves are fitted to prevent the flow of exhaust gases back into the control valve and air filter housing.

3 The system is not adjustable and requires no maintenance, except to ensure that the hoses are in good condition and are securely connected at each end, and that there is no build-up of carbon fouling the reed valves. Replace any hoses that are cracked, split or generally deteriorated. The reed valves can be checked for any build-up of carbon by unscrewing the cover screws - if any is found, clean the valves and their housings.

Testing

Control valve

4 Remove the valve from the motorcycle (see below).

5 Check the operation of the control valve or air switching valve by blowing through the air filter housing hose union; air should flow freely through the valve.

6 Apply vacuum to the vacuum hose fitting with a vacuum pump; no air should now flow through the valve if it is functioning correctly. Replace the valve with a new one if faulty.

Reed valves

7 Disconnect each reed valve hose from the control valve. Check the valve by blowing and sucking on the hose end. Air should flow through the hose only when blown down it and not when sucked back up. If this is not the case the reed valve is faulty. Check the other valve in the same way.

Control valve replacement

8 Remove the PAIR cover.
9 Disconnect the control valve hoses and remove it from the motorcycle.
10 Installation is the reverse of removal.

15 Evaporative emission control system (California models) - removal and installation

General information

1 This system prevents the escape of fuel vapor into the atmosphere by storing it in a charcoal-filled canister.

2 When the engine is not running, excess fuel vapor from the tank passes into the canister. When the engine is started, intake manifold vacuum draws the vapor back from the canister into the throttle bodies to be burned during the normal combustion process.

3 The canister has a one-way valve which allows air to be drawn into the system as the volume of fuel decreases in the tank. A shut-off valve also prevents any fuel escaping through it in the event of the bike falling over.

4 The system is not adjustable and can only be properly tested by a Suzuki dealer. However the owner can check that all the hoses are in good condition and are securely connected at each end. Renew any hoses that are cracked, split or generally deteriorated.

Removal and installation

5 The canister on S50 models is mounted at the right rear of the bike below the fender **(see illustration)**. To access the canister hoses, remove the trim cover.

6 To access the canister on a Volusia, remove the seat, fuel tank, frame head cover and speedometer (see Chapters 4, 8 and 9). The canister is mounted on the frame beneath the seat.

7 Label and disconnect the hoses, then remove the clamp screw and take the canister out. Make sure the hoses are correctly reconnected on installation.

8 The shut-off valve is located in the hose between the fuel tank and the canister.

16 Fuel pump - testing and replacement

1 Intruder, S50 and Marauder models use an electric fuel pump to transfer gasoline from the tank to the carburetors. Volusia models use a vacuum-operated fuel pump.

Testing

 Warning: Refer to the Warning at the beginning of Section 2 before starting this procedure.

Intruder and S50 models

2 Locate the fuel pump **(see illustration)**. Follow its wiring harness to the connector and disconnect it. Connect an ohmmeter between the terminals on the fuel pump side of the connector. If the reading is not 1 to 2 ohms, replace the fuel pump.

Warning: Do not use gasoline for this step. Use kerosene only.

3 If the pump resistance is within the

Fuel and exhaust systems - carbureted models 4A•19

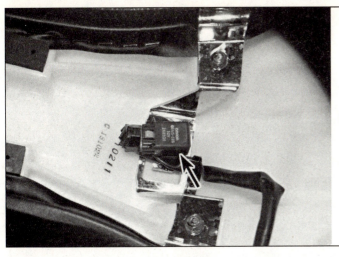

16.4 The fuel pump relay (arrow) is attached to the underside of the seat

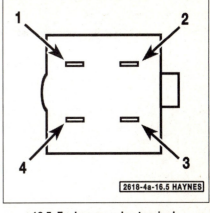

16.5 Fuel pump relay terminals

range listed in this Chapter's Specifications, remove it from the motorcycle (see below). Connect a length of hose to the inlet and outlet fittings on the pump. Place the inlet hose in a container of kerosene and place the outlet hose in a graduated container. Connect a 12-volt battery to the pump's electrical terminals for 30 seconds to run the pump. The pump should flow 300 cc (3/4 pint) or more. if it's less than this, or if the pump doesn't run at all, replace the pump.

4 Remove the rear seat (see Chapter 8). Remove the fuel pump relay from its mount and unplug its wiring connector **(see illustration)**.

5 Using an ohmmeter set to the k-ohms range, test the relay resistance as follows **(see illustration)**:

a) *Terminal 1 to terminal 2: Infinite resistance.*
b) *Terminal 1 to terminal 3: 0.5 to 10.0 k-ohms.*
c) *Terminal 1 to terminal 4: 2 to 20 k-ohms.*
d) *Terminal 2 to terminal 3: 20 to 100 k-ohms.*
e) *Terminal 2 to terminal 4: 20 to 100 k-ohms.*
f) *Terminal 3 to terminal 4: 0.5 to 10.0 k-ohms.*

6 If the relay doesn't perform as described, replace it.

Marauder models

7 To test it, disconnect the outlet hose from the fuel pump. Connect a length of hose to the fitting and place the end of the hose in a container. Crank the engine with the starter and check fuel flow. If no fuel, or only a little. Flows form the hose, replace the fuel pump.

8 The relay is built into the fuel pump. If fuel flows while the engine is cranking, but cuts off when the engine starts, the relay inside the pump may be defective. The fuel pump receives current directly while the engine is cranking, then through the relay after the engine starts. If the relay is defective, the pump must be replaced.

Volusia models

9 Test the pump as described in Step 7 above.

Replacement

10 Remove the fuel tank (see Section 2). If you're working on a bike with an electric fuel pump, disconnect the negative cable from the battery and disconnect the fuel pump electrical connector.

11 Disconnect the fuel lines (and vacuum line on Volusia models). Detach the pump from its mount and remove it from the motorcycle.

12 Installation is the reverse of the removal steps.

Notes

Chapter 4 Part B
Fuel, engine management and exhaust systems - fuel injected models

Contents

Air filter check, cleaning and renewal	see Chapter 1	Fuel pump - removal, disassembly and installation	5
Air filter housing and intake duct - removal and installation	8	Fuel pump relay - check, removal and installation	4
Catalytic converter	19	Fuel rails and injectors - removal and installation	13
Electronic control module (ECM)	see Chapter 5	Fuel strainer and filter - removal and installation	6
EVAP system (California models)	18	Fuel system check	see Chapter 1
Exhaust system - removal and installation	16	Fuel tank - removal and installation	2
Fast idle speed - check and adjustment	15	General information and precautions	1
Fuel injection system components - check, removal and installation	11	Idle speed check and adjustment	see Chapter 1
		PAIR system	17
Fuel injection system description	9	Throttle and fast idle cable check and adjustment	see Chapter 1
Fuel injection system troubleshooting	10	Throttle body - removal, cleaning, inspection and installation	12
Fuel pressure check	3	Throttle body synchronization	see Chapter 1
Fuel pressure regulator - removal and installation	7	Throttle cables - removal and installation	14

Degrees of difficulty

| Easy, suitable for novice with little experience | Fairly easy, suitable for beginner with some experience | Fairly difficult, suitable for competent DIY mechanic | Difficult, suitable for experienced DIY mechanic 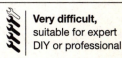 | Very difficult, suitable for expert DIY or professional |

Specifications

Fuel supply system
Fuel tank capacity .... See *Dimensions and Weights* at the end of the manual
Operating pressure .... 43 psi (3.0 Bar)
Pump flow rate .... Approximately 168 cc (5.7 US fl oz, 5.9 Imp fl oz) in 10 seconds

Component test data
Air pressure (AP) sensor
   Input voltage .... 4.5 to 5.5 V
   Output voltage .... Approximately 2.6 V at idle speed
Crankshaft position (CKP) sensor
   Resistance .... 184 to 276 ohms
   Peak voltage
     2008 and earlier .... Above 4.0V
     2009 and later .... Above 1.5 volts
Engine coolant temperature (ECT) sensor
   Input voltage .... 4.5 to 5.5V
   Resistance .... Approximately 2.45 k-ohms @ 20-degrees C (68-degrees F)
Gear position switch voltage
   2008 and earlier .... Above 0.6V
   2009 and later .... Above 0.2V
Injector voltage .... Battery voltage
Injector resistance .... 9.5 to 11.5 ohms @ 20-degrees C (68-degrees F)
Idle speed control valve resistance .... 80 ohms

Component test data (continued)

Oxygen sensor resistance (UK, Europe and Australia, 2008 and earlier)
    Output voltage - engine running
        At idle speed.. Less than 0.2 volts
        At 5000 rpm... More than 0.7 volt
Heated oxygen sensor (UK,
 output voltage
    At idle speed.. Less than 0.3 volts
    At 5000 rpm... More than 0.6 volt
Heated oxygen sensor resistance.. 6.7 to 9.5 ohms @ 23-degrees C (73.4-degrees F)
Intake air pressure (IAP) sensor
    Input voltage.. 4.5 to 5.5 V
    Output voltage.. Approximately 2.6 V at idle speed
Intake air temperature (IAT) sensor
    Input voltage.. 4.5 to 5.5V
    Resistance... Approximately 2.6 k-ohms @ 20-degrees C (68-degrees F)
PAIR solenoid valve resistance.. 20 to 24 ohms @ 20 to 30-degrees C (68 to 86-degrees F)
Secondary throttle position (STP) sensor
    Input voltage.. 4.5 to 5.5V
    Output voltage
        Closed.. 0.5V
        Open... 3.9V
    Resistance
        Yellow to black
            Closed.. Approximately 0.5 k-ohms
            Open... Approximately 3.9 k-ohms
        Blue to black
            2008 and earlier... Approximately 4.69 k-ohms
            2009 and later.. Not specified
Secondary throttle valve actuator resistance... Approximately 6.5 ohms
Throttle position (TP) sensor
    Input voltage.. 4.5 to 5.5V
    Output voltage
        Closed.. Approximately 1.1V
        Open... Approximately 4.4V
    Resistance
        Closed.. Approximately 1.1 ohms
        Open... Approximately 4.4 ohms
Tip-over (TO) sensor
    Resistance... 19.1 to 19.7 k-ohms
    Voltage
        Upright.. Approximately 0.4 to 1.4V
        Leaning at 65-degrees or more... Approximately 3.7 to 4.4V

Throttle body
Idle speed.. 1100 rpm
Fast idle speed.. 1800 rpm (engine cold)

PAIR system
Control valve resistance.. 20 to 24 ohms @ 20 to 30-degrees C (68 to 86-degrees F)

Torque settings
Intake air temperature (IAT) sensor... 18 Nm (13 ft-lbs)
Secondary throttle position (STP) sensor screw....................................... 3.5 Nm (30 inch-lbs)
Throttle position (TP) sensor screws... 3.5 Nm (30 inch-lbs)
Fuel pump mounting screws... 10 Nm (84 inch-lbs)
Fuel rail mounting screws.. 3.5 Nm (30 inch-lbs)
Crankshaft position sensor mounting bolt... 8 Nm (72 inch-lbs)

Fuel, engine management and exhaust systems - fuel injected models 4B•3

1 General information and precautions

General information

The fuel injection system, used on C50 and M50 models, consists of the fuel tank, incorporating the fuel pump and filter, the fuel hose to the fuel rail on the throttle body, and the injectors that are located in the throttle body. All models have a dual valve throttle body with one injector per cylinder.

The fuel pump is activated initially by the ignition switch and continues to deliver fuel while the engine is running. Fuel pressure is controlled within the pump by a pressure regulator. In the event of the machine falling over, a tip-over sensor cuts power to the fuel pump, injectors and ignition coils.

The entire fuel injection system is controlled by the engine control module (ECM) which monitors data sent from the various system sensors and adjusts fuel delivery to the engine accordingly. If a fault develops in the injection system, the FI warning LED illuminates on the instrument cluster and an LCD code is displayed. In the case of a minor fault the engine will continue to run enabling the machine to be ridden, although performance will be significantly reduced. For comprehensive fault diagnosis and certain service procedures, a Suzuki mode select switch (Part No. 09930-82710) is useful (and inexpensive), though not essential as its function can be copied using a simple jumper wire as described later in this Chapter.

The Suzuki Dual Throttle Valve fuel injection system uses two throttle valves per cylinder. The main valve is actuated by the throttle cables from the handlebar twistgrip; the secondary valve is actuated by an actuator controlled by the ECM for the purpose of smoothing air flow into the throttle body.

All models feature a PAIR system which introduces filtered air into the exhaust ports to promote the burning of excess fuel in the exhaust gases. California models feature an evaporative emission control system that prevents fuel vapor from escaping into the atmosphere.

Precautions

Warning: Gasoline is extremely flammable, so take extra precautions when you work on any part of the fuel system. Don't smoke or allow open flames or bare light bulbs near the work area, and don't work in a garage where a gas-type appliance is present. If you spill any fuel on your skin, rinse it off immediately with soap and water. When you perform any kind of work on the fuel system, wear safety glasses and have a fire extinguisher suitable for a class B type fire (flammable liquids) on hand.

Always perform service procedures in a well-ventilated area to prevent a build-up of fumes.

Never work in a building containing a gas appliance with a pilot light, or any other form of naked flame. Ensure that there are no naked light bulbs or any sources of flame or sparks nearby.

Do not smoke (or allow anyone else to smoke) while in the vicinity of petrol (gasoline) or of components containing it. Remember the possible presence of vapor from these sources and move well clear before smoking.

Check all electrical equipment belonging to the house, garage or workshop where work is being undertaken (see the *Safety first!* section of this manual). Remember that certain electrical appliances such as drills, cutters etc. create sparks in the normal course of operation and must not be used near petrol (gasoline) or any component containing it. Again, remember the possible presence of fumes before using electrical equipment.

Always mop up any spilt fuel and safely dispose of the rag used.

Any stored fuel that is drained off during servicing work must be kept in sealed containers that are suitable for holding gasoline (petrol), and clearly marked as such; the containers themselves should be kept in a safe place. Note that this last point applies equally to the fuel tank if it is removed from the machine; also remember to keep its filler cap closed at all times.

Read the *Safety first!* section of this manual carefully before starting work.

Owners of machines used in the US, particularly California, should note that their machines must comply at all times with Federal or State legislation governing the permissible levels of noise and of pollutants such as unburnt hydrocarbons, carbon monoxide etc. that can be emitted by those machines. All vehicles offered for sale must comply with legislation in force at the date of manufacture and must not subsequently be altered in any way which will affect their emission of noise or of pollutants.

In practice, this means that adjustments may not be made to any part of the fuel, ignition or exhaust systems by anyone who is not authorized or mechanically qualified to do so, or who does not have the tools, equipment and data necessary to properly carry out the task. Also if any part of these systems is to be renewed it must be renewed with only genuine Suzuki components or by components which are approved under the relevant legislation. The machine must never be used with any part of these systems removed, modified or damaged.

2 Fuel tank - removal and installation

Warning: Refer to the precautions given in Section 1 before starting work.

Raise

1 Make sure the fuel cap is secure. Remove the seat (see Chapter 8).
2 Remove the fuel tank mounting bolt **(see illustration)**.
3 Raise the rear of the tank about 4 inches and support it with the prop supplied with the bike, or use a block of wood if it's not available **(see illustration)**.

2.2 Remove the fuel tank mounting bolt and washer; be sure the metal bushing is in place before installing the bolt

2.3 Support the tank with the prop tool or a block of wood

2.6 Disconnect the electrical connector (right arrow) and fuel hose (left arrow) . . .

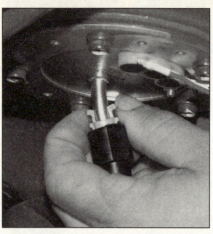
2.7a Squeeze the tabs to disconnect the fuel hose

2.7b Disconnect the vent hose (if equipped)

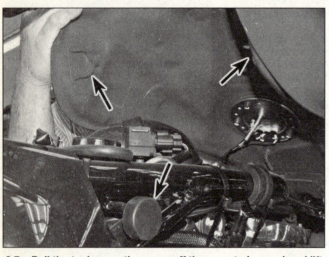
2.7c Pull the tank mounting cups off the mounts (arrows) and lift the tank

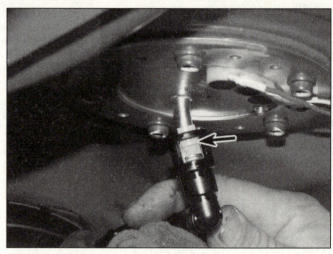
2.9 Be sure the tabs (arrow) are securely engaged after installing the hose

Removal

4 Make sure the ignition switch is OFF. Raise the tank (see above).
5 If you're working on a C50, remove the speedometer (see Chapter 9).
6 Disconnect the fuel pump wiring connector **(see illustration)**.
7 Place a rag underneath the fuel supply hose to catch any residual fuel, then release the clip on the hose connector and disconnect it from its union on the bottom of the tank **(see illustration 2.6 and the accompanying illustration)**. Disconnect the vent hose **(see illustration)** and lift the tank off the motorcycle **(see illustration)**.
8 Inspect the mounting bushings for signs of damage or deterioration and replace them with new ones if necessary.

Installation

9 Installation is the reverse of removal, noting the following:
  a) Check that the tank mounting bushings are installed.
  b) Refer to Chapter 1 and check the condition of the fuel system hoses before installing the tank.
  c) Align the fuel supply hose connector with its union on the tank and push it on fully so that the clip engages **(see illustration)**.
  d) Start the engine and check that there is no sign of fuel leakage.

Cleaning and repair

10 All repairs to the fuel tank should be carried out by a professional who has experience in this critical and potentially dangerous work. Even after cleaning and flushing the fuel system, explosive fumes can remain and ignite during repair of the tank.
11 If the fuel tank is removed from the bike, it should not be placed in an area where sparks or open flames could ignite the fumes coming out of the tank. Be especially careful inside garages where a gas-type appliance is located, because it could cause an explosion.

3 Fuel pressure check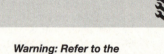

 Warning: Refer to the precautions given in Section 1 before starting work.

1 The fuel pump is located inside the fuel tank. When the ignition is switched ON, it should be possible to hear the pump run for a few seconds until the system is up to pressure. If you can't hear anything, first check the fuse (see Chapter 9), then check the relay (see Section 4) and the tip-over (TO) sensor (see Section 11). If they are good, check the wiring and terminals for physical damage or loose or corroded connections and repair as necessary (see the *Wiring Diagrams* at the end of Chapter 9). If the pump still will not run, fit a new pump assembly.
2 To check the fuel pressure, a suitable gauge, gauge hose and adapters are needed.

Fuel, engine management and exhaust systems - fuel injected models 4B•5

4.1 The fuel pump relay (arrow) is near the coolant reservoir

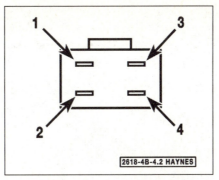

4.2 Fuel pump relay terminals

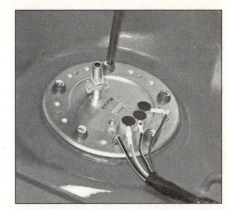

5.2a Remove the screws . . .

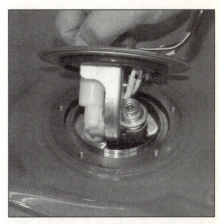

5.2b . . . and lift the pump assembly out . . .

Suzuki provides service tools (part nos. 09940-40211 and 09940-40220 for all models; 09915-74511 for M50 models; 09915-77331 and 09915-74521 for C50 models) for this purpose.

3 Raise the fuel tank (see Section 2).
4 Release the clip on the hose connector and disconnect it from its union on the bottom of the tank **(see illustrations 2.6 and 2.7a)**. Connect the gauge between the fuel tank and the fuel supply hose.
5 Turn the ignition switch ON and check the pressure reading on the gauge. The pressure should be as specified at the beginning of this Chapter.
6 Turn the ignition OFF and disconnect the gauge and adapters. Use a rag to catch any residual fuel as before. Align the fuel supply hose connector with its union on the tank and push it on fully so that the clip engages.
7 If the pressure is too low, check for a leak in the fuel supply system, a blocked fuel filter (see Section 6), a faulty pressure regulator (see Section 7) or a faulty fuel pump.
8 If the pressure is too high, either the pressure regulator or the fuel pump check valve is faulty.
9 On completion run the engine and check for leaks in the fuel hoses.

4 Fuel pump relay - check, removal and installation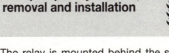

1 The relay is mounted behind the secondary gearcase cover (lower left side cover) **(see illustration)** - remove the cover to access it (see Chapter 8).
2 Pull the relay off its mounting and disconnect the wiring connector. Using a multimeter or test light, check for continuity between terminals 1 and 2 on the relay **(see illustration)**. There should be no continuity. Now use jumper wires to connect the positive terminal of a fully charged 12 volt battery to terminal 3 on the relay and the negative battery terminal to relay terminal 4. There should be continuity shown across terminals 1 and 2. If the relay fails either of the checks, replace it with a new one.

5 Fuel pump - removal, disassembly and installation

⚠ **Warning: Refer to the precautions given in Section 1 before starting work.**

Removal

1 The fuel pump is located inside the fuel tank. Remove the tank and drain it (see Section 2).

2 Turn the tank upside down and rest it on clean rags to protect the paintwork. Undo the bolts securing the pump base to the underside of the tank and lift out the pump **(see illustrations)**. If you're working on a 2009 or later model, disconnect the fuel gauge sender harness as you lift the pump out. **Note:** *You will need to lift the pump partway, turn and tilt it to get it out of the opening. Discard the O-ring as a new one must be fitted on reassembly.*

Disassembly

3 Refer to Section 6 and remove the strainer.
4 Disconnect the fuel pump wiring con-

5.2c . . . you'll need to turn and tilt it more than once to get it out of the opening

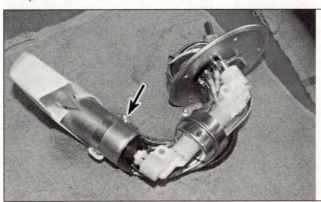

5.4a Remove the retaining band screw (arrow) . . .

4B•6 Fuel, engine management and exhaust systems - fuel injected models

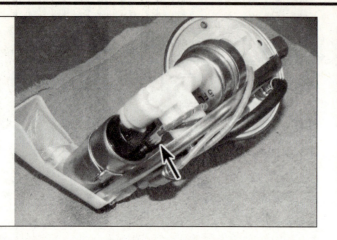

5.4b ... disconnect the electrical connector (arrow) and separate the pump from the plastic fitting

5.6 Use a new O-ring and lubricate it with grease

nector. Remove its securing screws and separate it from the plastic fitting that connects to the filter **(see illustrations)**.

5 Assembly is the reverse of the removal steps. Check that the wiring terminals for the fuel pump and the level sensor(s) are tight.

Installation

6 Fit a new O-ring into the recess around the aperture on the underside of the fuel tank and smear the O-ring lightly with grease **(see illustration)**. Install the pump and align the holes in the pump base with the threaded holes in the tank. Clean the threads of the bolts, then apply a suitable thread locking compound and install them finger-tight. Now tighten them gradually in a criss-cross pattern to the torque setting specified at the beginning of this Chapter.

7 Install the fuel tank (see Section 2) and refill it. Ensure there are no signs of fuel leakage around the pump base.

6 Fuel strainer and filter - removal and installation

⚠ **Warning:** Refer to the precautions given in Section 1 before starting work.

Fuel strainer

1 Remove the fuel pump unit from the tank (see Section 5).

C50 models

2 Refer to the accompanying illustrations to remove the strainer from the pump **(see illustrations)**.

3 Clean any sediment from the strainer with a soft brush or low pressure compressed air. If the strainer is very clogged with dirt and/or rust, or if there is evidence that some has made its way through the gauze, detach the strainer and rubber cushion from the pump and install a new one.

4 Installation is the reverse of the removal steps. Use a new rubber bushing to secure the pump to the assembly.

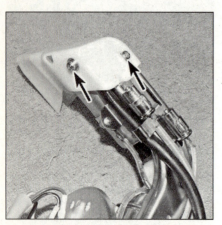

6.2a Remove the strainer cover screws (arrows) ...

6.2b ... take the cover off the strainer ...

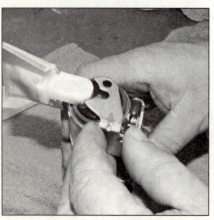

6.2c ... remove the retainer bracket ...

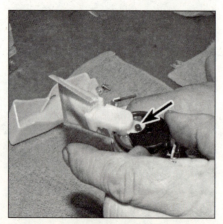

6.2d ... remove the strainer bracket, noting how it fits over the pin (arrow) ...

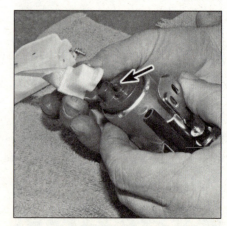

6.2e ... and detach the strainer from the pump - note how the strainer tab fits over the pin on the pump (arrow)

Fuel, engine management and exhaust systems - fuel injected models 4B•7

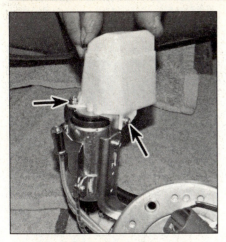
6.5a Remove the strainer cover screws (arrows) . . .

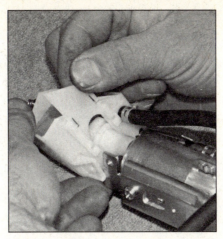
6.5b . . . slip the cover out of its slot . . .

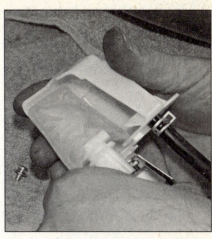
6.5c . . . take the cover off the strainer . . .

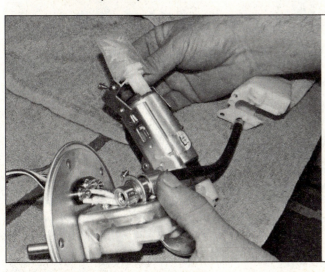
6.5d . . . remove the strainer bracket . . .

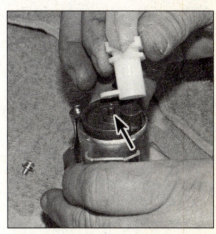
6.5e . . . and detach the strainer from the pump - note how the strainer tab fits over the pin on the pump (arrow)

M50 models

5 Refer to the accompanying illustrations to remove the strainer from the pump **(see illustrations)**.

Fuel filter

6 Remove the fuel strainer as described above and remove the fuel pump (see Section 5).

7 Remove the fuel filter retaining band screw and separate the filter from the plastic fitting **(see illustrations)**.

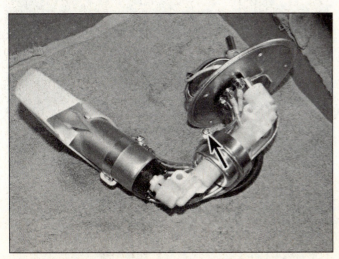
6.7a Here's the C50 filter retaining band screw (arrow)

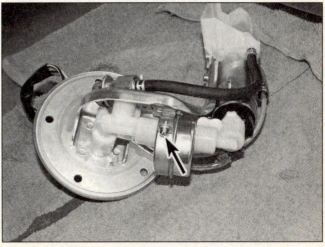
6.7b Here's the M50 filter retaining band screw (arrow)

4B•8 Fuel, engine management and exhaust systems - fuel injected models

6.8a Be sure the OUT mark (arrow) faces the proper direction - this is a C50 . . .

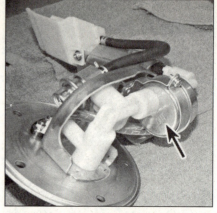

6.8b . . . and this is an M50

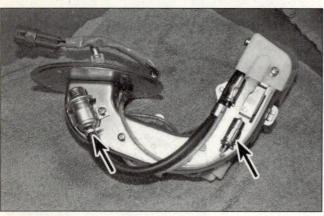

7.3a Here are the C50 pressure regulator (left arrow) and thermistor (right arrow)

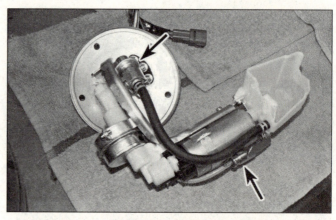

7.3b Here are the M50 pressure regulator (upper arrow) and thermistor (lower arrow)

8 Installation is the reverse of the removal steps. Be sure the OUT mark on the filter faces the proper direction (away from the fuel pump) **(see illustrations)**.

7 Fuel pressure regulator - removal and installation

 Warning: Refer to the precautions given in Section 1 before starting work.

Check

1 Suzuki provides no test procedure for the pressure regulator, which is mounted on the plate assembly in the fuel tank. However, if it is stuck open, it will be possible to blow through it with a low pressure air source. If it is stuck closed, then a high pressure air source with a gauge can be used to check the pressure at which it does open, if at all.
2 The definitive test is to substitute the suspect regulator with a known good one, repeat the fuel pressure check and assess any difference.

Removal and installation

3 Remove the fuel pump unit from the tank (see Section 5). Release the clip securing the fuel pressure regulator holder to the pump assembly then pull the regulator out of its socket and disconnect it from the hose **(see illustrations)**.
4 Installation is the reverse of the removal steps. Note that if the regulator is faulty a new pump assembly must be installed as the regulator is not available as a separate component.

8 Air filter housing and intake duct - removal and installation

Removal

1 Remove the fuel tank (see Section 2).
2 Remove the air filter housing bolts and loosen the screw that secures the clamp at the small-diameter end of the air intake tube **(see illustration)**. Disconnect the IAT sensor electrical connector and PAIR hose from the back of the housing and take it off **(see illustration)**.
3 If you're working on a C50, disconnect

8.2a Unscrew the mounting bolts and loosen the clamp screw (arrow) - it's hidden behind the duct

the PAIR hose and disconnect the wiring connector from the intake air temperature (IAT) sensor **(see illustration)**. Remove the IAP sensors (see Section 11, disconnect the PCV hose, loosen the clamp at the large end and remove the air intake tube.
3 If you're working on an M50, disconnect the wiring connector from the intake air pressure (IAP) sensor (see Section 11). Disconnect the PAIR hose, loosen the clamp and

Fuel, engine management and exhaust systems - fuel injected models 4B•9

8.2b Take the housing off and disconnect the electrical connector and hose (arrows) from the back side

8.3 Disconnect the PAIR hose (right arrow) and IAT connector (left arrow), then loosen the clamp screw (lower arrow) and take the duct off

10.2 The diagnostic connector (arrow) is on the left side of the bike

remove the air intake duct **(see illustration)**.
4 Make sure the foam seals around the rim of the duct are in good condition.

Installation

5 Installation is the reverse of removal. Make sure all hoses are in good condition and are securely connected. Make sure all wiring connectors are securely connected.

9 Fuel injection system description

1 The fuel injection system consists of two main component groups, the fuel supply circuit and the electronic control circuit.
2 The fuel supply circuit consists of the tank, pump and filter, pressure regulator and injectors. Fuel is pumped under pressure from the tank to the two fuel rails (one for each injector), from which the injectors are fed. Operating pressure is maintained initially by the pump check valve (a one-way valve that maintains pressure in the system even when the pump has stopped), and, once the engine is running, by the pressure regulator. The pump also incorporates a pressure relief valve, which releases fuel back into the tank should the system become over-pressurized. The injectors spray pressurized fuel into the throttle body where it mixes with air and vaporizes, before entering the cylinder where it is compressed and ignited.
3 The electronic control circuit consists of the engine control module (ECM), which operates and coordinates both the fuel injection and ignition systems, and the various sensors which provide the ECM with information on engine operating conditions.
4 The ECM monitors signals from the following sensors:

 a) Intake air temperature (IAT) sensor
 b) Intake air pressure (IAP) sensor
 c) Throttle position (TP) sensor
 d) Crankshaft position (CKP) sensor
 e) Engine coolant temperature (ECT) sensor

 f) Atmospheric pressure (AP) sensor
 g) Gear position (GP) sensor
 h) Tip over (TO) sensor
 i) Idle-speed Control (ISC) valve (2009 and later)

5 Based on the information it receives, the ECM calculates the appropriate ignition and fuel requirements of the engine. By varying the length of the electronic pulse it sends to each injector, the ECM controls the length of time the injectors are held open and thereby the amount of fuel that is supplied to the engine. Fuel supply varies according to the engine's needs for starting, warming-up, idling, cruising and acceleration.
6 In the event of an abnormality in any of the sensor signals, the ECM will determine whether the engine can still be run safely. If it can, a back-up mode replaces the sensor signal with a fixed signal, restricting performance but allowing the bike to be ridden home or to a dealer. When this occurs, the LCD display in the instrument cluster will indicate the letters FI every two seconds (alternating with the odometer reading), and the FI LED will come on. If the fault is too serious, the appropriate system will be shut down and the engine will not run. When this occurs, the LCD display in the instrument cluster will indicate the letters FI continuously, and the FI LED will flash. See Section 10 for troubleshooting.
7 In the event of no signal being received from the ECM within 3 seconds of the ignition being switched ON the LCD panel will display the letters CHEC. This is not a fault code in itself, but will occur if the ignition is ON for the stated time but if the kill switch is in the OFF position, or if the starter interlock circuit has a fault, or if the ignition fuse has blown (see Chapter 9). It will also occur if a wiring connector between the ECM and instrument cluster has become disconnected.
8 The system incorporates two safety circuits. When the ignition is switched ON, the fuel pump runs for three seconds and pressurizes the system. Thereafter the pump automatically switches off until the engine is started. The second circuit incorporates a tip-over sensor, which automatically switches off the fuel pump and cuts the ignition and injection circuits if the motorcycle falls over.

10 Fuel injection system troubleshooting

1 The system incorporates a self-diagnostic function whereby any faults are stored in the ECM memory. To access the appropriate fault code, and to perform certain tests, the Suzuki mode select switch (part no. 09930-82710) is very useful, though its function can easily be replicated using a short piece of auxiliary wire, either bared at the ends or with suitable terminals that will fit into the terminals on the connector, to jump between the two terminals in the connector that the switch plugs into. The mode select switch is not expensive.
2 Remove the right-hand side panel (see Chapter 8) and locate the mode select switch wiring connector (it has white/red and black/white wires going to it) **(see illustration)**. Remove the connector cover, ensure the ignition and the select switch are OFF, then connect the select switch. If a piece of auxiliary wire is being used in place of the switch, connect one end of the wire to one of the wire terminals in the connector, but leave the other end free for the moment.
3 Start the engine, or if it will not start, crank the engine on the electric starter for at least 4 seconds. Turn the mode select switch ON or connect the free end of the wire to the other terminal in the diagnostic connector. The fault code(s) will be displayed on the LCD panel on the instrument cluster, in ascending order if there are more than one. Note the codes and identify the faults from the following table. **Note:** *Do not disconnect the ECM wiring connectors, battery leads or main fuse before recording the fault codes. The ECM memory is erased when the connectors are disconnected.*

Fault code	Faulty component – symptoms	Possible causes
CHEC	No ECM signal – engine will not run	Kill switch OFF Faulty wiring or wiring connector Faulty ignition safety interlock system (clutch switch, sidestand switch, diode or gear position switch) Damaged ignition fuse
C00	No fault	System clear
C12	Crankshaft position (CKP) sensor – engine will not run	Faulty wiring or wiring connector Damaged sensor or timing rotor
C13, C17	Intake air pressure (IAP) sensor – engine will run, air pressure signal fixed at 760 mmHg	Faulty wiring or wiring connector Damaged sensor
C14	Throttle position (TP) sensor – engine will run, throttle position signal and ignition timing fixed	Faulty wiring or wiring connector Damaged sensor
C15	Engine coolant temperature (ECT) sensor – engine will run, coolant temperature signal fixed at 80°C	Faulty wiring or wiring connector Damaged sensor
C21	Intake air temperature (IAT) sensor – engine will run, air temperature signal fixed at 40°C	Faulty wiring or wiring connector Damaged sensor
C23	Tip-over (TO) sensor – engine will not run	Faulty wiring, wiring connector or damaged sensor
C24	Front cylinder ignition coil – engine will run on other cylinder, ignition signal to No. 1 cylinder cut	Faulty wiring or wiring connector Damaged ignition coil Faulty power supply for the ignition system *(see Chapter 5 for details)*
C25	Rear cylinder ignition coil – engine will run on other cylinder, ignition signal to No. 2 cylinder cut	Faulty wiring or wiring connector Damaged ignition coil Faulty power supply for the ignition system *(see Chapter 5 for details)*
C28	Secondary throttle valve (STV) actuator – engine will run, valve fixed in half open position	Damaged actuator motor
C29	Secondary throttle position (STP) sensor – engine will run, sensor fixed in half open position	Faulty wiring or wiring connector Damaged sensor
C31	Gear position (GP) sensor – engine will run, signal fixed to 6th gear	Faulty wiring or wiring connector Damaged sensor Faulty gearshift mechanism
C32	Front cylinder fuel injector – engine will run on other cylinder	Faulty wiring, wiring connector or damaged fuel injector
C33	Rear cylinder fuel injector – engine will run on other cylinder	Faulty wiring, wiring connector or damaged fuel injector
C40	Idle speed control (ISC) valve (2009 and later) Idle speed too high or too low	Clogged or stuck ISC valve Hose loose or broken Valve circuit open or shorted Misadjusted ISC valve
C41	Fuel pump control system – engine will not run	Faulty wiring or wiring connector to pump and/or pump relay Faulty pump relay *(see Section 4)* Damaged fuel pump *(see Section 5)*
C42	Ignition switch – engine will not run	Faulty wiring, wiring connector or damaged switch *(see Chapter 9 for details)*
C44	Oxygen sensor – engine will run, fuel/air compensation ratio fixed to normal condition	Faulty wiring or wiring connector Faulty sensor

Fuel, engine management and exhaust systems - fuel injected models 4B•11

11.8a The IAP sensors are on the air intake duct (arrows) (C50 shown) . . .

11.8b . . . each has an electrical connector and vacuum hose (air intake duct removed for clarity)

11.11 Slip the mounting tab out of the slot (arrows)

4   To check the fuel injection system components see Section 11.
5   Once the fault has been corrected, turn the ignition switch ON. If the fault has been cleared, the instrument display will indicate the code C00. Turn the mode select switch OFF or remove the jumper wire, then turn the ignition switch OFF and disconnect the mode select switch. Reinstall the wiring connector cover (see Chapter 8).

11 Fuel injection system components - check, removal and installation

1   If a fault is indicated on any of the system components, first check the wiring and connectors between the appropriate component and the engine control module (ECM); see *Wiring Diagrams* at the end of Chapter 9. A continuity test of all wires will locate a break or short in any circuit. Inspect the terminals inside the wiring connectors and ensure they are not loose or corroded. Spray the inside of the connectors with an electrical terminal cleaner before reconnection.
2   It is possible to undertake some checks on system components using a multimeter and comparing the results with the specifications at the beginning of this Chapter. **Note:** *Different meters may give slightly different results to those specified even though the component being tested is not faulty - do not consign a component to the bin before having it double-checked.* However, some faults will only become evident when a component is tested with a peak voltage tester, in which case the checks should be undertaken by a Suzuki dealer.
3   If after a thorough check the source of a fault has not been identified, it is possible that the ECM itself is faulty. Suzuki provides no test specifications for the ECM. In order to determine conclusively that the unit is defective, it should be substituted with a known good one. If the problem is then rectified, the original unit is proven faulty.

Crankshaft position (CKP) sensor

4   Make sure the ignition is OFF. To access the CKP sensor wiring connector remove the left side cover, lower left frame cover and toolbox (see Chapter 8). The sensor itself is in the alternator cover and is actuated by a trigger on the alternator rotor. Before testing the sensor it is worth removing the alternator cover (see Chapter 9) and cleaning the sensor - a build-up of dirt and/or debris can affect the signal sent to the ECM. Also check the trigger on the rotor for damage.
5   Trace the wiring from the alternator cover and disconnect it at the wiring connector. Using an ohmmeter or multimeter set to the ohms scale, measure the resistance between the terminals on the sensor side of the connector. If the result is as specified, check that there is no continuity between each terminal and earth (ground).
6   If the results are good, have the sensor peak voltage tested by a Suzuki dealer.
7   To remove the sensor, see Chapter 9 - it is part of the alternator stator in the valve cover and is not available separately.

Intake air pressure (IAP) sensor

8   Make sure the ignition is OFF. Raise the fuel tank (see Section 2). The IAP sensors (one for each cylinder) are on the back of the air intake duct **(see illustrations)**. Check the condition of the vacuum hose between the sensors and the throttle body. If a hose is cracked or deteriorated replace it with a new one. Ensure the hose is a tight fit on the sensor union, the hose joint pieces and the throttle body.
9   To check the input voltage, disconnect the sensor wiring connector and turn the ignition ON. Connect the positive probe of a voltmeter to the red wire terminal on the harness side of the wiring connector and the negative probe first to ground, then to the black/brown wire terminal to check the input voltage. Turn the ignition OFF. If input voltage is not as specified in both cases, check the wiring to the ECM and the ECM connector terminals.
10   If the input voltage is good, reconnect the wiring to the sensor, then start the engine and allow it idle. Insert the positive probe of a voltmeter into the green/white (rear cylinder) or green/black (front cylinder) wire terminal in the connector and the negative probe into the black/brown wire terminal to check the output voltage. If the result is as specified, take the sensor to a Suzuki dealer for vacuum testing. Note that the output voltage can vary between 2.4 and 4.0 volts depending on the altitude and atmospheric pressure at which the test is being carried out.
11   To remove the IAP sensor, first disconnect the vacuum hose and the wiring connector. Pull the sensor mounting tab out of the slot on the air intake tube **(see illustration)**. On installation, ensure the wiring connector terminals are clean and that the vacuum hose is a tight fit on the sensor union.

Throttle position (TP) sensor

Note: *The STP is secured by a special Torx security screw (it has a raised center to prevent a standard Torx bit from being used) which will require the appropriate Torx security bit to turn it.*

12   Make sure the ignition is OFF. Remove the air filter housing (see Section 8) - the TP sensor is located on the throttle body **(see illustration)**. Disconnect the sensor wiring

11.12 Here are the throttle position sensor (lower arrow) and secondary throttle position sensor (upper arrow) (2008 and earlier shown)

11.29 The tip-over switch is mounted under the fuel tank (arrow)

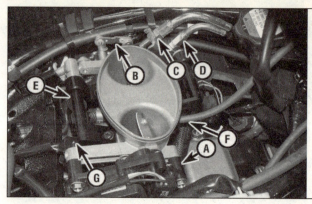

11.32 Throttle body details (2008 and earlier shown; 2009 and later similar)

- A Secondary throttle valve actuator
- B Fast idle link
- C Throttle pull cable
- D Throttle return cable
- E Fuel rail
- F Vacuum hose
- G Injector electrical connector

connector. Turn the ignition ON and connect the positive probe of a voltmeter to the red wire terminal on the loom side of the wiring connector and the negative probe first to ground, and then to the black/brown wire terminal to check the input voltage. Turn the ignition OFF. If the input voltage is not as specified in both cases, check the wiring to the ECM, the multi-pin wiring connector for the injector loom and the ECM connector terminals.

13 If the input voltage is good, check for continuity between the yellow wire terminal on the sensor and earth (ground). There should be no continuity.

14 Using an ohmmeter set to the K-ohms scale, measure the resistance between the yellow and black wire terminals on the sensor, first with the throttle closed, then with the throttle fully open. If the results are as specified, reconnect the wiring connector.

15 Turn the ignition ON and connect the probes of a voltmeter between the blue/black and black/brown wire terminals in the connector to check the output voltage, first with the throttle closed, then with the throttle fully open. Turn the ignition OFF. If the results are not as specified, the sensor is faulty.

16 To remove the TP sensor, first disconnect its wiring connector. Mark the position of the sensor to aid installation, then undo the Torx screws (see **Note** above) securing the sensor and remove it. Note how the end of the throttle shaft engages the slot in the sensor.

17 Installation is the reverse of removal. Apply some grease to the seal in the sensor socket in the throttle body. Ensure that the throttle shaft engages correctly in the slot in the sensor and align any register marks before lightly tightening the Torx screws. Ensure the wiring connector terminals are clean. If both the TP and STP sensors have been removed, make sure you correctly identify them before installation - the TP sensor has three wire terminals and the STP has four. The STP check, removal and installation procedure is covered later in this Section.

18 To check and adjust the position of the TP sensor, first check the engine idle speed and adjust it if necessary (see Chapter 1). Turn the engine OFF and connect the mode select switch to the wiring connector (see Section 11).

19 Turn the select switch ON. A code C00 will be displayed on the LCD panel on the instrument cluster with a line in front of it. If the line is in the mid-way position i.e. -C00, the TP sensor is adjusted correctly. If the line is above or below the mid-way position (¯C00 or _C00), loosen the Torx screws and carefully rotate the sensor until the line is in the mid-way position. Tighten the Torx screws to the specified torque setting.

Engine coolant temperature (ECT) sensor

20 Make sure the ignition is OFF. The engine coolant temperature (ECT) sensor is mounted on top of the engine (see Chapter 3).

21 Remove the fuel tank (see Section 2).

22 Disconnect the sensor wiring connector and turn the ignition ON. Connect the positive probe of a voltmeter to the black/blue wire terminal on the loom side of the connector and the negative probe first to ground, then to the black/brown wire terminal to check the input voltage. Turn the ignition OFF. If the input voltage is not as specified in both cases, check the wiring to the ECM and the ECM connector terminals.

23 Using an ohmmeter or multimeter set to the K-ohms scale, measure the resistance between the terminals on the sensor itself with the engine cold. If the result is not as specified, the sensor is faulty.

24 If the sensor is working correctly, the resistance should drop as the engine warms up. A check for sensor performance is described in Chapter 3. Also refer to Chapter 3 for the removal and installation procedure.

Intake air temperature (IAT) sensor

25 Make sure the ignition is OFF. Remove the air cleaner housing (see Section 8). The IAT sensor is mounted on the air filter housing **(see illustration 8.2b)**. Disconnect the sensor wiring connector and turn the ignition ON. Connect the positive probe of a voltmeter to the dark green wire terminal on the harness side of the wiring connector and the negative probe first to ground, then to the black/brown wire terminal to check the input voltage. Turn the ignition OFF. If the input voltage is not as specified in both cases, check the wiring to the ECM and the ECM connector terminals.

26 Using an ohmmeter or multimeter set to the K-ohms scale, measure the resistance between the terminals on the sensor itself. If the result is not as specified, the sensor is faulty.

27 To remove the sensor, first disconnect the wiring connector, then unscrew the sensor's mounting screw. Note the O-ring on the sensor body and replace it with a new one on installation if it is damaged. Tighten the sensor screw securely, but don't overtighten it and damage the threads.

Tip-over (TO) sensor

28 Make sure the ignition is OFF. Remove the seat and right side cover (see Chapter 8).

29 Trace the wiring from the sensor and disconnect it at the connector **(see illustration)**. Using an ohmmeter or multimeter set to the K-ohms scale, measure the resistance between the terminals on the sensor. Compare the result to that given in the Specifications at the beginning of this Chapter; if the result is good, reconnect the wiring connector.

30 With the connector reconnected, turn the ignition ON and insert the probes of a voltmeter into the brown/white and black/brown wire terminals on the harness side of the wiring connector to check the voltage. If the result is good, carefully unclip the sensor from its bracket and check the voltage reading when the sensor is leaned 65° to one side and then to the other; this simulates the cut-off point reached if the motorcycle falls over - at each point the voltage should read 3.7 to 4.4 volts. If not the sensor is faulty.

31 To remove the sensor, first disconnect the wiring connector. Unclip the sensor holder from its bracket and remove the sensor from the holder, noting which way it fits. Installation is the reverse of removal.

Secondary throttle valve (STV) actuator

32 Make sure the ignition is OFF. Remove the air filter (see Chapter 1) in order to view the secondary throttle valves. The STV actuator is on the left-hand side of the throttle body **(see illustration)**.

33 Turn the ignition ON and check the

Fuel, engine management and exhaust systems - fuel injected models 4B•13

operation of the secondary throttle valves in start-up mode. From 95 per cent open the valves should open fully, then return to the 95 per cent position. Turn the ignition OFF. If the valves do not move as described, check the wiring from the actuator to the ECM and check the ECM connector terminals.

34 Trace the wiring from the actuator to the wiring connector and disconnect it. Check that there is no continuity between either wire terminal on the actuator side of the connector and ground.

35 Using an ohmmeter or multimeter set to the ohms scale, connect the positive probe to the pink wire terminal on the sensor side of the connector and the negative probe to the black wire terminal and measure the actuator resistance. Do the same between the green wire terminal and the white/black wire terminal. If the result is not as specified, the actuator is faulty. If the result is as specified, have the ECM checked by a Suzuki dealer.

36 The actuator is not available separately from the throttle body - if the actuator is faulty a new throttle body must be installed (see Section 12).

Secondary throttle position (STP) sensor

Note: *The STP is secured by a special Torx security screw (it has a raised center to prevent a standard Torx bit from being used) which will require the appropriate Torx security bit to turn it.*

37 Make sure the ignition is OFF. Raise the fuel tank (see Section 2).

38 Remove the air filter housing (see Section 8). The secondary throttle position sensor is attached to the secondary throttle valve actuator (the TP sensor is attached directly to the throttle body) **(see illustration 11.12)**. Disconnect the sensor wiring connector. Turn the ignition ON and connect the positive probe of a voltmeter to the red wire terminal on the harness side of the wiring connector and the negative probe first to ground, and then to the black/brown wire terminal to check the input voltage. Turn the ignition OFF. If the input voltage is not as specified in both cases, check the wiring to the ECM, the multi-pin wiring connector for the injector harness and the ECM connector terminals.

39 If the input voltage is good, check for continuity between the yellow wire terminal and ground. There should be no continuity.

40 Remove the air filter (see Chapter 1). If you're working on a C50, close the secondary throttle valves by finger pressure on the fast idle link **(see illustration 11.32)**. If you're working on an M50, close the valves by pressing directly on them with a finger. Using an ohmmeter or multimeter set to the K-ohms scale, connect the positive probe to the yellow wire terminal on the sensor and the negative probe to the black wire terminal and measure the sensor resistance. Now open the secondary throttle valves by finger pressure and measure the resistance. Turn the ignition OFF.

11.46 Remove the screws (arrows) and detach the gear position switch

41 If the results are as specified, connect the ohmmeter between the blue and black wire terminals and repeat Step 40. If the results are now as specified, go to Step 42.

42 If the results are not as specified, first check the sensor adjustment as follows. Close the secondary throttle valves and loosen the sensor Torx screw. Connect the ohmmeter or multimeter to the yellow and black wire terminals, then adjust the position of the sensor until the resistance reading is within specification (valves closed); tighten the sensor screws. If the specified resistance cannot be obtained, loosen the locknut on the adjuster screw on the STV actuator, then turn the adjuster screw until the reading is as specified. Tighten the locknut on completion. If the specified resistance still cannot be obtained, the STP sensor is faulty.

43 If the results are as specified, reconnect the sensor wiring connector and disconnect the STP sensor wiring connector, then turn the ignition ON. Insert the probes of a voltmeter into the yellow/white and black/brown wire terminals on the harness side of the connector to check the output voltage while carefully closing and opening the throttle valves by finger pressure (use pins or similar probes to backprobe the terminals while the connector is connected). If the output voltage is not as specified the STP sensor is faulty. If the output voltage is good, have the ECM checked by a Suzuki dealer.

44 To remove the sensor, first disconnect the wiring connector. Mark the position of the sensor to aid installation, then undo the Torx screw (see **Note** above) securing the sensor to the STV actuator and remove the sensor. Note how the end of the throttle shaft engages the slot in the sensor.

45 Installation is the reverse of removal. Apply some grease to the seal in the sensor socket in the throttle body. Ensure that the throttle shaft engages correctly in the slot in the sensor and align any register marks before lightly tightening the Torx screws. Ensure the wiring connector terminals are clean. If both the TP and STP sensors have been removed, make sure you correctly identify them before installation. After installation adjust the sensor as described in Step 42.

11.53 Unplug the electrical connector (left arrow) to expose the injector terminals (right arrow) (there's a separate connector for each of the two injectors)

Gear position (GP) switch

46 Support the bike on an auxiliary stand and raise the sidestand. Ensure the engine kill switch is in the RUN position. If you're working on a C50, remove the left side cover (see Chapter 8). On all models, remove the secondary gearcase cover (lower left side cover) (see Chapter 8). The GP switch connector is a 3-pin with blue, pink and black/white wires **(see illustration)**.

47 Trace the wiring from the switch to the connector and disconnect it. Connect the probes of an ohmmeter or continuity tester between the blue and black/white wire terminals on the switch side of the connector. With the transmission in neutral there should be continuity. If not, remove the switch and check the contacts on its inside and the plungers in the end of the selector drum.

48 Reconnect the wiring connector. Turn the ignition switch ON and insert the positive probe of a voltmeter into the pink wire terminal in the connector and connect the negative probe to ground to check the output voltage. Select each gear in turn and check that the voltage is above the specified minimum in each gear. Turn the ignition OFF.

49 If the output voltage is not as specified, either the pink wire to the GP switch or the GP switch itself is faulty.

50 If the output voltage is as specified check the wiring from the switch to the ECM and check the ECM connector terminals.

51 To replace the switch, unscrew its mounting screws **(see illustration 11.46)**.

52 On installation make sure the plunger(s) move(s) freely in the bore(s). Apply a smear of sealant to the wiring grommet, and apply a suitable non-permanent thread locking compound to the wiring clamp and switch screws.

Fuel injectors

53 Make sure the ignition is OFF. Remove the air filter housing (see Section 8). Identify the faulty injector by the trouble code and disconnect the injector wiring connector **(see illustration)**. Using an ohmmeter or

12.3 Disconnect the vacuum hoses

12.5a Loosen the clamp (arrow) . . .

multimeter set to the ohms scale, measure the resistance between the terminals on the injector. If the result is as specified, check that there is no continuity between each terminal and ground. If there is continuity, the injector is faulty and a new one must be installed (see Section 13).

54 Turn the ignition ON. Connect the positive probe of a voltmeter to the yellow/red wire terminal on the loom side of the harness connector and the negative probe to ground to check the input voltage. **Note:** *Injector voltage can only be detected for 3 seconds after the ignition has been turned ON.* Turn the ignition OFF. If the input voltage is not as specified, refer to the Wiring Diagrams at the end of Chapter 9 and check for a fault in the yellow/red wire.

55 If the input voltage is as specified, refer to the Wiring Diagrams at the end of Chapter 9 and check for a fault in the individual injector wires.

Oxygen (O2) sensor

56 Make sure the ignition is OFF. Remove the right frame cover (see Chapter 8).
57 Trace the wiring from the sensor in the exhaust system to the wiring connector and disconnect it. Check that there is no continuity between the white/black wire terminal on the harness side of the connector and ground.
58 Reconnect the sensor wiring connector. Start the engine and warm it up to normal operating temperature.
59 With the engine idling insert the positive probe of a voltmeter into the white/black wire terminal in the connector and connect the negative probe to the black/brown wire terminal and check the output voltage. Now increase engine speed to 5000 rpm and check the output voltage again. Turn the engine OFF. If the readings are not as specified replace the sensor with a new one.
60 Check for battery voltage at the white/black wire terminal in the connector with the ignition ON and the connector connected,

bearing in mind that the voltage will only register for a few seconds - connect the meter probes between the terminal and ground before turning the ignition on. If there is no voltage check the wiring and connectors between the connector and the ECM. If the wiring is good, either the sensor or the ECM is faulty. Turn the ignition OFF.
61 Disconnect the sensor wiring connector. Measure the resistance between the two white wire terminals on the sensor side of the wiring connector. If it is not as specified the sensor is faulty. Bear in mind that the resistance will vary with temperature, so try to take the reading at the temperature specified.
62 If the resistance is good, and all the wiring and connectors to the ECM are good, the ECM could be faulty and should be checked by a Suzuki dealer.
63 To remove the sensor, first make sure it is cold, then disconnect the wiring connectors. Unscrew the sensor from the exhaust. On installation tighten the sensor to the specified torque setting.

Idle speed control (ISC) valve (2009 and later)

64 Locate the ISC valve on the front side of the throttle body. Disconnect its connector. Unplug the connector from the ECM.
65 Identify the ISC valve wires in the wiring harness side of the ECM connector (blue, yellow, green/white and brown). Locate the other end of each wire at the ISC valve. Connect an ohmmeter between the ends of each wire and check for continuity. If there is no continuity, check the wire for a break. Also check the wire terminals for corrosion or damage.
66 Remove the throttle body from the engine (see Section 12).
67 Measure resistance between the two outermost terminals in the ISC valve connector (the valve side, not the harness side) and compare the reading with the value listed in this Chapter's Specifications. Measure resis-

tance between the two inner most terminals and again compare the reading with the value listed in this Chapter's Specifications. If the resistance is not as listed, the ISC valve must be replaced.
68 Valve replacement requires that the ISC valve be pre-set using the special Suzuki diagnostic scanner. Have the job done by a dealer service department or other qualified shop.

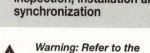

12 Throttle body - removal, inspection, installation and synchronization

Warning: Refer to the precautions given in Section 1 before starting work.

Removal

1 Remove the fuel tank and air intake tube (see Sections 2 and 8).
2 Disconnect the electrical connectors for the throttle position sensor, secondary throttle position sensor, secondary throttle valve actuator and fuel injectors.
3 There are various vacuum hoses coming from the throttle body and connecting via unions to various vacuum actuated components. Disconnect the hoses from their unions as required (but where the hose has already been detached from the component it actuates, e.g. the sensors on the air filter housing, there is no need - the hoses can be removed with the throttle bodies), making a note or color-coding them as you do to avoid confusion on installation **(see illustration)**.
4 Disconnect the throttle cables (see Section 14) - this can be done after partially removing the throttle body to improve access if required.
5 Loosen the clamp screw securing the throttle body to the intake manifold, then ease the throttle body up off the manifold and remove it **(see illustrations)**.

Fuel, engine management and exhaust systems - fuel injected models 4B•15

12.5b ... and lift the throttle body up off the intake manifold

12.5c If necessary, unbolt the intake manifold from the engine - note what direction the notches face

Cleaning

Caution: *Use only a petroleum based solvent or dedicated injector cleaner for throttle body cleaning. Don't use caustic cleaners.*

6 Before using a cleaner on the throttle body, remove the external components as described above.

Caution: *Do not remove the secondary throttle valve actuator or throttle valves.*

7 Ensure that only metal components are submerged in cleaning solvent and always follow the manufacturer's recommendations as to cleaning time. If a spray cleaner is used, direct the spray into all passages.

8 After the cleaner has loosened and dissolved most of the varnish and other deposits, use a nylon-bristled brush to remove the stubborn deposits. Rinse the throttle body again, then dry it with compressed air.

9 Use compressed air to blow out all of the fuel and air passages.

Caution: *Never clean the jets or passages with a piece of wire or a drill bit, as they will be enlarged, causing the fuel and air metering rates to be upset.*

Inspection

10 Check the throttle body for cracks or any other damage which may result in air getting in.

11 Check that the throttle valves and linkages move smoothly and freely in the bodies. Inspect the valve shafts and throttle bodies for wear. Check the condition of the valve shaft springs.

Installation

12 Installation is the reverse of removal, noting the following:

a) *Ensure the throttle bodies are fully engaged with the inlet stubs on the cylinder heads before tightening the clamps.*
b) *Ensure the fuel injector and throttle body wiring connectors are securely connected.*
c) *Make sure all detached vacuum hoses are secured back on their correct unions. Make sure all hoses are in good condition, correctly routed and not pinched.*
d) *Check the operation of the throttle cable and adjust it as necessary (see Chapter 1).*
e) *Check the operation of the STV actuator (see Section 11).*
f) *Check the engine idle speed and adjust as necessary (see Chapter 1) If the throttle linkage has been removed or if the bodies have been disassembled, synchronize them (see Chapter 1).*

Synchronization

13 Connect a synchronizing gauge into the vacuum hose on the left rear corner of the throttle body below the fast idle cam link, using a T-fitting.

14 Connect a second gauge tube to the vacuum hose on the other side of the throttle body.

15 Run the engine at 1100 rpm. If necessary, adjust by turning the synchronizing screws. These are the two brass screws set into the lower rear edge of the throttle body.

13 Fuel rails and injectors - removal and installation

 Warning: *Refer to the precautions given in Section 1 before proceeding.*

2008 and earlier

Removal

Note: *The fuel injectors on 2008 and earlier models can be removed with the throttle body in place. If the body has been removed, ignore the Steps which do not apply.*

1 Make sure the ignition is OFF. Remove the fuel tank and air intake pipe (see Sections 2 and 8).

2 Disconnect the negative cable from the battery.

3 Disconnect the electrical connectors from the fuel injectors **(see illustration 11.53)**.

4 Undo the screws securing the fuel rails to the throttle body **(see illustration)**. Carefully lift the fuel rails off - the injectors may come away with the rails.

13.4 Loosen the fuel rail screws (arrows)

4B•16 Fuel, engine management and exhaust systems - fuel injected models

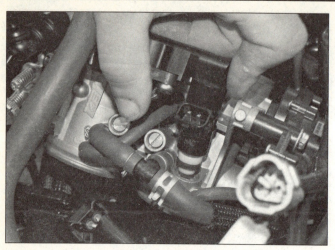

13.5a Work the injector free of the engine

13.5b Inspect the seals and spacer (arrows)

5 Pull each injector out of the fuel rail or throttle body (see illustrations). Discard the injector O-ring, spacer and seal as new ones must be fitted on reassembly.

6 Modern fuels contain detergents which should keep the injectors clean and free of gum or varnish from fuel residue. If an injector is suspected of being blocked, clean it with injector cleaner. If the injector is clean but its performance is suspect, take it to a Suzuki dealer for assessment.

Installation

Note: *Apply a smear of clean engine oil to all new seals and O-rings before reassembly.*

7 Fit a new seal onto the bottom of each injector, and a new spacer and O-ring onto the top, and smear them with clean oil **(see illustration 13.5b)**. Carefully press the injectors into the throttle bodies, aligning them so the wiring connectors face away from the throttle body **(see illustration 13.5a)**. **Note:** *Avoid twisting the injectors as this may damage the seals.* If the injectors are difficult to locate in the throttle body because of the bottom seals, remove the seals and fit them into the throttle body, then fit the injector into the seal.

8 Locate the fuel rail assembly over the injectors and press it down until the O-rings are felt to seat. Install the fuel rail screws and tighten them to the specified torque setting.

9 Install the remaining components in the reverse order of removal. On completion, start the engine and check carefully that there are no fuel leaks.

2009 and later models

10 Remove the throttle body (see Section 12).

11 Disconnect the fuel feed hose from the metal fuel tube on the rear fuel rail.

12 Remove the retaining screw from the rear fuel rail's retaining plate, then take the retaining plate off. Pull the plug straight out of the rear fuel rail (don't let it cock sideways or the O-ring seat may be damaged).

13 Thread an 8mm by 0.5 thread pitch bolt into the joint fitting in the rear fuel rail. The bolt must be threaded in at least 10 turns. Pull on the bolt to remove the joint fitting from the fuel rail. As with the plug, pull the joint fitting straight out of the rear fuel rail (don't let it cock sideways or the O-ring seat may be damaged).

14 Remove two screws from the top of each fuel rail, then pull the fuel rail straight off its injector.

Caution: *Don't remove the L-shaped metal fuel fitting from the rear fuel rail.*

15 Pull each injector straight out of its fuel rail.

16 Installation is the reverse of the removal steps. Use new O-rings, lightly coated with clean engine oil. Be careful not to twist the injectors when installing them.

14 Throttle cables - removal and installation

Removal

1 Remove the air filter housing (see Section 8).

2 Loosen the locknuts securing the throttle cable adjusters in the bracket, then slip them out of the bracket and detach them from the throttle pulley, noting how they fit - the lower cable is the throttle opening cable, the upper cable is the throttle closing cable **(see illustration)**.

3 Disconnect the cables from the throttle pulley at the handlebar. This is basically the same as for carbureted models (see Chapter 4A).

4 Remove the cables from the machine, noting their correct routing.

Installation

5 Thread the cables through to the throttle bodies and up to the handlebars, making sure they are correctly routed - they must not interfere with any other component and should not be kinked or bent sharply.

6 Reverse the disconnection procedure to connect the cables to the throttle body and handlebar twistgrip.

7 Start the engine and check the action of the throttle, and that the idle speed does not rise as the handlebars are turned. If it does, correct the problem before riding the motorcycle.

14.2 Loosen the locknuts (left arrows), slip the cables out of the bracket and free the ends from the pulley (right arrows)

Fuel, engine management and exhaust systems - fuel injected models 4B•17

15.6 Fast idle screw

17.8 Disconnect the electrical connector (upper arrow); remove the screws (lower arrows) and take off the cover

15 Fast idle speed - check and adjustment

Note: *The fast idle mechanism is actuated by the STV actuator when the engine is cold and should cancel automatically when the engine warms up. If the idle speed cannot be adjusted correctly (see Chapter 1), check for a possible fault in the coolant temperature sensor or sensor wiring (see Section 11).*

1 Warm the engine to normal operating temperature.
2 Set the idle speed to 1100 rpm by turning the throttle stop screw (see Chapter 1).
3 Check the throttle position sensor adjustment and correct it if necessary (see Section 11).
4 Raise and support the fuel tank (see Section 2).
5 Start the engine and check the output voltage of the throttle position sensor (see Section 11). Write the number down.
6 Disconnect the wiring connector from the STV actuator **(see illustration 11.32)**. Open the secondary throttle valve all the way by pushing on the fast idle link **(see illustration 11.32)**. Now recheck the TP sensor output voltage and write it down. Calculate the difference between this measurement and the measurement in Step 6. If the difference is not within the range listed in this Chapter's Specifications, adjust it by turning the fast idle screw **(see illustration)**.
7 Let the engine cool, then restart it and check fast idle speed. It should be within the range listed in this Chapter's Specifications, and should drop to idle speed within the specified time. If not, the problem may be in the engine coolant temperature or its harness or in the secondary throttle valve actuator.

16 Exhaust system - removal and installation

 Warning: If the engine has been running the exhaust system will be very hot. Allow the system to cool before carrying out any work.

1 If the motorcycle is equipped with oxygen sensors, trace the wiring from the oxygen sensor and disconnect it at the connector.
2 Remove the exhaust system mounting nuts and bolts. Detach the front exhaust pipes from the exhaust ports in the cylinders and remove the exhaust system from the vehicle.
3 Installation is the reverse of the removal steps. Use new gaskets at all connections. Run the engine and check that there are no exhaust gas leaks.

17 PAIR system

General information

1 To reduce the amount of unburned hydrocarbons released in the exhaust gases, a pulse secondary air (PAIR) system is fitted on some California, Canada, Europe and UK models The system consists of the control valve (mounted under the air filter housing, the reed valves incorporated in the control valve) and the hoses. The control valve is actuated electronically by the ECM.
2 Under certain operating conditions, the PAIR control valve allows filtered air to be drawn through it, the reed valves and cylinder head passages and into the exhaust ports. The air mixes with the exhaust gases, causing any unburned particles of the fuel in the mixture to be burned in the exhaust port/pipes. This process changes a considerable amount of hydrocarbons and carbon monoxide into relatively harmless carbon dioxide and water. The reed valves are fitted to prevent the flow of exhaust gases back into the control valve and air filter housing.
3 The system is not adjustable and requires no maintenance, except to ensure that the hoses are in good condition and are securely connected at each end, and that there is no build-up of carbon fouling the reed valves. Replace any hoses that are cracked, split or generally deteriorated. The reed valves can be checked for any build-up of carbon by unscrewing the cover screws - if any is found, clean the valves and their housings.

Testing

Control valve

4 Remove the valve from the motorcycle (see below).
5 Check the operation of the control valve by blowing through the air filter housing hose union; air should flow freely through the valve.
6 Connect a 12V battery across the valve wiring connector terminals and repeat the check; no air should now flow through the valve if it is functioning correctly. If an ohmmeter is available, check the resistance of the control valve windings by connecting an ohmmeter between its wiring connector terminals and compare the reading obtained to that given in the Specifications. Replace the valve with a new one if faulty.

Reed valves

7 Disconnect each reed valve hose from the control valve. Check the valve by blowing and sucking on the hose end. Air should flow through the hose only when blown down it and not when sucked back up. If this is not the case the reed valve is faulty. Check the other valve in the same way.

Control valve replacement

8 Remove the solenoid cover from the left side of the motorcycle **(see illustration)**.

17.9 Disconnect the vacuum hoses (arrows)

18.5 The EVAP canister is mounted on the frame

9 Unplug the electrical connector from the solenoid, disconnect its hoses and remove it from the motorcycle (see illustration).
10 Installation is the reverse of removal.

18 EVAP system (California models)

General information

1 This system prevents the escape of fuel vapor into the atmosphere by storing it in a charcoal-filled canister.
2 When the engine is not running, excess fuel vapor from the tank passes into the canister. When the engine is started, intake manifold vacuum draws the vapor back from the canister into the throttle bodies to be burned during the normal combustion process.
3 The canister has a one-way valve which allows air to be drawn into the system as the volume of fuel decreases in the tank. A shut-off valve also prevents any fuel escaping through it in the event of the bike falling over.
4 The system is not adjustable and can only be properly tested by a Suzuki dealer. However the owner can check that all the hoses are in good condition and are securely connected at each end. Renew any hoses that are cracked, split or generally deteriorated.

Removal and installation

5 The canister is mounted on the frame (see illustration). Label and disconnect the hoses, then remove the clamp screw and take the canister out. Make sure the hoses are correctly reconnected on installation.
6 The shut-off valve is located in the hose between the fuel tank and the canister.

19 Catalytic converter

Note: *A catalytic converter is fitted as standard on European and Australian market models.*

General information

1 A catalytic converter is incorporated in each silencer to minimize the level of exhaust pollutants released into the atmosphere.
2 The catalytic converter consists of a canister containing a fine mesh impregnated with a catalyst material, over which the hot exhaust gases pass. The catalyst speeds up the oxidation of harmful carbon monoxide, unburned hydrocarbons and soot, effectively reducing the quantity of harmful products released into the atmosphere via the exhaust gases.
3 The catalytic converter is of the closed-loop type with exhaust gas oxygen content information being fed back to the ECM by the oxygen sensor.
4 The oxygen sensor contains a heating element which is controlled by the ECM. When the engine is cold, the ECM switches on the heating element which warms the sensor. This brings the sensor quickly up to its normal operating temperature. Once the engine is sufficiently warmed up, the ECM switches off the heating element.
5 Refer to Section 16 for exhaust system removal and installation, and Section 11 for oxygen sensor removal and installation information.

Precautions

6 The catalytic converter is a reliable and simple device which needs no maintenance in itself, but there are some facts of which an owner should be aware if the converter is to function properly for its full service life.

a) DO NOT use leaded or lead replacement gasoline - the additives will coat the precious metals, reducing their converting efficiency and will eventually destroy the catalytic converter.
b) Always keep the ignition and fuel systems well-maintained in accordance with the manufacturer's schedule - if the fuel/air mixture is suspected of being incorrect have it checked on an exhaust gas analyzer.
c) If the engine develops a misfire, do not ride the bike at all (or at least as little as possible) until the fault is cured.
d) DO NOT use fuel or engine oil additives - these may contain substances harmful to the catalytic converter.
e) DO NOT continue to use the bike if the engine burns oil to the extent of leaving a visible trail of blue smoke.
f) Remember that the catalytic converter and oxygen sensor are FRAGILE - do not strike them with tools during servicing work.

Chapter 5
Ignition system

Contents

General information 1	Ignition (main) switch and key lock cylinder - check, removal
IC igniter - removal, check and installation 5	and installation .... See Chapter 9
Ignition coils - check, removal and installation 3	Pickup coils - check, removal and installation 4
Ignition stop switch - check, removal and installation .. See Chapter 9	Spark plug replacement .... See Chapter 1
Ignition system - check 2	Crankshaft position sensor testing and replacement.. See Chapter 4B

Degrees of difficulty

Easy, suitable for novice with little experience	**Fairly easy,** suitable for beginner with some experience	**Fairly difficult,** suitable for competent DIY mechanic	**Difficult,** suitable for experienced DIY mechanic	**Very difficult,** suitable for expert DIY or professional 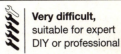

Specifications

Ignition coil
Intruder
    Primary resistance .... 2 to 6 ohms
    Secondary resistance .... 15 to 40 k-ohms

S50
    Primary resistance .... 1.8 to 2.6 ohms
    Secondary resistance .... 16 to 26 k-ohms

Volusia and Marauder
    Primary resistance .... 2 to 6 ohms
    Secondary resistance .... 15 to 30 k-ohms

C50
    Primary resistance .... 2.8 to 4.7 ohms
    Secondary resistance .... 24 to 36 k-ohms

M50
    Primary resistance .... 2 to 6 ohms
    Secondary resistance .... 15 to 30 k-ohms

Pickup coil resistance
Intruder and S50... 50 to 200 ohms
Volusia .... Not specified
Marauder .... 170 to 280 ohms

Ignition timing .... Not adjustable

1 General information

These motorcycles are equipped with a battery operated, fully transistorized, breakerless ignition system. The system consists of the following components:

    Pickup coil or crankshaft position sensor
    IC igniter unit or engine control module
    Battery and fuse
    Ignition coils
    Spark plugs
    Stop and main (key) switches
    Primary and secondary circuit wiring

The transistorized ignition system functions on the same principle as a breaker point DC ignition system with the pickup unit and igniter performing the tasks previously associated with the breaker points and mechanical advance system. As a result, adjustment and maintenance of ignition components is eliminated (with the exception of spark plug replacement). 2009 and later C50 models sold in the UK, Europe, Australia and California have two ignition coils and two spark plugs per cylinder.

Because of their nature, the individual ignition system components can be checked but not repaired. If ignition system troubles occur, and the faulty component can be isolated, the only cure for the problem is to replace the part with a new one. Keep in mind that most electrical parts, once purchased, can't be returned. To avoid unnecessary expense, make very sure the faulty component has been positively identified before buying a replacement part.

5•2 Ignition system

2.5 Unscrew the spark plug caps from the plug wires and measure their resistance with an ohmmeter

2.13 A simple spark gap testing fixture can be made from a block of wood, a large alligator clip, two nails, a screw and a piece of wire

2 Ignition system - check

Warning: Because of the very high voltage generated by the ignition system, extreme care should be taken to avoid electrical shock when these checks are performed.

1 If the ignition system is the suspected cause of poor engine performance or failure to start, a number of checks can be made to isolate the problem.
2 Make sure the ignition stop switch is in the Run or On position.

Engine will not start

3 Disconnect one of the spark plug wires, connect the wire to a spare spark plug and lay the plug on the engine with the threads contacting the engine. If it's necessary to hold the spark plug, use an insulated tool. Crank the engine over and make sure a well-defined, blue spark occurs between the spark plug electrodes.

Warning: DO NOT remove one of the spark plugs from the engine to perform this check - atomized fuel being pumped out of the open spark plug hole could ignite, causing severe injury!

4 If no spark occurs, the following checks should be made:
5 Unscrew a spark plug cap from a plug wire and check the cap resistance with an ohmmeter **(see illustration)**. If the resistance is infinite, replace it with a new one. Repeat this check on the other plug cap.
6 Make sure all electrical connectors are clean and tight. Refer to the wiring diagrams at the end of this book and check all wires for shorts, opens and correct installation.

7 Check the battery voltage with a voltmeter and the specific gravity with a hydrometer (see Chapter 1). If the voltage is less than 12-volts or if the specific gravity is low, recharge the battery.
8 Check the ignition fuse and the fuse connections. If the fuse is blown, replace it with a new one; if the connections are loose or corroded, clean or repair them.
9 Refer to Section 3 and check the ignition coil primary and secondary resistance.
10 If you're working on a carbureted model, refer to Section 4 and check the pickup coil resistance. If you're working on a fuel injected model, refer to Section 11 in Chapter 4B to check the crankshaft position sensor.
11 If the preceding checks produce positive results but there is still no spark at the plug, have the IC igniter checked by a Suzuki dealer service department or other repair shop equipped with the special tester required.

Engine starts but misfires

12 If the engine starts but misfires, make the following checks before deciding that the ignition system is at fault.
13 The ignition system must be able to produce a spark across an 8-millimeter (5/16-inch) gap (minimum). A simple test fixture **(see illustration)** can be constructed to make sure the minimum spark gap can be jumped. Make sure the fixture electrodes are positioned seven millimeters apart.
14 Connect one of the spark plug wires to the protruding test fixture electrode, then attach the fixture's alligator clip to a good engine ground/earth.
15 Crank the engine over (it may start and run on the remaining cylinder) and see if well-defined, blue sparks occur between the test fixture electrodes. If the minimum spark gap test is positive, the ignition coil for that cylinder is functioning properly. Repeat the check on the spark plug wire that is connected to the other coil. If the spark will not jump the gap during either test, or if it is weak (orange colored), refer to Steps 5 through 11 of this Section and perform the component checks described.

3 Ignition coils - check, removal and installation

Check

1 In order to determine conclusively that the ignition coils are defective, they should be tested by an authorized Suzuki dealer service department which is equipped with the special electrical tester required for this check.
2 However, the coils can be checked visually (for cracks and other damage) and the primary and secondary coil resistances can be measured with an ohmmeter. If the coils are undamaged, and if the resistances are as specified, they are probably capable of proper operation.
3 To check the coils for physical damage, they must be removed (see Step 9). To check the resistances, simply remove the fuel tank (see Chapter 4), unplug the primary circuit electrical connectors from the coil(s) and remove the spark plug wire from the plug that is connected to the coil being checked. Mark the locations of all wires before disconnecting them.
4 To check the coil primary resistance, attach one ohmmeter lead to one of the primary terminals and the other ohmmeter lead to the other primary terminal **(see illustrations)**.
5 Place the ohmmeter selector switch in the Rx1 position and compare the measured resistance to the value listed in this Chapter's Specifications.
6 If the coil primary resistance is as specified, check the coil secondary resistance by

Ignition system 5•3

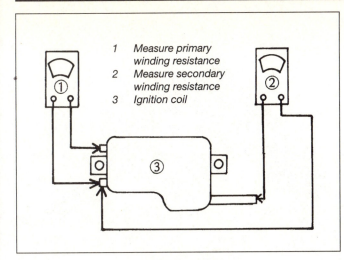

3.4a Ignition coil test

1. Measure primary winding resistance
2. Measure secondary winding resistance
3. Ignition coil

3.4b Ignition coil primary terminals (arrows) (S50 shown)

disconnecting the meter leads from the primary terminals and attaching one of them to the spark plug wire terminal and the other to either of the primary terminals **(see illustration 3.4a)**.

7 Place the ohmmeter selector switch in the Rx100 position and compare the measured resistance to the values listed in this Chapter's Specifications.

8 If the resistances are not as specified, unscrew the spark plug wire retainers from the coil, detach the wires and check the resistance again. If it is now within specifications, one or both of the wires are bad. If it's still not as specified, the coil is probably defective and should be replaced with a new one.

Removal and installation

9 Remove the fuel tank for access to the coils (see Chapter 4).

10 To remove the coils, disconnect the spark plug wires from the plugs. After labeling them with tape to aid in reinstallation, unplug the coil primary circuit electrical connectors.

11 Support the coil with one hand and remove the coil mounting screws **(see illustration 3.4b)**, then remove the coil.

12 Installation is the reverse of removal. If a new coil is being installed, disconnect the spark plug wire terminal from the coil, disconnect the wire and transfer it to the new coil. Make sure the primary circuit electrical connectors are attached to the proper terminals.

4 Pickup coil(s) - check and replacement

Check

1 Remove the left side cover (see Chapter 8).

2 Follow the pickup coil wiring harness from the point where it leaves the alternator cover to the electrical connector, then disconnect the connector for the pickup coil(s).

3 Connect an ohmmeter to the terminals in the pickup coil connector and compare the resistance reading with the value listed in this Chapter's Specifications.

4 Set the ohmmeter on the highest resistance range. Measure the resistance between a good ground and each terminal in the electrical connector. The meter should read infinity.

5 If a pickup coil fails either of the above tests, it must be replaced. On Intruder models, replace both coils as a set.

Replacement

6 The pickup coil is replaced as a unit with the alternator stator (see Chapter 9).

5 IC igniter or ECM - removal, check and installation

5.2 The ECM is mounted under the seat (S50 shown)

Removal

1 Remove the seat.

2 Disconnect the igniter electrical connector. Free the igniter or engine control module (ECM) from its mount and take it out **(see illustration)**.

Check

3 A special tester is required to accurately measure the resistance values across the various terminals of the IC igniter. Take the unit to a Suzuki dealer service department or other repair shop equipped with this tester.

Installation

4 Installation is the reverse of the removal steps.

Notes

Chapter 6
Steering, suspension and final drive

Contents

Drive chain - removal, cleaning, inspection and installation 13
Drive chain and sprockets... See Chapter 1
Final drive unit and driveshaft (shaft drive models) -
  removal, inspection and installation.. 11
Fork oil - replacement .... See Chapter 1
Forks - disassembly, inspection and reassembly 4
Forks - removal and installation... 3
Front bevel gears (shaft drive models) - removal, inspection
  and installation... 12
General information.. 1
Handlebars - removal and installation... 2

Rear shock absorbers - removal and installation......................... 6
Rear suspension linkage (single-shock models) - removal,
  inspection and installation 7
Rear wheel coupling/rubber damper - check and replacement ... 15
Sprockets - check and replacement 14
Steering head bearings - check and replacement .... See Chapter 1
Steering head bearings - replacement... 5
Suspension - check... See Chapter 1
Swingarm - removal and installation... 9
Swingarm bearings - check.. 8
Swingarm bearings - replacement.. 10

Degrees of difficulty

Easy, suitable for novice with little experience	Fairly easy, suitable for beginner with some experience	Fairly difficult, suitable for competent DIY mechanic	Difficult, suitable for experienced DIY mechanic 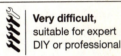	Very difficult, suitable for expert DIY or professional

Specifications

Front suspension

Fork oil
  Type
    Intruder and S50... 10W fork oil
    Marauder .... 15W fork oil
    Volusia and C50.. Suzuki fork oil SS-08 or equivalent
    M50.. Suzuki fork oil L01 or equivalent
  Amount
    Intruder and S50
      1985 and 1986 .... 337 cc (11.4 US fl oz, 11.9 Imp oz)
      1987 .... 355 cc (12.0 US fl oz, 12.5 Imp oz)
      1988 and later .... 413 cc (14.0 US fl oz, 14.5 Imp oz)
    Marauder .... 838 cc (28.3 US fl oz, 29.5 Imp oz)
    Volusia and C50.. 412 cc (24 US fl oz, 25 Imp oz)
    M50.. 490 cc (16.6 US fl oz, 17.3 Imp oz)
  Level
    Intruder and S50... Not specified
    Marauder (outer tube raised 177 mm/6.97 inches) ..... 154 mm (6.06 inches)
    Volusia and C50 (without spring)............................ 177 mm (6.96 inches)
    M50 (without spring)... 153 mm (6.02 inches)
Damper free length (Marauder) .... 156 mm (6.14 inches)
Fork spring length
  Intruder and S50 models .... Not specified
  Volusia and C50 models (service limit) .... 540 mm (21.26 inches)
  Marauder models .... Not specified
  M50 models .... 372 mm (14.6 inches)
Damper height (Marauder only).................................... 156 mm (6.1 inches)

Rear suspension and final drive

Final drive oil type and quantity (shaft drive models)............. See Chapter 1
Drive chain 20-link length limit (chain drive models)............. 319.4 mm (12.6 inches)

Torque specifications

Intruder and S50 models

Handlebar clamp bolts	
1986 through 1997 models	12 to 20 Nm (102 to 174 inch-lbs)
1998 and later models	15 to 25 Nm (11 to 18 ft-lbs)
Handlebar bracket-to-post Allen bolts	
1986 through 1997 models	12 to 20 Nm (102 to 174 inch-lbs)*
1998 and later models	40 to 50 Nm (29 to 36 ft-lbs)
Handlebar bracket-to-triple clamp nuts	
All except 1999 models	40 to 50 Nm (29 to 36 ft-lbs)
1999 models	80 to 100 Nm (58 to 72 ft-lbs)
Steering head nut	
1986 through 1997 models	60 to 100 Nm (43.5 to 72.5 ft-lbs)
1998 and later models	80 to 100 Nm (58 to 72.5 ft-lbs)
Steering stem adjusting nut	
Initial torque	40 to 50 Nm (29 to 36 ft-lbs)
Final torque	Hand tight
Lower triple clamp bolts	
1986 through 1997 models	20 to 30 Nm (14.5 to 21.5 ft-lbs)
1998 and later models	25 to 40 Nm (18 to 29 ft-lbs)
Fork cap bolt	25 to 30 Nm (18 to 21.5 ft-lbs)
Fork damper rod bolt	15 to 25 Nm (11 to 18 ft-lbs)*
Rear shock absorber mounting nuts	20 to 30 Nm (14.5 to 21.5 ft-lbs)
Swingarm pivot shaft nut	50 to 80 Nm (36 to 58 ft-lbs)
Final drive unit to swingarm nuts	35 to 45 Nm (25.5 to 32.5 ft-lbs)
Front driven gear Allen bolts	18 to 28 Nm (13 to 20 ft-lbs)
Front driven gearcase bolts	Not specified
Front drive gear unit bolts	18 to 28 Nm (13 to 20 ft-lbs)

Volusia and C50 models

Handlebar clamp bolts	23 Nm (16.5 ft-lbs)
Handlebar bracket bolt and nut	70 Nm (50.5 ft-lbs)
Steering head nut	90 Nm (65 ft-lbs)
Steering stem adjusting nut	
Initial torque	45 Nm (32.5 ft-lbs)
Final torque	Loosen 1/4 to 1/2 turn from initial torque
Fork cap bolt	45 Nm (32.5 ft-lbs)
Lower triple clamp bolts	33 Nm (24 ft-lbs)
Fork damper rod bolt	20 Nm (14.5 ft-lbs)*
Rear shock absorber mounting nuts/bolts	50 Nm (36 ft-lbs)
Rear suspension linkage bolts/nuts	78 Nm (56.5 ft-lbs)
Swingarm left pivot shaft	100 Nm (72.5 ft-lbs)
Swingarm right pivot shaft	9.5 Nm (84 inch-lbs)
Swingarm left pivot shaft locknut	100 Nm (72.5 ft-lbs)
Final drive unit to swingarm nuts	40 Nm (29 ft-lbs)
Front driven gear Allen bolts	23 Nm (16.5 ft-lbs)
Front driven gearcase bolts	Not specified
Front drive gear unit bolts	23 Nm (16.5 ft-lbs)

Marauder models

Handlebar mounting nuts	54 Nm (39 ft-lbs)
Steering head nut	90 Nm (65 ft-lbs)
Steering stem adjusting nut	
Initial torque	45 Nm (32.5 ft-lbs)
Second step	Loosen 1/4 to 1/2 turn from initial torque
Final step	Tighten by hand to eliminate play
Fork cap bolt	23 Nm (16.5 ft-lbs)
Upper triple clamp bolts	23 Nm (16.5 ft-lbs)
Lower triple clamp bolts	33 Nm (24 ft-lbs)
Rear shock absorber upper bolts	23 Nm (16.5 ft-lbs)
Rear shock absorber lower nuts	50 Nm (36 ft-lbs)
Swingarm pivot shaft nut	100 Nm (72.5 ft-lbs)
Rear sprocket nuts	50 Nm (36 ft-lbs)
Engine sprocket nut	115 Nm (83 ft-lbs)

Steering, suspension and final drive

M50 models

Handlebar clamp bolts	23 Nm (16.5 ft-lbs)
Handlebar bracket nuts	54 Nm (39 ft-lbs)
Steering head nut	90 Nm (65 ft-lbs)
Steering stem adjusting nut	
Initial torque	45 Nm (32.5 ft-lbs)
Final torque	Loosen 1/4 to 1/2 turn from initial torque
Fork cap bolt	23 Nm (16.5 ft-lbs)
Upper triple clamp bolts	23 Nm (16.5 ft-lbs)
Lower triple clamp bolts	33 Nm (24 ft-lbs)
Fork damper rod bolt	39 Nm (28 ft-lbs)*
Rear shock absorber mounting nuts/bolts	50 Nm (36 ft-lbs)
Rear suspension linkage bolts/nuts	78 Nm (56.5 ft-lbs)
Swingarm left pivot shaft	100 Nm (72.5 ft-lbs)
Swingarm right pivot shaft	9.5 Nm (84 inch-lbs)
Swingarm left pivot shaft locknut	100 Nm (72.5 ft-lbs)
Final drive unit to swingarm nuts	40 Nm (29 ft-lbs)
Front driven gear Allen bolts	23 Nm (16.5 ft-lbs)
Front driven gearcase bolts	22 Nm (16 ft-lbs)
Front drive gear unit bolts	23 Nm (16.5 ft-lbs)

*Apply non-permanent thread locking agent to the threads.

1 General information

The front forks on these models are of the conventional coil spring, hydraulically-damped telescopic type. Marauder and Boulevard M50 models use cartridge forks. All other have damper rod forks.

The steering stem is supported by tapered roller bearings (Intruder, S50 and Marauder) or caged ball bearings (all others).

The rear suspension on Intruder, S50 and Marauder models consists of two coil spring/shock absorbers and a swingarm. On Intruder and S50 models, the swingarm contains a passage for the driveshaft.

The rear suspension on Volusia, C50 and M5 models is a simulated rigid frame, consisting of a rocker-type swingarm, single coil-over shock absorber and progressive rising rate linkage.

The final drive on all models except the Marauder uses a bevel gear at the engine, a driveshaft and a rear differential. Final drive on Marauder models uses a chain. Rubber dampers are installed between the rear wheel coupling and the wheel on all models.

2 Handlebars - removal and installation

1 These motorcycles use a one-piece handlebar, secured to the upper triple clamp by upper and lower brackets on all except Marauder models. The Marauder handlebar has integral mounting posts, which are threaded on the bottom and secured to the upper triple clamp by nuts.

2 On all except Marauders, before removing the handlebars, look for a punch mark indicating the position of the handlebar in the brackets (see illustration). Make your own mark if you can't see one.

3 On all except Marauders, pry the trim plugs out of the handlebar bolt holes (see illustration).

4 If the handlebars must be removed for access to other components, such as the forks or the steering head, simply remove the bracket nuts (Marauder models) or the upper bolts (all others) and lift the handlebar off (see illustration). It's not necessary to disconnect the cables, wires or hoses, but it is a good idea to support the assembly with a piece of wire or rope, to avoid unnecessary strain on the cables, wires and (on the right side) the brake hose.

2.2 Look for a punch mark (arrow) that indicates handlebar alignment; if there isn't one, make your own mark

2.3 Pry out the trim buttons (arrows) for access to the handlebar bolts

6•4 Steering, suspension and final drive

2.4 The handlebar brackets are secured to the triple clamp by a nut on each side (arrow)

3.6a Loosen, but DO NOT remove, the fork cap bolt . . .

3.6b . . . or sudden release of the spring pressure will jam the spring into the handlebar like this

5 Check the handlebar for cracks and distortion and replace it if any undesirable conditions are found.

6 Installation is the reverse of the removal steps, with the following additions:

a) If you're working on a Marauder, tighten the bracket nuts to the torque listed in this Chapter's Specifications.

b) If you're working on an Intruder or S50, tighten the bracket bolts evenly, in two or three stages, to the torque listed in this Chapter's Specifications. This will leave a small clearance between the upper and lower brackets. The clearance should be the same on the front and rear sides of the bracket. Don't try to close the gap by tightening the bolts further or the brackets will break.

c) On Volusia, C50 and M50 models, tighten the forward bolt on each bracket to the torque listed in this Chapter's Specifications, then tighten the rear bolt. This will leave a gap at the rear of the bracket. Don't try to close the gap by tightening the bolts further or the brackets will break.

3 Forks - removal and installation

Removal

1 Support the bike securely upright. Jack up the front of the frame to take the weight off the front wheel.

2 Remove the brake caliper and hang it from the bike with a piece of rope or wire (see Chapter 7). It's not necessary to disconnect the caliper brake hose for fork removal.

3 Remove the wheel (see Chapter 7).

4 Remove the front fender (see Chapter 8).

5 Remove any wiring harness clamps or straps from the fork tubes.

Warning: *Do not remove the fork cap completely in this step or the spring may fly out and jam against the handlebar.*

6 If you plan to disassemble the forks, loosen the cap bolts now (this will be easier while the fork leg is still mounted in the triple clamps) **(see illustrations)**. On Intruder, S50 and M50 models, this is a good time to loosen the damper rod Allen bolt in the bottom end of each fork tube, as the spring pressure should keep the damper rod from spinning inside the fork tube when the bolt is turned **(see illustration)**. **Note:** *if the damper rod bolt just spins without loosening, refer to the disassembly procedure to remove it.*

7 Loosen the upper and lower triple clamp bolts **(see illustration)**. Twist the fork tubes and slide them downward and out of the triple clamps.

Installation

8 Slide each fork leg into the lower triple clamp.

9 Slide the fork legs up, installing the tops of the tubes into the upper triple clamp.

a) If you're working on an Intruder, S50, Volusia or C50, push the fork leg up until it stops against the ridge inside the upper triple clamp.

b) If you're working on a Marauder or M50, the end of each tube should be flush with the top surface of the upper triple clamp **(see illustration)**.

3.6c Loosen the damper rod bolt (arrow) in the underside of the fork leg

3.7 Remove the triple clamp bolts (arrows)

3.9 The upper fork tube should be flush with the upper triple clamp surface (arrow)

Steering, suspension and final drive 6•5

4.2a Remove the metal and rubber washers from the underside of the upper trim cover . . .

4.2b . . . and slide the lower washers off of the fork leg

10 The remainder of installation is the reverse of the removal steps, with the following additions:
   a) Be sure to tighten the triple clamp bolts to the torque listed in this Chapter's Specifications.
   b) Tighten the caliper mounting bolts to the torque listed in the Chapter 7 Specifications.
   c) If you're working on a Marauder, tighten the fender brace mounting bolts finger-tight. Pump the forks up and down several times, then tighten the bolts securely.

11 Pump the front brake lever several times to bring the pads into contact with the disc.

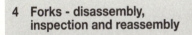

4 Forks - disassembly, inspection and reassembly

Intruder, S50, Volusia and C50
Disassembly

1 Remove the forks following the procedure in Section 3. Work on one fork leg at a time to avoid mixing up the parts.
2 If you're working on a Volusia or C50, remove the cover from the inner fork tube. Slide the rubber washer, metal washer and cover stopper ring off the inner fork tube **(see illustrations)**. Remove the cover guide ring from the top of the outer fork tube **(see illustration)**.

 Warning: On models without a spring stopper nut inside the fork tube, be careful of spring pressure as you remove the cap bolt. The spring is under considerable compression and will come out forcefully.

3 On all models, remove the fork cap bolt (if you haven't already done so).
4 On Volusia models so equipped,

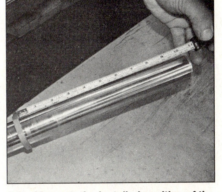

4.2c Measure the installed position of the clamp before removing it

4.2d Remove the ring from the groove in the lower fork leg

unscrew the spring stopper nut with a 14 mm hex bit.
5 On all models, remove the fork spring **(see illustration)**.
6 Invert the fork assembly over a con-

4.5 Pull the spring out of the fork

tainer and allow the oil to drain out.
7 Prevent the damper rod from turning using a holding handle (part no. 09950-34520) and adapter (09940-34561) or equivalents **(see illustration)**. Unscrew the Allen bolt at

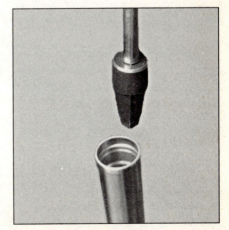

4.7a This is the Suzuki tool that keeps the damper rod from turning

6•6 Steering, suspension and final drive

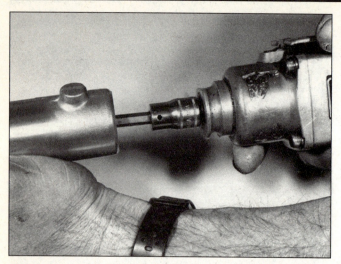

4.7b Loosen the Allen bolt - if you don't have an air wrench, refer to the tool suggestions in the text

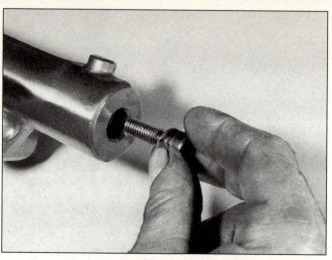

4.7c Remove the damper rod bolt and washer - use a new washer on assembly

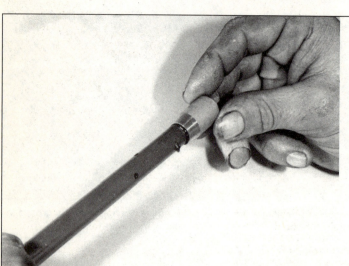

4.8 Take the oil lock piece off the end of the damper rod . . .

the bottom of the outer tube and retrieve the copper washer **(see illustrations)**.
8 Take the oil lock piece off the damper rod **(see illustration)**.
9 Pull out the damper rod and its spring **(see illustration)**. Don't remove the Teflon ring from the damper rod unless you plan to replace it.
10 Pry the dust seal from the outer tube **(see illustration)**.
11 Pry the retaining ring from its groove in the outer tube **(see illustration)**.
12 Hold the outer tube and yank the inner tube upward repeatedly (like a slide hammer), until the seal, washer and outer tube guide bushing pop loose.
13 Slide the seal, washer and outer tube guide bushing from the inner tube **(see illustration)**.

Inspection

14 Clean all parts in solvent and blow

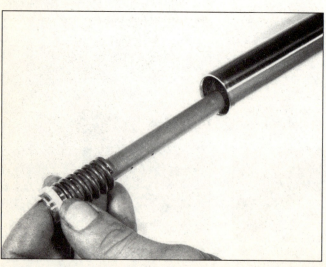

4.9 . . . and remove the damper rod from the inner fork tube

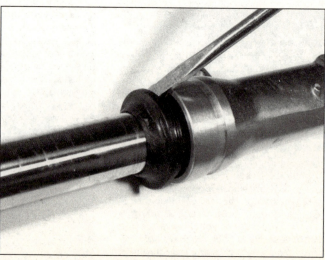

4.10 Pry the dust seal out of the outer fork tube

Steering, suspension and final drive 6•7

4.11 Pry the retaining ring out of its groove and slide it off the inner fork tube

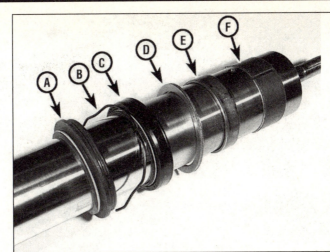

4.13 Seal and bushing details

- A Dust seal
- B Backup ring
- C Oil seal
- D Backup ring
- E Outer tube bushing
- F Inner tube bushing

4.18 Place the damper rod in the inner fork tube so it protrudes from the bottom . . .

4.20 . . . then place the oil lock piece on the end of the damper rod and install the assembly in the outer fork tube

them dry with compressed air, if available. Check the inner and outer fork tubes, the guide bushings and the damper rod for score marks, scratches, flaking of the chrome and excessive or abnormal wear. Look for dents in the tubes and replace them if any are found. Check the fork seal seat for nicks, gouges and scratches. If damage is evident, leaks will occur around the seal-to-outer tube junction. Replace worn or defective parts with new ones.

15 Have the fork inner tube checked for runout at a dealer service department or other repair shop.

 Warning: *If it is bent, it should not be straightened; replace it with a new one.*

16 Measure the overall length of the long spring and check it for cracks and other damage. Compare the length to the minimum length listed in this Chapter's Specifications. If it's defective or sagged, replace both fork springs with new ones. Never replace only one spring.

Reassembly

17 If it's necessary to replace the inner guide bushing (the one that won't come off that's on the bottom of the inner tube), pry it apart at the slit and slide it off. Make sure the new one seats properly.

18 Place the rebound spring over the damper rod and slide the rod assembly into the inner fork tube until it protrudes from the lower end of the tube **(see illustration)**.

19 If you haven't already done so, install the oil lock piece onto the end of the damper rod **(see illustration 4.10)**.

20 Insert the inner tube/damper rod assembly into the outer tube **(see illustration)** until the Allen-head bolt (with copper washer) can be threaded into the damper rod from the lower end of the outer tube **(see illustration 4.7c)**. **Note:** *Apply a non-permanent thread locking compound to the threads of the bolt. Keep the two tubes fairly horizontal so the damper rod base doesn't fall off. Using the tool described in Step 4, hold the damper rod and tighten the Allen bolt to the torque listed in this Chapter's Specifications.*

21 Slide the outer guide bushing down the inner tube. Using a special bushing driver or equivalent and a used guide bushing placed on top of the guide bushing being installed, drive the bushing into place until it is fully seated. If you don't have access to one of these tools, it is highly recommended that you take the assembly to a Suzuki dealer service department or other motorcycle repair shop to have this done. It is possible, however, to drive the bushing into place using a section of tubing and an old guide bushing.

Wrap tape around the ends of the tubing to prevent it from scratching the fork tube **(see illustration)**.

22 Slide the washer down the inner tube,

4.21 If you don't have a seal driver, use a section of pipe to tap the seal in - be sure to tape the ends of the pipe so it doesn't scratch the fork tube

6•8 Steering, suspension and final drive

4.24 Make sure the retaining ring seats in its groove

4.25 Push the dust seal down until it seats in the outer fork tube

4.27a Pour the specified amount of oil into the fork

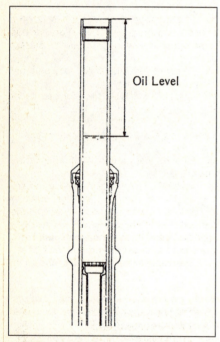

4.27b Measure the oil level in the fork with a stiff tape measure; add or drain oil to correct the level

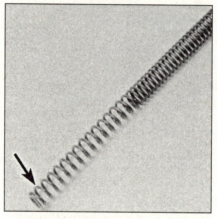

4.28 The end of the spring with widely spaced coils (arrow) goes toward the bottom

4.35 Hold the fork cap with one wrench and loosen the locknut with another

into position over the guide bushing.

23 Lubricate the lips and the outer diameter of the fork seal with the recommended fork oil (see Chapter 1) and slide it down the inner tube, with the lips facing down. Drive the seal into place with a special seal driver (Suzuki part no. 09940-50112). If you don't have access to one of these, it is recommended that you take the assembly to a Suzuki dealer service department or other motorcycle repair shop to have the seal driven in. If you are very careful, the seal can be driven in with a hammer and a drift punch. Work around the circumference of the seal, tapping gently on the outer edge of the seal until it's seated. Be careful - if you distort the seal, you'll have to disassemble the fork again and end up taking it to a dealer anyway!

24 Install the retaining ring, making sure the ring is completely seated in its groove **(see illustration)**.
25 Install the dust seal, making sure it seats completely **(see illustration)**.
26 Install the drain screw and a new gasket, if it was removed.
27 Compress the fork fully and add the recommended type and quantity of fork oil **(see illustrations)**.
28 Install the fork spring with the widely spaced coils at the bottom **(see illustration)**.
29 If you're working on a Volusia or C50, install the spring stopper nut (if equipped) and tighten it slightly. Install the fork tube cover guide ring in its groove at the top of the outer fork tube. Position the outer cover stopper on the inner fork tube, 246.6 mm (9.7 inches) from the top of the tube. Install the metal washer, rubber washer and fork tube cover.
30 Install the fork by following the procedure outlined in Section 3. If you won't be installing the fork right away, store it in an upright position to prevent leakage.
31 If the fork has a spring stopper nut, tighten it to the torque listed in this Chapter's Specifications, using a 14 mm hex bit.

32 Tighten the fork cap bolt to the torque listed in this Chapter's Specifications.

Marauder models

Disassembly

33 Remove the forks following the procedure in Section 3. Work on one fork leg at a time to avoid mixing up the parts.
34 Unscrew the cap bolt from the fork tube.
35 Hold the locknut with a wrench and unscrew the cap bolt from the fork cartridge **(see illustration)**. Unscrew the locknut and remove the rubber damper.
36 Invert the fork over a drain pan and pull the inner tube slowly outward to drain the oil. This will probably take several minutes. Pull the inner tube all the way out of the outer tube.
37 Pump the damper rod several times to drain the oil from the damper.
38 Remove the dust seal and oil seal stopper ring **(see illustrations 4.10 and 4.11)**.
39 Remove the oil seal from the outer fork tube with a slide hammer equipped with puller jaws. Remove the seal retainer if it's worn or damaged.

Steering, suspension and final drive

Inspection

40 Hold the inner fork tube and damper in an upright position and measure how far the damper protrudes from the fork tube. If it's less than 156 mm (6.1 inches), the damper and inner fork tube must be replaced as a unit (they can't be disassembled).

41 Check the outer tube for wear or damage and replace it if problems are found. This fork design does not have replaceable bushings.

Assembly

42 install the oil seal retainer (if removed). Install a new oil seal as described in Steps 22 and 23 above. Secure the oil seal with the stopper ring, making sure it's securely seated in its groove.

43 Install the dust seal, using the same tool that was used to install the oil seal.

44 Coat the surface of the inner fork tube with fork oil and install it in the outer tube.

45 Cut a piece of cardboard 177.0 mm (7 inches) long, and wide enough to wrap around the inner fork tube.

46 Hold the fork tube upright. Extend the upper (outer) tube so there's a distance of 177 mm (7 inches) and wrap the cardboard holder around the inner tube to hold the outer tube up.

47 Pour approximately 800 cc of the specified fork oil into the top of the fork, then remove the cardboard holder.

48 Install the rubber damper and locknut on the damper rod threads. Thread the locknut all the way on.

49 Install the cap bolt on the damper rod threads, then tighten the locknut against the cap bolt.

50 With the fork still upright, slowly compress and extend the fork tubes 15 times, then hold the fork tube upright for five more minutes.

51 Remove the fork cap bolt and locknut.

52 Extend the fork tubes and install the cardboard holder again.

53 Raise the outer fork tube an additional 50 mm (2 inches) above the cardboard holder. **Note:** *Don't raise it higher than this, or oil will leak out of the damper and the procedure will have to be done over.* This will pull fork oil into the damper's oil chamber. Hold it in this position until no air bubbles can be seen in the fork oil.

54 Once the fork oil is free of bubbles, slowly lower the outer tube down to the cardboard holder, taking care not to compress the cardboard.

55 Fill the outer fork tube to the top with specified fork oil.

56 Slowly lift the outer fork tube 50 mm (2 inches) above the cardboard, then slowly lower it back to the cardboard. Hold the fork tube in this position for five more minutes.

57 With the outer fork tube resting on the cardboard, measure the oil level from the top of the outer fork tube. It should be 149 mm (5.9 inches). Add more oil if necessary (or pull some out with a syringe) to get the correct level.

58 Clean the oil off the damper threads (blow it off if compressed air is available).

59 Install the rubber damper on the threads with its tapered side down.

60 Thread the locknut all the way onto the damper. Finger-tighten the cap bolt against the locknut. Tighten the locknut against the cap bolt to the torque listed in this Chapter's Specifications.

61 Install the fork leg as described in Section 3. Once it's securely installed, tighten the cap bolt to the torque listed in this Chapter's Specifications.

M50 models

Disassembly

62 Remove the forks following the procedure in Section 3. Work on one fork leg at a time to avoid mixing up the parts.

63 Unscrew the cap bolt from the fork tube.

64 Compress the fork spring and install a holder tool on the damper rod underneath the locknut. A Suzuki special tool is available for this (part no. 09940-94922), but if you don't have it, you can make a substitute by cutting a slot in the piece of steel plate. Hold the locknut with a wrench and unscrew the cap bolt from the fork cartridge. Unscrew the locknut, then remove the spring spacer and spring.

65 Invert the fork over a drain pan and pump the damper rod several times to drain the oil from the damper. Let the oil drain for several minutes.

66 If the damper rod Allen bolt wouldn't come loose during fork removal, hold the damper rod with a holding tool (Suzuki part no. 09940-30221) and unscrew the Allen bolt from the bottom of the fork leg.

67 Pull the damper rod and cartridge out of the fork tube.

68 Pull the upper and lower fork legs apart, taking care not to damage the bushings. They can't be replaced separately.

69 Remove the dust seal and oil seal stopper ring **(see illustrations 4.10 and 4.11)**.

70 Remove the oil seal from the outer fork tube with a slide hammer equipped with puller jaws. Remove the seal retainer if it's worn or damaged.

Inspection

71 Measure the free length of the fork spring. If it's less than the limit listed in this Chapter's Specifications, replace it. Always replace both springs if one must be replaced.

72 Check the inner and outer tubes for wear or damage and replace them if problems are found. This fork design does not have replaceable bushings.

73 Pump the damper rod and check it for smooth movement. If movement is rough or uneven, replace the damper rod (cartridge) with a new one.

Assembly

74 install the oil seal retainer (if removed). Install a new oil seal as described in Steps 22 and 23 above. Secure the oil seal with the stopper ring, making sure it's securely seated in its groove.

75 Install the dust seal, using the same tool that was used to install the oil seal.

76 Compress the fork all the way and hold it upright. Fill the fork to the top with the oil listed in this Chapter's Specifications.

77 Pump the damper rod slowly through its full travel until the oil is free of bubbles (at least 10 times). You'll need a Suzuki tool (part no 09940-52841) or equivalent to hold onto the end of the damper rod.

78 Repeat Steps 77 and 78 until the fluid is free of bubbles. **Note:** *Be sure not to let the oil level drop below the top of the damper cartridge, or air will be sucked in and you'll have to repeat the procedure.*

79 Measure the oil level from the top of the outer fork tube. It should be 153 mm (6.2 inches). Add more oil if necessary (or pull some out with a syringe) to get the correct level.

80 Thread the locknut all the way onto the damper if it was removed.

81 Install the fork spring and spacer.

82 Pull the damper rod all the way up. Compress the fork spring and install the holding tool beneath the damper rod locknut.

83 Finger-tighten the cap bolt against the locknut.

84 Install the fork leg as described in Section 3. With the upper triple clamp bolts slightly loose, tighten the locknut against the cap bolt to the torque listed in this Chapter's Specifications. Then tighten the upper triple clamp bolts to the torque listed in this Chapter's Specifications.

5 Steering head bearings - replacement and adjustment

1 If the steering head bearing check (see Chapter 1) indicates excessive play in the steering head bearings, adjust tem as described below. If the check indicates excessive roughness, or if adjustment doesn't help with excessive play, the entire front end must be disassembled and the bearings and races replaced with new ones.

2 Refer to Chapter 7 and remove the front wheel.

3 Remove the handlebar and front forks (see Sections 2 and 3).

4 Remove the headlight assembly and disconnect the speedometer wires or cable (see Chapter 9). If you're working on a Marauder, remove the speedometer from the bike.

5 Disconnect the brake hose and wiring harness retainers from the triple clamps.

6 If you're working on a Volusia or C50, remove the cover from the front of the lower triple clamp.

6•10 Steering, suspension and final drive

5.7a Steering stem nut (upper arrow) and adjusting nut (lower arrow)

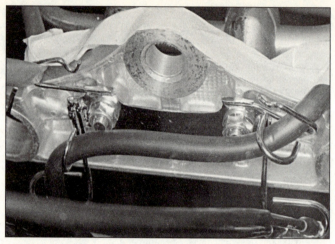

5.7b Lift off the triple clamp; note the tape used to protect it from scratches

5.12a Unscrew the adjusting nut . . .

5.12b . . . lift off the bearing cover and upper bearing (tapered roller bearing shown) . . .

5.13 . . . and lower the steering stem and lower bearing out of the head

7 Remove the steering stem head nut and washer **(see illustration)**, then lift off the upper triple clamp (sometimes called the fork bridge or crown) **(see illustration)**.

Adjustment

8 Tighten the steering stem adjusting nut to the torque listed in this Chapter's Specifications, using a special 4-point socket. These are available from aftermarket tool suppliers or Suzuki dealers.
9 Turn the lower triple clamp back and forth through its full travel 5 or 6 times to seat the bearings, then loosen the adjusting nut 1/4-turn.
10 Tighten the adjusting nut, using the special socket and your fingers (not a ratchet or breaker bar) just enough to eliminate any play in the bearings.
11 Recheck play as described in Chapter 1. If it's now acceptable, reverse Steps 2 through 7 above to reinstall the removed components. If it's still loose or rough, continue with bearing removal as described below.

Removal

12 Remove the stem adjusting nut while supporting the steering head from the bottom **(see illustration)**. Lift off the race cover and upper bearing **(see illustration)**. **Note:** *The illustrations show tapered roller bearings. Service procedures are the same for the caged ball bearings used on some models.*
13 Remove the steering stem and lower triple clamp assembly together with the lower bearing **(see illustration)**. If it's stuck, gently tap on the top of the steering stem with a plastic mallet or a hammer and a wood block.
14 Clean all the parts with solvent and dry them thoroughly, using compressed air, if available. If you do use compressed air, don't let the bearings spin as they're dried - it could ruin them. Wipe the old grease out of the frame steering head and bearing races.
15 Examine the races in the steering head for cracks, dents, and pits. If even the slightest amount of wear or damage is evident, the races should be replaced with new ones.
16 To remove the races, drive them out of the steering head with Suzuki tool no. 90041-54911 or equivalent **(see illustration)**. A slide hammer with the proper internal-jaw puller will also work. Since the races are an inter-

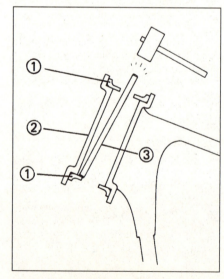

5.16a Drive out the bearing races with a hammer and drift

1 Outer races
2 Steering head
3 Drift

Steering, suspension and final drive 6•11

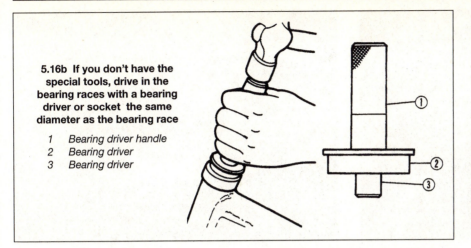

5.16b If you don't have the special tools, drive in the bearing races with a bearing driver or socket the same diameter as the bearing race

1 Bearing driver handle
2 Bearing driver
3 Bearing driver

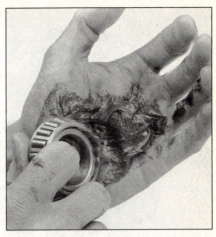

5.22 Work the grease completely into the rollers

ference fit in the frame, installation will be easier if the new races are left overnight in a refrigerator. This will cause them to contract and slip into place in the frame with very little effort. When installing the races, use Suzuki puller tool 09941-74910 or equivalent, or tap them gently into place with a hammer and bearing driver or a large socket **(see illustration)**. Do not strike the bearing surface or the race will be damaged.

Inspection

17 Check the bearings for wear. Look for cracks, dents, and pits in the races and flat spots on the bearings. Replace any defective parts with new ones. If a new bearing is required, replace both of them as a set.
18 To remove the lower bearing from the steering stem, use a hammer and chisel, taking care not to damage the steering stem. Don't remove this bearing unless it, or the grease seal underneath, must be replaced.
19 Check the grease seal under the lower bearing and replace it with a new one if necessary.
20 Inspect the steering stem/lower triple clamp for cracks and other damage. Do not attempt to repair any steering components. Replace them with new parts if defects are found.
21 Check the bearing cover - if it's worn or deteriorated, replace it.

Installation

22 Pack the bearings with high-quality grease (preferably a moly-based grease) **(see illustration)**. Coat the outer races with grease also.
23 Install the grease seal and lower bearing onto the steering stem. Drive the lower bearing onto the steering stem using Suzuki stem bearing driver no. 09941-74910 **(see illustration)**. If you don't have access to this tool, a section of pipe with a diameter the same as the inner race of the bearing can be used. Drive the bearing on until it is fully seated.
24 Insert the steering stem/lower triple clamp into the frame head. Install the upper bearing and the race cover **(see illustration 5.12b)**.

25 Install the adjusting nut with its shoulder down (against the bearing). If you're using an adjustable spanner, tighten the nut while moving the lower triple clamp back and forth. Continue to tighten the nut to the torque listed in this Chapter's Specifications. Once the nut is tightened to the initial torque, make sure there is no more play (don't overtighten, though, or the steering will be too tight and the bearings may be damaged). Make sure the steering head turns smoothly.
26 Turn the steering stem from full left to full right lock 5 or 6 times to seat the bearings, then loosen it 1/4 turn.
27 Tighten the nut by hand, just enough to eliminate play in the bearing.
28 Install the fork tubes and the upper triple clamp. The tops of the fork tubes should be even with the upper triple clamp. Tighten the lower triple clamp bolts to the torque listed in this Chapter's Specifications.
29 Install the steering head nut and tighten it securely, but not completely, yet. Tighten the upper triple clamp bolts to the torque listed in this Chapter's Specifications.
30 Tighten the steering head nut to the torque listed in this Chapter's Specifications.
31 The remainder of installation is the reverse of the removal steps.

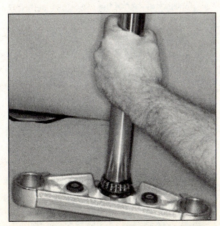

5.23 Drive the grease seal and lower bearing on with a hollow driver (or an equivalent piece of pipe) and a hammer

32 Check the alignment of the handlebars and the front wheel. If necessary, loosen the triple clamp bolts, have an assistant hold the front wheel, then turn the handlebars to align them with the front wheel. Tighten the triple clamp bolts to the torque listed in this Chapter's Specifications.

6 Rear shock absorbers - removal and installation

Intruder, S50 and Marauder

Removal

1 Set the bike on its centerstand (if equipped). If the bike doesn't have a centerstand, support it in an upright position so it can't be knocked over during this procedure.
2 Remove the shock absorber upper and lower nuts (Intruder and S50) or upper bolt and lower nut (Marauder) and lift the shock off the motorcycle **(see illustration)**.

6.2 Rear shock absorber fasteners (arrows) (S50 right shock shown)

6•12 Steering, suspension and final drive

6.5a Here's the upper shock bolt on the M50 (Volusia and C50 similar)

6.5b Lower shock absorber and linkage bolts (arrows) (single-shock models)

Installation

3 Installation is the reverse of the removal procedure. Tighten the shock absorber fasteners to the torque values listed in this Chapter's Specifications.

Volusia, C50 and M50

4 Remove the seat, fuel tank and battery case (see Chapters 8, 4 and 9).
5 Support the motorcycle and remove the shock absorber mounting bolts (see illustrations).
6 Installation is the reverse of the removal steps. Be sure the bolt heads are facing in the proper directions. Tighten the bolts to the torque listed in this Chapter's Specifications.

7 Rear suspension linkage (single-shock models) - removal, inspection and installation

Removal

1 Support the bike securely upright.
2 Remove the seat, battery and battery tray (see Chapters 8 and 9).
3 Remove the linkage mounting bolts and nuts and take the linkage out (see illustration 6.5b).

Inspection

4 Remove the spacers and needle bearings from the rocker arm. Check the bearings for wear or damage. If the bearings are good, pack them with molybdenum disulfide grease and reinstall them (see illustration).

Installation

5 Installation is the reverse of the removal steps. Tighten the nuts and bolts to the torque listed in this Chapter's Specifications.

8 Swingarm bearings - check

1 Refer to Chapter 7 and remove the rear wheel. If you're working on a twin-shock model, refer to Section 6 and remove the rear shock absorbers.
2 Grasp the rear of the swingarm with one hand and place your other hand at the junction of the swingarm and the frame. Try to move the rear of the swingarm from side-to-side. Any wear (play) in the bearings should be felt as movement between the swingarm and the frame at the front. The swingarm will actually be felt to move forward and backward at the front (not from side-to-side). If any play is noted, the bearings should be replaced with new ones (see Section 10).
3 Next, move the swingarm up and down through its full travel. It should move freely, without any binding or rough spots. If it does not move freely, refer to Section 10 for servicing procedures.

9 Swingarm - removal and installation

Intruder and S50 models

Removal

1 Raise the bike and support it securely so it can't be knocked over during this procedure.

7.4 Remove the collars for access to the bearings

9.5a Loosen the clamp . . .

Steering, suspension and final drive 6•13

9.5b ... and remove the universal joint cover

9.6 The longer end of the universal joint goes toward the engine (driveshaft removed for clarity)

2 Remove the shock absorbers (see Section 6).
3 Remove the rear wheel (see Chapter 7).
4 Remove the final drive unit and driveshaft (see Section 11).
5 Loosen the clamp on the universal joint cover boot and remove the cover **(see illustrations)**.
6 Remove the swingarm cover and take the universal joint out through the opening **(see illustration)**.
7 Pry the cap off the swingarm pivot **(see illustration)**. Support the swingarm. Unscrew the pivot shaft nut, then pull the pivot shaft out through the swingarm cover opening.
8 Remove the swingarm to the rear of the vehicle.
9 Check the pivot bearings in the swingarm for dryness or deterioration. If they're in need of lubrication or replacement, refer to Section 10.

Installation

10 Support the swingarm so its pivot holes are aligned with the holes in the frame. Install the pivot shaft and tighten its nut to the torque listed in this Chapter's Specifications.

11 Raise and lower the swingarm to make sure it moves freely without binding or interference. Check swingarm bearing play as described in Section 8.
12 The remainder of installation is the reverse of the removal steps. Lubricate the bearings and universal joint with Suzuki super grease "A" or equivalent.

Volusia, C50 and M50 models
Removal
13 If you're working on an M50, remove the fuel tank (see Chapter 3).
14 Remove the rear wheel (see Chapter 7).
15 Remove the final drive unit and driveshaft (see Section 11).
16 Remove the secondary gear cover and rear clutch cover (see Chapter 2).
17 Remove the battery case (see Chapter 9).
18 Remove the toolbox and lower right frame cover (see Chapter 8).
19 If you're working on an M50, remove the fuse and relay box and its support bracket (see Chapter 9).
20 Unbolt the suspension linkage and the upper end of the shock absorber **(see illus-**

9.7 Pry off the trim cover (arrow) for access to the swingarm pivot bolt

trations 6.5a and 65b).
21 Hold the right swingarm pivot bolt with an Allen wrench and unscrew the locknut **(see illustrations)**.

9.21a Unscrew the locknut (left arrow) from the pivot bolt (right arrow) ...

9.21b ... with a socket, then remove the pivot bolt ...

6•14 Steering, suspension and final drive

22 Support the swingarm and remove the pivot bolt **(see illustration)**. Lower the swingarm and take it out, together with the rear suspension.
23 Remove rear suspension components from the swingarm as necessary (see Section 7).

Installation
24 If you removed the universal joint, its rubber boot or any suspension components from the swingarm, install them (see Sections 7 and 11).
25 Make sure the swingarm bearings are lubricated and in position.
26 Raise the swingarm into position and install its pivot bolts. Thread the bolts in, but don't tighten them yet.
27 Tighten the left pivot bolt to the torque listed in this Chapter's Specifications.
28 Tighten the right pivot bolt to the torque listed in this Chapter's Specifications, then tighten the locknut to the torque listed in this Chapter's Specifications.
29 Raise and lower the swingarm to make sure it moves smoothly and without binding. If it doesn't, find out why before proceeding further.
30 The remainder of installation is the reverse of the removal steps.

Marauder models
Removal
31 Remove the rear wheel (see Chapter 7).
32 Remove the swingarm pivot covers.
33 Remove the nuts that secure the bottom ends of the shock absorbers and the rear brake torque link to the swingarm.
34 Hold the swingarm pivot shaft and unscrew the pivot shaft nut.
35 Support the swingarm and remove the pivot shaft. Separate the swingarm from the motorcycle.
36 Refer to Section 10 and inspect the swingarm bearings (they remain in the frame when the swingarm is removed).

Installation
37 Installation is the reverse of the removal steps. Tighten the swingarm pivot shaft nut to the torque listed in this Chapter's Specifications.

10 Swingarm bearings - replacement

Intruder and Marauder models
1 Bearing replacement isn't complicated, but it requires a blind hole (expanding) puller and a slide hammer, as well as a shouldered drift to tap the bearings in without damaging them. The puller and slide hammer can be rented if you don't have them, but compare the cost of having the bearings replaced by a dealer service department or other qualified shop to that of renting the equipment before you proceed.
2 Remove the swingarm (see Section 9).
3 Pry the dust covers off the swingarm pivot point in the frame. Remove the washer and bearing spacer from each side.
4 Remove the bearings with a blind hole (expanding) puller and slide hammer. Remove the center spacer.
5 Drive new inner races into the swingarm with a shouldered drift. The drift should just fit inside the bearing and its shoulder should be the same diameter as the bearing outer race.
6 Pack the bearing with molybdenum disulfide grease.

C50 and M50 models
7 Take the bearings out of the swingarm.
8 If the bearing races need to be replaced, pass a drift through the opposite side of the swingarm and tap evenly around the race to drive it out.
9 Drive in new races with a socket or bearing driver the same diameter as the race.
10 Pack the bearing with molybdenum disulfide grease.
11 Refer to Section 9 and install the swingarm.

11 Final drive unit and driveshaft (shaft drive models) - removal, inspection and installation

Removal
1 Raise the bike and set it on its centerstand (if equipped). If the bike doesn't have a centerstand, support it securely so it can't be knocked over during this procedure.
2 Remove the final drive unit nuts and pull it off the swingarm, together with the driveshaft.
3 Remove the mounting plate.
4 Pry the oil seal off, taking care not to damage its mounting surface.
5 Remove the driveshaft snap-ring. Pull the driveshaft out of the final drive unit and remove the spring.

9.22 . . . then remove the left pivot bolt (arrow)

Inspection
6 Check for signs of oil leakage around the pinion and drive coupling. Turn the pinion by hand and check for rough or noisy movement. Remove the filler plug and look into the hole, using a flashlight if necessary, for obvious signs of damage such as broken gear teeth.
7 Final drive unit overhaul is a complicated procedure that requires several special tools, for which there are no readily available substitutes. If there's visible wear or damage, or if rotation is rough or noisy, take it to a Suzuki dealer for disassembly and further inspection.
8 Check the driveshaft for bending or other visible damage such as step wear of the splines. If the shaft is bent, replace it. If the splines at either end of the shaft are worn, replace the shaft.
9 Hold the universal joint firmly in one hand and try to twist it. If there's play in the joint, replace the universal joint as an assembly (but don't confuse play in the joint with its normal motion).

Installation
10 Installation is the reverse of the removal steps, with the following additions:
 a) Don't forget to reinstall the spring between the differential pinion and the rear end of the driveshaft.
 b) Wipe all the old grease off the final drive pinion and put a coating of high-temperature grease on the splines.
 c) Align the tab on the retaining plate with one of the notches in the bearing retainer.
 d) If the universal joint pulled off of the front pinion when the final drive unit was removed, pull back the rubber cover at the front end of the driveshaft **(see illustrations 9.5a and 9.5b)**. Place the universal joint on the driveshaft **(see illustration 9.6)**, then align the universal joint with the front pinion and push the final drive unit into its installed position.
 e) Tighten the mounting nuts to the torque listed in this Chapter's Specifications.
 f) Fill the final drive unit with oil (see Chapter 1).

Steering, suspension and final drive 6•15

12.3 Remove the secondary gearcase cover (arrow)

12.4a Unscrew the Allen bolts (arrows) . . .

12 Front bevel gears (shaft drive models) - removal, inspection and installation

Driven gear

Removal

1 Raise the bike and support it securely so it can't be knocked over during this procedure.
2 Remove the final drive unit, driveshaft and swingarm (see Sections 9 and 11).
3 Remove the secondary gearcase cover **(see illustration)**.
4 Unbolt the secondary driven gear housing and the secondary gearcase **(see illustrations)**.
5 Take the secondary gearcase off the engine and remove the driven gear unit **(see illustrations)**.

12.4b . . . and the hex bolts (arrows) . . .

12.4c . . . noting that one of them has a copper washer (arrow)

12.5a Remove the secondary gearcase and locate the dowels and oil jet (arrows) . . .

6•16 Steering, suspension and final drive

Inspection

6 Rotate the splined shaft in the driven gear housing with fingers and check for rough or noisy movement. Check for signs of oil leakage around the shaft. Visual inspection of the internal components isn't possible without disassembling the unit.

7 Driven gear housing overhaul is a complicated procedure that requires several special tools, for which there are no readily available substitutes. If there's visible wear or damage, or if differential rotation is rough or noisy, take it to a Suzuki dealer for disassembly and further inspection.

Installation

8 Installation is the reverse of the removal steps, with the following additions:
   a) Use a new copper washer on the secondary gearcase bolt (see illustration 12.4c).
   b) Make sure both dowel pins are in place and use a new O-ring when installing the secondary driven gear and gearcase.
   c) Check the engine oil level and add some if necessary (see Chapter 1).

Drive gear

9 Inspection of the secondary drive gear requires removal of the engine and disassembly of the crankcase (see Chapter 2).

13 Drive chain - removal, cleaning, inspection and installation

Note: *Suzuki recommends replacing the chain and sprockets as a set.*

Removal

1 Remove the chain guard.
2 If you plan to remove the engine sprocket, bend back the tab on the engine sprocket lockwasher (see illustration 14.6a). While an assistant holds the rear brake on, loosen the engine sprocket nut.
3 Remove the rear wheel (see Chapter 7).

12.5b . . . and remove the secondary driven gear with its shims and O-rings (right arrows); note the location of the bearing dowel (left arrow)

4 Remove the swingarm (see Section 9).
5 Lift the chain off the engine sprocket and remove it from the bike.
6 Unscrew the engine sprocket nut and take the sprocket off.
7 Check the chain guard on the swingarm for wear or damage and replace it as necessary.

Cleaning and inspection

8 Soak the chain in a high flash point solvent for approximately five or six minutes. Use a brush to work the solvent into the spaces between the links and plates.
9 Wipe the chain dry, then check it carefully for worn or damaged links. Replace the chain if wear or damage is found at any point.
10 Stretch the chain taut and measure its length between the number of pins listed in this Chapter's Specifications. Compare the measured length to the specified value replace the chain if it's beyond the limit. If the chain needs to be replaced, refer to Section 14 and check the sprockets. If they're worn, replace them also. If a new chain is installed on worn sprockets, it will wear out quickly.
11 Lubricate the chain with spray chain lube compatible with O-ring chains.

Installation

12 Installation is the reverse of the removal steps. Refer to Chapter 1 and adjust the chain.

14 Sprockets - check and replacement

1 Support the bike securely so it can't be knocked over during this procedure.
2 Whenever the sprockets are inspected, the chain should be inspected also and replaced if it's worn. Installing a worn chain on new sprockets will cause them to wear quickly.
3 Remove the engine sprocket cover. Check the teeth on the engine sprocket and rear sprocket for wear (see illustration).
4 If the sprockets are worn, remove the rear wheel (see Chapter 7) and the chain (see Section 13).
5 Remove the collar from the center of the hub on the sprocket side. Remove the bolts or nuts and detach the sprocket from the rear wheel hub.
6 Bend back the lockwasher, then unscrew the nut from the transmission shaft

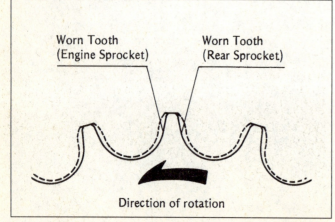

14.3 Check the sprockets in the areas indicated to see if they're worn excessively

14.6a Bend back the lockwasher . . .

Steering, suspension and final drive 6•17

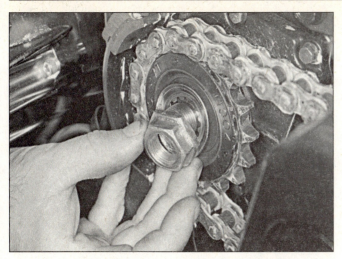

14.6b ... unscrew the nut and remove the lockwasher ...

14.6c ... then pull the sprocket off and disengage it from the chain

and remove the lockwasher. Pull the sprocket off the transmission shaft, together with the chain **(see illustrations)**.

7 Inspect the seal behind the engine sprocket. If it has been leaking, remove the seal cover. Pry the seal out (taking care not to scratch the seal bore) and tap in a new seal with a socket the same diameter as the seal. Reinstall the cover, using a new gasket.

8 Installation is the reverse of the removal steps, with the following additions:

a) *Use a new lockwasher on the engine sprocket nut. Tighten the sprocket nuts to the torques listed in this Chapter's Specifications.*
b) *Refer to Chapter 1 and adjust the chain.*
c) *If you removed the seal cover, check the engine oil level and add some if necessary (see Chapter 1).*

15 Rear wheel coupling/ rubber damper - check and replacement

Shaft drive models

1 Remove the rear wheel (see Chapter 7).
2 Bend back the lockwasher tabs, unscrew the nuts and lift the rear wheel coupling from the wheel.
3 Check the rubber dampers in the wheel for cracks, hardening and general deterioration. Replace them if necessary. Pry out the old dampers with a screwdriver and drive new ones in.
4 Installation is the reverse of the removal procedure.

Chain drive models

5 Remove the rear wheel and sprocket (see Chapter 7 and Section 14).
6 Remove the spacer from the center of the dust seal. Pry the seal out of the hub.
7 Turn the hub over and take the rubber dampers out of their pockets. If they're worn or deteriorated, replace them with new ones.
8 Checking and replacement procedures for the coupling bearing are similar to those described for the wheel bearings. Refer to Chapter 7.
9 Installation is the reverse of the removal steps.

Notes

Chapter 7
Brakes, wheels and tires

Contents

Brake caliper - removal, overhaul and installation	3
Brake disc - inspection, removal and installation	4
Brake hoses and lines - inspection and replacement	7
Brake light switches - check and replacement	See Chapter 9
Brake pads - replacement	2
Brake pads and linings - wear check	See Chapter 1
Brake pedal and linkage - removal and installation	9
Brake pedal position and play - check and adjustment	See Chapter 1
Brake system - general check	See Chapter 1
Brake system bleeding	8
Front wheel - removal, inspection and installation	11
General information	1
Master cylinder - removal, overhaul and installation	5
Rear drum brake - removal, inspection and installation	6
Rear wheel - removal, inspection and installation	12
Tires/wheels - general check	See Chapter 1
Tube tires - removal and installation	15
Tubeless tires - general information	14
Tubes - repair	16
Wheel bearings - inspection and maintenance	13
Wheels - inspection, repair and alignment check	10

Degrees of difficulty

Easy, suitable for novice with little experience	**Fairly easy,** suitable for beginner with some experience	**Fairly difficult,** suitable for competent DIY mechanic	**Difficult,** suitable for experienced DIY mechanic	**Very difficult,** suitable for expert DIY or professional

Specifications

Brakes

Brake fluid type	See Chapter 1
Brake pad minimum thickness	See Chapter 1
Front disc thickness	
Intruder, S50, Volusia, C50	
Standard	5.0 +/- 0.2 mm (0.197 +/- 0.008 inch)
Minimum*	4.5 mm (0.18 inch)
Marauder, M50	
Standard	4.5 +/- 0.2mm (0.18 +/- 0.01 inch)
Minimum*	4.0 mm (0.16 inch)

* Refer to marks stamped into the disc (they supersede information printed here)

Disc runout (maximum)	0.3 mm (0.012 inch)
Brake pedal position and freeplay	See Chapter 1
Rear brake lining thickness limit	
Intruder, S50, Marauder	1.5 mm (1/16 inch)
Volusia, C50, M50	Refer to wear indicator (Chapter 1)
Brake drum diameter limit	180.7 mm (7.11 inch)

Wheels and tires

Wheel runout limit	
Axial (side-to-side)	2.0 mm (0.08 inch)
Radial (out-of-round)	2.0 mm (0.08 inch)
Axle runout limit (front and rear)	0.25 mm (0.10 inch)
Tire pressures	See Chapter 1

Torque specifications

Intruder and S50
Caliper mounting bolts	25 to 40 Nm (18 to 29 ft-lbs)
Caliper assembly bolts	15 to 20 Nm (11.0 to 14.5 ft-lbs)
Union bolts	Not specified
Brake disc-to-wheel bolts	15 to 25 Nm (11 to 18 ft-lbs)
Master cylinder mounting bolts	Not specified
Front brake lever pivot pin locknut	Not specified
Caliper bleed valve	6 to 9 Nm (54 to 78 inch-lbs)
Brake pedal pinch bolt	Not specified
Rear brake cam lever bolt	5 to 8 Nm (44 to 72 inch-lbs)
Brake torque link nuts	20 to 30 Nm (14.5 to 21.5 ft-lbs)
Front axle nut	36 to 52 Nm (26.0 to 37.5 ft-lbs)
Front axle pinch bolt	15 to 25 Nm (11 to 18 ft-lbs)
Rear axle nut	50 to 80 Nm (36 to 58 ft-lbs)

Volusia and C50
Caliper mounting bolts	39 Nm (28 ft-lbs)
Union bolts	23 Nm (16.5 ft-lbs)
Brake disc-to-wheel bolts	23 Nm (16.5 ft-lbs)
Master cylinder mounting bolts	10 Nm (84 inch-lbs)
Caliper bleed valve	7.5 Nm (66 inch-lbs)
Brake pedal bolt	11 Nm (96 inch-lbs)
Rear brake cam lever bolt	5 to 8 Nm (44 to 72 inch-lbs)
Brake torque link nuts	
Front	35 Nm (25.5 ft-lbs)
Rear	25 Nm (18 ft-lbs)
Front axle nut	65 Nm (47 ft-lbs)
Front axle pinch bolt	33 Nm (24 ft-lbs)
Rear axle nut	65 Nm (47 ft-lbs)

Marauder
Caliper mounting bolts	39 Nm (28 ft-lbs)
Union bolts	23 Nm (16.5 ft-lbs)
Brake disc-to-wheel bolts	23 Nm (16.5 ft-lbs)
Master cylinder mounting bolts	10 Nm 984 inch-lbs)
Caliper bleed valve	7.5 Nm (66 inch-lbs)
Brake pedal bolt	Not specified
Rear brake cam lever bolt	10 Nm (84 inch-lbs)
Brake torque link nuts	
Front	35 Nm (25.5 ft-lbs)
Rear	25 Nm (18 ft-lbs)
Front axle nut	65 Nm (47 ft-lbs)
Front axle pinch bolt	23 Nm (16.5 ft-lbs)
Rear axle nut	65 Nm (47 ft-lbs)

M50
Caliper mounting bolts	39 Nm (28 ft-lbs)
Union bolts	23 Nm (16.5 ft-lbs)
Brake disc-to-wheel bolts	23 Nm (16.5 ft-lbs)
Master cylinder mounting bolts	10 Nm (84 inch-lbs)
Caliper bleed valve	7.5 Nm (66 inch-lbs)
Brake pedal bolt	11 Nm (96 inch-lbs)
Rear brake cam lever bolt	10 Nm (84 inch-lbs)
Brake torque link nuts	
Front	35 Nm (25.5 ft-lbs)
Rear	25 Nm (18 ft-lbs)
Front axle nut	65 Nm (47 ft-lbs)
Front axle pinch bolt	23 Nm (16.5 ft-lbs)
Rear axle nut	65 Nm (47 ft-lbs)

Brakes, wheels and tires

2.2 Pad cover screws (right arrows) and bleed valve (left arrow) on an opposed-piston caliper

2.3a Remove the pad cover and pull out the retaining pin clips (arrows) . . .

2.3b . . . slide the pins partway out . . .

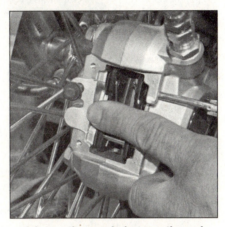

2.3c . . . then push down on the pad spring and pull the pins the rest of the way out

2.4a Pull out the pads and shims . . .

1 General information

The motorcycles covered by this manual are equipped with hydraulic disc brakes on the front wheel. All models use a single caliper, equipped with either one or two pistons. All models use a mechanical drum brake on the rear wheel.

Either wire or cast aluminum wheels are used, depending on model.

Caution: Disc brake components rarely require disassembly. Do not disassemble components unless absolutely necessary. If any hydraulic brake line connection in the system is loosened, the entire system should be disassembled, drained, cleaned and then properly filled and bled upon reassembly. Do not use solvents on internal brake components. Solvents will cause seals to swell and distort. Use only clean brake fluid or alcohol for cleaning. Use care when working with brake fluid as it can injure your eyes and it will damage painted surfaces and plastic parts.

2 Brake pads - replacement

Warning: The dust created by the brake system is harmful to your health. Never blow it out with compressed air and don't inhale any of it. An approved filtering mask should be worn when working on the brakes.

1 Support the bike securely upright so it can't fall over.

Opposed-piston calipers

2 Remove the dust cover from the back of the caliper **(see illustration)**.
3 Remove the retaining clips from the pad pins **(see illustration)**. Push the springs away from the retaining pins, then pull the retaining pins out **(see illustrations)**.
4 Pull the brake pads and shims out of the caliper **(see illustrations)**.
5 Check the condition of the brake disc (see Section 4). If it is in need of machining or replacement, follow the procedure in that

2.4b . . . and separate them

Section to remove it. If it is okay, deglaze it with sandpaper or emery cloth, using a swirling motion.

6 Remove the cap from the master cylinder reservoir and siphon out some fluid. Push the piston into the caliper as far as possible, while checking the master cylinder reservoir to make sure it doesn't overflow. If you can't depress the piston with thumb pressure, try

7•4 Brakes, wheels and tires

2.11a Caliper mounting details (opposed piston calipers)

- A Mounting bolts
- B Bleed valve
- C Brake hose banjo fitting

2.11b Cut the tie-wrap that holds the cable to the brake line . . .

2.11c . . . slip the cable out of its groove in the fork leg . . .

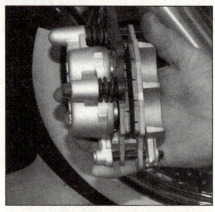

2.11d . . . take the caliper off for access to the pads

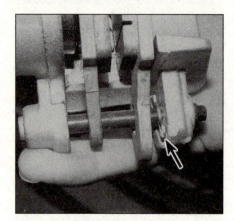

2.13a Pull off the pad pin clip (arrow) . . .

using a C-clamp. If the piston sticks, remove the caliper and overhaul it as described in Section 3.

7 Reverse Steps 1 through 3 to install the shims, pads, spring and retaining pins. Be sure the retaining pins are securely held by the clips.

8 Refill the master cylinder reservoir (see Chapter 1) and install the diaphragm and cap.

9 Operate the brake lever several times to bring the pads into contact with the disc. Check the operation of the brakes carefully before riding the motorcycle.

Pin slider calipers

10 Remove the reflector (US and Canada) or cable guide hook (all others) from the right front fork leg.

11 Remove the caliper mounting bolts **(see illustration)**. Cut the tie-wrap that secures the speed sensor cable to the brake line **(see illustrations)**. Slide the caliper and pads off the disc **(see illustration)**.

12 Support the caliper with rope or wire so it doesn't hang by the brake hose. It's a good idea to wrap the caliper with rags and tape to protect the caliper and wheel from scratches.

13 Remove the clip and pad pin **(see illustrations)**. Lift the inner and outer pads out of the caliper, noting their different shapes **(see illustrations)**.

2.13b . . . pull out the retaining pin . . .

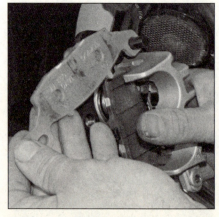

2.13c . . . swivel the pad up and slip it off the bracket post . . .

2.13d . . . and remove the remaining pad from the clip on the bracket (arrow)

Brakes, wheels and tires 7•5

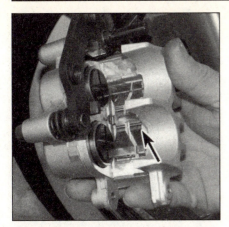

2.14 Remove the pad spring (arrow) if it's corroded or damaged

14 Remove the anti-rattle spring **(see illustration)**. If it appears damaged, replace it.
15 Check the pad support clip on the caliper bracket **(see illustration 2.13d)**. If it's missing or distorted, replace it.
16 Check the condition of the brake disc (see Section 4). If it is in need of machining or replacement, follow the procedure in that Section to remove it. If it is okay, deglaze it with sandpaper or emery cloth, using a swirling motion.
17 Remove the cap from the master cylinder reservoir and siphon out some fluid. Push the piston into the caliper as far as possible, while checking the master cylinder reservoir to make sure it doesn't overflow. If you can't depress the piston with thumb pressure, try using a C-clamp. If the piston sticks, remove the caliper and overhaul it as described in Section 3.
18 Install the anti-rattle spring in the caliper.
19 Install the inner and outer pads in the caliper, making sure to install them in the correct locations.
20 Install the caliper, tightening the mounting bolts to the torque listed in this Chapter's Specifications.
21 Refill the master cylinder reservoir (see Chapter 1) and install the diaphragm and cap.
22 Operate the brake lever several times to bring the pads into contact with the disc. Check the operation of the brakes carefully before riding the motorcycle.

3 Brake caliper - removal, overhaul and installation

⚠ **Warning:** *If a caliper indicates the need for an overhaul (usually due to leaking fluid or sticky operation), all old brake fluid should be flushed from the system. Also, the dust created by the brake system is harmful to your health. Never blow it out with compressed air*

3.3 Caliper mounting details (opposed piston caliper)

A Mounting bolts
B Brake hose fitting
C Brake hose retainer
D Bleed valve

and don't inhale any of it. An approved filtering mask should be worn when working on the brakes. Do not, under any circumstances, use petroleum-based solvents to clean brake parts. Use clean brake fluid, brake cleaner or denatured alcohol only!

Note: *If you are removing the caliper only to replace or inspect the brake pads, don't disconnect the hose from the caliper.*

Removal

1 Support the bike securely upright. If you're planning to overhaul the caliper and don't have a source of compressed air to blow out the piston, use the bike's hydraulic system instead. **Note:** *On opposed-piston calipers, this method will loosen the pistons, but you'll need to separate the caliper halves as described below to get them all the way out.* To do this, remove the pads (see Section 2) and operate the brake lever to force the piston out of the cylinder. Block one piston with a piece of wood in the brake pad cavity, then push the other piston almost all the way out. Hold the exposed piston with a C-clamp, then operate the brake lever to push the other piston all the way out. Grip the exposed piston with a rag and twist and pull it out the rest of the way. **Note**: *Brake fluid will run out of the caliper if you remove the piston(s) in this manner. Try to keep it off the bike by holding the caliper over a pan. Be sure to wipe any spilled fluid off painted or plastic surfaces immediately and clean the area with soap and water.*
2 If you're working on a pin slider caliper, remove the brake hose banjo fitting bolt and separate the hose from the caliper **(see illustration 2.11a)**. If you're working on an opposed-piston caliper, unscrew the hose from the fitting on the caliper after the caliper is removed from the bike. Discard the sealing washers. Plug the end of the hose or wrap a plastic bag tightly around it to prevent excessive fluid loss and contamination.
3 If you're working on an opposed-piston caliper, loosen the caliper assembly bolts (they're on the opposite side of the caliper from the mounting bolts). This will be easier to do while the caliper is still bolted to the bike. Remove the caliper mounting bolts **(see illustration)**. Take the caliper off the bike.

Overhaul

4 If you're working on an opposed-piston caliper, remove the caliper assembly bolts. Pull the caliper halves apart.
5 If you're working on a pin slider caliper, remove the brake pads and anti-rattle spring from the caliper if you haven't already done so (see Section 2, if necessary).
6 Clean the exterior of the caliper with denatured alcohol or brake system cleaner.
7 If you're working on a pin slider caliper, remove the caliper bracket and the slider pin boots from the caliper.
8 If you didn't force out the piston with the bike's hydraulic system in Step 1, place a few rags between the piston and the caliper frame to act as a cushion, then use compressed air, directed into the fluid inlet, to remove the piston. Use only enough air pressure to ease the piston out of the bore. If a piston is blown out, even with the cushion in place, it may be damaged.

⚠ **Warning:** *Never place your fingers in front of the piston in an attempt to catch or protect it when applying compressed air, as serious injury could occur.*

9 Using a wood or plastic tool, remove

3.9 Remove the dust seal with a plastic or wooden tool (such as a pencil) to avoid damage to the seal groove

3.17a Install the slider pin boots

3.17b Apply a thin coat of the specified grease to the slider pins on the caliper bracket

4.4 The minimum allowable thickness is stamped into the disc

4.6 Loosen the disc retaining bolts a little at a time to prevent distortion

the dust seal **(see illustration)**. Metal tools may cause bore damage.

10 Using a wood or plastic tool, remove the piston seal from the groove in the caliper bore.

11 Clean the piston and the bore with denatured alcohol, clean brake fluid or brake system cleaner and blow dry them with filtered, unlubricated compressed air. Inspect the surface of the piston for nicks and burrs and loss of plating. Check the caliper bore, too. If surface defects are present, the caliper must be replaced. If the caliper is in bad shape, the master cylinder should also be checked.

12 If you're working on a pin slider caliper, temporarily reinstall the caliper bracket. Make sure it slides smoothly in-and-out of the caliper. If it doesn't, check the slider pins for burrs or excessive wear. Also check the slider pin bores in the caliper for wear and scoring. Replace the bracket, the caliper, or both if necessary.

13 Lubricate the new piston seal with clean brake fluid and install it in its groove in the caliper bore. Make sure it seats completely and isn't twisted.

14 Lubricate the new dust seal with clean brake fluid and install it in its groove, making sure it seats correctly.

15 Lubricate the piston with clean brake fluid and install it in the caliper bore. Using your thumbs, push the piston all the way in, making sure it doesn't get cocked in the bore.

16 If you're working on an opposed-piston caliper, assemble the caliper halves, using a new O-ring on the fluid passage. Tighten the caliper assembly bolts to the torque listed in this Chapter's Specifications.

17 If you're working on a pin slider caliper, install the slider pin boots **(see illustration)**. Apply a thin coat of PBC (poly butyl cuprysil) grease, or silicone grease designed for high-temperature brake applications, to the slider pins on the caliper bracket **(see illustration)**. Install the caliper bracket to the caliper and seat the boots over the lips on the bracket.

Installation

18 Install the anti-rattle spring (pin slider caliper only) and the brake pads (see Section 2).

19 Install the caliper, tightening the mounting bolts to the torque listed in this Chapter's Specifications.

20 Connect the brake hose to the caliper, using a new sealing washer on each side of the fitting. Tighten the banjo fitting bolt to the torque listed in this Chapter's Specifications.

21 Fill the master cylinder with the recommended brake fluid (see Chapter 1) and bleed the system (see Section 8). Check for leaks.

22 Check the operation of the brakes carefully before riding the motorcycle.

4 Brake disc - inspection, removal and installation

Inspection

1 Set the bike on its centerstand (if equipped). Otherwise prop it securely with the front wheel off the ground.

2 Visually inspect the surface of the disc for score marks and other damage. Light scratches are normal after use and won't affect brake operation, but deep grooves and heavy score marks will reduce braking efficiency and accelerate pad wear. If the disc is badly grooved it must be machined or replaced.

3 To check disc runout, mount a dial indicator to a fork leg (front disc) or frame (rear disc) with the plunger on the indicator touching the surface of the disc about 1/2-inch from the outer edge. Slowly turn the wheel and watch the indicator needle, comparing your reading with the limit listed in this Chapter's Specifications. If the runout is greater than allowed, check the hub bearings for play (see Chapter 1). If the bearings are worn, replace them and repeat this check. If the disc runout is still excessive, it will have to be replaced.

4 The disc must not be machined or allowed to wear down to a thickness less than the minimum allowable thickness listed in this Chapter's Specifications. The thickness of the disc can be checked with a micrometer. If the thickness of the disc is less than the minimum allowable, it must be replaced. The minimum thickness is also stamped into the disc **(see illustration)**.

Removal

5 Remove the wheel (see Section 11).

Caution: Don't lay the wheel down and allow it to rest on the disc - the disc could become warped.

6 Mark the relationship of the disc to the wheel, so it can be installed in the same position. Remove the Allen bolts that retain the disc to the wheel **(see illustration)**. Loosen the bolts a little at a time, in a criss-cross pattern, to avoid distorting the disc.

7 Take note of any paper shims that may be present where the disc mates to the wheel. If there are any, mark their position and be sure to include them when installing the disc.

Installation

8 Position the disc on the wheel, aligning the previously applied matchmarks (if you're reinstalling the original disc). Make sure the arrow (stamped on the disc) marking the direction of rotation is pointing in the proper direction.

Brakes, wheels and tires 7•7

5.4 Unscrew the banjo bolt (right arrow); use new sealing washers on both sides of the fitting (lower arrows)

5.5 Unscrew the locknut (arrow) and remove the bolt to detach the brake lever

5.6 Remove the trim plugs (arrows) for access to the master cylinder screws

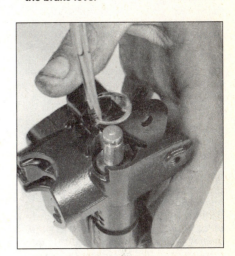

5.9a Remove the snap-ring from the cylinder bore . . .

9   Apply a non-hardening thread locking compound to the threads of the bolts. Install the bolts, tightening them a little at a time, in a criss-cross pattern, until the torque listed in this Chapter's Specifications is reached. Clean off all grease from the brake disc using acetone or brake system cleaner.
10   Install the wheel.
11   Operate the brake lever several times to bring the pads into contact with the disc. Check the operation of the brakes carefully before riding the motorcycle.

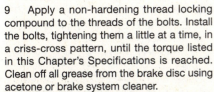

5   Master cylinder - removal, overhaul and installation

1   If the master cylinder is leaking fluid, or if the lever does not produce a firm feel when the brake is applied, and bleeding the brakes does not help, master cylinder overhaul is recommended. Before disassembling the master cylinder, read through the entire procedure and make sure that you have the correct rebuild kit. Also, you will need some new, clean brake fluid of the recommended type, some clean rags and internal snap-ring pliers.

Caution: To prevent damage to the paint from spilled brake fluid, always cover the fuel tank when working on the master cylinder.

2   Loosen, but do not remove, the screws holding the reservoir cap in place.

Caution: Disassembly, overhaul and reassembly of the brake master cylinder must be done in a spotlessly clean work area to avoid contamination and possible failure of the brake hydraulic system components.

Removal

3   Refer to Chapter 9 and remove the brake light switch.
4   Unscrew the banjo fitting bolt **(see illustration)** and separate the brake hose from the master cylinder. Wrap the end of the hose in a clean rag and suspend the hose in an upright position or bend it down carefully and place the open end in a clean container. The objective is to prevent excess loss of brake fluid, fluid spills and system contamination.
5   Remove the locknut from the underside of the lever pivot bolt, then unscrew the bolt **(see illustration)**.
6   Look for a punch mark in the upper side of the handlebar next to the clamp seam. If you don't see one, make your own mark. Pry out the trim plugs that cover the master cylinder mounting screws **(see illustration)**. Remove the screws and separate the master cylinder from the handlebar.

Caution: Do not tip the master cylinder upside down or brake fluid will run out.

7   Disconnect the electrical connectors from the brake light switch.

Overhaul

8   Detach the reservoir cap and the rubber diaphragm, then drain the brake fluid into a suitable container. Wipe any remaining fluid out of the reservoir with a clean rag.
9   Carefully remove the rubber dust boot from the end of the piston. Remove the snap-ring and slide out the piston and spring **(see**

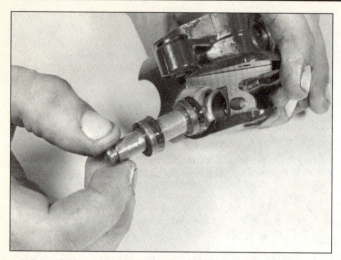
5.9b ... then pull out the piston assembly ...

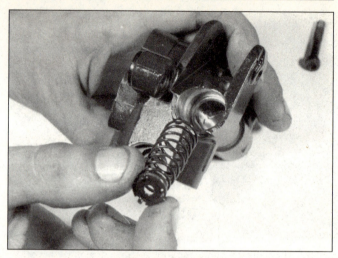
5.9c ... and spring

illustrations). Lay the parts out in the proper order to prevent confusion during reassembly.

10 Clean all of the parts with brake system cleaner (available at auto parts stores), denatured alcohol or clean brake fluid.

Caution: Do not, under any circumstances, use a petroleum-based solvent to clean brake parts. If compressed air is available, use it to dry the parts thoroughly (make sure it's filtered and unlubricated). Check the master cylinder bore for corrosion, scratches, nicks and score marks. If damage is evident, the master cylinder must be replaced with a new one. If the master cylinder is in poor condition, then the caliper should be checked as well. Make sure the ports in the bottom of the master cylinder are clear. If the small relief port is clogged, the brakes will drag.

11 Remove the old cup seals from the piston and spring and install the new ones. If a new piston is included in the rebuild kit, use it regardless of the condition of the old one.

12 Before reassembling the master cylinder, soak the piston and the rubber cup seals in clean brake fluid for ten to fifteen minutes. Lubricate the master cylinder bore with clean brake fluid, then carefully insert the piston and related parts in the reverse order of disassembly. Make sure the lips on the cup seals do not turn inside out when they are slipped into the bore

13 Depress the piston, then install the snap-ring (make sure the snap-ring is properly seated in the groove with the sharp edge facing out). Install the rubber dust boot (make sure the lip is seated properly in the piston groove).

Installation

14 Attach the master cylinder to the handlebar with the clamp. Align the clamp seam with the positioning mark o the handlebar. Tighten the bolts to the torque listed in this

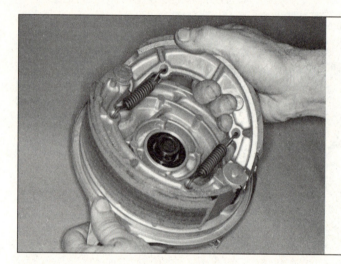
6.4 Fold the shoes off the panel to remove them

Chapter's Specifications. **Note**: *Tighten the upper bolt first, then the lower bolt. There will be a gap at the bottom between the clamp and master cylinder body. Don't try to close the gap by overtightening the lower bolt or you'll break the clamp.*

15 Install the brake lever and tighten the pivot bolt locknut.

16 Connect the brake hose to the master cylinder, using new sealing washers. Tighten the banjo fitting bolt to the torque listed in this Chapter's Specifications. Refer to Section 8 and bleed the air from the system.

6 Rear drum brake - removal, inspection and installation

Warning: The dust collected by the brake system is harmful to your health. Never blow it out with compressed air and don't inhale any of it. An approved filtering mask should be worn when working on the brakes.

Removal

1 Before you start, inspect the rear brake wear indicator (see Chapter 1).
2 Remove the rear wheel (see Section 12).
3 Lift the brake panel out of the wheel.
4 Fold the shoes toward each other to release the spring tension **(see illustration)**. Remove the shoes and springs from the brake panel.

Inspection

5 Check the linings for wear, damage, and signs of contamination from road dirt or water. If the linings are visibly defective, replace them.
6 Measure the thickness of the lining material (just the lining material, not the metal backing) and compare with the value listed in this Chapter's Specifications. Replace the shoes if the material is worn to less than the minimum.
7 Check the ends of the shoes where they contact the brake cam and pivot post. Replace the shoes if there's visible wear.
8 Check the brake cam and pivot post for wear and damage. If necessary, make

Brakes, wheels and tires 7•9

6.9 The brake drum diameter limit is cast into the drum

match marks on the cam and cam lever, then remove the pinch bolt, lever, wear indicator pointer, seal, spring and cam.

9 Check the brake drum (inside the wheel) for wear or damage (see illustration). Measure the diameter at several points with a brake drum micrometer (or have this done by a dealer service department). If the measurements are uneven (indicating that the drum is out-of-round) or if there are scratches deep enough to snag a fingernail, have the drum turned (skimmed) by a dealer to correct the surface. If the drum has to be turned (skimmed) beyond the wear limit to remove the defects, replace it.

10 Check the brake cam for looseness in the brake panel hole. If it feels loose, measure the diameter of the cam and hole and compare them with those listed in this Chapter's Specifications. Replace worn parts.

Installation

11 Apply high temperature brake grease to the ends of the springs, the cam and the anchor pin.

12 Hook the springs to the shoes. Position the shoes in a V on the brake panel, then fold them down into position (see illustration 6.4). Make sure the ends of the shoes fit correctly in the cam and on the pivot post.

13 The remainder of installation is the reverse of the removal steps.

14 Check the position of the brake pedal (see Chapter 1) and adjust it if necessary. Check the operation of the brakes carefully before riding the motorcycle.

7 Brake hoses and lines - inspection and replacement

Inspection

1 Once a week, or if the motorcycle is used less frequently, before every ride, check the condition of the brake hose that runs from the master cylinder to the caliper.

2 Twist and flex the rubber hose while looking for cracks, bulges and seeping fluid. Check extra carefully around the areas where the hose connects to the banjo fittings, as these are common areas for hose failure.

Replacement

3 Each brake hose has banjo fittings on each end. Cover the surrounding area with plenty of rags and unscrew the banjo bolts on either end of the hose. Remove any retainers that secure the hose to other components, detach the hose from the clips and remove the hose.

4 Position the new hose, making sure it isn't twisted or otherwise strained, between the two components. Install the banjo bolts, using new sealing washers on both sides of the fittings, and tighten them to the torque listed in this Chapter's Specifications.

5 Flush the old brake fluid from the system, refill the system with the recommended fluid (see Chapter 1) and bleed the air from the system (see Section 8). Check the operation of the brakes carefully before riding the motorcycle.

8 Brake system bleeding

1 Bleeding the brake is simply the process of removing all the air bubbles from the brake fluid reservoir, the hose and the brake caliper. Bleeding is necessary whenever a brake system hydraulic connection is loosened, when a component or hose is replaced, or when the master cylinder or caliper is overhauled. Leaks in the system may also allow air to enter, but leaking brake fluid will reveal their presence and warn you of the need for repair.

2 To bleed the brake, you will need some new, clean brake fluid of the recommended type (see Chapter 1), a length of clear vinyl or plastic tubing, a small container partially filled with clean brake fluid, some rags and a wrench to fit the brake caliper bleed valve.

3 Cover the fuel tank and other painted components to prevent damage in the event that brake fluid is spilled.

4 Remove the reservoir cap and slowly pump the brake lever a few times, until no air bubbles can be seen floating up from the holes at the bottom of the reservoir. Doing this bleeds the air from the master cylinder end of the line. Reinstall the reservoir cap.

5 Attach one end of the clear vinyl or plastic tubing to the brake caliper bleeder valve and submerge the other end in the brake fluid in the container (see illustration 2.11a or 3.3).

6 Remove the reservoir cap and check the fluid level. Do not allow the fluid level to drop below the lower mark during the bleeding process.

7 Carefully pump the brake lever three or four times and hold it while opening the caliper bleeder valve. When the valve is opened, brake fluid will flow out of the caliper into the clear tubing and the lever will move toward the handlebar.

8 Retighten the bleeder valve, then release the brake lever gradually. Repeat the process until no air bubbles are visible in the brake fluid leaving the caliper and the lever is firm when applied. Remember to add fluid to the reservoir as the level drops. Use only new, clean brake fluid of the recommended type. Never reuse the fluid lost during bleeding; it absorbs moisture from the air, which can lead to brake failure.

9 Replace the reservoir cap, wipe up any spilled brake fluid and check the entire system for leaks. Note: *If bleeding is difficult, it may be necessary to let the brake fluid in the system stabilize for a few hours (it may be aerated). Repeat the bleeding procedure when the tiny bubbles in the system have settled out.*

9 Brake pedal and linkage - removal and installation

Gear-type brake linkage

1 Support the motorcycle securely upright.

2 Unhook the brake pedal spring.

3 Fully unscrew the brake free play adjusting nut from the wheel end of the brake rod and disengage the threaded rod from the brake cam lever.

4 Remove the brake gear cover.

5 Remove the front footpeg (see Chapter 8).

6 Remove the battery (see Chapter 9). Remove the regulator/rectifier and unscrew the battery case bolts, but don't remove the case yet.

7 Remove the front exhaust pipe (see Chapter 4), then remove the battery case.

8 Unhook the brake pedal spring.

9 Remove the cotter pin from the brake pedal clevis pin, then remove the clevis pin.

10 Look for alignment marks on the brake pedal gears. If they aren't visible, make your own. Remove the cotter pins that secure the

7•10 Brakes, wheels and tires

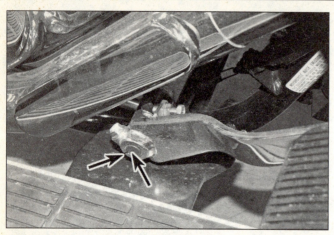

9.19a Mark the brake pedal and shaft (arrows) if there aren't any marks visible; this is a C50 . . .

9.19b . . . and this is an M50 (others similar)

shafts of the brake pedal gears.
11 Remove the gears and brake pedal assembly.
12 Check all parts for wear and damage. If necessary, remove the cotter pins and separate the brake pedal and link rod from the footpeg bracket.
13 Assembly and installation are the reverse of the removal steps, with the following additions:

a) Use new cotter pins.
b) Lubricate the shafts and gears with multi-purpose grease.
c) Check brake pedal height and freeplay and adjust as necessary (see Chapter 1).
d) Tighten the footrest bracket bolts securely.
e) Adjust the brake pedal (see Chapter 1). Test the brakes and make sure they work correctly before riding the bike.

Rod and pivot linkage

14 Support the motorcycle securely upright so it can't be knocked over during this procedure.
15 Remove the exhaust system (see Chapter 4).
16 Remove the rear clutch cover (see Chapter 8).
17 Remove the lower rear cover from the right side of the frame.
18 Unhook the spring from the brake light switch.
19 Look for alignment marks on the brake pedal and shaft **(see illustrations)**. If you can't see them, make your own.
20 Remove the brake pedal pinch bolt and pull the pedal off the shaft. Remove the pedal shaft from the motorcycle.
21 Unscrew the rear brake adjusting nut completely and take it off the brake rod (see Chapter 1). Remove the cotter pin and pivot pin and disconnect the front end of the front brake rod **(see illustration)**.
22 Unscrew the brake link shaft with an Allen wrench **(see illustration)**. Pull the shaft out and remove the brake link, together with the rods.
23 Check all parts for wear and damage and replace as needed. If necessary, remove the cotter pins and separate the brake cable and rod from the link.
24 Installation is the reverse of the removal steps, with the following additions:

a) Lubricate the shafts with multi-purpose grease.
b) Use new cotter pins if they were removed.
c) Align the punch mark on the brake pedal shaft with the split in the pedal.
d) Adjust the brake pedal (see Chapter 1). Test the brakes and make sure they work correctly before riding the bike.

Cable linkage

25 Support the motorcycle securely upright so it can't be knocked over during this procedure.
26 Remove the trim piece that covers the right swingarm pivot.
27 Unscrew the brake pedal adjusting nut completely and take it off the brake cable.
28 Loosen the brake light switch adjusting nuts and free the switch spring and cable from the bracket.
29 Detach the brake cable retainers from

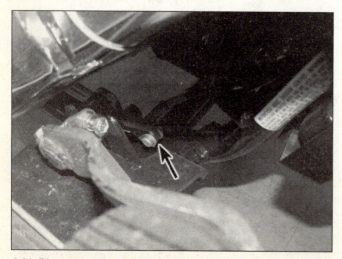

9.21 Disconnect the forward end of the pedal linkage rod (arrow)

9.22 Disconnect the rods from the links and remove the pivot bolt (arrows)

Brakes, wheels and tires

the motorcycle.
30 Unbolt the footrest bracket and remove it together with the brake pedal.
31 Check all parts for wear and damage. If necessary, remove the cotter pins and separate the brake cable, switch cable and pedal from the footrest bracket.
32 Installation is the reverse of the removal steps, with the following additions:
a) Lubricate the shafts with multi-purpose grease.
b) Use new cotter pins if they were removed.
c) Adjust the brake pedal (see Chapter 1). Test the brakes and make sure they work correctly before riding the bike.

10 Wheels - inspection, repair and alignment check

Inspection and repair

1 Clean the wheels thoroughly to remove mud and dirt that may interfere with the inspection procedure or mask defects. Make a general check of the wheels and tires as described in Chapter 1.
2 Place the motorcycle on the centerstand (if equipped). Otherwise, jack the bike up and support it so the wheel you're inspecting is off the ground. With the wheel in the air, attach a dial indicator to the fork slider or the swingarm and position the pointer against the side of the rim. Spin the wheel slowly and check the side-to-side (axial) runout of the rim, then compare your readings with the value listed in this Chapter's Specifications. In order to accurately check radial runout with the dial indicator, the wheel would have to be removed from the machine and the tire removed from the wheel. With the axle clamped in a vise, the wheel can be rotated to check the runout.
3 An easier, though slightly less accurate, method is to attach a stiff wire pointer to the fork slider or the swingarm and position the end a fraction of an inch from the wheel (where the wheel and tire join). If the wheel is true, the distance from the pointer to the rim will be constant as the wheel is rotated. Repeat the procedure to check the runout of the rear wheel. **Note**: *If wheel runout is excessive, refer to the appropriate Section in this Chapter and check the wheel bearings very carefully before replacing the wheel.*
4 The wheels should also be visually inspected for cracks, flat spots on the rim and other damage. Since tubeless tires are involved, look very closely for dents in the area where the tire bead contacts the rim. Dents in this area may prevent complete sealing of the tire against the rim, which leads to deflation of the tire over a period of time.
5 If damage is evident, or if runout in either direction is excessive, the wheel will have to be replaced with a new one. Never attempt to repair a damaged wheel.

Alignment check

6 Misalignment of the wheels, which may be due to a cocked rear wheel or a bent frame or triple clamps, can cause strange and possibly serious handling problems. If the frame or triple clamps are at fault, repair by a frame specialist or replacement with new parts are the only alternatives.
7 To check the alignment you will need an assistant, a length of string or a perfectly straight piece of wood and a ruler graduated in 1/64 inch increments. A plumb bob or other suitable weight will also be required.
8 Support the motorcycle securely upright, then measure the width of both tires at their widest points. Subtract the smaller measurement from the larger measurement, then divide the difference by two. The result is the amount of offset that should exist between the front and rear tires on both sides.
9 If a string is used, have your assistant hold one end of it about half way between the floor and the rear axle, touching the rear sidewall of the tire.
10 Run the other end of the string forward and pull it tight so that it is roughly parallel to the floor. Slowly bring the string into contact with the front sidewall of the rear tire, then turn the front wheel until it is parallel with the string. Measure the distance from the front tire sidewall to the string.
11 Repeat the procedure on the other side of the motorcycle. The distance from the front tire sidewall to the string should be equal on both sides.
12 As was previously pointed out, a perfectly straight length of wood may be substituted for the string. The procedure is the same.
13 If the distance between the string and tire is greater on one side, or if the rear wheel appears to be cocked, refer to Chapter 6, *Swingarm bearings - check,* and make sure the swingarm is tight. Also refer to the chain adjustment procedure in Chapter 1 and make sure the adjusters are set evenly.
14 If the front-to-back alignment is correct, the wheels still may be out of alignment vertically.

15 Using the plumb bob, or other suitable weight, and a length of string, check the rear wheel to make sure it is vertical. To do this, hold the string against the tire upper sidewall and allow the weight to settle just off the floor. When the string touches both the upper and lower tire sidewalls and is perfectly straight, the wheel is vertical. If it is not, place thin spacers under one leg of the centerstand.
16 Once the rear wheel is vertical, check the front wheel in the same manner. If both wheels are not perfectly vertical, the frame and/or major suspension components are bent.

11 Front wheel - removal, inspection and installation

Removal

1 Support the motorcycle securely upright so it can't be knocked over during this procedure. Raise the front wheel off the ground by placing a floor jack, with a wood block on the jack head, under the engine.
2 Remove the front brake caliper (see Section 3).
3 If the bike has a mechanical speedometer, unscrew the speedometer cable from the drive unit.
4 If the axle has a cotter pin and nut, remove them.
5 Loosen the axle clamp bolt. On models with a nut and cotter pin, it's on the same side as the nut. On models without a nut and cotter pin, it's on the same side as the axle bolt head **(see illustration)**.
6 Support the wheel. On models with an axle nut, insert a punch or similar tool into the hole in the right side of the axle and pull it out. On models without a nut, unscrew the axle with an Allen wrench and pull it out **(see illustration 11.5)**.
7 Carefully lower the wheel. Don't lose the spacers that fit between the hub and fork legs **(see illustration)**.

11.5 Pry out the trim plug, remove the pinch bolt and unscrew the axle (arrow)

11.7 Note the locations of the spacers (arrow) when removing the wheel

7•12 Brakes, wheels and tires

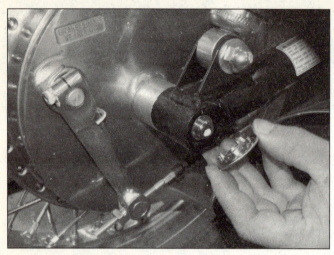

12.2a Remove the trim cap for access to the axle nut

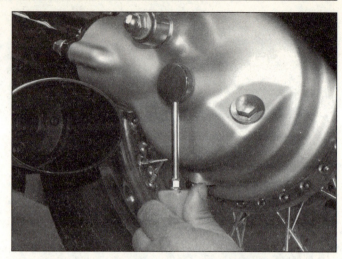

12.2b Pry out the trim cap for access to the axle bolt

Caution: *Don't lay the wheel down and allow it to rest on a disc - the disc could become warped. Set the wheel on wood blocks so the disc doesn't support the weight of the wheel. If the axle is corroded, remove the corrosion with fine emery cloth.*

Note: *Do not operate the front brake lever with the wheel removed. To prevent accidental operation of the brake, slip a piece of wood between the brake pads.*

Inspection

8 Check the axle for straightness (see Section 12).
9 Check the condition of the wheel bearings (see Section 13).

Installation

10 Installation is the reverse of removal. Don't forget to install the spacers. Tighten the axle nut (if equipped) and pinch bolt to the torque listed in this Chapter's Specifications.
11 Reinstall the brake caliper.

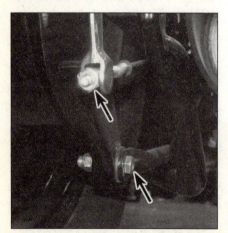

12.9 Unscrew the brake rod adjusting nut (upper arrow) and detach the rear end of the torque link (lower arrow)

12 Apply the front brake, pump the forks up and down several times and check for binding and proper brake operation.

12 Rear wheel - removal, inspection and installation

Removal

Intruder models

1 Support the bike securely so it can't be knocked over during this procedure and raise the rear wheel off the ground.
2 Remove the trim covers from the axle nut and bolt **(see illustrations)**. Remove the cotter pin from the axle nut and loosen the nut.
3 Unscrew the brake free play adjusting nut all the way (see Chapter 1). Slide out the pin and remove the cotter pin from the torque link nut, then remove the nut and disconnect the torque link from the brake panel.
4 Remove the axle nut and the washer.
5 Support the wheel and slide the axle out. Pull the wheel to the right to clear the

differential, lower the wheel and remove it from the swingarm, being careful not to lose the spacer on the right side of the hub.

Volusia and Boulevard C50/M50 models

6 If you're working on a Volusia or C50, and if you have a way to raise the bike securely high enough so the rear wheel can be lowered out from under the fender, the rear wheel can be removed with the rear fender in place. If not, refer to Chapter 8 and remove the seat and rear fender. The rear fender need not be removed on M50 models.
7 Support the bike securely so it can't be knocked over during this procedure and raise the rear wheel off the ground.
8 Remove the exhaust system (see Chapter 4).
9 Unscrew the brake free play adjusting nut all the way **(see illustration)**. Slide out the pin and remove the cotter pin from the torque link nut, then remove the nut and disconnect the torque link from the brake panel.
10 Remove the left side cover and lower frame cover (see Chapter 8). Remove the trim

12.10 Pry out the trim cap for access to the axle bolt

Brakes, wheels and tires 7•13

12.12 Remove the cotter pin (arrow) and unscrew the locknut - use a new cotter pin on installation

13.5a Insert the split end of the tool into the bearing and drive the wedge into the split end to lock it to the bearing . . .

cover from the axle bolt head (if equipped) **(see illustration)**.

11 Unbolt the left swingarm cover and take it off the swingarm (see Chapter 8).

12 Remove the cotter pin (if equipped) and unscrew the axle shaft locknut **(see illustration)**.

13 Support the wheel and slide the axle out. Pull the wheel to the right to clear the differential, lower the wheel and remove it from the swingarm, being careful not to lose the spacer on the right side of the hub **(see illustration 12.12)**.

2001 through 2004 Marauder models

14 Support the bike securely so it can't be knocked over during this procedure and raise the rear wheel off the ground.

15 Unscrew the brake free play adjusting nut all the way, then pull the cable out of the brake arm. Slide out the pin and remove the cotter pin from the torque link nut, then remove the nut and disconnect the torque link from the brake panel **(see illustration 12.9)**.

16 If the rear axle nut (on the right side of the bike) has a cotter pin, remove it. Unscrew the nut.

17 Unbolt the chain guard and take it off the motorcycle (see Chapter 6 if necessary).

18 Remove the axle and lower the wheel. Roll it forward enough to disengage the chain from the driven sprocket, then roll the wheel out from under the bike.

Inspection

19 Before installing the wheel, check the axle for straightness. If the axle is corroded, first remove the corrosion with fine emery cloth. Set the axle on V-blocks and check it for runout using a dial indicator. If the axle exceeds the maximum allowable runout limit listed in this Chapter's Specifications, it must be replaced.

20 Check the condition of the wheel bearings (see Section 13).

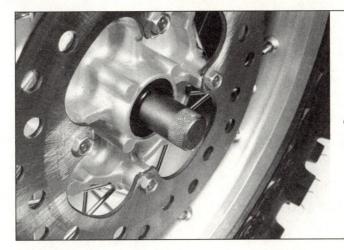

13.5b . . . then tap on the wedge to drive the tool out of the hub, together with the bearing

Installation

21 Installation is the reverse of the removal steps, with the following additions:

a) If you're working on a chain drive model, adjust the drive chain slack (see Chapter 1).

b) Tighten the axle nut to the torque listed in this Chapter's Specifications. Install a new cotter pin, tightening the axle nut an additional amount, if necessary, to align the hole in the axle with the castellations on the nut.

c) Use a new cotter pin on the torque link nut and tighten it to the torque listed in this Chapter's Specifications.

d) Adjust the brake pedal height and free-play (see Chapter 1).

e) Check the operation of the brakes carefully before riding the motorcycle.

13 Wheel bearings - inspection and maintenance

1 The front wheel uses two ball bearings, which are permanently lubricated and sealed on both sides. The rear wheel hub uses two ball bearings, which are sealed on the outer side. On chain drive models the drive chain sprocket coupling uses one unsealed ball bearing.

2 Support the bike securely upright so it can't be knocked over during this procedure. Remove the wheel (see Section 11 or 12).

3 Set the wheel on blocks so as not to allow the weight of the wheel to rest on the brake disc or drive chain sprocket.

Front wheel bearings

4 If you haven't already done so, remove the speedometer gear housing (if equipped) and axle spacer(s).

 You can make the tool described in the next step by cutting a slot in the shaft of a bolt that just fits inside the bearings, and grinding a wedge shape on the end of a metal rod.

5 Drive out the bearings with a bearing remover tool (Suzuki part no. 0941-50111) **(see illustrations)**. Remove the bearing spacer from the hub.

6   Thoroughly clean the inside of the hub with high-flash point solvent and blow it out with compressed air, if available.

7   Drive in the new bearings with a bearing driver or a socket the same diameter as the bearing outer race. Don't forget to install the spacer after you've installed the first bearing.

8   The remainder of installation is the reverse of the removal steps.

Coupling bearing (chain drive models)

9   Remove the coupling from the rear wheel and remove the coupling collar (see Chapter 6).

10   Remove the spacer and pry the grease seal out of the coupling to expose the bearing.

11   Tap against the back side of the bearing with a bearing driver or a socket to drive it out of the coupling.

12   Thoroughly clean the bearing with solvent. Blow it dry with compressed air, if available, but don't spin the bearing with compressed air while it's dry. Hold the inner race with fingers and spin the outer race. If the bearing feels rough, loose, or makes noise (more than a slight whirring), replace it.

13   Drive the bearing into the coupling with a bearing driver or a socket the same diameter as the outer race.

14   Pack the bearing with grease.

15   Tap in a new grease seal with a brass or plastic mallet. Tap evenly so the seal doesn't tilt. If necessary, lay a block of wood across the seal so the hammer's force will be spread evenly.

16   Check the rubber dampers in the rear wheel; if they shows signs of wear or deterioration they must be replaced.

Rear wheel bearings

17   If you haven't already done so, remove the coupling from the hub.

18   Insert a brass drift into the hub and place it against the opposite bearing. Tap evenly around the inner race to drive the bearing from the hub. The bearing spacer will also come out. If there isn't room to insert a drift and catch the edge of the bearing, use the tools described for front wheel bearings. **Note:** *On Boulevard M50 models, there are two bearings on the left side of the hub.*

19   Lay the wheel on its other side and remove the remaining bearing using the same technique.

20   Refer to Step 17 and inspect the bearings.

21   If the bearings check out okay and will be reused, wash them in solvent once again and dry them, then pack the bearings from the open side with medium weight, lithium-based multi-purpose grease.

22   Thoroughly clean the hub area of the wheel. Install the right-hand bearing into the recess in the hub, with the sealed side facing out. **Note:** *On Intruder and Boulevard S50 models, the right bearing has a metal seal plate and the left bearing has a rubber seal plate.* Using a bearing driver or a socket large enough to contact the outer race of the bearing, drive it in until it bottoms in the bore.

23   Turn the wheel over and install the bearing spacer and bearing, driving the bearing into place as described in Step 22 until it contacts the spacer. There will be a small amount of clearance between the bottom of the bore and the bearing when the bearing touches the spacer. Don't try to close the gap by driving the bearing farther in.

24   On chain drive models, press a little grease into the bearing in the rear wheel coupling (if you haven't just repacked it). Install the coupling to the wheel, making sure the coupling collar is located in the inside of the inner race (between the wheel and the coupling).

25   The remainder of installation is the reverse of the removal steps.

14 Tubeless tires - general information

1   Tubeless tires are used as standard equipment on models with cast wheels. They are generally safer than tube-type tires but if problems do occur they require special repair techniques.

2   The force required to break the seal between the rim and the bead of the tire is substantial, and is usually beyond the capabilities of an individual working with normal tire irons.

3   Also, repair of the punctured tire and replacement on the wheel rim requires special tools, skills and experience that the average do-it-yourselfer lacks.

4   For these reasons, if a puncture or flat occurs with a tubeless tire, the wheel should be removed from the motorcycle and taken to a dealer service department or a motorcycle repair shop for repair or replacement of the tire.

15 Tube tires - removal and installation

1   To properly remove and install tires, you will need at least two motorcycle tire irons, some water and a tire pressure gauge.

2   Begin by removing the wheel from the motorcycle. If the tire is going to be re-used, mark it next to the valve stem, wheel balance weight or rim lock.

3   Deflate the tire by removing the valve stem core. When it is fully deflated, push the bead of the tire away from the rim on both sides. In some extreme cases, this can only be accomplished with a bead breaking tool, but most often it can be carried out with tire irons. Riding on a deflated tire to break the bead is not recommended, as damage to the rim and tire will occur.

4   Dismounting a tire is easier when the tire is warm, so an indoor tire change is recommended in cold climates. The rubber gets very stiff and is difficult to manipulate when cold.

5   Place the wheel on a thick pad or old blanket. This will help keep the wheel and tire from slipping around.

6   Once the bead is completely free of the rim, lubricate the inside edge of the rim and the tire bead with soap and water or rubber lubricant (do not use any type of petroleum-based lubricant, as it will cause the tire to deteriorate). Remove the locknut and push the tire valve through the rim.

7   Insert one of the tire irons under the bead of the tire at the valve stem and lift the bead up over the rim. This should be fairly easy. Take care not to pinch the tube as this is done. If it is difficult to pry the bead up, make sure that the rest of the bead opposite the valve stem is in the dropped center section of the rim.

8   Hold the tire iron down with the bead over the rim, then move about 1 or 2 inches to either side and insert the second tire iron. Be careful not to cut or slice the bead or the tire may split when inflated. Also, take care not to catch or pinch the inner tube as the second tire iron is levered over. For this reason, tire irons are recommended over screwdrivers or other implements.

9   With a small section of the bead up over the rim, one of the levers can be removed and reinserted 1 or 2 inches farther around the rim until about 1/4 of the tire bead is above the rim edge. Make sure that the rest of the bead is in the dropped center of the rim. At this point, the bead can usually be pulled up over the rim by hand.

10   Once all of the first bead is over the rim, the inner tube can be withdrawn from the tire and rim. Push in on the valve stem, lift up on the tire next to the stem, reach inside the tire and carefully pull out the tube. It is usually not necessary to completely remove the tire from the rim to repair the inner tube. It is sometimes recommended though, because checking for foreign objects in the tire is difficult while it is still mounted on the rim.

11   To remove the tire completely, make sure the bead is broken all the way around on the remaining edge, then stand the tire and wheel up on the tread and grab the wheel with one hand. Push the tire down over the same edge of the rim while pulling the rim away from the tire. If the bead is correctly positioned in the dropped center of the rim, the tire should roll off and separate from the rim very easily. If tire irons are used to work this last bead over the rim, the outer edge of the rim may be marred. If a tire iron is necessary, be sure to pad the rim as described earlier.

12   Refer to Section 16 for inner tube repair procedures.

13   Mounting a tire is basically the reverse of removal. Some tires have a balance mark and/or directional arrows molded into the tire sidewall. Look for these marks so that the

tire can be installed properly. The dot should be aligned with the valve stem.

14 If the tire was not removed completely to repair or replace the inner tube, the tube should be inflated just enough to make it round. Sprinkle it with talcum powder, which acts as a dry lubricant, then carefully lift up the tire edge and install the tube with the valve stem next to the hole in the rim. Once the tube is in place, push the valve stem through the rim and start the locknut on the stem.

15 Lubricate the tire bead, then push it over the rim edge and into the dropped center section opposite the inner tube valve stem. Work around each side of the rim, carefully pushing the bead over the rim. The last section may have to be levered on with tire irons. If so, take care not to pinch the inner tube as this is done.

16 Once the bead is over the rim edge, check to see that the inner tube valve stem is pointing to the center of the hub. If it's angled slightly in either direction, rotate the tire on the rim to straighten it out. Run the locknut the rest of the way onto the stem but don't tighten it completely.

17 Inflate the tube to approximately 1-1/2 times the pressure listed in the Chapter 1 Specifications and check to make sure the guidelines on the tire sidewalls are the same distance from the rim around the circumference of the tire.

 Warning: Do not overinflate the tube or the tire may burst, causing serious injury.

18 After the tire bead is correctly seated on the rim, allow the tire to deflate. Replace the valve core and inflate the tube to the recommended pressure, then tighten the valve stem locknut securely and tighten the cap.

16 Tubes - repair

1 Tire tube repair requires a patching kit that's usually available from motorcycle dealers, accessory stores or auto parts stores. Be sure to follow the directions supplied with the kit to ensure a safe repair. Patching should be done only when a new tube is unavailable. Replace the tube as soon as possible. Sudden deflation can cause loss of control and an accident.

2 To repair a tube, remove it from the tire, inflate and immerse it in a sink or tub full of water to pinpoint the leak. Mark the position of the leak, then deflate the tube. Dry it off and thoroughly clean the area around the puncture.

3 Most tire patching kits have a buffer to rough up the area around the hole for proper adhesion of the patch. Roughen an area slightly larger than the patch, then apply a thin coat of the patching cement to the roughened area. Allow the cement to dry until tacky, then apply the patch.

4 It may be necessary to remove a protective covering from the top surface of the patch after it has been attached to the tube. Keep in mind that tubes made from synthetic rubber may require a special patch and adhesive if a satisfactory bond is to be achieved.

5 Before replacing the tube, check the inside of the tire to make sure the object that caused the puncture is not still inside. Also check the outside of the tire, particularly the tread area, to make sure nothing is projecting through the tire that may cause another puncture. Check the rim for sharp edges or damage. Make sure the rubber trim band is in good condition and properly installed before inserting the tube.

TIRE CHANGING SEQUENCE - TUBELESS TIRES

Deflate tire. After releasing beads, push tire bead into well of rim at point opposite valve. Insert lever next to valve and work bead over edge of rim.

Use two levers to work bead over edge of rim. Note use of rim protectors.

When first bead is clear, remove tire as shown.

Before installing, ensure that tire is suitable for wheel. Take note of any sidewall markings such as direction of rotation arrows.

Work first bead over the rim flange.

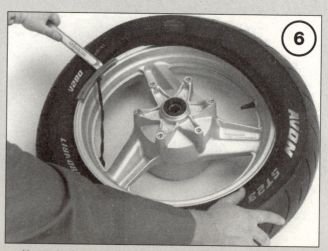

Use a tire lever to work the second bead over rim flange.

TIRE CHANGING SEQUENCE - TUBED TIRES

1. Deflate tire. After pushing tire beads away from rim flanges push tire bead into well of rim at point opposite valve. Insert tire lever adjacent to valve and work bead over edge of rim.

2. Use two levers to work bead over edge of rim. Note use of rim protectors.

3. Remove inner tube from tire.

4. When first bead is clear, remove tire as shown.

5. When fitting, partially inflate inner tube and insert in tire.

6. Work first bead over rim and feed valve through hole in rim. Partially screw on retaining nut to hold valve in place.

7. Check that inner tube is positioned correctly and work second bead over rim using tire levers. Start at a point opposite valve.

8. Work final area of bead over rim while pushing valve inwards to ensure that inner tube is not trapped.

Notes

Chapter 8
Frame and bodywork

Contents

Footpegs, floorboards and brackets - removal and installation...	3
Frame - inspection and repair	2
Front fender - removal and installation......................................	9
General information	1
Rear fender - removal and installation	11
Rear view mirrors - removal and installation	5
Saddlebags (Volusia and C50) - removal and installation	10
Seat - removal and installation..	6
Side covers - removal and installation	7
Sidestand - maintenance	4
Steering head covers - removal and installation	8

Degrees of difficulty

Easy, suitable for novice with little experience	**Fairly easy,** suitable for beginner with some experience	**Fairly difficult,** suitable for competent DIY mechanic	**Difficult,** suitable for experienced DIY mechanic 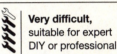	**Very difficult,** suitable for expert DIY or professional

1 General information

The machines covered by this manual use a double cradle frame, constructed of steel tubing. This Chapter covers the procedures necessary to remove and install the side covers and other body parts. Since many service and repair operations on these motorcycles require removal of the side covers and/or other body parts, the procedures are grouped here and referred to from other Chapters.

2 Frame - inspection and repair

1 The frame should not require attention unless accident damage has occurred. In most cases, frame replacement is the only satisfactory remedy for such damage. A few frame specialists have the jigs and other equipment necessary for straightening the frame to the required standard of accuracy, but even then there is no simple way of assessing to what extent the frame may have been over stressed.
2 After the machine has accumulated a lot of miles, the frame should be examined closely for signs of cracking or splitting at the welded joints. Rust can also cause weakness at these joints. Loose engine mount bolts can cause ovaling or fracturing of the mounting tabs. Minor damage can often be repaired by welding, depending on the extent and nature of the damage.
3 Remember that a frame which is out of alignment will cause handling problems. If misalignment is suspected as the result of an accident, it will be necessary to strip the machine completely so the frame can be thoroughly checked.

3 Footpegs, floorboards and brackets - removal and installation

1 If it's only necessary to detach the footpeg or floorboard from the bracket, pry the clip off the pivot pin or remove the pivot bolt **(see illustrations)**, slide out the pin(s) and detach the footpeg or floorboard from the

3.1a Remove the clip and pivot pin (arrow) or pivot bolt

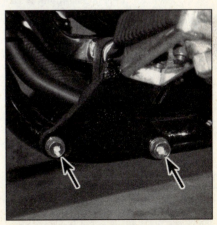

3.1b Unbolt the bracket if necessary

8•2 Frame and bodywork

3.2 The S50 footpeg bracket is secured under the frame by Allen bolts of different lengths; label them for installation

4.1 Make sure the sidestand pivot bolt is tight and the spring is in good condition (arrows)

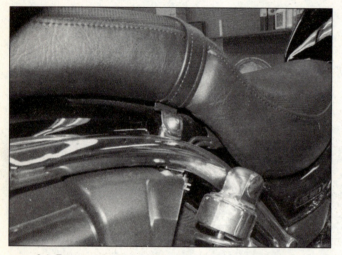

6.1 Remove the bolts at the front and sides of the seat

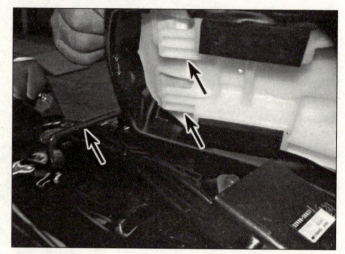

6.2 Disengage the tabs at the rear from the bracket (arrows)

bracket. Be careful not to lose the spring. Installation is the reverse of removal, but be sure to install the spring correctly.
2 If the entire bracket is bolted to the frame, remove the bolts that secure the bracket to the frame, then detach the footpeg and bracket (see illustrations 3.1a, 3.1b and the accompanying illustration). Welded footpeg brackets can't be detached.
3 Installation is the reverse of removal.

4 Sidestand - maintenance

1 The sidestand is bolted to a bracket on the frame (see illustration). An extension spring anchored to the bracket ensures that the stand is held in the retracted position.
2 Make sure the pivot bolt is tight and the extension spring is in good condition and not over stretched. An accident is almost certain to occur if the stand extends while the machine is in motion.

5 Rear view mirrors - removal and installation

1 To remove a mirror, loosen its locknut. Unscrew the mirror from the bracket on the handlebar.
2 Installation is the reverse of removal. Position the mirror.

6 Seat - removal and installation

Intruder and S50

1 Remove the bolt(s) from each side of he seat (see illustration).
2 Disengage the tabs at the rear of the seat and lift the seat off (see illustration).
3 Installation is the reverse of removal. Engage the tabs at the rear of the seat with the bracket on the frame (see illustration 6.2).

Volusia, C50, Marauder and M50

4 Unlock the seat with the ignition key. Remove the bolt at the rear of the passenger seat (see illustration).

6.4 Remove the bolt at the rear of the seat . . .

Frame and bodywork 8•3

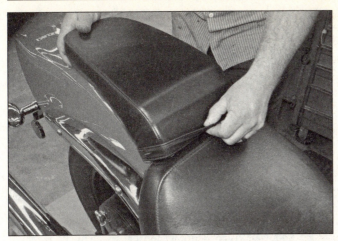

6.5 ... pull the strap off the rear seat ...

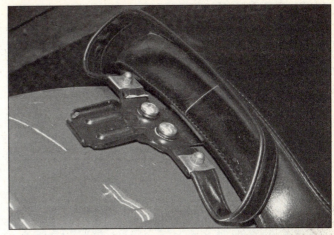

6.6a ... remove the screws at the rear of the front seat ...

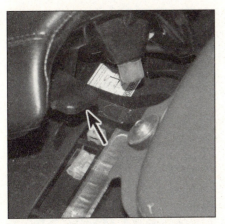

6.6b ... and pull the tab (arrow) from under the fuel tank

7.1a Remove the screw (arrow) and disengage the hooks to remove the S50 right side cover

7.1b Remove the screw (arrow) and disengage the hooks to remove the S50 left side cover

5   Pull the grab strap down off the rear seat, then lift the seat off **(see illustration)**.
6   Remove the two screws at the rear of the front seat **(see illustration)**. Lift the seat up and disengage the tab at the front from the back of the fuel tank **(see illustration)**.
7   Installation is the reverse of the removal steps.

7 Side covers - removal and installation

Intruder and S50

1   Remove the side cover mounting screw from the bottom (left cover) or front (right cover) **(see illustrations)**.
2   Carefully pull the securing lugs out of the grommets and lift the cover off.

Caution: *Don't use force. If the cover won't come off with a light pull, make sure all fasteners have been removed.*

3   Installation is the reverse of the removal steps.

Volusia and M50

Lower left side cover

4   Remove the screws, unhook the tabs and take the cover off **(see illustration)**.

Caution: *Don't use force. If the cover won't come off with a light pull, make sure all fasteners have been removed.*

7.4 Remove the screws (arrows) to detach the M50 lower left side cover

5   Installation is the reverse of the removal steps.

Lower rear covers (frame covers)

6   Carefully pull off the cover, disengaging the posts from the grommets **(see illustration)**.
7   Installation is the reverse of the removal steps.

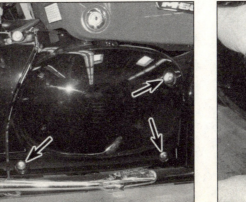

7.6 Carefully pull the frame cover off to disengage the posts (arrows)

8•4 Frame and bodywork

7.8 Unlock the M50 left side cover with the key and disengage the hooks

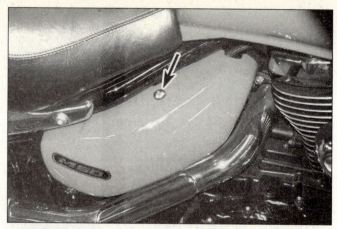

7.9 Remove the screw (arrow) and disengage the hooks to remove the M50 right side cover

8.2a Here are the S50 frame head cover front screws (arrows) . . .

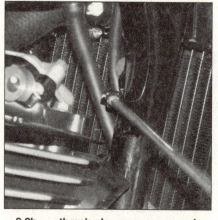

8.2b . . . there's also a screw on each side (arrow)

Upper side covers

8 On the left side, use the ignition key to unlock the cover. Disengage the hooks at the upper and rear corners and take the cover off **(see illustration)**.

9 On the right side, remove the screw at the top of the cover **(see illustration)**. Disengage the hooks at the upper and rear corners and take the cover off.

10 Installation is the reverse of the removal steps.

Marauder

Side covers

11 Remove the Allen bolt from the upper front corner of the cover. Disengage the two hooks and take the cover off.

12 Installation is the reverse of the removal steps.

Swingarm pivot covers

13 Remove the Allen bolts and take the cover off the frame.

14 Installation is the reverse of the removal steps.

8 Steering head covers - removal and installation

1 Remove the fuel tank (see Chapter 4).
2 Remove the mounting screws (if equipped) **(see illustrations)**. These are on the front or side, depending on model.
3 Spread the cover halves apart and lift it off the frame **(see illustration)**.
4 Installation is the reverse of the removal steps.

9 Front fender - removal and installation

1 Unbolt the fender from the fork legs and take it off **(see illustrations)**. The wheel need not be removed.

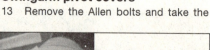

8.3 Carefully spread the cover and remove it from the frame

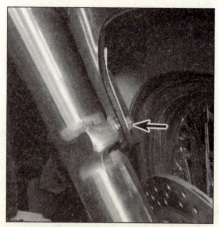

9.1a The front fender bolts (two per side) are on the inside of the fender (arrow) (C50 shown)

Frame and bodywork 8•5

9.1b The Volusia and M50 fender bolts (arrows) are accessible from outside the fender

10.2a Remove the saddlebag mounting bolts (arrows) . . .

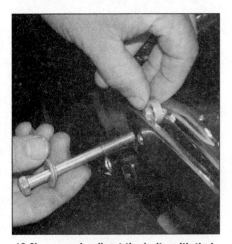

10.2b . . . and pull out the bolts with their washers - there's a spacer between the bracket and fender

11.2 Place blocks on the C50 rear tire to support the fender (fender removed for clarity)

11.4 Remove the seatback screws (arrows) from each side

2 Installation is the reverse of the removal steps.

10 Saddlebags (Volusia and C50) - removal and installation

1 Open the saddlebag being removed.
2 Remove the mounting bolts (see illustration). Take the saddlebag off and collect the spacers that go between the bracket and fender (see illustration).
3 Installation is the reverse of the removal steps.

11 Rear fender - removal and installation

1 Support the bike securely upright.
2 If you're working on a C50, which has a heavy rear fender, make some wooden blocks to support it and place them on top of the rear tire (see illustration).
3 Remove the seat (see Section 6).
4 Disconnect the electrical connectors for the turn signal lights. If you're working on a C50 so equipped, unbolt the seat back frame and take it off (see illustration).
5 Remove the mounting bolts and take the rear fender off of the motorcycle (see illustration).

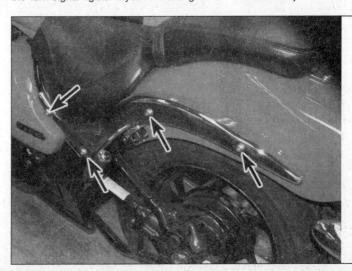

11.5 Remove the fender mounting screws and bolts (arrows) (M50 shown)

8•6 Frame and bodywork

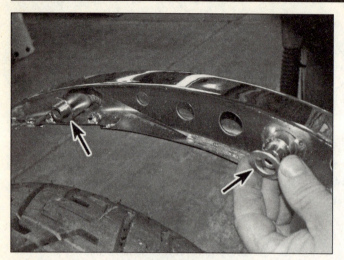

11.6a Don't forget to reinstall the inside washers (arrows) on C50 models

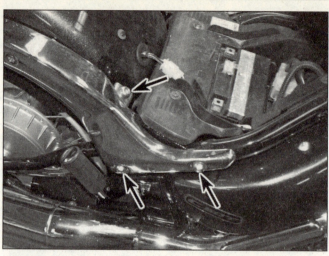

11.6b The front three bolts on each side on C50 models (arrows) use non-permanent thread locking agent on the threads

6   Installation is the reverse of the removal procedure. On C50 models, be sure to reinstall the washers that go on the inside of the fender braces **(see illustration)** and use non-permanent thread locking agent on the threads of the forward three bolts on each side **(see illustration)**. Tighten them to 50 Nm (36 ft-lbs).

Chapter 9
Electrical system

Contents

Alternator - coil replacement	32
Alternator - testing	29
Alternator rotor and starter clutch - removal and installation	31
Battery - charging	4
Battery - inspection and maintenance	3
Battery electrolyte level/specific gravity check	See Chapter 1
Brake light switches - check and replacement	12
Charging system - running voltage test	28
Charging system testing - general information and precautions	27
Electrical troubleshooting	2
Fuses - check and replacement	5
General information	1
Handlebar switches - check	18
Handlebar switches - removal and installation	19
Headlight aim - check and adjustment	9
Headlight assembly - removal and installation	8
Headlight bulb - replacement	7
Horn - check, replacement and adjustment	22
Ignition main (key) switch - check and replacement	17
Instrument and warning light bulbs - replacement	14
Instrument and warning light housings - removal and installation	13
Lighting system - check	6
Meters and gauges - check and replacement	15
Neutral switch - check and replacement	20
Oil pressure switch - check and replacement	16
Sidestand switch - check and replacement	21
Starter motor - disassembly, inspection and reassembly	25
Starter motor - removal and installation	24
Starter reduction gears - removal, inspecton and installation	26
Starter relay - check and replacement	23
Turn signal circuit - check	11
Turn signal, tail/brake light and license plate light bulbs - replacement	10
Voltage regulator/rectifier - check and replacement	30
Wiring diagrams	33

Degrees of difficulty

| Easy, suitable for novice with little experience | Fairly easy, suitable for beginner with some experience | Fairly difficult, suitable for competent DIY mechanic | Difficult, suitable for experienced DIY mechanic | Very difficult, suitable for expert DIY or professional |

Specifications

Battery
Intruder and S50
  Type... 12 volt, 16Ah (amp hours), fillable
  Specific gravity................................... 1.280 at 68-degrees F (20-degrees C)
All others
  Type... 12 volt, 10 Ah (amp hours), maintenance free
  Open circuit voltage........................... 12.5 volts minimum

Charging system
Charging system output
  Intruder, S50, Marauder..................... 13.5 to 15.5 volts DC at 5000 rpm
  Volusia, C50, M50.............................. 14.0 to 15.5 volts DC at 5000 rpm
Alternator output
  Intruder and S50................................. 65 volts AC at 5000 rpm
  Marauder... 75 volts AC at 5000 rpm
  Volusia, C50, M50.............................. 70 volts AC at 5000 rpm
Stator coil resistance
  Intruder and S50................................. Continuity (no specified ohms setting)
  All others... 0.2 to 1.5 ohms

Starter

Brush length limit
    Intruder and S50 .... 9 mm (5/16 inch)
    All others .... Not specified
Commutator diameter .... Not specified
Mica undercut limit
    Intruder and S50 .... 0.2 mm (0.008 inch)
    All others .... Not specified
Starter relay resistance
    Intruder and S50 .... 2 to 6 ohms
    Marauder... 3 to 6 ohms
    Volusia, C50, M50 .... 3 to 7 ohms

Circuit fuse ratings

All except main fuse
    Intruder, S50, Marauder 10A
    Volusia, C50, M50
        Ignition fuse
            All except 2009 and later M50 .... 15 amps
            2009 and later M50 .... 20 amps
        All except ignition fuse .... 10 amps
Main fuse
    Intruder and S50
        1985 through 1992 .... 30A
        1993 and later... 25A
    All others 30A

Bulb wattage

Intruder and S50

Headlight 60/55
Parking light (except US and Canada)
    1985 through 1991 .... 3.4
    1992 and later 4
Front turn signals
    1985
        Canada 23/8
        UK.. 23
    1986 and 1987
        US and Canada 23
        All others... 21
    1988 and 1989 .... 21/5
    1990 and later
        US and Canada 21/5
        All others... 21
Rear turn signals
    1985 23
    1986 and 1987
        US and Canada 23
        All others... 21
    1988 and later 21
Speedometer light
    1985 .... 3.4
    1986
        US and Canada 3.0
        All others... 3.4
    1987 and later 3.4
Indicator lights
    All except high beam 3.0
    High beam.. 1.7
Tail/brake lights
    1985 through 1987 .... 23/8
    1988 and later
        Intruder, Marauder and S50..................................... 21/5
        C50
            2008 and earlier... 21/5
            2009 and later .... LED
        M50... LED

Electrical system

License plate light	
1985	8
1986 through 2003	
US and Canada	8
All others	5
2004 and later	
Intruder and S50	8
Volusia and C50	
2008 and earlier	Not applicable
2009 and later	5
Marauder	Not applicable
M50	5

Marauder

Headlight	60/55
Parking light (except US and Canada)	4
Front turn signals	
US and Canada	21/5
All others	21
Rear turn signals	21
Speedometer light	3.4
Indicator lights	
All except high beam	3.0
High beam	1.7
Tail/brake lights	21/5
License plate light	
US and Canada	8
All others	5

Volusia, C50, M50

Headlight	60/55
Parking light (except US and Canada)	4
Front turn signals	
US and Canada	21/5
All others	21
Rear turn signals	21
Speedometer light	3.4
Indicator lights	LED
License plate light (M50 only)	5

Torque specifications

Alternator rotor bolt	
Intruder and S50	140 to 160 Nm (102 to 115 ft-lbs)*
All others	160 Nm (115 ft-lbs)*
Alternator stator screws	
Marauder	10 Nm (84 inch-lbs)
All others	Not specified*
Stator harness clamp screws	
Marauder	10 Nm (84 inch-lbs)
All others	Not specified*
Signal generator/crankshaft position sensor clamp screws	
Marauder	4.5 Nm (42 inch-lbs)*
All others	Not specified*
Starter clutch screws	
Intruder and S50	23 to 28 Nm (17 to 20 ft-lbs)*
All others	26 Nm (19 ft-lbs)*
Starter mounting bolts	
Marauder	10 Nm (84 inch-lbs)
All others	Not specified

Apply non-permanent thread locking agent to the threads.

9•4 Electrical system

1 General information

The machines covered by this manual are equipped with a 12-volt electrical system. The components include a crankshaft mounted permanent magnet alternator and a solid state voltage regulator/rectifier unit.

The regulator maintains the charging system output within the specified range to prevent overcharging. The rectifier converts the AC (alternating current) output of the alternator to DC (direct current) to power the lights and other components and to charge the battery.

The alternator consists of a multi-coil stator (bolted to the left-hand crankcase cover) and a permanent magnet rotor mounted on the crankshaft.

An electric starter mounted to the engine case is standard equipment. The starting system includes the motor, the battery, the solenoid and the various wires and switches. If the engine stop switch and the main key switch are both in the On position, the circuit relay allows the starter motor to operate only if the transmission is in Neutral (Neutral switch on) or the clutch lever is pulled to the handlebar (clutch switch on) and the sidestand is up (sidestand switch on). **Note:** *Keep in mind that electrical parts, once purchased, can't be returned. To avoid unnecessary expense, make very sure the faulty component has been positively identified before buying a replacement part.*

2 Electrical troubleshooting

A typical electrical circuit consists of an electrical component, the switches, relays, etc. related to that component and the wiring and connectors that hook the component to both the battery and the frame. To aid in locating a problem in any electrical circuit, complete wiring diagrams of each model are included at the end of this Chapter.

Before tackling any troublesome electrical circuit, first study the appropriate diagrams thoroughly to get a complete picture of what makes up that individual circuit. Trouble spots, for instance, can often be narrowed down by noting if other components related to that circuit are operating properly or not. If several components or circuits fail at one time, chances are the fault lies in the fuse or ground connection, as several circuits often are routed through the same fuse and ground connections.

Electrical problems often stem from simple causes, such as loose or corroded connections or a blown fuse. Prior to any electrical troubleshooting, always visually check the condition of the fuse, wires and connections in the problem circuit.

If testing instruments are going to be utilized, use the diagrams to plan where you will make the necessary connections in order to accurately pinpoint the trouble spot.

The basic tools needed for electrical troubleshooting include a test light or voltmeter, a continuity tester (which includes a bulb, battery and set of test leads) and a jumper wire, preferably with a circuit breaker incorporated, which can be used to bypass electrical components. Specific checks described later in this Chapter may also require an ohmmeter.

Voltage checks should be performed if a circuit is not functioning properly. Connect one lead of a test light or voltmeter to either the negative battery terminal or a known good ground (earth). Connect the other lead to a connector in the circuit being tested, preferably nearest to the battery or fuse. If the bulb lights, voltage is reaching that point, which means the part of the circuit between that connector and the battery is problem-free. Continue checking the remainder of the circuit in the same manner. When you reach a point where no voltage is present, the problem lies between there and the last good test point. Most of the time the problem is due to a loose connection. Keep in mind that some circuits only receive voltage when the ignition key is in the On position.

One method of finding short circuits is to remove the fuse and connect a test light or voltmeter in its place to the fuse terminals. There should be no load in the circuit. Move the wiring harness from side-to-side while watching the test light. If the bulb lights, there is a short to ground somewhere in that area, probably where insulation has rubbed off a wire. The same test can be performed on other components in the circuit, including the switch.

A ground check should be done to see if a component is grounded properly. Disconnect the battery and connect one lead of a self-powered test light (continuity tester) to a known good ground. Connect the other lead to the wire or ground connection being tested. If the bulb lights, the ground is good. If the bulb does not light, the ground is not good.

A continuity check is performed to see if a circuit, section of circuit or individual component is capable of passing electricity through it. Disconnect the battery and connect one lead of a self-powered test light (continuity tester) to one end of the circuit being tested and the other lead to the other end of the circuit. If the bulb lights, there is continuity, which means the circuit is passing electricity through it properly. Switches can be checked in the same way.

Remember that all electrical circuits are designed to conduct electricity from the battery, through the wires, switches, relays, etc. to the electrical component (light bulb, motor, etc.). From there it is directed to the frame (ground) where it is passed back to the battery. Electrical problems are basically an interruption in the flow of electricity from the battery or back to it.

3 Battery - inspection and maintenance

1 Most battery damage is caused by heat, vibration, and/or low electrolyte levels, so keep the battery securely mounted, check the electrolyte level frequently and make sure the charging system is functioning properly.

Fillable batteries

1 Fillable batteries are used on Intruder and S50 models. The battery is mounted in a carrier under the motorcycle and is removed from below.
2 Disconnect the negative cable from the battery (the terminal is on the left side of the motorcycle, just above the regulator/rectifier) **(see illustration)**.

> **Warning:** *Always disconnect the negative cable first and reconnect it last to prevent sparks that could cause the battery to explode.*

3 Remove the screw and detach the positive terminal cover (it's on the right side of the motorcycle, just in front of the battery) **(see illustration)**.
4 Disconnect the positive cable **(see illustration)**.
5 Remove the battery tray bolts, swing the tray down and lower the battery out of the motorcycle **(see illustrations)**.
6 Check the electrolyte level as described in Chapter 1. If it is low, remove the cell caps and fill each cell to the upper level mark with distilled water. Do not use tap water (except in an emergency), and do not overfill. The cell holes are quite small, so it may help to use a plastic squeeze bottle with a small spout to add the water. If the level is within the marks on the case, additional water is not necessary.
7 Next, check the specific gravity of the electrolyte in each cell with a small hydrometer made especially for motorcycle batteries. These are available from most dealer parts departments or motorcycle accessory stores.
8 Remove the caps, draw some electrolyte from the first cell into the hydrometer **(see illustration)** and note the specific gravity. Compare the reading to the Specifications listed in this Chapter. **Note:** *Add 0.004 points to the reading for every 10-degrees F above 68-degrees F (20-degrees C) - subtract 0.004 points from the reading for every 10-degrees below 68-degrees F (20-degrees C). Return the electrolyte to the appropriate cell and repeat the check for the remaining cells. When the check is complete, rinse the hydrometer thoroughly with clean water.*
9 If the specific gravity of the electro-

Electrical system 9•5

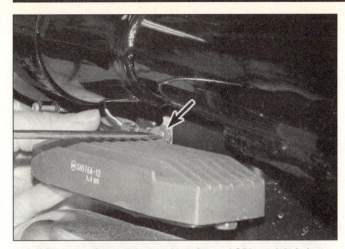

3.2 The negative terminal on Intruder and S50 models is just above the regulator/rectifier (arrow)

3.3 Remove the cover from the positive terminal . . .

3.4 . . . and disconnect the cable (arrow)

3.5a Remove the battery tray bolts (arrow) (one on each side of the bike) . . .

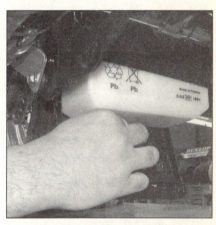

3.5b . . . swing the tray down and lower the battery out

lyte in each cell is as specified, the battery is in good condition and is apparently being charged by the machine's charging system.

10 If the specific gravity is low, the battery is not fully charged. This may be due to corroded battery terminals, a dirty battery case, a malfunctioning charging system, or loose or corroded wiring connections. On the other hand, it may be that the battery is worn out, especially if the machine is old, or that infrequent use of the motorcycle prevents normal charging from taking place.

11 Be sure to correct any problems and charge the battery if necessary. Refer to Section 4 for additional battery maintenance and charging procedures.

12 Install the battery cell caps, tightening them securely. Be sure the terminal blocks are in place or you won't be able to connect the cables to the battery once it's installed (see illustration). Reconnect the cables to the battery, attaching the positive cable first and the negative cable last. Make sure to install the plastic cap over the positive terminal. Be very careful not to pinch or otherwise restrict the battery vent tube (see illustration), as the battery may build up enough

3.8 On Intruder and S50 models, check the specific gravity with a hydrometer

3.12a Be sure the terminal blocks are installed in the terminals

3.12b Connect the vent tube (arrow) securely to the battery . . .

9•6 Electrical system

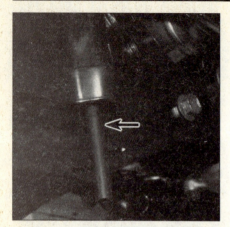

3.12c ... and route the tube (arrow) through the passage on the right of the battery case

internal pressure during normal charging system operation to explode. Be sure the tube is routed correctly **(see illustration)**.

Maintenance free batteries

13 Remove the seat (see Chapter 8). Check around the base inside of the battery for sediment, which is the result of sulfation caused by low electrolyte levels. These deposits will cause internal short circuits, which can quickly discharge the battery. Look for cracks in the case and replace the battery if either of these conditions is found.

 Warning: Always disconnect the negative cable first and reconnect it last to prevent sparks that could cause the battery to explode.

14 Check the battery terminals and cable ends for tightness and corrosion. If corrosion is evident, remove the cables from the battery and clean the terminals and cable ends with a wire brush or knife and emery paper. If you need to remove the battery, lift it out of the carrier **(see illustration)**. Reconnect the cables and apply a thin coat of petroleum jelly to the connections to slow further corrosion.

15 The battery case should be kept clean

3.16 Route the positive cable as shown

3.14 The battery on all except Intruder and S50 models is under the seat

to prevent current leakage, which can discharge the battery over a period of time (especially when it sits unused). Wash the outside of the case with a solution of baking soda and water. Do not get any baking soda solution in the battery cells. Rinse the battery thoroughly, then dry it.

16 If acid has been spilled on the frame or battery box, neutralize it with the baking soda and water solution, dry it thoroughly, then touch up any damaged paint. If you're working on a C50 or M50, make sure the positive cable is routed correctly **(see illustration)**.

17 If the motorcycle sits unused for long periods of time, disconnect the cables from the battery terminals. Refer to Section 4 and charge the battery approximately once every month.

4 Battery - charging

1 If the machine sits idle for extended periods or if the charging system malfunctions, the battery can be charged from an external source. Charging procedures for the fillable battery used on Intruder and S50 models are different from the procedures for maintenance-free batteries, which are used on all other models.

Fillable batteries (Intruder and S50)

2 To properly charge the battery, you will need a charger of the correct rating, a hydrometer, a clean rag and a syringe for adding distilled water to the battery cells.

3 The maximum charging rate for any battery is 1/10 of the rated amp/hour capacity. As an example, the maximum charging rate for a 14 amp/hour battery would be 1.4 amps. If the battery is charged at a higher rate, it could be damaged.

4 Do not allow the battery to be subjected to a so-called quick charge (high rate of charge over a short period of time) unless you are prepared to buy a new battery. The heat will warp the plates inside the battery until they touch each other, causing a short circuit.

5 When charging the battery, always remove it from the machine and be sure to check the electrolyte level before hooking up the charger. Add distilled water to any cells that are low.

6 Loosen the cell caps, hook up the battery charger leads (red to positive, black to negative), cover the top of the battery with a clean rag, then, and only then, plug in the battery charger.

 Warning: Remember, the gas escaping from a charging battery is explosive, so keep open flames and sparks well away from the area. If the gas ignites, the entire battery can explode and spray acid. Also, the electrolyte is extremely corrosive and will damage anything it comes in contact with.

7 Allow the battery to charge until the specific gravity is as specified (refer to Chapter 1 for specific gravity checking procedures). The charger must be unplugged and disconnected from the battery when making specific gravity checks. If the battery overheats or gases excessively, the charging rate is too high. Either disconnect the charger or lower the charging rate to prevent damage to the battery.

8 If one or more of the cells do not show an increase in specific gravity after a long slow charge, or if the battery as a whole does not seem to want to take a charge, it is time for a new battery.

9 When the battery is fully charged, unplug the charger first, then disconnect the leads from the battery. Install the cell caps and wipe any electrolyte off the outside of the battery case.

Maintenance-free batteries (all except Intruder and S50)

10 Charging the maintenance-free battery used on these models requires a digital voltmeter and a variable-voltage charger with a built-in ammeter.

Electrical system

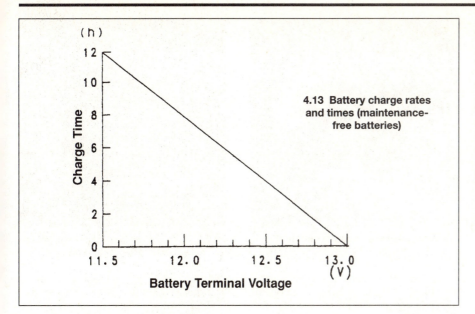

4.13 Battery charge rates and times (maintenance-free batteries)

5.1a The Intruder/S50 fuses are under this cover on the left side of the bike . . .

11 When charging the battery, always remove it from the machine and be sure to check the electrolyte level by looking through the translucent battery case before hooking up the charger. If the electrolyte level is low, the battery must be discarded; never remove the sealing plug to add water.

12 Disconnect the battery cables (negative cable first), then connect a digital voltmeter between the battery terminals and measure the voltage.

13 If terminal voltage is 12.6 volts or higher, the battery is fully charged. If it's lower, recharge the battery **(see illustration)**.

14 A quick charge can be used in an emergency, provided the maximum charge rates and times are not exceeded (exceeding the maximum rate or time may ruin the battery). A quick charge should always be followed as soon as possible by a charge at the standard rate and time.

15 Hook up the battery charger leads (positive lead to battery positive terminal and negative lead to battery negative terminal),

then, and only then, plug in the battery charger.

 Warning: The gas escaping from a charging battery is explosive, so keep open flames and sparks well away from the area. Also, the electrolyte is extremely corrosive and will damage anything it comes in contact with.

16 Start charging at a high voltage setting (no more than 25 volts) and watch the ammeter for about 5 minutes. If the charging current doesn't increase, replace the battery with a new one.

17 When the charging current increases beyond the specified maximum, reduce the charging voltage to reduce the charging current to the rate listed on the battery's label. Do this periodically as the battery charges.

18 Allow the battery to charge for the specified time listed on the battery's label. If the battery overheats or gases excessively, the charging rate is too high. Either discon-

nect the charger or lower the charging rate to prevent damage to the battery.

19 After the specified time, unplug the charger first, then disconnect the leads from the battery.

20 Wait 30 minutes, then measure voltage between the battery terminals. If it's 12.6 volts or higher, the battery is fully charged. If it's between 12.0 and 12.6 volts, charge the battery again (refer to this Chapter's Specifications and illustration 4.13 for charge rate and time).

5 Fuses - check and replacement

1 On Intruder, S50 and Marauder models, the fuse box is under the left side cover **(see illustrations)**. It contains the main and accessory fuses.

2 On Volusia, C50 and M50 models, the accessory fuses are located under the cover on the left side of the motorcycle **(see illustration)**. The main fuse is located under the

5.1b . . . remove the cover for access to the fuses

5.2a Here are the C50/M50 fuse box (left arrow) and turn signal/sidestand relay (right arrow)

9•8 Electrical system

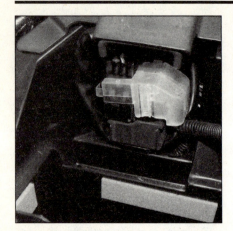

5.2b The C50/M50 main fuse and starter relay are under the fuel tank

5.2c Unplug the wiring connector and remove the cover . . .

5.2d . . . to expose the main fuse, spare fuse and starter relay terminals

seat in front of the battery (see illustrations).
3 Spare fuses are installed next to the main and accessory fuses.
4 If you have a test light, the fuses can be checked without removing them. Turn the ignition to the On position, connect one end of the test light to a good ground, then probe each terminal on top of the fuse. If the fuse is good, there will be voltage available at both terminals. If the fuse is blown, there will only be voltage present at one of the terminals.
5 The "plug-in" type fuses can be pulled from position. If you can't pull the fuse out with your fingertips, use a pair of needle-nose pliers. A blown fuse is easily identified by a break in the element (see illustration).
6 If a fuse blows, be sure to check the wiring harnesses very carefully for evidence of a short circuit. Look for bare wires and chafed, melted or burned insulation. If a fuse is replaced before the cause is located, the new fuse will blow immediately.
7 Never, under any circumstances, use a higher rated fuse or bridge the fuse block terminals, as damage to the electrical system - including melted wires, ruined components, and fire - could result.
8 Occasionally a fuse will blow or cause an open circuit for no obvious reason. Corrosion of the fuse ends and fuse block terminals may occur and cause poor fuse contact.

If this happens, remove the corrosion with a wire brush or emery paper, then spray the fuse end and terminals with electrical contact cleaner.

6 Lighting system - check

1 The battery provides power for operation of the headlight, taillight, brake light, license plate light and instrument cluster lights. If none of the lights operate, always check battery voltage before proceeding. Low battery voltage indicates either a faulty battery, low battery electrolyte level or a defective charging system. Refer to Chapter 1 for battery checks and Sections 27 through 30 for charging system tests. Also, check the condition of the fuses and replace any blown fuses with new ones.

Headlight
2 If the headlight is out when the engine is running (US, Canadian models) or with the lighting switch On (all other models), check the fuse first with the key On (see Section 5), then unplug the electrical connector for the headlight and use jumper wires to connect the bulb directly to the battery terminals. If

the light comes on, the problem lies in the wiring or one of the switches in the circuit. Refer to Sections 18 and 19 for switch testing and replacement procedures, and also the wiring diagrams at the end of this Chapter.

Taillight/license plate light
3 If the taillight fails to work, check the bulbs and the bulb terminals first, then check for battery voltage at the red wire in the taillight. If voltage is present, check the ground (earth) circuit for an open or poor connection.
4 If no voltage is indicated, check the wiring between the taillight and the main (key) switch, then check the switch.

Brake light
5 See Section 12 for the brake light circuit checking procedure.

Neutral indicator light
6 If the neutral light fails to operate when the transmission is in Neutral, check the fuses and the bulb (see Section 14 for bulb removal procedures). If the bulb and fuses are in good condition, check for battery voltage at the wire attached to the neutral switch on the left side of the engine. If battery voltage is present, refer to Section 20 for the neutral switch check and replacement procedures.
7 If no voltage is indicated, check the wires between the junction box and the bulb, the junction box and the switch and between the switch and the bulb for open circuits and poor connections.

Oil pressure warning light
8 See Section 16 for the oil pressure warning light circuit check.

Coolant temperature warning light
9 See Chapter 3, Section 3 for the coolant temperature warning light circuit check.

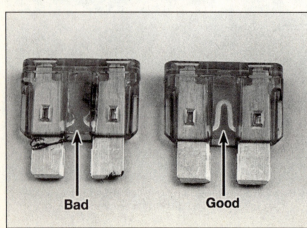

5.5 A blown "plug-in" type fuse can be identified by a broken element - be sure to replace a blown fuse with one of the same amperage rating

Electrical system

7.1a There's an adjusting screw (left) and retaining screw (right) on each side of the headlight ring

7.1b Pull the retaining ring and lens away from the housing

7 Headlight bulb - replacement

1 Remove the headlight ring securing screw from each side of the housing (see illustration). Take off the ring and lens (see illustration). Pull out the assembly and disconnect the electrical connector.
2 Pull up the tab and remove the dust cover (see illustration).
3 Lift up the retaining clip and swing it out of the way (see illustration).

Warning: *If the headlight has just been on, let the bulb cool before you continue. It will be hot to enough to cause burns.*

4 Remove the bulb holder (see illustration).
5 When installing the new bulb, reverse the removal procedure. Be sure not to touch the bulb with your fingers - oil from your skin will cause the bulb to overheat and fail prematurely. If you do touch the bulb, wipe it off with a clean rag dampened with rubbing alcohol. Make sure the clip is securely seated (see illustration).
6 During installation, make sure the tab at the top of the ring is engaged with the housing (see illustration).

8 Headlight assembly - removal and installation

1 Remove the headlight bulb holder housing (see Section 7).
2 Disconnect the electrical connectors

7.2 Be sure the TOP mark on the dust cover is upward when you install it

7.3 Unhook the clip and move it aside ...

7.4 ... then pull the bulb holder out of the socket

7.5 The clip should like this after it's installed

7.6 Engage the hook (left arrow) with the tab (right arrow)

9•10 Electrical system

8.2 Remove the nuts and bolts (arrows)

10.1 Remove the lens screws (arrows) for access to the turn signal bulb

inside the headlight housing and remove the headlight assembly mounting bolts and nuts **(see illustration)**.

3 Installation is the reverse of removal. Be sure the Top mark on the lens is up. Adjust the headlight aim (see Section 9).

9 Headlight aim - check and adjustment

1 An improperly adjusted headlight may cause problems for oncoming traffic or provide poor, unsafe illumination of the road ahead. Before adjusting the headlight, be sure to consult with local traffic laws and regulations.

2 The headlight beam can be adjusted both vertically and horizontally. Before performing the adjustment, make sure the fuel tank has at least a half tank of fuel, and have an assistant sit on the seat.

3 Start by adjusting the vertical position of the beam. To do this, insert a screwdriver into the adjuster hole in the lower left of the headlight rim and turn the adjuster **(see illustration 7.1a)**.

10 Turn signal, tail/brake light and license plate light bulbs - replacement

Turn signals

1 On early models with visible securing screws in the lens, remove the lens securing screw(s) and take off the lens **(see illustrations)**.

2 On later models, remove the screw from the underside of the bulb housing **(see illustrations)**.

3 Push the bulb in and turn it counterclockwise to remove it **(see illustration)**. Check the socket terminals for corrosion and clean them if necessary. Line up the pins on the new bulb with the slots in the socket, push in and turn the bulb clockwise until it locks in place. It is a good idea to use a paper towel or dry cloth when handling the new bulb to prevent injury if the bulb should break and to increase bulb life.

Tail/brake light

4 On all except M50 models, remove the lens securing screws and take off the

10.2a On later models, remove the screw from the underside of the housing (arrow) . . .

lens **(see illustrations)**. Push the bulb into the socket and turn it counterclockwise to remove it. Installation is the reverse of the removal steps.

5 On M50 models, the taillight is a long-life LED assembly that's replaced as a unit. Remove its screws, take it off, install a new one and tighten the screws.

10.2b . . . twist the lens to align the notch and tab (arrows) and pull the lens off

10.3 Push the bulb into the socket, turn counterclockwise to align the pins with the grooves (arrow) and pull the bulb out

10.4a Remove the lens screws (arrows)

10.4b Remove the lens screws (arrows)

10.6 Remove the license plate light nuts (arrows) or screws

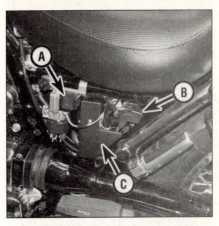

11.3 Left side electrical components (Intruder and S50)

A Turn signal relay
B Starter relay
C Fuse box

License plate light

6 Remove the lens securing nuts (Intruder and S50) **(see illustration)** or screws (all others) and take off the lens. Push the bulb into the socket and turn it counterclockwise to remove it. Installation is the reverse of the removal steps.

11 Turn signal circuit - check

1 The battery provides power for operation of the signal lights, so if they do not operate, always check the battery voltage and specific gravity first. Low battery voltage indicates either a faulty battery, low electrolyte level or a defective charging system. Refer to Chapter 1 for battery checks and Sections 27 through 30 for charging system tests. Also, check the fuses (see Section 5).
2 Most turn signal problems are the result of a burned out bulb or corroded socket. This is especially true when the turn signals function properly in one direction, but fail to flash in the other direction. Check the bulbs and the sockets (see Section 10).
3 If the bulbs and sockets check out okay, refer to the wiring diagrams at the end of this manual and check for power at the turn signal relay with the ignition On. On all except Marauder models, it's under the left side cover **(see illustration 5.2a and the accompanying illustration)**. On Marauders, it's under the right side cover.
4 If the switch is okay, check the wiring between the turn signal relay and the turn signal lights (see the wiring diagrams at the end of this manual).
5 If the wiring checks out okay, replace the turn signal relay.

12 Brake light switches - check and replacement

Circuit check

1 Before checking any electrical circuit, check the fuses (see Section 5).

2 Using a test light (or voltmeter) connected to a good ground, check for voltage at the brown wire terminal in the electrical connector at the brake light switch. If there's no voltage present, check the brown wire between the switch and the junction box (see the wiring diagrams at the end of this manual).
3 If voltage is available, touch the probe of the test light to the other terminal of the switch, then pull the brake lever or depress the brake pedal - if the test light doesn't light up, replace the switch.
4 If the test light does light, check the wiring between the switch and the brake lights (see the wiring diagrams at the end of this manual).

Switch replacement

Brake lever switch

5 Disconnect the electrical connectors from the switch.
6 Remove the mounting screw **(see illustration)** and detach the switch from the brake lever bracket/front master cylinder.
7 Installation is the reverse of the removal procedure. The brake lever switch isn't adjustable.

Brake pedal switch

8 Locate the switch at the brake pedal, follow its wiring harness to the electrical connector and disconnect it.
9 Where necessary for access, remove the footpeg bracket from the motorcycle.
10 Unhook the switch spring **(see illustration)**. Loosen the adjuster nut, compress the retainer prongs and remove the switch from the bracket.
11 Install the switch by reversing the removal procedure.
12 Adjust the switch by following the procedure described in Chapter 1.

12.6 Remove the screw (arrow) and take the brake light switch off

12.10 Turn the nut (arrow), not the switch body, to detach the switch from the bracket

9•12 Electrical system

13.1a Unscrew the speedometer cable (lower arrow) and screws (upper arrows) . . .

13.1b . . . remove the screws and washers . . .

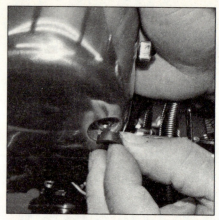

13.1c . . . and remove the grommets from the screw holes

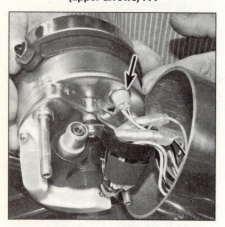

13.2 Pull out the speedometer, disconnect the wires and pull out the bulb socket (arrow)

13.5a Remove the cover screw and take the cover off . . .

13.5b . . . and note how the wiring harnesses are routed

13 Instrument and warning light housings - removal and installation

Caution: Keep the gauge housing in an upright position while it's off the motorcycle or the gauge(s) will be ruined.

Intruder and S50

Speedometer

1 Unscrew the speedometer cable knurled nut from the speedometer and pull the speedometer cable free **(see illustration)**. Remove the speedometer case screws, washers and grommets **(see illustrations)**.
2 Remove the speedometer **(see illustration)**.

3 Disconnect the instrument electrical connectors.
4 Installation is the reverse of the removal steps.

Warning light housing

5 Remove the screw that secures the warning light cover and take it off, noting how the wiring harnesses are routed inside the cover **(see illustrations)**.

13.6a Remove the screws (arrows) . . .

13.6b . . . and pull the speedometer and indicator housings off the triple clamp

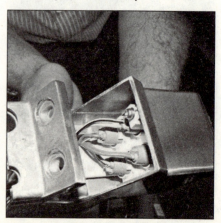

13.6c Turn the housing over for access to the bulb sockets

Electrical system 9•13

13.14a Remove the pilot box screws (arrows) (upper screw hidden)

13.14b Lift the pilot box and disconnect the wiring connector

13.17a Remove one screw (arrow) from each side of the cover . . .

6 Remove the warning light housing screws and take the housing off the upper triple clamp (see illustrations).
7 Installation is the reverse of the removal steps.

Marauder

8 Remove the fuel tank (see Chapter 4).
9 Disconnect the speedometer connector (it's just behind the V of the upper frame members).
10 Unscrew the knurled nut and detach the speedometer cable from the speedometer.
11 Remove the single screw from the bottom of the speedometer housing and lift the speedometer out.
12 Remove the screws from the back of the warning light housing and lift it out of the bracket.

C50

13 The speedometer and warning light are contained in a pilot box on top of the fuel tank.
14 Remove the pilot box screws (see illustration). Lift it off the tank and unplug its connector (see illustration).
15 Installation is the reverse of the removal steps. The rear pilot box screw is shorter than the front two screws.

M50

Speedometer

16 Remove the headlight housing (see Section 8). Working inside the housing, disconnect the speedometer electrical connectors.
17 Remove one Allen screw from each side of the speedometer cover (see illustration). Slide the cover forward to disengage the hook under the front end, then lift it off (see illustration).
18 Remove the front wheel (see Chapter 6). Slide the speed sensor out from between the wheel and fork leg (see illustrations).
19 Remove one bolt at the top of the speedometer and two from underneath (see illustration). Lift off the speedometer.
20 Installation is the reverse of the removal steps. Be sure the speed sensor tabs engage the slots in the front hub (see illustration 13.18b).

13.17b . . . then slide the cover forward to disengage the hook (arrow) and lift it off

Pilot box

21 If you need to remove the pilot box completely, partially remove the fuel tank and support in the raised position (see Chapter 4). Reach under the tank and disconnect the pilot box electrical connector. This

13.18a The speed sensor fits between the fork and hub (arrow)

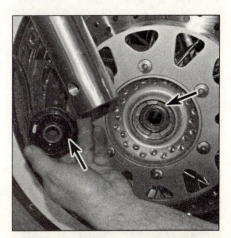

13.18b On installation, fit the tabs (left arrow) into the hub slots (right arrow)

13.19 Remove one upper bolt (arrow) and two lower bolts (not shown) and lift off the speedometer

9•14 Electrical system

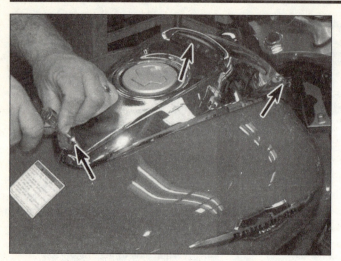

13.22 Remove the M50 pilot box screws (arrows, upper screw hidden)...

13.23 ... if you're just removing it for access to other components, hang it out of the way...

isn't necessary if you're just removing it for access to other components.

22 Remove the pilot box screws **(see illustration)**.

23 Lift the pilot box off. If you're just removing the pilot box for access to other components, hang it from the frame **(see illustration)**.

24 If necessary, remove the warning light cluster screws and take the cluster out **(see illustration)**.

25 Installation is the reverse of the removal steps.

14 Instrument and warning light bulbs - replacement

Note: *the speedometer and cluster lights in Volusia, C50 and M50 models are non-replaceable light emitting diodes. If a light doesn't work, the speedometer or cluster must be replaced.*

1 To replace a bulb, remove the speedometer or indicator housing (see Section 13),

pull the appropriate rubber socket out of the back of the instrument housing, then pull the bulb out of the socket **(see illustrations)**. If the socket contacts are dirty or corroded, they should be scraped clean and sprayed with electrical contact cleaner before new bulbs are installed.

2 Carefully push the new bulb into position, then push the socket into the instrument housing.

15 Meters and gauges - check and replacement

Check

Temperature gauge (if equipped)

1 Disconnect the electrical connector from the temperature sender on top of the cylinder head (see Chapter 3).

2 Connect a variable resistor between the terminals of the sensor harness.

3 Change the setting on the resistor and

note the temperature gauge reading:

   a) *2.45 K-ohms and above - light off, temperature 66-degrees F (19-degrees C)*
   b) *0.811 k-ohms - light off, temperature 122-degrees F (50-degrees C)*
   c) *Approximately 100 ohms - light flickering, temperature 248 to 282-degrees F*
   d) *No resistance (plain jumper wire) - light flickering, temperature 284-degrees F (140-degrees C) or above*

4 If the light or gauge don't operate as specified, replace the speedometer as an assembly.

Speedometer and tachometer (if equipped)

5 Special instruments are required to properly check the operation of these meters. Take the instrument cluster to a Suzuki dealer service department or other qualified repair shop for diagnosis.

Speedometer cable replacement

6 This procedure applies to Intruder, S50 and Marauder models. The speed sensor

13.24 ... but if you need to remove it completely, raise the fuel tank and unplug the connector (arrow)

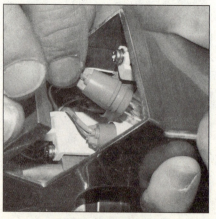

14.1a Pull out the bulb socket ...

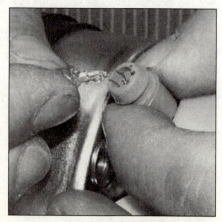

14.1b ... and pull the bulb straight out of the socket

Electrical system 9•15

15.8 Unscrew the knurled nut (arrow) to detach the speedometer cable

cable on other models is removed as part of speedometer removal (see Section 13).
7 Disconnect the speedometer cable from the speedometer **(see illustration 13.1a)**.
8 Disconnect the lower end of the speedometer cable from the drive at the front wheel **(see illustration)**. Note carefully how the cable is routed, then remove it.
9 Pull the cable out of the drive.

All models
10 Installation is the reverse of the removal steps.

16 Oil pressure switch - check and replacement

1 If the oil pressure warning light fails to operate properly, check the oil level and make sure it is correct.
2 If the oil level is correct, disconnect the wire from the oil pressure switch, which is located on the left front corner of the crankcase near the oil filter **(see illustration)**. Turn the main switch On and ground the end of the wire. If the light comes on, the oil pressure switch is defective and must be replaced with a new one (only after draining the engine oil).
3 If the light does not come on, check the oil pressure warning light bulb, the wiring between the oil pressure switch and the light, and the light ground circuit (see the wiring diagrams at the end of this manual).
4 To replace the switch, drain the engine oil (see Chapter 1) and unscrew the switch from the crankcase. Coat the threads of the new switch with silicone sealant, then screw the unit into its hole, tightening it to the torque listed in this Chapter's Specifications.
5 Fill the crankcase with the recommended type and amount of oil (see Chapter 1) and check for leaks.

17 Ignition main (key) switch - check and replacement

Check
1 Disconnect the ignition switch electrical connector.
2 Using an ohmmeter, check the continuity of the terminal pairs indicated in the wiring diagrams at the end of this manual. Continuity should exist between the terminals connected by a solid line when the switch is in the indicated position.
3 If the switch fails any of the tests, replace it.

Replacement
4 Remove bodywork components as necessary for access to the switch mounting screw. On Intruder and S50 models, the switch is on the lest side of the bike **(see illustration)**. On all other models, the switch is mounted on the right of the frame just behind the steering head.
5 If you haven't already done so, disconnect the switch electrical connector.
6 Turn the switch to the ON position, using the key. Remove the screw and remove the switch.
7 Installation is the reverse of the removal steps.

18 Handlebar switches - check

1 Generally speaking, the switches are reliable and trouble-free. Most troubles, when they do occur, are caused by dirty or corroded contacts, but wear and breakage of internal parts is a possibility that should not be overlooked. If breakage does occur, the entire switch and related wiring harness will have to be replaced with a new one, since individual parts are not usually available.
2 The switches can be checked for continuity with an ohmmeter or a continuity test light. Always disconnect the battery ground cable, which will prevent the possibility of a short circuit, before making the checks.
3 Trace the wiring harness of the switch in question and unplug the electrical connectors.
4 Refer to the wiring diagrams at the end of this manual for switch continuity diagrams. Using the ohmmeter or test light, check for continuity between the terminals of the switch harness with the switch in the various positions. Continuity should exist between the terminals connected by a solid line when the switch is in the indicated position.
5 If the continuity check indicates a problem exists, refer to Section 19, disassemble the switch and spray the switch contacts with electrical contact cleaner. If they are accessible, the contacts can be scraped clean with a knife or polished with crocus cloth. If switch components are damaged or broken, it will be obvious when the switch is disassembled.

16.2 The oil pressure switch (arrow) is at the left front of the engine

17.4 The Intruder and S50 key switch is secured by an Allen screw (arrow)

9•16 Electrical system

19.1a Remove the screws (arrows) . . .

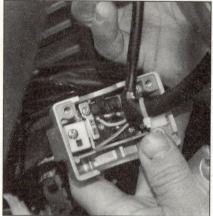

19.1b . . . and separate the housing halves for access to the switches

20.2 The neutral switch is secured by two screws (arrows)

19 Handlebar switches - removal and installation

1 The handlebar switches are composed of two halves that clamp around the bars. They are easily removed for cleaning or inspection by taking out the clamp screws and pulling the switch halves away from the handlebars **(see illustrations)**.
2 To completely remove the switches, the mounting screws should be removed **(see illustration 19.1a)** and the electrical connectors in the wiring harness should be unplugged.
3 When installing the switches, make sure the wiring harnesses are properly routed to avoid pinching or stretching the wires. If there's an alignment tab on the switch housing, make sure it engages with the hole in the handlebar.

20 Neutral switch - check and replacement

Note: *This Section applies to the neutral switch on carbureted models. Testing and replacement procedures for the gear position switch on fuel injected models are included in Chapter 4B.*

Check

1 Remove the cover from the clutch slave cylinder (see Chapter 2).
2 Disconnect the wire from the neutral switch **(see illustration)**. Connect one lead of an ohmmeter to a good ground and the other lead to the post on the switch.
3 When the transmission is in neutral, the ohmmeter should read 0 ohms - in any other gear, the meter should read infinite resistance.
4 If the switch doesn't check out as described, replace it.

Replacement

5 Remove the switch mounting screws and take it off the engine **(see illustration 20.2)**.
6 Install the switch with a new sealing washer and tighten it securely.

21 Sidestand switch - check and replacement

Check

1 Support the bike upright so you can raise or lower the sidestand. Locate the switch **(see illustration)**.
2 Follow the wiring harness from the switch to the connector, then disconnect the connector.
3 Connect the leads of an ohmmeter to the wire terminals on the switch side of the connector.
4 With the sidestand in the up position, there should be continuity through the switch (0 ohms). With the sidestand down, there should be no continuity (infinite resistance).
5 If the switch fails either of these tests, replace it.

21.1 The sidestand switch is secured by two screws (arrows)

Replacement

6 Support the bike and raise the sidestand.
7 Remove the switch mounting bolts **(see illustration 21.1)**. Follow the wiring harness to the electrical connector, disconnect it and remove the switch.
8 Installation is the reverse of the removal procedure.

22 Horn - check and replacement

Check

1 Disconnect the electrical connectors from the horn. Using two jumper wires, apply battery voltage directly to the terminals on the horn. If the horn sounds, check the switch (see Section 18) and the wiring between the switch and the horn (see the wiring diagrams at the end of this manual).
2 If the horn doesn't sound, replace it.

Replacement

3 Detach the electrical connectors and unbolt the horn bracket from the frame **(see illustration 8.2)**.
4 Detach the horn from the bracket and transfer the bracket to the new horn.
5 Installation is the reverse of removal.

23 Starter relay - check and replacement

Check

1 Locate the starter relay (see Section 5).
2 Disconnect the battery positive cable and the starter cable from the terminals on the starter relay.

Electrical system 9•17

24.2 On all except Marauder models, remove the starter cover (arrow)

24.3a Disconnect the cable and remove the nuts (arrows) . . .

24.3b . . . lift the starter out and inspect the O-ring (arrow)

Caution: *Don't let the battery positive cable make contact with anything, as it would be a direct short to ground.*

3 Connect the leads of an ohmmeter to the terminals of the starter relay.
4 Turn the ignition switch to On and the engine stop switch to Run. Place the transmission in Neutral.

25.4 Remove the brush plate from the housing

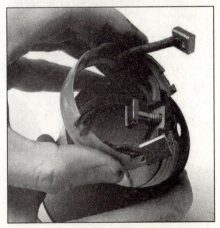

25.5 Push the terminal bolt through the housing and remove the plastic brush holder

5 Press the starter button - the relay should click and the ohmmeter should indicate 0 ohms.
6 If the meter doesn't read 0 ohms or the relay doesn't click, replace it.

Replacement

7 Disconnect the cable from the negative terminal of the battery.
8 Detach the battery positive cable, the starter cable and electrical connector from the relay.
9 Pull the relay holder off its mounting tabs.
10 Installation is the reverse of removal. Reconnect the negative battery cable after all the other electrical connections are made.

24 Starter motor - removal and installation

Removal

1 Disconnect the cable from the negative terminal of the battery.
2 On all except Marauder models, remove

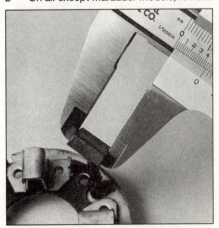

25.6 Measure the length of the brushes and compare the length of the shortest brush with the length listed in this Chapter's Specifications

the starter cover from behind the rear cylinder **(see illustration)**.
3 Remove the nut and washer retaining the starter wires to the starter, then remove the starter mounting bolts and pull the starter out of the engine **(see illustrations)**.
4 Check the condition of the O-ring on the end of the starter and replace it if necessary.

Installation

5 Apply a little engine oil to the O-ring and install the starter by reversing the removal procedure.

25 Starter motor - disassembly, inspection and reassembly

1 Remove the starter motor (see Section 24).

Disassembly

2 Mark the position of the housing to each end cover. Remove the two through-bolts and detach the end and reduction covers.
3 Pull the armature out of the housing (toward the reduction gear side).
4 Remove the brush plate from the housing **(see illustration)**.
5 Remove the nut and push the terminal bolt through the housing. Remove the two brushes with the plastic holder from the housing **(see illustration)**.

Inspection

6 The parts of the starter motor that most likely will require attention are the brushes. Measure the length of the brushes and compare the results to the brush length listed in this Chapter's Specifications **(see illustration)**. If any of the brushes are worn beyond the specified limits, replace the brush holder assembly with a new one. If the brushes are not worn excessively, cracked, chipped, or otherwise damaged, they may be reused.

25.7 Check the commutator for cracks and discoloring, then measure the diameter and compare it with the minimum diameter listed in this Chapter's Specifications

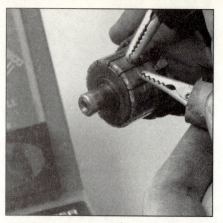

25.8a Continuity should exist between the commutator bars

25.8b There should be no continuity between the commutator bars and the armature shaft

7 Inspect the commutator **(see illustration)** for scoring, scratches and discoloration. The commutator can be cleaned and polished with crocus cloth, but do not use sandpaper or emery paper. After cleaning, wipe away any residue with a cloth soaked in an electrical system cleaner or denatured alcohol. Measure the commutator diameter and compare it to the diameter listed in this Chapter's Specifications. If it is less than the service limit, the motor must be replaced with a new one.

8 Using an ohmmeter or a continuity test light, check for continuity between the commutator bars **(see illustration)**. Continuity should exist between each bar and all of the others. Also, check for continuity between the commutator bars and the armature shaft **(see illustration)**. There should be no continuity between the commutator and the shaft. If the checks indicate otherwise, the armature is defective.

9 Check for continuity between the brush plate and the brushes **(see illustration)**. The meter should read close to 0 ohms. If it doesn't, the brush plate has an open and must be replaced.

10 Using the highest range on the ohmmeter, measure the resistance between the brush holders and the brush plate **(see illustration)**. The reading should be infinite. If there is any reading at all, replace the brush plate.

11 Check the starter reduction gears for worn, cracked, chipped and broken teeth. If the gears are damaged or worn, replace the starter motor.

Reassembly

12 Install the plastic brush holder into the housing. Make sure the terminal bolt and washers are assembled correctly **(see illustration)**. Tighten the terminal nut securely.

13 Detach the brush springs from the brush plate (this will make armature installation much easier). Install the brush plate into the housing, routing the brush leads into the notches in the plate **(see illustration)**. Make sure the tongue on the brush plate fits into the notch in the housing.

14 Install the brushes into their holders and slide the armature into place. Install the brush springs **(see illustrations)**.

25.9 There should be almost no resistance (0 ohms) between the brushes and the brush plate

15 Install any washers that were present on the end of the armature shaft. Install the end and reduction covers, aligning the protrusions with the notches. Install the two through-bolts and tighten them securely.

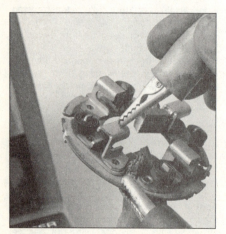

25.10 There should be no continuity between the brush plate and the brush holders (the resistance should be infinite)

25.12 Install the washers on the starter terminal as shown

25.13 When installing the brush plate, make sure the brush leads fit into the notches in the plate (arrow) - also, make sure the tongue on the plate fits into the notch in the housing (arrows)

Electrical system 9•19

25.14a Install each brush spring on the post in this position . . .

25.14b . . . then pull the end of the spring 1/2 turn clockwise and seat the end of it in the groove in the end of the brush

26 Starter reduction gears - removal, inspection and installation

1 Remove the alternator cover (see Section 31).
2 Slip the reduction gears off their shafts **(see illustration)**.
3 Pull out the pivot pins, noting their different lengths **(see illustration)**.
4 Check the gears and pivots for wear and damage and replace any parts with problems.
5 Installation is the reverse of the removal steps.

27 Charging system testing - general information and precautions

1 If the performance of the charging system is suspect, the system as a whole should be checked first, followed by testing of the individual components (the alternator and the voltage regulator/rectifier). **Note**: *Before beginning the checks, make sure the battery is fully charged and that all system connections are clean and tight.*
2 Checking the output of the charging system and the performance of the various components within the charging system requires the use of special electrical test equipment. A voltmeter or a multimeter is the absolute minimum equipment required. In addition, an ohmmeter is generally required for checking the remainder of the system.
3 When making the checks, follow the procedures carefully to prevent incorrect connections or short circuits, as irreparable damage to electrical system components may result if short circuits occur. Because of the special tools and expertise required, it is recommended that the job of checking the charging system be left to a dealer service department or a reputable motorcycle repair shop.

28 Charging system - running voltage test

Caution: Never disconnect the battery cables from the battery while the engine is running. If the battery is disconnected, the alternator and regulator/rectifier will be damaged.

1 To check the charging system output, you will need a voltmeter or a multimeter with a voltmeter function.
2 The battery must be fully charged (charge it from an external source if necessary) and the engine must be at normal operating temperature to obtain an accurate reading.
3 On all except Intruder and S50 models, remove the seat (see Chapter 8).
4 Attach the positive voltmeter lead to the battery positive terminal and the negative lead to the battery negative terminal (refer to Section 3 if necessary). The voltmeter selector switch (if so equipped) must be in a DC volt range greater than 15 volts.
5 Start the engine. Run it at 5,000 rpm, with the headlight high beam switched on.
6 The charging system voltage should be within the range listed in this Chapter's Specifications.
7 If the output is as specified, the alternator is functioning properly. If the charging system as a whole is not performing as it should, refer to Section 30 and check the voltage regulator/rectifier.
8 Low voltage output may be the result of damaged windings in the alternator stator coils, loss of magnetism in the alternator rotor or wiring problems. Make sure all electrical connections are clean and tight, then refer to Section 29 for specific alternator tests.
9 High voltage output, above the specified range, may indicate a defective regulator/rectifier.

26.2 Remove the starter reduction gears (arrows) - they may come off with the alternator cover

26.3 The shafts have different lengths

9•20 Electrical system

30.4 The Intruder/S50 regulator/rectifier is secured by two bolts (arrows)

30.6a For access to the regulator/rectifier on Volusia, C50 and M50 models, remove the bracket bolts (arrows) (upper bolt hidden) ...

29 Alternator - testing

No-load output test

1 Follow the wiring harness from the alternator housing to the connector, then disconnect the connector.
2 Connect a voltmeter with a 100-volt AC scale to two of the yellow wire terminals in the alternator connector (at this point, you're measuring the alternator output before it has been rectified from alternating current to direct current, so the voltmeter must be able to measure AC).
3 Run the engine at 5,000 rpm and note the voltage reading.
4 Take three different measurements between different pairs of wires. In all cases, the voltage should be as listed in this Chapter's Specifications. **Note:** *If only one of the readings is low, one stator coil is probably defective. This will produce an occasional failure to start due to insufficient battery charge.*
   a) *If the voltage reading is correct, the rectifier/regulator is probably defective. Refer to Section 30 for test procedures.*
   b) *If the voltage reading is low, the alternator may be defective. Test the stator coils as described in Section 29. If the stator coils test out OK, the rotor magnets have probably lost magnetism. This can be caused by dropping or hitting the alternator, by leaving the alternator near another source of magnetism, or by age.*

Continuity test

5 If charging system output is low or non-existent, the alternator stator coil windings and leads should be checked for proper continuity. The test can be made with the stator in place on the machine.
6 Using an ohmmeter (preferred) or a continuity test light, check for continuity between each of the wires coming from the alternator stator (the same connector that was disconnected in Section 29 for the output test). Continuity should exist between any one wire and each of the others. If you're using an ohmmeter, the resistance should be within the range listed in this Chapter's Specifications.
7 Check for continuity between each of the wires and the engine. No continuity should exist between any of the wires and the engine.
8 If there is no continuity between any two of the wires, or if there is continuity between the wires and an engine ground, an open circuit or a short exists within the stator coils. Since repair of the stator is not feasible, it must be replaced with a new one. **Note:** *An open or shorted stator coil will cause low output or no output. Weak or damaged rotor magnets will cause low output.*

30 Voltage regulator/rectifier - check and replacement

Check

1 Testing of the voltage regulator/rectifier requires a special Suzuki tester. Ordinary ohmmeters will produce a wide variety of readings which may indicate that the regulator/rectifier is defective when it is actually good.
2 If the charging system running voltage in Section 29 was too high, the regulator/rectifier may be defective. It may also be defective if the output was too low and no other cause (alternator or wiring problems) can be found.
3 If you suspect the regulator/rectifier, take it to a dealer service department or other repair shop for further checks, or substitute a known good unit and recheck the charging system output.

Replacement

4 The regulator/rectifier on Intruder and S50 models is mounted on the left side of the motorcycle **(see illustration)**. Remove its mounting bolts, lift the regulator out, and disconnect its wiring connector.
5 The regulator/rectifier on Marauder models is mounted between the frame rails at the rear of the frame, just forward of the exhaust crossover pipe. Unbolt the regulator, lower it out of its bracket and disconnect its wiring connector.
6 The regulator/rectifier on Volusia, C50 and M50 models is mounted behind the fuse and relay bracket. Remove the lower left side cover (see Chapter 8). Remove the bracket bolts and pull it out, disconnect the wiring connector and remove the mounting screws **(see illustrations)**.
7 Installation is the reverse of the removal steps.

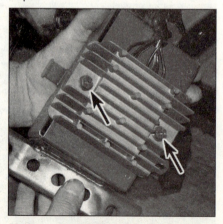

30.6b ... take the bracket off, remove the regulator/rectifier screws (arrows) and detach the regulator/rectifier from the bracket

Electrical system 9•21

31.3a Remove the alternator cover screws (arrows) (Intruder/S50 shown, others similar)

31.3b Disengage the grommet (arrow) as the cover is removed

31 Alternator rotor and starter clutch - removal and installation

Note: *This procedure requires an alternator rotor puller, for which there are no good substitutes. Rotor pullers are normally available at motorcycle dealers, but the puller for this engine may be very difficult to find, even for Suzuki dealers. Before starting, check with your dealer's parts department to make sure they have the correct puller for sale. If not, they may have one in the service department, in which case you can save money by doing most of the work yourself and having the dealer's service department remove the rotor. Be sure you will be able to remove the rotor before starting the job.*

Removal

Rotor

1 Disconnect the cable from the negative terminal of the battery.
2 On all except Marauder models, remove the clutch slave cylinder or release mechanism cover (see Chapter 2). On Marauders, remove the drive chain front sprocket cover.
3 Remove the alternator cover screws **(see illustration)**. Pull the cover off the engine, disengaging the wiring harness grommet as you go **(see illustrations)**. The rotor magnets will create some resistance, so you will need to pull firmly. Don't pry the cover off; if it's stuck, check again to make sure all fasteners have been removed. Strike the cover with a soft mallet to break the gasket seal if necessary.
4 Locate the cover dowels; they may have come off with the cover or stayed in the engine **(see illustration)**.
5 Prevent the alternator rotor from turning. There are two easy ways to do this: wedge a copper penny or washer into the space between the starter reduction gear and alternator rotor or place the transmission in first gear and have an assistant firmly apply the rear brake.
6 Remove the rotor bolt **(see illustration 31.4)**.
7 Hold the rotor from turning again, and using a rotor puller (Suzuki tool no. 09930-33730 or equivalent), remove the rotor from the crankshaft **(see illustration)**.

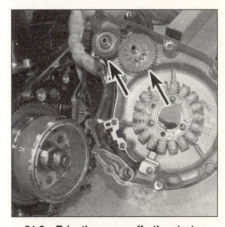

31.3c Take the cover off - the starter reduction gears (arrows) may stay in the cover

Caution: *Don't try to remove the rotor without a puller, as it can easily be damaged. Do not pound on it or you'll weaken the rotor magnets.*

8 Remove the Woodruff key from the crankshaft **(see illustration)**.

31.4 Locate the cover dowels (arrows) - use a new gasket on installation

31.7 Hold the puller flats and turn the bolt to remove the rotor

9•22 Electrical system

31.8 Remove the rotor and locate the Woodruff key (arrow)

31.10 Try to turn the gear while holding the starter clutch - it should turn in one direction only

31.12 Be sure the directional arrow (arrow) faces the right way

Starter clutch

9   Remove the rotor as described above.

10 Hold the starter clutch in one hand and try to turn the driven gear on both directions with the other hand **(see illustration)**. It should rotate in one direction only. If it turns both ways or neither way, replace the starter clutch.

11 Remove the Allen screws (inside the rotor) that secure the starter clutch to the back of the rotor **(see illustration 31.4)**. Take the starter clutch off.

12 Assembly is the reverse of disassembly. Be sure the starter clutch is facing the right way **(see illustration)**. Use non-permanent thread locking agent on the threads of the starter clutch bolts and tighten them to the torque listed in this Chapter's Specifications.

Installation

13 Clean all dirt from the crankshaft and the inside of the rotor with high flash point solvent.

14 Position the rotor on the engine. Install the bolt, tightening it to the torque listed in this Chapter's Specifications.

15 The remainder of installation is the reverse of the removal steps. Before you install the right crankcase cover, make sure the rotor magnets haven't picked up any pieces of metal that could damage the alternator.

32 Alternator - coil replacement

1   Remove the alternator cover (see Section 31).

2   To remove the stator coils, remove the stator screws **(see illustrations)**, remove the wiring harness retainer and lift the stator coils out of the alternator housing.

3   To remove the charging coil and pickup coil or crankshaft position sensor, remove their screws and take them out of the cover **(see illustrations 32.2a or 32.2b)**.

4   Installation is the reverse of the removal steps. Tighten the stator screws to the torque listed in this Chapter's Specifications.

33 Wiring diagrams

Prior to troubleshooting a circuit, check the fuses to make sure they're in good condition. Make sure the battery is fully charged and check the cable connections.

When checking a circuit, make sure all connectors are clean, with no broken or loose terminals or wires. When disconnecting a connector, don't pull on the wires - pull only on the connector housings themselves.

32.2a Remove the screws (arrows) and lift the retainer off of the tab (A) to detach the coils - this is an Intruder/S50 . . .

32.2b . . . and this is a C50/M50

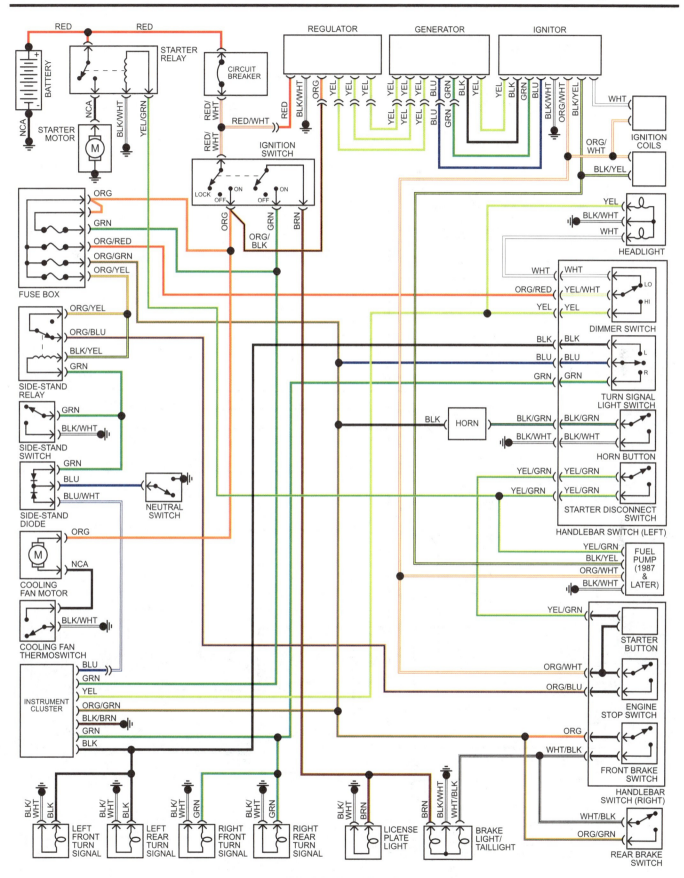

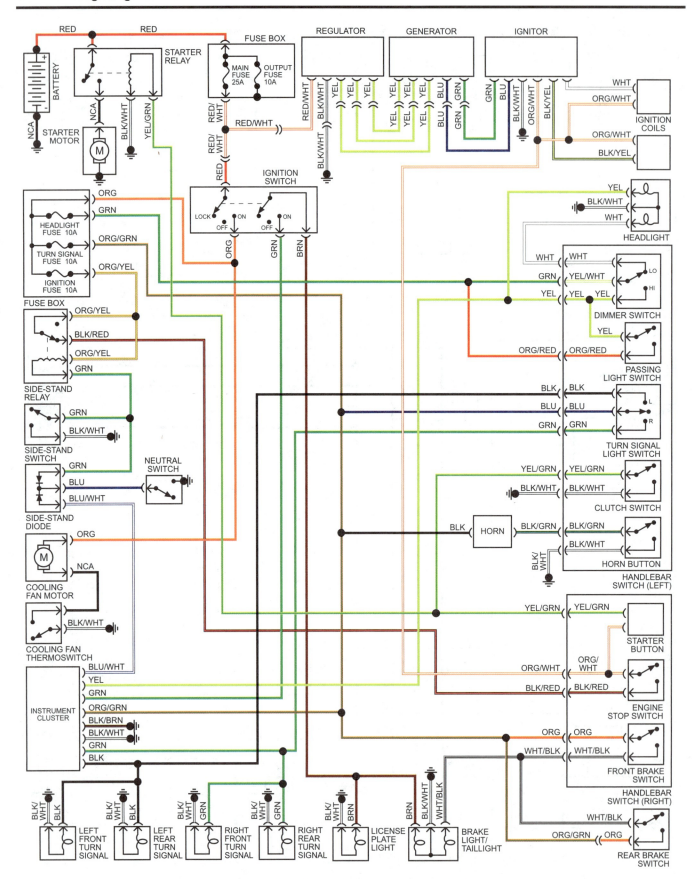

1992 and later Suzuki Intruder and Boulevard S50

Wiring diagrams 9•25

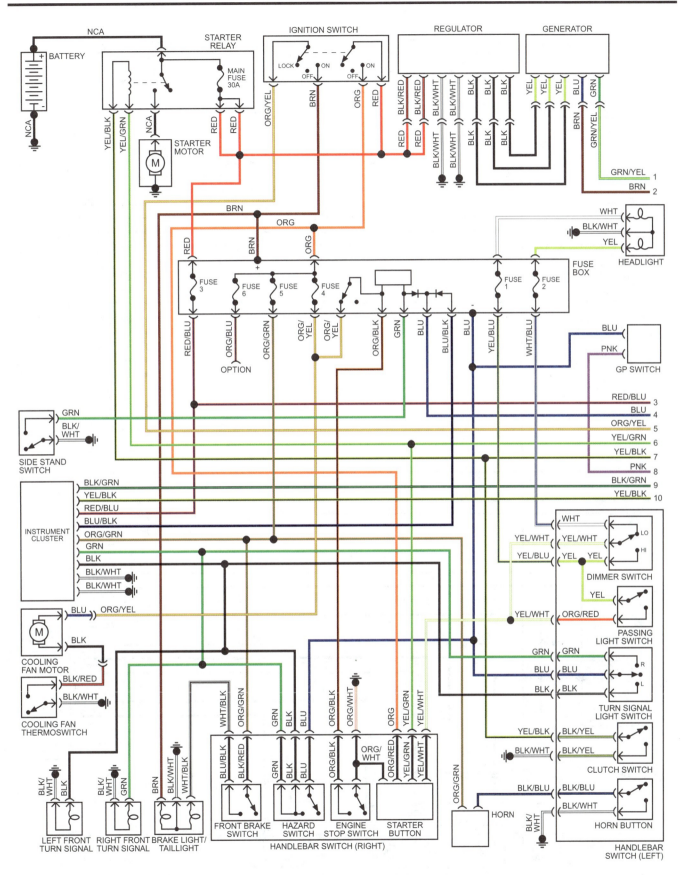

2005 and later Boulevard C50 and M50 (page 1 of 2)

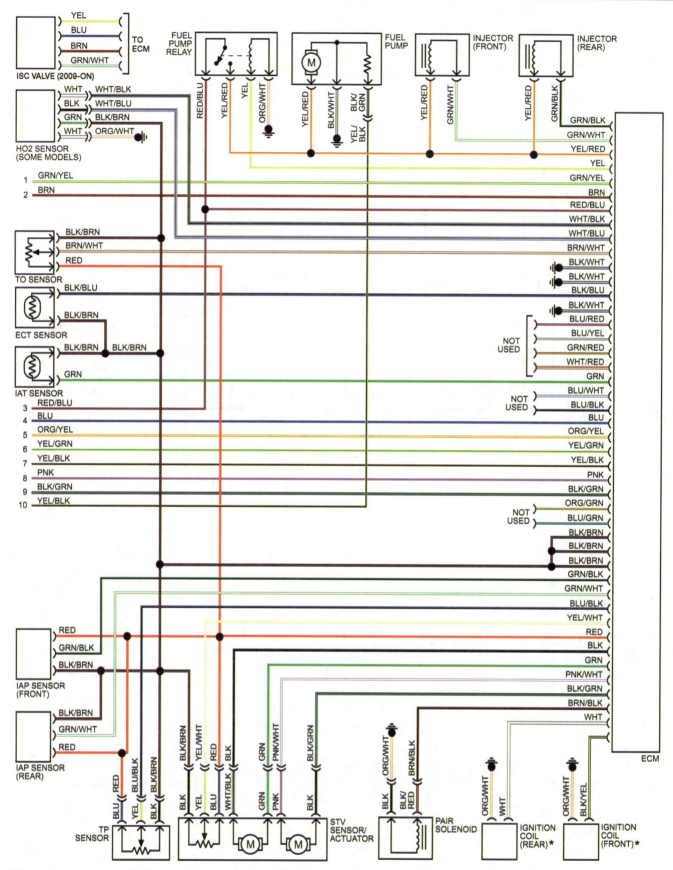

2005 and later Boulevard C50 and M50 (page 2 of 2) - *2009-on wire colors: front main coil, BLK/YEL and ORH/WHT; front sub coil, WHT and ORG/WHT; rear main coil, BLK/BLU and ORG/WHT; rear sub coil, BLK/RED and ORG/WHT

Reference REF•1

Dimensions and Weights .... **REF•1**	Troubleshooting .... **REF•27**
Tools and Workshop Tips.................. **REF•4**	Troubleshooting Equipment .... **REF•36**
Conversion Factors .... **REF•22**	Technical Terms Explained................. **REF•41**
Motorcycle Chemicals and Lubricants........ **REF•23**	Index.................................. **REF•49**
Storage............................... **REF•24**	

Dimensions and weights

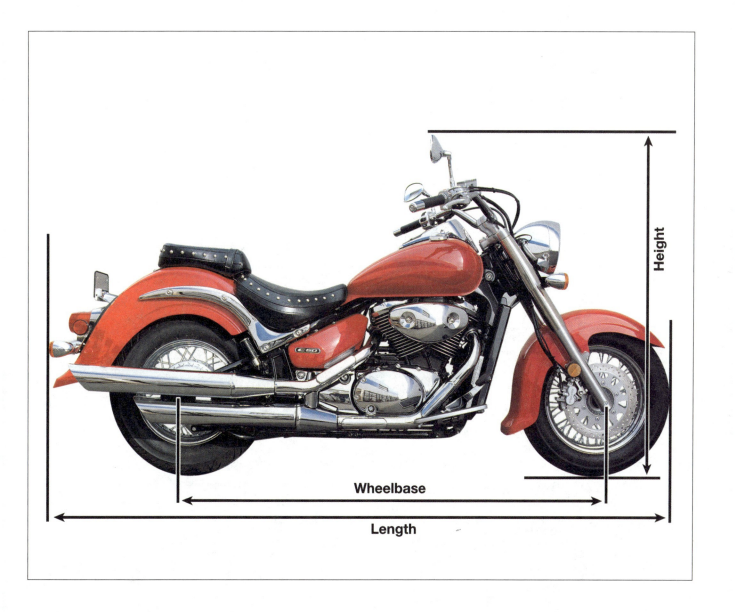

Wheelbase
Intruder and S50
    1985 and 1986 .... 1545 mm (61.0 inches)
    1987 and later .... 1560 mm (61.4 inches)
Marauder .... 1645 mm (64.8 inches)
Volusia and C50
    2002 and earlier .... 1650 mm (64.9 inches)
    2003 and later .... 1655 mm (65.2 inches)
M50 .... 1655 mm (65.2 inches)

Overall length
Intruder and S50
    1985 and 1986 .... 2225 mm (87.6 inches)
    1987 .... 2235 mm (88.0 inches)
    1988 through 1991 .... 2255 mm (88.78 inches)
    1992 through 1997
        Switzerland .... 2280 mm (89.8 inches)
        All others .... 2255 mm (88.8 inches)
    1998 and 1999
        Switzerland .... 2290 mm (89.8 inches)
        All others .... 2255 mm (88.8 inches)
    2000 and later .... 2250 mm (88.6 inches)
Marauder
    1997 through 2003
        Europe .... 2405 mm (94.7 inches)
        All others .... 2365 mm (93.1 inches)
    2004 .... 2405 mm (94.7 inches)
Volusia and C50
    2008 and earlier .... 2510 mm (98.8 inches)
    2009 and later .... 2500 mm (98.4 inches)
M50 .... 2370 mm (93.3 inches)

Overall width
Intruder and S50
    1985 through 1991
        GLF, GLEF .... 710 mm (28.0 inches)
        GLP, GLEP .... 750 mm (29.5 inches)
    1992 through 1999 .... 770 mm (30.3 inches)
    2000 through 2004 .... 885 mm (34.8 inches)
    2005 and later .... 765 mm (30.1 inches)
Marauder .... 750 mm (29.5 inches)
Volusia and C50
    2006 and earlier .... 985 mm (38.8 inches)
    2007 and later .... 970 mm (38.3 inches)
M50 .... 920 mm (36.2 inches)

Overall height
Intruder and S50
    1985 and 1986
        GLF, GLEF .... 1000 mm (43.3 inches)
        GLP, GLEP .... 1085 mm (46.7 inches)
    1987
        GLF, GLEF .... 1110 mm (43.7 inches)
        GLP, GLEP .... 1190 mm (46.9 inches)
    1988 through 1991
        GLF, GLEF .... 1115 mm (43.9 inches)
        GLP, GLEP .... 1220 mm (48.0 inches)
    1992 through 1997 .... 1200 mm (47.2 inches)
    1998 and 1999 .... 1215 mm (47.8 inches)
    2000 through 2004 .... 1180 mm (46.5 inches)
    2005 and later .... 1125 mm (44.3 inches)
Marauder .... 1110 mm (43.7 inches)
Volusia and C50
    2006 and earlier .... 1110 mm (43.7 inches)
    2007 and later .... 1105 mm (43.5 inches)
M50 .... 1125 mm (44.3 inches)

Reference REF•3

Minimum ground clearance
Intruder and S50
- 1985 and 1986 .... 125 mm (4.9 inches)
- 1987 .... 130 mm (5.1 inches)
- 1988 through 1991 .... 135 mm (5.3 inches)
- 1992 and later .... 125 mm (4.9 inches)

Marauder .... 135 mm (5.3 inches)
Volusia and C50 .... 140 mm (5.5 inches)
M50 .... 140 mm (5.5 inches)

Weight (dry)
Intruder and S50
- 1985
  - GLF .... 185 kg (408 lbs)
  - GLP .... 186 kg (410 lbs)
- 1986
  - GLF
    - Spoke wheels .... 185 kg (408 lbs)
    - Cast wheels .... 187 kg (412 lbs)
  - GLP
    - Spoke wheels .... 186 kg (410 lbs)
    - Cast wheels .... 188 kg (414 lbs)
- 1987
  - GLF .... 185 kg (408 lbs)
  - GLEF .... 188 kg (414 lbs)
  - GLP .... 186 kg (410 lbs)
  - GLEP .... 189 kg (416 lbs)
- 1988 through 1991
  - GLF .... 198 kg (436 lbs)
  - GLP .... 199 kg (438 lbs)
- 1992 through 2000
  - California .... 201 kg (443 lbs)
  - All others .... 200 kg (440 lbs)
- 2001 and later
  - California .... 202 kg (445 lbs)
  - All others .... 201 kg (443 lbs)

Marauder .... 207 kg (456 lbs)
Volusia and C50
- 2001 and 2002 .... 239 kg (526 lbs)
- 2003 and 2004 .... 241 kg (531 lbs)
- 2005 through 2008 .... 246 kg (542 lbs)
- 2009 and later (curb weight) .... 277 kg (611 lbs)

M50 .... 247 kg (545 lbs)

Seat height
Intruder and S50
- 1985 through 1987 .... Not specified
- 1988 through 1991 .... 685 mm (26.9 inches)
- 1992 through 1995
  - Germany .... 755 mm (29.7 inches)
  - All others .... 685 mm (27.0 inches)
- 1996 and later .... 700 mm (27.6 inches)

Marauder .... 700 mm (27.6 inches)
Volusia and C50 .... 700 mm (27.6 inches)
M50 .... 700 mm (27.6 inches)

Fuel tank capacity
VS700/750/800 Intruder, Boulevard S50
- Capacity (including reserve), all except California .... 12 liters (3.2 US gal, 2.7 Imp gal)
- Capacity (including reserve), California .... 11 liters (2.9 US gal, 2.4 Imp gal)
- Reserve (all models) .... 3.0 liters (3.4 US qt, 5.9 Imp pt)

VL800 Volusia
- Capacity, including reserve .... 17 liters (4.5 US gal, 3.7 Imp gal)
- Reserve .... Not specified

VL800 Boulevard C50
- Capacity, including reserve .... 15.5 liters (4.1 US gal, 3.4 Imp gal)
- Reserve .... Not specified

VZ800 Marauder
- Capacity, including reserve .... 13 liters (3.4 US gal, 2.9 Imp gal)
- Reserve .... Not specified

VZ800 Boulevard M50
- Capacity (including reserve), all except California .... 15.5 liters (4.1 US gal, 3.4 Imp gal)
- Capacity (including reserve), California .... 15.0 liters (4.0 US gal, 3.3 Imp gal)
- Reserve (all models) .... 3.0 liters (3.4 US qt, 5.9 Imp pt)

REF•4 Tools and Workshop Tips

Buying tools

A good set of tools is a fundamental requirement for servicing and repairing a motorcycle. Although there will be an initial expense in building up enough tools for servicing, this will soon be offset by the savings made by doing the job yourself. As experience and confidence grow, additional tools can be added to enable the repair and overhaul of the motorcycle. Many of the special tools are expensive and not often used so it may be preferable to rent them, or for a group of friends or motorcycle club to join in the purchase.

As a rule, it is better to buy more expensive, good quality tools. Cheaper tools are likely to wear out faster and need to be replaced more often, nullifying the original savings.

Warning: To avoid the risk of a poor quality tool breaking in use, causing injury or damage to the component being worked on, always aim to purchase tools which meet the relevant national safety standards.

The following lists of tools do not represent the manufacturer's service tools, but serve as a guide to help the owner decide which tools are needed for this level of work. In addition, items such as an electric drill, hacksaw, files, soldering iron and a workbench equipped with a vise, may be needed. Although not classed as tools, a selection of bolts, screws, nuts, washers and pieces of tubing always come in useful.

For more information about tools, refer to the Haynes *Motorcycle Workshop Practice Techbook* (Bk. No. 3470).

Manufacturer's service tools

Inevitably certain tasks require the use of a service tool. Where possible an alternative tool or method of approach is recommended, but sometimes there is no option if personal injury or damage to the component is to be avoided. Where required, service tools are referred to in the relevant procedure.

Service tools can usually only be purchased from a motorcycle dealer and are identified by a part number. Some of the commonly-used tools, such as rotor pullers, are available in aftermarket form from mail-order motorcycle tool and accessory suppliers.

Maintenance and minor repair tools

1 Set of flat-bladed screwdrivers
2 Set of Phillips head screwdrivers
3 Combination open-end and box wrenches
4 Socket set (3/8 inch or 1/2 inch drive)
5 Set of Allen keys or bits
6 Set of Torx keys or bits
7 Pliers, cutters and self-locking grips (vise grips)
8 Adjustable wrenches
9 C-spanners
10 Tread depth gauge and tire pressure gauge
11 Cable oiler clamp
12 Feeler gauges
13 Spark plug gap measuring tool
14 Spark plug wrench or deep plug sockets
15 Wire brush and emery paper
16 Calibrated syringe, measuring cup and funnel
17 Oil filter adapters
18 Oil drainer can or tray
19 Pump type oil can
20 Grease gun
21 Straight-edge and steel rule
22 Continuity tester
23 Battery charger
24 Hydrometer (for battery specific gravity check)
25 Anti-freeze tester (for liquid-cooled engines)

Tools and Workshop Tips

Repair and overhaul tools

1 Torque wrench (small and mid-ranges)
2 Conventional, plastic or soft-faced hammers
3 Impact driver set
4 Vernier caliper
5 Snap-ring pliers (internal and external, or combination)
6 Set of cold chisels and punches
7 Selection of pullers
8 Breaker bars
9 Chain breaking/riveting tool set
10 Wire stripper and crimper tool
11 Multimeter (measures amps, volts and ohms)
12 Stroboscope (for dynamic timing checks)
13 Hose clamp (wingnut type shown)
14 Clutch holding tool
15 One-man brake/clutch bleeder kit

Special tools

 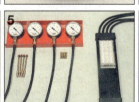  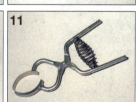 
   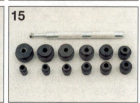

1 Micrometers (external type)
2 Telescoping gauges
3 Dial gauge
4 Cylinder compression gauge
5 Vacuum gauges (left) or manometer (right)
6 Oil pressure gauge
7 Plastigage kit
8 Valve spring compressor (4-stroke engines)
9 Piston pin drawbolt tool
10 Piston ring removal and installation tool
11 Piston ring clamp
12 Cylinder bore hone (stone type shown)
13 Stud extractor
14 Screw extractor set
15 Bearing driver set

Tools and Workshop Tips

1 Workshop equipment and facilities

The workbench

● Work is made much easier by raising the bike up on a ramp - components are much more accessible if raised to waist level. The hydraulic or pneumatic types seen in the dealer's workshop are a sound investment if you undertake a lot of repairs or overhauls **(see illustration 1.1)**.

1.1 Hydraulic motorcycle ramp

● If raised off ground level, the bike must be supported on the ramp to avoid it falling. Most ramps incorporate a front wheel locating clamp which can be adjusted to suit different diameter wheels. When tightening the clamp, take care not to mark the wheel rim or damage the tire - use wood blocks on each side to prevent this.

● Secure the bike to the ramp using tie-downs **(see illustration 1.2)**. If the bike has only a sidestand, and hence leans at a dangerous angle when raised, support the bike on an auxiliary stand.

1.2 Tie-downs are used around the passenger footrests to secure the bike

● Auxiliary (paddock) stands are widely available from mail order companies or motorcycle dealers and attach either to the wheel axle or swingarm pivot **(see illustration 1.3)**. If the motorcycle has a centerstand, you can support it under the crankcase to prevent it toppling while either wheel is removed **(see illustration 1.4)**.

1.3 This auxiliary stand attaches to the swingarm pivot

1.4 Always use a block of wood between the engine and jack head when supporting the engine in this way

Fumes and fire

● Refer to the Safety first! page at the beginning of the manual for full details. Make sure your workshop is equipped with a fire extinguisher suitable for fuel-related fires (Class B fire - flammable liquids) - it is not sufficient to have a water-filled extinguisher.

● Always ensure adequate ventilation is available. Unless an exhaust gas extraction system is available for use, ensure that the engine is run outside of the workshop.

● If working on the fuel system, make sure the workshop is ventilated to avoid a build-up of fumes. This applies equally to fume build-up when charging a battery. Do not smoke or allow anyone else to smoke in the workshop.

Fluids

● If you need to drain fuel from the tank, store it in an approved container marked as suitable for the storage of gasoline **(see illustration 1.5)**. Do not store fuel in glass jars or bottles.

● Use proprietary engine degreasers or solvents which have a high flash-point, such as kerosene, for cleaning off oil, grease and dirt - never use gasoline for cleaning. Wear rubber gloves when handling solvent and engine degreaser. The fumes from certain solvents can be dangerous - always work in a well-ventilated area.

Dust, eye and hand protection

● Protect your lungs from inhalation of dust particles by wearing a filtering mask over the nose and mouth. Many frictional materials still contain asbestos which is dangerous to your health. Protect your eyes from spouts of liquid and sprung components by wearing a pair of protective goggles **(see illustration 1.6)**.

1.6 A fire extinguisher, goggles, mask and protective gloves should be at hand in the workshop

● Protect your hands from contact with solvents, fuel and oils by wearing rubber gloves. Alternatively apply a barrier cream to your hands before starting work. If handling hot components or fluids, wear suitable gloves to protect your hands from scalding and burns.

What to do with old fluids

● Old cleaning solvent, fuel, coolant and oils should not be poured down domestic drains or onto the ground. Package the fluid up in old oil containers, label it accordingly, and take it to a garage or disposal facility. Contact your local disposal company for location of such sites.

1.5 Use an approved can only for storing gasoline

> *Note: It is illegal to dump oil down the drain. Check with your local auto parts store, disposal facility or environmental agency to see if they accept the oil for recycling.*

Tools and Workshop Tips

2 Fasteners - screws, bolts and nuts

Fastener types and applications

Bolts and screws

● Fastener head types are either of hexagonal, Torx or splined design, with internal and external versions of each type (see illustrations 2.1 and 2.2); splined head fasteners are not in common use on motorcycles. The conventional slotted or Phillips head design is used for certain screws. Bolt or screw length is always measured from the underside of the head to the end of the item (see illustration 2.11).

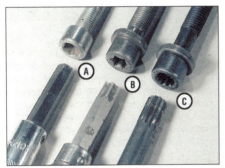

2.1 Internal hexagon/Allen (A), Torx (B) and splined (C) fasteners, with corresponding bits

2.2 External Torx (A), splined (B) and hexagon (C) fasteners, with corresponding sockets

● Certain fasteners on the motorcycle have a tensile marking on their heads, the higher the marking the stronger the fastener. High tensile fasteners generally carry a 10 or higher marking. Never replace a high tensile fastener with one of a lower tensile strength.

Washers (see illustration 2.3)

● Plain washers are used between a fastener head and a component to prevent damage to the component or to spread the load when torque is applied. Plain washers can also be used as spacers or shims in certain assemblies. Copper or aluminum plain washers are often used as sealing washers on drain plugs.

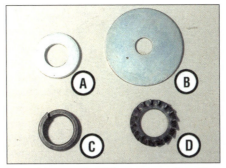

2.3 Plain washer (A), penny washer (B), spring washer (C) and serrated washer (D)

● The split-ring spring washer works by applying axial tension between the fastener head and component. If flattened, it is fatigued and must be replaced. If a plain (flat) washer is used on the fastener, position the spring washer between the fastener and the plain washer.
● Serrated star type washers dig into the fastener and component faces, preventing loosening. They are often used on electrical ground connections to the frame.
● Cone type washers (sometimes called Belleville) are conical and when tightened apply axial tension between the fastener head and component. They must be installed with the dished side against the component and often carry an OUTSIDE marking on their outer face. If flattened, they are fatigued and must be replaced.
● Tab washers are used to lock plain nuts or bolts on a shaft. A portion of the tab washer is bent up hard against one flat of the nut or bolt to prevent it loosening. Due to the tab washer being deformed in use, a new tab washer should be used every time it is removed.
● Wave washers are used to take up endfloat on a shaft. They provide light springing and prevent excessive side-to-side play of a component. Can be found on rocker arm shafts.

Nuts and cotter pins

● Conventional plain nuts are usually six-sided (see illustration 2.4). They are sized by thread diameter and pitch. High tensile nuts carry a number on one end to denote their tensile strength.

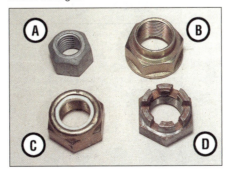

2.4 Plain nut (A), shouldered locknut (B), nylon insert nut (C) and castellated nut (D)

● Self-locking nuts either have a nylon insert, or two spring metal tabs, or a shoulder which is staked into a groove in the shaft - their advantage over conventional plain nuts is a resistance to loosening due to vibration. The nylon insert type can be used a number of times, but must be replaced when the friction of the nylon insert is reduced, i.e. when the nut spins freely on the shaft. The spring tab type can be reused unless the tabs are damaged. The shouldered type must be replaced every time it is removed.
● Cotter pins are used to lock a castellated nut to a shaft or to prevent loosening of a plain nut. Common applications are wheel axles and brake torque arms. Because the cotter pin arms are deformed to lock around the nut a new cotter pin must always be used on installation - always use the correct size cotter pin which will fit snugly in the shaft hole. Make sure the cotter pin arms are correctly located around the nut (see illustrations 2.5 and 2.6).

2.5 Bend cotter pin arms as shown (arrows) to secure a castellated nut

2.6 Bend cotter pin arms as shown to secure a plain nut

Caution: If the castellated nut slots do not align with the shaft hole after tightening to the torque setting, tighten the nut until the next slot aligns with the hole - never loosen the nut to align its slot.

● R-pins (shaped like the letter R), or slip pins as they are sometimes called, are sprung and can be reused if they are otherwise in good condition. Always install R-pins with their closed end facing forwards (see illustration 2.7).

REF•8 Tools and Workshop Tips

2.7 Correct fitting of R-pin. Arrow indicates forward direction

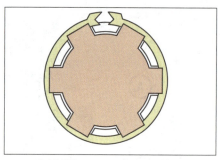

2.10 Align snap-ring opening with shaft channel

2.12 Using a thread gauge to measure pitch

Snap-rings (see illustration 2.8)

● Snap-rings (sometimes called circlips) are used to retain components on a shaft or in a housing and have corresponding external or internal ears to permit removal. Parallel-sided (machined) snap-rings can be installed either way round in their groove, whereas stamped snap-rings (which have a chamfered edge on one face) must be installed with the chamfer facing away from the direction of thrust load (see illustration 2.9).

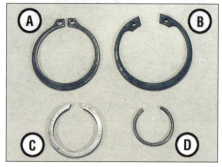

2.8 External stamped snap-ring (A), internal stamped snap-ring (B), machined snap-ring (C) and wire snap-ring (D)

● Always use snap-ring pliers to remove and install snap-rings; expand or compress them just enough to remove them. After installation, rotate the snap-ring in its groove to ensure it is securely seated. If installing a snap-ring on a splined shaft, always align its opening with a shaft channel to ensure the snap-ring ends are well supported and unlikely to catch (see illustration 2.10).

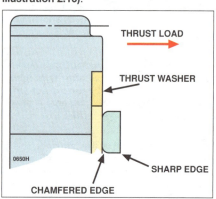

2.9 Correct fitting of a stamped snap-ring

● Snap-rings can wear due to the thrust of components and become loose in their grooves, with the subsequent danger of becoming dislodged in operation. For this reason, replacement is advised every time a snap-ring is disturbed.

● Wire snap-rings are commonly used as piston pin retaining clips. If a removal tang is provided, long-nosed pliers can be used to dislodge them, otherwise careful use of a small flat-bladed screwdriver is necessary. Wire snap-rings should be replaced every time they are disturbed.

Thread diameter and pitch

● Diameter of a male thread (screw, bolt or stud) is the outside diameter of the threaded portion (see illustration 2.11). Most motorcycle manufacturers use the ISO (International Standards Organization) metric system expressed in millimeters. For example, M6 refers to a 6 mm diameter thread. Sizing is the same for nuts, except that the thread diameter is measured across the valleys of the nut.

● Pitch is the distance between the peaks of the thread (see illustration 2.11). It is expressed in millimeters, thus a common bolt size may be expressed as 6.0 x 1.0 mm (6 mm thread diameter and 1 mm pitch). Generally pitch increases in proportion to thread diameter, although there are always exceptions.

● Thread diameter and pitch are related for conventional fastener applications and the accompanying table can be used as a guide. Additionally, the AF (Across Flats), wrench or socket size dimension of the bolt or nut (see illustration 2.11) is linked to thread and pitch specification. Thread pitch can be measured with a thread gauge (see illustration 2.12).

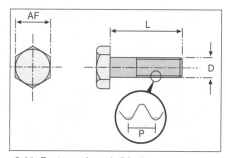

2.11 Fastener length (L), thread diameter (D), thread pitch (P) and head size (AF)

AF size	Thread diameter x pitch (mm)
8 mm	M5 x 0.8
8 mm	M6 x 1.0
10 mm	M6 x 1.0
12 mm	M8 x 1.25
14 mm	M10 x 1.25
17 mm	M12 x 1.25

● The threads of most fasteners are of the right-hand type, ie they are turned clockwise to tighten and counterclockwise to loosen. The reverse situation applies to left-hand thread fasteners, which are turned counterclockwise to tighten and clockwise to loosen. Left-hand threads are used where rotation of a component might loosen a conventional right-hand thread fastener.

Seized fasteners

● Corrosion of external fasteners due to water or reaction between two dissimilar metals can occur over a period of time. It will build up sooner in wet conditions or in countries where salt is used on the roads during the winter. If a fastener is severely corroded it is likely that normal methods of removal will fail and result in its head being ruined. When you attempt removal, the fastener thread should be heard to crack free and unscrew easily - if it doesn't, stop there before damaging something.

● A smart tap on the head of the fastener will often succeed in breaking free corrosion which has occurred in the threads (see illustration 2.13).

● An aerosol penetrating fluid (such as WD-40) applied the night beforehand may work its way down into the thread and ease removal. Depending on the location, you may be able to make up a modeling-clay well around the fastener head and fill it with penetrating fluid.

2.13 A sharp tap on the head of a fastener will often break free a corroded thread

Tools and Workshop Tips

- If you are working on an engine internal component, corrosion will most likely not be a problem due to the well lubricated environment. However, components can be very tight and an impact driver is a useful tool in freeing them **(see illustration 2.14)**.

2.14 Using an impact driver to free a fastener

- Where corrosion has occurred between dissimilar metals (e.g. steel and aluminum alloy), the application of heat to the fastener head will create a disproportionate expansion rate between the two metals and break the seizure caused by the corrosion. Whether heat can be applied depends on the location of the fastener - any surrounding components likely to be damaged must first be removed **(see illustration 2.15)**. Heat can be applied using a paint stripper heat gun or clothes iron, or by immersing the component in boiling water - wear protective gloves to prevent scalding or burns to the hands.

2.15 Using heat to free a seized fastener

- As a last resort, it is possible to use a hammer and cold chisel to work the fastener head unscrewed **(see illustration 2.16)**. This will damage the fastener, but more importantly extreme care must be taken not to damage the surrounding component.

> **Caution:** Remember that the component being secured is generally of more value than the bolt, nut or screw - when the fastener is freed, do not unscrew it with force, instead work the fastener back and forth when resistance is felt to prevent thread damage.

2.16 Using a hammer and chisel to free a seized fastener

Broken fasteners and damaged heads

- If the shank of a broken bolt or screw is accessible you can grip it with self-locking grips. The knurled wheel type stud extractor tool or self-gripping stud puller tool is particularly useful for removing the long studs which screw into the cylinder mouth surface of the crankcase or bolts and screws from which the head has broken off **(see illustration 2.17)**. Studs can also be removed by locking two nuts together on the threaded end of the stud and using a wrench on the lower nut **(see illustration 2.18)**.

2.17 Using a stud extractor tool to remove a broken crankcase stud

2.18 Two nuts can be locked together to unscrew a stud from a component

- A bolt or screw which has broken off below or level with the casing must be extracted using a screw extractor set. Centerpunch the fastener to centralize the drill bit, then drill a hole in the fastener **(see illustration 2.19)**. Select a drill bit which is approximately half to three-quarters the diameter of the fastener and drill to a depth which will accommodate the extractor. Use the largest size extractor possible, but avoid leaving too small a wall thickness otherwise the extractor will merely force the fastener walls outwards wedging it in the casing thread.

- If a spiral type extractor is used, thread it counterclockwise into the fastener. As it is screwed in, it will grip the fastener and unscrew it from the casing **(see illustration 2.20)**.

2.19 When using a screw extractor, first drill a hole in the fastener . . .

2.20 . . . then thread the extractor counterclockwise into the fastener

- If a taper type extractor is used, tap it into the fastener so that it is firmly wedged in place. Unscrew the extractor (counter-clockwise) to draw the fastener out.

>  **Warning:** Stud extractors are very hard and may break off in the fastener if care is not taken - ask a machine shop about spark erosion if this happens.

- Alternatively, the broken bolt/screw can be drilled out and the hole retapped for an oversize bolt/screw or a diamond-section thread insert. It is essential that the drilling is carried out squarely and to the correct depth, otherwise the casing may be ruined - if in doubt, entrust the work to a machine shop.
- Bolts and nuts with rounded corners cause the correct size wrench or socket to slip when force is applied. Of the types of wrench/socket available always use a six-point type rather than an eight or twelve-point type - better grip

REF•10 Tools and Workshop Tips

2.21 Comparison of surface drive box wrench (left) with 12-point type (right)

is obtained. Surface drive wrenches grip the middle of the hex flats, rather than the corners, and are thus good in cases of damaged heads **(see illustration 2.21)**.

- Slotted-head or Phillips-head screws are often damaged by the use of the wrong size screwdriver. Allen-head and Torx-head screws are much less likely to sustain damage. If enough of the screw head is exposed you can use a hacksaw to cut a slot in its head and then use a conventional flat-bladed screwdriver to remove it. Alternatively use a hammer and cold chisel to tap the head of the fastener around to loosen it. Always replace damaged fasteners with new ones, preferably Torx or Allen-head type.

HAYNES HiNT

A dab of valve grinding compound between the screw head and screwdriver tip will often give a good grip.

Thread repair

- Threads (particularly those in aluminum alloy components) can be damaged by overtightening, being assembled with dirt in the threads, or from a component working loose and vibrating. Eventually the thread will fail completely, and it will be impossible to tighten the fastener.
- If a thread is damaged or clogged with old locking compound it can be renovated with a thread repair tool (thread chaser) **(see illustrations 2.22 and 2.23)**; special thread

2.22 A thread repair tool being used to correct an internal thread

2.23 A thread repair tool being used to correct an external thread

chasers are available for spark plug hole threads. The tool will not cut a new thread, but clean and true the original thread. Make sure that you use the correct diameter and pitch tool. Similarly, external threads can be cleaned up with a die or a thread restorer file **(see illustration 2.24)**.

2.24 Using a thread restorer file

- It is possible to drill out the old thread and retap the component to the next thread size. This will work where there is enough surrounding material and a new bolt or screw can be obtained. Sometimes, however, this is not possible - such as where the bolt/screw passes through another component which must also be suitably modified, also in cases where a spark plug or oil drain plug cannot be obtained in a larger diameter thread size.
- The diamond-section thread insert (often known by its popular trade name of Heli-Coil) is a simple and effective method of replacing the thread and retaining the original size. A kit can be purchased which contains the tap, insert and installing tool **(see illustration 2.25)**. Drill out the damaged thread with the size drill specified **(see illustration 2.26)**. Carefully retap the thread **(see illustration 2.27)**. Install the

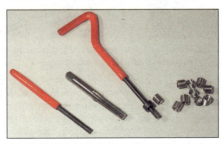

2.25 Obtain a thread insert kit to suit the thread diameter and pitch required

2.26 To install a thread insert, first drill out the original thread . . .

2.27 . . . tap a new thread . . .

2.28 . . . fit insert on the installing tool . . .

2.29 . . . and thread into the component . . .

2.30 . . . break off the tang when complete

insert on the installing tool and thread it slowly into place using a light downward pressure **(see illustrations 2.28 and 2.29)**. When positioned between a 1/4 and 1/2 turn below the surface withdraw the installing tool and use the break-off tool to press down on the tang, breaking it off **(see illustration 2.30)**.

- There are epoxy thread repair kits on the market which can rebuild stripped internal threads, although this repair should not be used on high load-bearing components.

Tools and Workshop Tips

Thread locking and sealing compounds

● Locking compounds are used in locations where the fastener is prone to loosening due to vibration or on important safety-related items which might cause loss of control of the motorcycle if they fail. It is also used where important fasteners cannot be secured by other means such as lockwashers or cotter pins.

● Before applying locking compound, make sure that the threads (internal and external) are clean and dry with all old compound removed. Select a compound to suit the component being secured - a non-permanent general locking and sealing type is suitable for most applications, but a high strength type is needed for permanent fixing of studs in castings. Apply a drop or two of the compound to the first few threads of the fastener, then thread it into place and tighten to the specified torque. Do not apply excessive thread locking compound otherwise the thread may be damaged on subsequent removal.

● Certain fasteners are impregnated with a dry film type coating of locking compound on their threads. Always replace this type of fastener if disturbed.

● Anti-seize compounds, such as copper-based greases, can be applied to protect threads from seizure due to extreme heat and corrosion. A common instance is spark plug threads and exhaust system fasteners.

3 Measuring tools and gauges

Feeler gauges

● Feeler gauges (or blades) are used for measuring small gaps and clearances **(see illustration 3.1)**. They can also be used to measure endfloat (sideplay) of a component on a shaft where access is not possible with a dial gauge.

● Feeler gauge sets should be treated with care and not bent or damaged. They are etched with their size on one face. Keep them clean and very lightly oiled to prevent corrosion build-up.

3.1 Feeler gauges are used for measuring small gaps and clearances - thickness is marked on one face of gauge

● When measuring a clearance, select a gauge which is a light sliding fit between the two components. You may need to use two gauges together to measure the clearance accurately.

Micrometers

● A micrometer is a precision tool capable of measuring to 0.01 or 0.001 of a millimeter. It should always be stored in its case and not in the general toolbox. It must be kept clean and never dropped, otherwise its frame or measuring anvils could be distorted resulting in inaccurate readings.

● External micrometers are used for measuring outside diameters of components and have many more applications than internal micrometers. Micrometers are available in different size ranges, typically 0 to 25 mm, 25 to 50 mm, and upwards in 25 mm steps; some large micrometers have interchangeable anvils to allow a range of measurements to be taken. Generally the largest precision measurement you are likely to take on a motorcycle is the piston diameter.

● Internal micrometers (or bore micrometers) are used for measuring inside diameters, such as valve guides and cylinder bores. Telescoping gauges and small hole gauges are used in conjunction with an external micrometer, whereas the more expensive internal micrometers have their own measuring device.

External micrometer

Note: *The conventional analogue type instrument is described. Although much easier to read, digital micrometers are considerably more expensive.*

● Always check the calibration of the micrometer before use. With the anvils closed (0 to 25 mm type) or set over a test gauge

3.2 Check micrometer calibration before use

(for the larger types) the scale should read zero **(see illustration 3.2)**; make sure that the anvils (and test piece) are clean first. Any discrepancy can be adjusted by referring to the instructions supplied with the tool. Remember that the micrometer is a precision measuring tool - don't force the anvils closed, use the ratchet (4) on the end of the micrometer to close it. In this way, a measured force is always applied.

● To use, first make sure that the item being measured is clean. Place the anvil of the micrometer (1) against the item and use the thimble (2) to bring the spindle (3) lightly into contact with the other side of the item **(see illustration 3.3)**. Don't tighten the thimble down because this will damage the micrometer - instead use the ratchet (4) on the end of the micrometer. The ratchet mechanism applies a measured force preventing damage to the instrument.

● The micrometer is read by referring to the linear scale on the sleeve and the annular scale on the thimble. Read off the sleeve first to obtain the base measurement, then add the fine measurement from the thimble to obtain the overall reading. The linear scale on the sleeve represents the measuring range of the micrometer (eg 0 to 25 mm). The annular scale

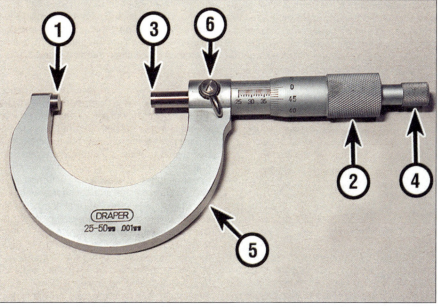

3.3 Micrometer component parts

1 Anvil
2 Thimble
3 Spindle
4 Ratchet
5 Frame
6 Locking lever

REF•12 Tools and Workshop Tips

on the thimble will be in graduations of 0.01 mm (or as marked on the frame) - one full revolution of the thimble will move 0.5 mm on the linear scale. Take the reading where the datum line on the sleeve intersects the thimble's scale. Always position the eye directly above the scale otherwise an inaccurate reading will result.

In the example shown the item measures 2.95 mm (see illustration 3.4):

Linear scale	2.00 mm
Linear scale	0.50 mm
Annular scale	0.45 mm
Total figure	**2.95 mm**

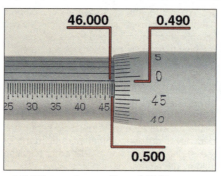

3.5 Micrometer reading of 46.99 mm on linear and annular scales . . .

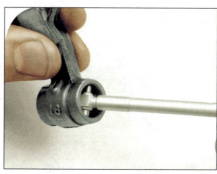

3.7 Expand the telescoping gauge in the bore, lock its position . . .

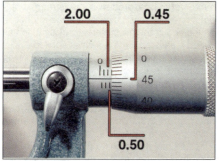

3.4 Micrometer reading of 2.95 mm

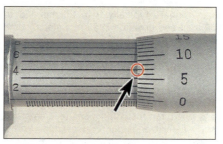

3.6 . . . and 0.004 mm on vernier scale

3.8 . . . then measure the gauge with a micrometer

Most micrometers have a locking lever (6) on the frame to hold the setting in place, allowing the item to be removed from the micrometer.
● Some micrometers have a vernier scale on their sleeve, providing an even finer measurement to be taken, in 0.001 increments of a millimeter. Take the sleeve and thimble measurement as described above, then check which graduation on the vernier scale aligns with that of the annular scale on the thimble
Note: *The eye must be perpendicular to the scale when taking the vernier reading - if necessary rotate the body of the micrometer to ensure this.* Multiply the vernier scale figure by 0.001 and add it to the base and fine measurement figures.

In the example shown the item measures 46.994 mm (see illustrations 3.5 and 3.6):

Linear scale (base)	46.000 mm
Linear scale (base)	00.500 mm
Annular scale (fine)	00.490 mm
Vernier scale	00.004 mm
Total figure	**46.994 mm**

Internal micrometer

● Internal micrometers are available for measuring bore diameters, but are expensive and unlikely to be available for home use. It is suggested that a set of telescoping gauges and small hole gauges, both of which must be used with an external micrometer, will suffice for taking internal measurements on a motorcycle.
● Telescoping gauges can be used to measure internal diameters of components. Select a gauge with the correct size range, make sure its ends are clean and insert it into the bore. Expand the gauge, then lock its position and withdraw it from the bore (see illustration 3.7). Measure across the gauge ends with a micrometer (see illustration 3.8).
● Very small diameter bores (such as valve guides) are measured with a small hole gauge. Once adjusted to a slip-fit inside the component, its position is locked and the gauge withdrawn for measurement with a micrometer (see illustrations 3.9 and 3.10).

Vernier caliper

Note: *The conventional linear and dial gauge type instruments are described. Digital types are easier to read, but are far more expensive.*
● The vernier caliper does not provide the precision of a micrometer, but is versatile in being able to measure internal and external diameters. Some types also incorporate a depth gauge. It is ideal for measuring clutch plate friction material and spring free lengths.
● To use the conventional linear scale vernier, loosen off the vernier clamp screws (1) and set its jaws over (2), or inside (3), the item to be measured (see illustration 3.11). Slide the jaw into contact, using the thumb-wheel (4) for fine movement of the sliding scale (5) then tighten the clamp screws (1). Read off the main scale (6) where the zero on the sliding scale (5) intersects it, taking the whole number to the left of the zero; this provides the base measurement. View along the sliding scale and select the division which lines up exactly

3.9 Expand the small hole gauge in the bore, lock its position . . .

3.10 . . . then measure the gauge with a micrometer

with any of the divisions on the main scale, noting that the divisions usually represents 0.02 of a millimeter. Add this fine measurement to the base measurement to obtain the total reading.

Tools and Workshop Tips

Plastigage

- Plastigage is a plastic material which can be compressed between two surfaces to measure the oil clearance between them. The width of the compressed Plastigage is measured against a calibrated scale to determine the clearance.
- Common uses of Plastigage are for measuring the clearance between crankshaft journal and main bearing inserts, between crankshaft journal and big-end bearing inserts, and between camshaft and bearing surfaces. The following example describes big-end oil clearance measurement.
- Handle the Plastigage material carefully to prevent distortion. Using a sharp knife, cut a length which corresponds with the width of the bearing being measured and place it carefully across the journal so that it is parallel with the shaft (see illustration 3.15). Carefully install both bearing shells and the connecting rod. Without rotating the rod on the journal tighten its bolts or nuts (as applicable) to the specified torque. The connecting rod and bearings are then disassembled and the crushed Plastigage examined.

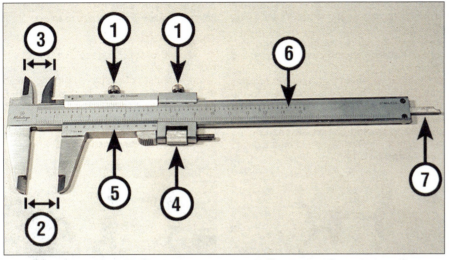

3.11 Vernier component parts (linear gauge)

1 Clamp screws
2 External jaws
3 Internal jaws
4 Thumbwheel
5 Sliding scale
6 Main scale
7 Depth gauge

In the example shown the item measures 55.92 mm (see illustration 3.12):

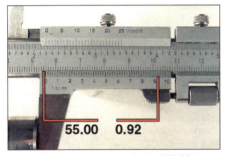

3.12 Vernier gauge reading of 55.92 mm

Base measurement	55.00 mm
Fine measurement	00.92 mm
Total figure	**55.92 mm**

- Some vernier calipers are equipped with a dial gauge for fine measurement. Before use, check that the jaws are clean, then close them fully and check that the dial gauge reads zero. If necessary adjust the gauge ring accordingly. Slacken the vernier clamp screw (1) and set its jaws over (2), or inside (3), the item to be measured (see illustration 3.13). Slide the jaws into contact, using the thumbwheel (4) for movement. Read off the main scale (5) where the edge of the sliding scale (6) intersects it, taking the whole number to the left of the zero; this provides the base measurement. Read off the needle position on the dial gauge (7) scale to provide the fine measurement; each division represents 0.05 of a millimeter. Add this fine measurement to the base measurement to obtain the total reading.

In the example shown the item measures 55.95 mm (see illustration 3.14):

Base measurement	55.00 mm
Fine measurement	00.95 mm
Total figure	**55.95 mm**

3.15 Plastigage placed across shaft journal

- Using the scale provided in the Plastigage kit, measure the width of the material to determine the oil clearance (see illustration 3.16). Always remove all traces of Plastigage after use using your fingernails.

Caution: Arriving at the correct clearance demands that the assembly is torqued correctly, according to the settings and sequence (where applicable) provided by the motorcycle manufacturer.

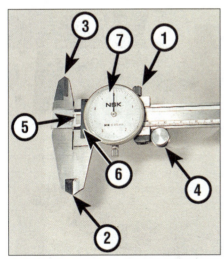

3.13 Vernier component parts (dial gauge)

1 Clamp screw
2 External jaws
3 Internal jaws
4 Thumbwheel
5 Main scale
6 Sliding scale
7 Dial gauge

3.14 Vernier gauge reading of 55.95 mm

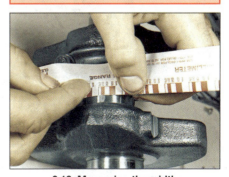

3.16 Measuring the width of the crushed Plastigage

Tools and Workshop Tips

Dial gauge or DTI (Dial Test Indicator)

● A dial gauge can be used to accurately measure small amounts of movement. Typical uses are measuring shaft runout or shaft endfloat (sideplay) and setting piston position for ignition timing on two-strokes. A dial gauge set usually comes with a range of different probes and adapters and mounting equipment.

● The gauge needle must point to zero when at rest. Rotate the ring around its periphery to zero the gauge.

● Check that the gauge is capable of reading the extent of movement in the work. Most gauges have a small dial set in the face which records whole millimeters of movement as well as the fine scale around the face periphery which is calibrated in 0.01 mm divisions. Read off the small dial first to obtain the base measurement, then add the measurement from the fine scale to obtain the total reading.

Base measurement	1.00 mm
Fine measurement	0.48 mm
Total figure	**1.48 mm**

3.17 Dial gauge reading of 1.48 mm

In the example shown the gauge reads 1.48 mm **(see illustration 3.17)**:

● If measuring shaft runout, the shaft must be supported in vee-blocks and the gauge mounted on a stand perpendicular to the shaft. Rest the tip of the gauge against the center of the shaft and rotate the shaft slowly while watching the gauge reading **(see illustration 3.18)**. Take several measurements along the length of the shaft and record the maximum gauge reading as the amount of runout in the shaft. **Note:** *The reading obtained will be total runout at that point - some manufacturers specify that the runout figure is halved to compare with their specified runout limit.*

● Endfloat (sideplay) measurement requires that the gauge is mounted securely to the surrounding component with its probe touching the end of the shaft. Using hand pressure, push and pull on the shaft noting the maximum endfloat recorded on the gauge **(see illustration 3.19)**.

3.19 Using a dial gauge to measure shaft endfloat

● A dial gauge with suitable adapters can be used to determine piston position BTDC on two-stroke engines for the purposes of ignition timing. The gauge, adapter and suitable length probe are installed in the place of the spark plug and the gauge zeroed at TDC. If the piston position is specified as 1.14 mm BTDC, rotate the engine back to 2.00 mm BTDC, then slowly forwards to 1.14 mm BTDC.

Cylinder compression gauges

● A compression gauge is used for measuring cylinder compression. Either the rubber-cone type or the threaded adapter type can be used. The latter is preferred to ensure a perfect seal against the cylinder head. A 0 to 300 psi (0 to 20 Bar) type gauge (for gasoline engines) will be suitable for motorcycles.

● The spark plug is removed and the gauge either held hard against the cylinder head (cone type) or the gauge adapter screwed into the cylinder head (threaded type) **(see illustration 3.20)**. Cylinder compression is measured with the engine turning over, but not running - carry out the compression test as described in *Troubleshooting Equipment*. The gauge will hold the reading until manually released.

Oil pressure gauge

● An oil pressure gauge is used for measuring engine oil pressure. Most gauges come with a set of adapters to fit the thread of the take-off point **(see illustration 3.21)**. If the take-off point specified by the motorcycle manufacturer is an external oil pipe union, make sure that the specified replacement union is used to prevent oil starvation.

3.21 Oil pressure gauge and take-off point adapter (arrow)

● Oil pressure is measured with the engine running (at a specific rpm) and often the manufacturer will specify pressure limits for a cold and hot engine.

Straight-edge and surface plate

● If checking the gasket face of a component for warpage, place a steel rule or precision straight-edge across the gasket face and measure any gap between the straight-edge and component with feeler gauges **(see illustration 3.22)**. Check diagonally across the component and between mounting holes **(see illustration 3.23)**.

3.22 Use a straight-edge and feeler gauges to check for warpage

3.18 Using a dial gauge to measure shaft runout

3.20 Using a rubber-cone type cylinder compression gauge

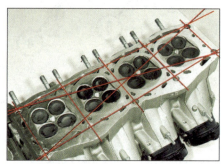

3.23 Check for warpage in these directions

Tools and Workshop Tips

- Checking individual components for warpage, such as clutch plain (metal) plates, requires a perfectly flat plate or piece of plate glass and feeler gauges.

4 Torque and leverage

What is torque?

- Torque describes the twisting force around a shaft. The amount of torque applied is determined by the distance from the center of the shaft to the end of the lever and the amount of force being applied to the end of the lever; distance multiplied by force equals torque.
- The manufacturer applies a measured torque to a bolt or nut to ensure that it will not loosen in use and to hold two components securely together without movement in the joint. The actual torque setting depends on the thread size, bolt or nut material and the composition of the components being held.
- Too little torque may cause the fastener to loosen due to vibration, whereas too much torque will distort the joint faces of the component or cause the fastener to shear off. Always stick to the specified torque setting.

Using a torque wrench

- Check the calibration of the torque wrench and make sure it has a suitable range for the job. Torque wrenches are available in Nm (Newton-meters), kgf m (kilograms-force meter), lbf ft (pounds-feet), lbf in (inch-pounds). Do not confuse lbf ft with lbf in.
- Adjust the tool to the desired torque on the scale (see illustration 4.1). If your torque wrench is not calibrated in the units specified, carefully convert the figure (see Conversion Factors). A manufacturer sometimes gives a torque setting as a range (8 to 10 Nm) rather than a single figure - in this case set the tool midway between the two settings. The same torque may be expressed as 9 Nm ± 1 Nm. Some torque wrenches have a method of locking the setting so that it isn't inadvertently altered during use.

4.1 Set the torque wrench index mark to the setting required, in this case 12 Nm

- Install the bolts/nuts in their correct location and secure them lightly. Their threads must be clean and free of any old locking compound. Unless specified the threads and flange should be dry - oiled threads are necessary in certain circumstances and the manufacturer will take this into account in the specified torque figure. Similarly, the manufacturer may also specify the application of thread-locking compound.
- Tighten the fasteners in the specified sequence until the torque wrench clicks, indicating that the torque setting has been reached. Apply the torque again to double-check the setting. Where different thread diameter fasteners secure the component, as a rule tighten the larger diameter ones first.
- When the torque wrench has been finished with, release the lock (where applicable) and fully back off its setting to zero - do not leave the torque wrench tensioned. Also, do not use a torque wrench for loosening a fastener.

Angle-tightening

- Manufacturers often specify a figure in degrees for final tightening of a fastener. This usually follows tightening to a specific torque setting.
- A degree disc can be set and attached to the socket (see illustration 4.2) or a protractor can be used to mark the angle of movement on the bolt/nut head and the surrounding casting (see illustration 4.3).

4.2 Angle tightening can be accomplished with a torque-angle gauge . . .

4.3 . . . or by marking the angle on the surrounding component

Loosening sequences

- Where more than one bolt/nut secures a component, loosen each fastener evenly a little at a time. In this way, not all the stress of the joint is held by one fastener and the components are not likely to distort.
- If a tightening sequence is provided, work in the REVERSE of this, but if not, work from the outside in, in a criss-cross sequence (see illustration 4.4).

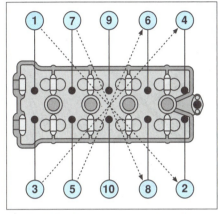

4.4 When loosening, work from the outside inwards

Tightening sequences

- If a component is held by more than one fastener it is important that the retaining bolts/nuts are tightened evenly to prevent uneven stress build-up and distortion of sealing faces. This is especially important on high-compression joints such as the cylinder head.
- A sequence is usually provided by the manufacturer, either in a diagram or actually marked in the casting. If not, always start in the center and work outwards in a criss-cross pattern (see illustration 4.5). Start off by securing all bolts/nuts finger-tight, then set the torque wrench and tighten each fastener by a small amount in sequence until the final torque is reached. By following this practice,

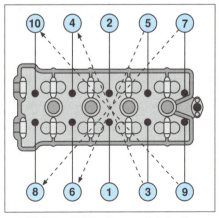

4.5 When tightening, work from the inside outwards

REF•16 Tools and Workshop Tips

the joint will be held evenly and will not be distorted. Important joints, such as the cylinder head and big-end fasteners often have two- or three-stage torque settings.

Applying leverage

● Use tools at the correct angle. Position a socket or wrench on the bolt/nut so that you pull it towards you when loosening. If this can't be done, push the wrench without curling your fingers around it **(see illustration 4.6)** - the wrench may slip or the fastener loosen suddenly, resulting in your fingers being crushed against a component.

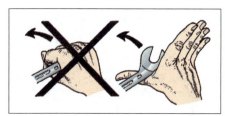

4.6 If you can't pull on the wrench to loosen a fastener, push with your hand open

● Additional leverage is gained by extending the length of the lever. The best way to do this is to use a breaker bar instead of the regular length tool, or to slip a length of tubing over the end of the wrench or socket.

● If additional leverage will not work, the fastener head is either damaged or firmly corroded in place (see *Fasteners*).

5 Bearings

Bearing removal and installation

Drivers and sockets

● Before removing a bearing, always inspect the casing to see which way it must be driven out - some casings will have retaining plates or a cast step. Also check for any identifying markings on the bearing and, if installed to a certain depth, measure this at this stage. Some roller bearings are sealed on one side - take note of the original installed position.

● Bearings can be driven out of a casing using a bearing driver tool (with the correct size head) or a socket of the correct diameter. Select the driver head or socket so that it contacts the outer race of the bearing, not the balls/rollers or inner race. Always support the casing around the bearing housing with wood blocks, otherwise there is a risk of fracture. The bearing is driven out with a few blows on the driver or socket from a heavy mallet. Unless access is severely restricted (as with wheel bearings), a pin-punch is not recommended unless it is moved around the bearing to keep it square in its housing.

● The same equipment can be used to install bearings. Make sure the bearing housing is supported on wood blocks and line up the bearing in its housing. Install the bearing as noted on removal - generally they are installed with their marked side facing outwards. Tap the bearing squarely into its housing using a driver or socket which bears only on the bearing's outer race - contact with the bearing balls/rollers or inner race will destroy it **(see illustrations 5.1 and 5.2)**.

● Check that the bearing inner race and balls/rollers rotate freely.

5.1 Using a bearing driver against the bearing's outer race

5.2 Using a large socket against the bearing's outer race

Pullers and slide-hammers

● Where a bearing is pressed on a shaft a puller will be required to extract it **(see illustration 5.3)**. Make sure that the puller clamp or legs fit securely behind the bearing and are unlikely to slip out. If pulling a bearing

5.3 This bearing puller clamps behind the bearing and pressure is applied to the shaft end to draw the bearing off

off a gear shaft for example, you may have to locate the puller behind a gear pinion if there is no access to the race and draw the gear pinion off the shaft as well **(see illustration 5.4)**.

> **Caution: Ensure that the puller's center bolt locates securely against the end of the shaft and will not slip when pressure is applied. Also ensure that puller does not damage the shaft end.**

5.4 Where no access is available to the rear of the bearing, it is sometimes possible to draw off the adjacent component

● Operate the puller so that its center bolt exerts pressure on the shaft end and draws the bearing off the shaft.

● When installing the bearing on the shaft, tap only on the bearing's inner race - contact with the balls/rollers or outer race will destroy the bearing. Use a socket or length of tubing as a drift which fits over the shaft end **(see illustration 5.5)**.

5.5 When installing a bearing on a shaft use a piece of tubing which bears only on the bearing's inner race

● Where a bearing locates in a blind hole in a casing, it cannot be driven or pulled out as described above. A slide-hammer with knife-edged bearing puller attachment will be required. The puller attachment passes through the bearing and when tightened expands to fit firmly behind the bearing **(see illustration 5.6)**. By operating the slide-hammer part of the tool the bearing is jarred out of its housing **(see illustration 5.7)**.

● It is possible, if the bearing is of reasonable weight, for it to drop out of its housing if the casing is heated as described opposite. If

Tools and Workshop Tips

5.6 Expand the bearing puller so that it locks behind the bearing . . .

5.7 . . . attach the slide hammer to the bearing puller

this method is attempted, first prepare a work surface which will enable the casing to be tapped face down to help dislodge the bearing - a wood surface is ideal since it will not damage the casing's gasket surface. Wearing protective gloves, tap the heated casing several times against the work surface to dislodge the bearing under its own weight **(see illustration 5.8)**.

5.8 Tapping a casing face down on wood blocks can often dislodge a bearing

● Bearings can be installed in blind holes using the driver or socket method described above.

Drawbolts

● Where a bearing or bushing is set in the eye of a component, such as a suspension linkage arm or connecting rod small-end, removal by drift may damage the component. Furthermore, a rubber bushing in a shock absorber eye cannot successfully be driven out of position. If access is available to a hydraulic press, the task is straightforward. If not, a drawbolt can be fabricated to extract the bearing or bushing.

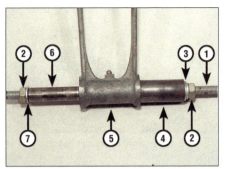

5.9 Drawbolt component parts assembled on a suspension arm

1 Bolt or length of threaded bar
2 Nuts
3 Washer (external diameter greater than tubing internal diameter)
4 Tubing (internal diameter sufficient to accommodate bearing)
5 Suspension arm with bearing
6 Tubing (external diameter slightly smaller than bearing)
7 Washer (external diameter slightly smaller than bearing)

5.10 Drawing the bearing out of the suspension arm

● To extract the bearing/bushing you will need a long bolt with nut (or piece of threaded bar with two nuts), a piece of tubing which has an internal diameter larger than the bearing/bushing, another piece of tubing which has an external diameter slightly smaller than the bearing/bushing, and a selection of washers **(see illustrations 5.9 and 5.10)**. Note that the pieces of tubing must be of the same length, or longer, than the bearing/bushing.

● The same kit (without the pieces of tubing) can be used to draw the new bearing/bushing back into place **(see illustration 5.11)**.

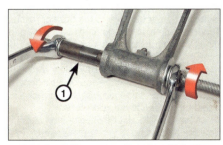

5.11 Installing a new bearing (1) in the suspension arm

Temperature change

● If the bearing's outer race is a tight fit in the casing, the aluminum casing can be heated to release its grip on the bearing. Aluminum will expand at a greater rate than the steel bearing outer race. There are several ways to do this, but avoid any localized extreme heat (such as a blow torch) - aluminum alloy has a low melting point.

● Approved methods of heating a casing are using a domestic oven (heated to 100°C/200°F) or immersing the casing in boiling water **(see illustration 5.12)**. Low temperature range localized heat sources such as a paint stripper heat gun or clothes iron can also be used **(see illustration 5.13)**. Alternatively, soak a rag in boiling water, wring it out and wrap it around the bearing housing.

> **Warning: All of these methods require care in use to prevent scalding and burns to the hands. Wear protective gloves when handling hot components.**

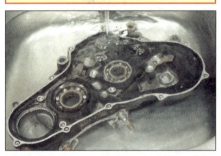

5.12 A casing can be immersed in a sink of boiling water to aid bearing removal

5.13 Using a localized heat source to aid bearing removal

● If heating the whole casing note that plastic components, such as the neutral switch, may suffer - remove them beforehand.

● After heating, remove the bearing as described above. You may find that the expansion is sufficient for the bearing to fall out of the casing under its own weight or with a light tap on the driver or socket.

● If necessary, the casing can be heated to aid bearing installation, and this is sometimes the recommended procedure if the motorcycle manufacturer has designed the housing and bearing fit with this intention.

REF•18 Tools and Workshop Tips

- Installation of bearings can be eased by placing them in a freezer the night before installation. The steel bearing will contract slightly, allowing easy insertion in its housing. This is often useful when installing steering head outer races in the frame.

Bearing types and markings

- Plain shell bearings, ball bearings, needle roller bearings and tapered roller bearings will all be found on motorcycles **(see illustrations 5.14 and 5.15)**. The ball and roller types are usually caged between an inner and outer race, but uncaged variations may be found.

5.16 Typical bearing marking

Bearing troubleshooting

- If a bearing outer race has spun in its housing, the housing material will be damaged. You can use a bearing locking compound to bond the outer race in place if damage is not too severe.
- Shell bearings will fail due to damage of their working surface, as a result of lack of lubrication, corrosion or abrasive particles in the oil **(see illustration 5.17)**. Small particles of dirt in the oil may embed in the bearing material whereas larger particles will score the bearing and shaft journal. If a number of short journeys are made, insufficient heat will be generated to drive off condensation which has built up on the bearings.

5.18 Example of ball journal bearing with damaged balls and cages

5.19 Hold outer race and listen to inner race when spun

5.14 Shell bearings are either plain or grooved. They are usually identified by color code (arrow)

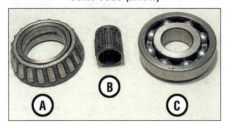

5.15 Tapered roller bearing (A), needle roller bearing (B) and ball journal bearing (C)

- Shell bearings (often called inserts) are usually found at the crankshaft main and connecting rod big-end where they are good at coping with high loads. They are made of a phosphor-bronze material and are impregnated with self-lubricating properties.
- Ball bearings and needle roller bearings consist of a steel inner and outer race with the balls or rollers between the races. They require constant lubrication by oil or grease and are good at coping with axial loads. Taper roller bearings consist of rollers set in a tapered cage set on the inner race; the outer race is separate. They are good at coping with axial loads and prevent movement along the shaft - a typical application is in the steering head.
- Bearing manufacturers produce bearings to ISO size standards and stamp one face of the bearing to indicate its internal and external diameter, load capacity and type **(see illustration 5.16)**.
- Metal bushings are usually of phosphor-bronze material. Rubber bushings are used in suspension mounting eyes. Fiber bushings have also been used in suspension pivots.

5.17 Typical bearing failures

- Ball and roller bearings will fail due to lack of lubrication or damage to the balls or rollers. Tapered-roller bearings can be damaged by overloading them. Unless the bearing is sealed on both sides, wash it in kerosene to remove all old grease then allow it to dry. Make a visual inspection looking to dented balls or rollers, damaged cages and worn or pitted races **(see illustration 5.18)**.
- A ball bearing can be checked for wear by listening to it when spun. Apply a film of light oil to the bearing and hold it close to the ear - hold the outer race with one hand and spin the inner race with the other hand **(see illustration 5.19)**. The bearing should be almost silent when spun; if it grates or rattles it is worn.

6 Oil seals

Oil seal removal and installation

- Oil seals should be replaced every time a component is dismantled. This is because the seal lips will become set to the sealing surface and will not necessarily reseal.
- Oil seals can be pried out of position using a large flat-bladed screwdriver **(see illustration 6.1)**. In the case of crankcase seals, check first that the seal is not lipped on the inside, preventing its removal with the crankcases joined.

6.1 Pry out oil seals with a large flat-bladed screwdriver

- New seals are usually installed with their marked face (containing the seal reference code) outwards and the spring side towards the fluid being retained. In certain cases, such as a two-stroke engine crankshaft seal, a double lipped seal may be used due to there being fluid or gas on each side of the joint.

Tools and Workshop Tips

- Use a bearing driver or socket which bears only on the outer hard edge of the seal to install it in the casing - tapping on the inner edge will damage the sealing lip.

Oil seal types and markings

- Oil seals are usually of the single-lipped type. Double-lipped seals are found where a liquid or gas is on both sides of the joint.
- Oil seals can harden and lose their sealing ability if the motorcycle has been in storage for a long period - replacement is the only solution.
- Oil seal manufacturers also conform to the ISO markings for seal size - these are molded into the outer face of the seal (see illustration

6.2 These oil seal markings indicate inside diameter, outside diameter and seal thickness

7 Gaskets and sealants

Types of gasket and sealant

- Gaskets are used to seal the mating surfaces between components and keep lubricants, fluids, vacuum or pressure contained within the assembly. Aluminum gaskets are sometimes found at the cylinder joints, but most gaskets are paper-based. If the mating surfaces of the components being joined are undamaged the gasket can be installed dry, although a dab of sealant or grease will be useful to hold it in place during assembly.
- RTV (Room Temperature Vulcanizing) silicone rubber sealants cure when exposed to moisture in the atmosphere. These sealants are good at filling pits or irregular gasket faces, but will tend to be forced out of the joint under very high torque. They can be used to replace a paper gasket, but first make sure that the width of the paper gasket is not essential to the shimming of internal components. RTV sealants should not be used on components containing gasoline.
- Non-hardening, semi-hardening and hard setting liquid gasket compounds can be used with a gasket or between a metal-to-metal joint. Select the sealant to suit the application: universal non-hardening sealant can be used on virtually all joints; semi-hardening on joint faces which are rough or damaged; hard setting sealant on joints which require a permanent bond and are subjected to high temperature and pressure. **Note:** *Check first if the paper gasket has a bead of sealant impregnated in its surface before applying additional sealant.*
- When choosing a sealant, make sure it is suitable for the application, particularly if being applied in a high-temperature area or in the vicinity of fuel. Certain manufacturers produce sealants in either clear, silver or black colors to match the finish of the engine. This has a particular application on motorcycles where much of the engine is exposed.
- Do not over-apply sealant. That which is squeezed out on the outside of the joint can be wiped off, whereas an excess of sealant on the inside can break off and clog oilways.

Breaking a sealed joint

- Age, heat, pressure and the use of hard setting sealant can cause two components to stick together so tightly that they are difficult to separate using finger pressure alone. Do not resort to using levers unless there is a pry point provided for this purpose (see illustration 7.1) or else the gasket surfaces will be damaged.
- Use a soft-faced hammer (see illustration 7.2) or a wood block and conventional hammer to strike the component near the mating surface. Avoid hammering against cast extremities since they may break off. If this method fails, try using a wood wedge between the two components.

Caution: If the joint will not separate, double-check that you have removed all the fasteners.

7.1 If a pry point is provided, apply gentle pressure with a flat-bladed screwdriver

7.2 Tap around the joint with a soft-faced mallet if necessary - don't strike cooling fins

Removal of old gasket and sealant

- Paper gaskets will most likely come away complete, leaving only a few traces stuck

HAYNES HINT

Most components have one or two hollow locating dowels between the two gasket faces. If a dowel cannot be removed, do not resort to gripping it with pliers - it will almost certainly be distorted. Install a close-fitting socket or Phillips screwdriver into the dowel and then grip the outer edge of the dowel to free it.

on the sealing faces of the components. It is imperative that all traces are removed to ensure correct sealing of the new gasket.
- Very carefully scrape all traces of gasket away making sure that the sealing surfaces are not gouged or scored by the scraper (see illustrations 7.3, 7.4 and 7.5). Stubborn deposits can be removed by spraying with an aerosol gasket remover. Final preparation of

7.3 Paper gaskets can be scraped off with a gasket scraper tool . . .

7.4 . . . a knife blade . . .

7.5 . . . or a household scraper

REF•20 Tools and Workshop Tips

7.6 Fine abrasive paper is wrapped around a flat file to clean up the gasket face

7.7 A kitchen scourer can be used on stubborn deposits

the gasket surface can be made with very fine abrasive paper or a plastic kitchen scourer **(see illustrations 7.6 and 7.7)**.

● Old sealant can be scraped or peeled off components, depending on the type originally used. Note that gasket removal compounds are available to avoid scraping the components clean; make sure the gasket remover suits the type of sealant used.

8 Chains

Breaking and joining final drive chains

● Drive chains for all but small bikes are continuous and do not have a clip-type connecting link. The chain must be broken using a chain breaker tool and the new chain securely riveted together using a new soft rivet-type link. Never use a clip-type connecting link instead of a rivet-type link, except in an emergency. Various chain breaking and riveting tools are available, either as separate tools or combined as illustrated in the accompanying photographs - read the instructions supplied with the tool carefully.

> ⚠ **Warning: The need to rivet the new link pins correctly cannot be overstressed - loss of control of the motorcycle is very likely to result if the chain breaks in use.**

● Rotate the chain and look for the soft link. The soft link pins look like they have been

8.1 Tighten the chain breaker to push the pin out of the link . . .

8.2 . . . withdraw the pin, remove the tool . . .

8.3 . . . and separate the chain link

deeply center-punched instead of peened over like all the other pins **(see illustration 8.9)** and its sideplate may be a different color. Position the soft link midway between the sprockets and assemble the chain breaker tool over one of the soft link pins **(see illustration 8.1)**. Operate the tool to push the pin out through the chain **(see illustration 8.2)**. On an O-ring chain, remove the O-rings **(see illustration 8.3)**. Carry out the same procedure on the other soft link pin.

> **Caution: Certain soft link pins (particularly on the larger chains) may require their ends to be filed or ground off before they can be pressed out using the tool.**

● Check that you have the correct size and strength (standard or heavy duty) new soft link - do not reuse the old link. Look for the size marking on the chain sideplates **(see illustration 8.10)**.

● Position the chain ends so that they are

8.4 Insert the new soft link, with O-rings, through the chain ends . . .

8.5 . . . install the O-rings over the pin ends . . .

8.6 . . . followed by the sideplate

engaged over the rear sprocket. On an O-ring chain, install a new O-ring over each pin of the link and insert the link through the two chain ends **(see illustration 8.4)**. Install a new O-ring over the end of each pin, followed by the sideplate (with the chain manufacturer's marking facing outwards) **(see illustrations 8.5 and 8.6)**. On an unsealed chain, insert the link through the two chain ends, then install the sideplate with the chain manufacturer's marking facing outwards.

● Note that it may not be possible to install the sideplate using finger pressure alone. If using a joining tool, assemble it so that the plates of the tool clamp the link and press the sideplate over the pins **(see illustration 8.7)**. Otherwise, use two small sockets placed over

8.7 Push the sideplate into position using a clamp

Tools and Workshop Tips

8.8 Assemble the chain riveting tool over one pin at a time and tighten it fully

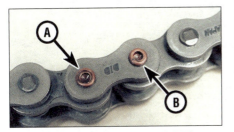

8.9 Pin end correctly riveted (A), pin end unriveted (B)

the rivet ends and two pieces of the wood between a C-clamp. Operate the clamp to press the sideplate over the pins.
● Assemble the joining tool over one pin (following the manufacturer's instructions) and tighten the tool down to spread the pin end securely (see illustrations 8.8 and 8.9). Do the same on the other pin.

> **Warning: Check that the pin ends are secure and that there is no danger of the sideplate coming loose. If the pin ends are cracked the soft link must be replaced.**

Final drive chain sizing

● Chains are sized using a three digit number, followed by a suffix to denote the chain type (see illustration 8.10). Chain type is either standard or heavy duty (thicker sideplates), and also unsealed or O-ring/X-ring type.
● The first digit of the number relates to the pitch of the chain, ie the distance from the center of one pin to the center of the next pin (see illustration 8.11). Pitch is expressed in eighths of an inch, as follows:

8.10 Typical chain size and type marking

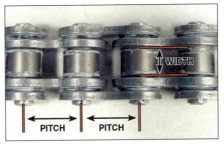

8.11 Chain dimensions

Sizes commencing with a 4 (for example 428) have a pitch of 1/2 inch (12.7 mm)

Sizes commencing with a 5 (for example 520) have a pitch of 5/8 inch (15.9 mm)

Sizes commencing with a 6 (for example 630) have a pitch of 3/4 inch (19.1 mm)

● The second and third digits of the chain size relate to the width of the rollers, for example the 525 shown has 5/16 inch (7.94 mm) rollers (see illustration 8.11).

9 Hoses

Clamping to prevent flow

● Small-bore flexible hoses can be clamped to prevent fluid flow while a component is worked on. Whichever method is used, ensure that the hose material is not permanently distorted or damaged by the clamp.
a) A brake hose clamp available from auto parts stores (see illustration 9.1).
b) A wingnut type hose clamp (see illustration 9.2).
c) Two sockets placed on each side of the hose and held with straight-jawed self-locking pliers (see illustration 9.3).
d) Thick card stock on each side of the hose held between straight-jawed self-locking pliers (see illustration 9.4).

9.1 Hoses can be clamped with an automotive brake hose clamp . . .

9.2 . . . a wingnut type hose clamp . . .

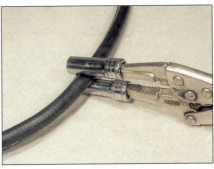

9.3 . . . two sockets and a pair of self-locking grips . . .

9.4 . . . or thick card and self-locking grips

Freeing and fitting hoses

● Always make sure the hose clamp is moved well clear of the hose end. Grip the hose with your hand and rotate it while pulling it off the union. If the hose has hardened due to age and will not move, slit it with a sharp knife and peel its ends off the union (see illustration 9.5).
● Resist the temptation to use grease or soap on the unions to aid installation; although it helps the hose slip over the union it will equally aid the escape of fluid from the joint. It is preferable to soften the hose ends in hot water and wet the inside surface of the hose with water or a fluid which will evaporate.

9.5 Cutting a coolant hose free with a sharp knife

Conversion Factors

Length (distance)
Inches (in)	X	25.4	= Millimeters (mm)	X 0.0394	= Inches (in)
Feet (ft)	X	0.305	= Meters (m)	X 3.281	= Feet (ft)
Miles	X	1.609	= Kilometers (km)	X 0.621	= Miles

Volume (capacity)
Cubic inches (cu in; in^3)	X	16.387	= Cubic centimeters (cc; cm^3)	X 0.061	= Cubic inches (cu in; in^3)
Imperial pints (Imp pt)	X	0.568	= Liters (l)	X 1.76	= Imperial pints (Imp pt)
Imperial quarts (Imp qt)	X	1.137	= Liters (l)	X 0.88	= Imperial quarts (Imp qt)
Imperial quarts (Imp qt)	X	1.201	= US quarts (US qt)	X 0.833	= Imperial quarts (Imp qt)
US quarts (US qt)	X	0.946	= Liters (l)	X 1.057	= US quarts (US qt)
Imperial gallons (Imp gal)	X	4.546	= Liters (l)	X 0.22	= Imperial gallons (Imp gal)
Imperial gallons (Imp gal)	X	1.201	= US gallons (US gal)	X 0.833	= Imperial gallons (Imp gal)
US gallons (US gal)	X	3.785	= Liters (l)	X 0.264	= US gallons (US gal)

Mass (weight)
Ounces (oz)	X	28.35	= Grams (g)	X 0.035	= Ounces (oz)
Pounds (lb)	X	0.454	= Kilograms (kg)	X 2.205	= Pounds (lb)

Force
Ounces-force (ozf; oz)	X	0.278	= Newtons (N)	X 3.6	= Ounces-force (ozf; oz)
Pounds-force (lbf; lb)	X	4.448	= Newtons (N)	X 0.225	= Pounds-force (lbf; lb)
Newtons (N)	X	0.1	= Kilograms-force (kgf; kg)	X 9.81	= Newtons (N)

Pressure
Pounds-force per square inch (psi; lbf/in^2; lb/in^2)	X	0.070	= Kilograms-force per square centimeter (kgf/cm^2; kg/cm^2)	X 14.223	= Pounds-force per square inch (psi; lbf/in^2; lb/in^2)
Pounds-force per square inch (psi; lbf/in^2; lb/in^2)	X	0.068	= Atmospheres (atm)	X 14.696	= Pounds-force per square inch (psi; lbf/in^2; lb/in^2)
Pounds-force per square inch (psi; lbf/in^2; lb/in^2)	X	0.069	= Bars	X 14.5	= Pounds-force per square inch (psi; lbf/in^2; lb/in^2)
Pounds-force per square inch (psi; lbf/in^2; lb/in^2)	X	6.895	= Kilopascals (kPa)	X 0.145	= Pounds-force per square inch (psi; lbf/in^2; lb/in^2)
Kilopascals (kPa)	X	0.01	= Kilograms-force per square centimeter (kgf/cm^2; kg/cm^2)	X 98.1	= Kilopascals (kPa)

Torque (moment of force)
Pounds-force inches (lbf in; lb in)	X	1.152	= Kilograms-force centimeter (kgf cm; kg cm)	X 0.868	= Pounds-force inches (lbf in; lb in)
Pounds-force inches (lbf in; lb in)	X	0.113	= Newton meters (Nm)	X 8.85	= Pounds-force inches (lbf in; lb in)
Pounds-force inches (lbf in; lb in)	X	0.083	= Pounds-force feet (lbf ft; lb ft)	X 12	= Pounds-force inches (lbf in; lb in)
Pounds-force feet (lbf ft; lb ft)	X	0.138	= Kilograms-force meters (kgf m; kg m)	X 7.233	= Pounds-force feet (lbf ft; lb ft)
Pounds-force feet (lbf ft; lb ft)	X	1.356	= Newton meters (Nm)	X 0.738	= Pounds-force feet (lbf ft; lb ft)
Newton meters (Nm)	X	0.102	= Kilograms-force meters (kgf m; kg m)	X 9.804	= Newton meters (Nm)

Vacuum
Inches mercury (in. Hg)	X	3.377	= Kilopascals (kPa)	X 0.2961	= Inches mercury
Inches mercury (in. Hg)	X	25.4	= Millimeters mercury (mm Hg)	X 0.0394	= Inches mercury

Power
Horsepower (hp)	X	745.7	= Watts (W)	X 0.0013	= Horsepower (hp)

Velocity (speed)
Miles per hour (miles/hr; mph)	X	1.609	= Kilometers per hour (km/hr; kph)	X 0.621	= Miles per hour (miles/hr; mph)

Fuel consumption*
Miles per gallon, Imperial (mpg)	X	0.354	= Kilometers per liter (km/l)	X 2.825	= Miles per gallon, Imperial (mpg)
Miles per gallon, US (mpg)	X	0.425	= Kilometers per liter (km/l)	X 2.352	= Miles per gallon, US (mpg)

Temperature
Degrees Fahrenheit = (°C x 1.8) + 32   Degrees Celsius (Degrees Centigrade; °C) = (°F - 32) x 0.56

*It is common practice to convert from miles per gallon (mpg) to liters/100 kilometers (l/100km), where mpg (Imperial) x l/100 km = 282 and mpg (US) x l/100 km = 235

Motorcycle Chemicals and Lubricants

A number of chemicals and lubricants are available for use in motorcycle maintenance and repair. They include a wide variety of products ranging from cleaning solvents and degreasers to lubricants and protective sprays for rubber, plastic and vinyl.

- **Contact point/spark plug cleaner** is a solvent used to clean oily film and dirt from points, grim from electrical connectors and oil deposits from spark plugs. It is oil free and leaves no residue. It can also be used to remove gum and varnish from carburetor jets and other orifices.

- **Carburetor cleaner** is similar to contact point/spark plug cleaner but it usually has a stronger solvent and may leave a slight oily residue. It is not recommended for cleaning electrical components or connections.

- **Brake system cleaner** is used to remove brake dust, grease and brake fluid from the brake system, where clean surfaces are absolutely necessary. It leaves no residue and often eliminates brake squeal caused by contaminants.

- **Silicone-based lubricants** are used to protect rubber parts such as hoses and grommets, and are used as lubricants for hinges and locks.

- **Multi-purpose grease** is an all purpose lubricant used wherever grease is more practical than a liquid lubricant such as oil. Some multi-purpose grease is colored white and specially formulated to be more resistant to water than ordinary grease.

- **Gear oil** (sometimes called gear lube) is a specially designed oil used in transmissions and final drive units, as well as other areas where high friction, high temperature lubrication is required. It is available in a number of viscosities (weights) for various applications.

- **Motor oil** is the lubricant formulated for use in engines. It normally contains a wide variety of additives to prevent corrosion and reduce foaming and wear. Motor oil comes in various weights (viscosity ratings) from 0 to 50. The recommended weight of the oil depends on the season, temperature and the demands on the engine. Light oil is used in cold climates and under light load conditions. Heavy oil is used in hot climates and where high loads are encountered. Multi-viscosity oils are designed to have characteristics of both light and heavy oils and are available in a number of weights from 0W-20 to 20W-50.

- **Gasoline additives** perform several functions, depending on their chemical makeup. They usually contain solvents that help dissolve gum and varnish that build up on carburetor and inlet parts. They also serve to break down carbon deposits that form on the inside surfaces of the combustion chambers. Some additives contain upper cylinder lubricants for valves and piston rings.

- **Brake and clutch fluid** is a specially formulated hydraulic fluid that can withstand the heat and pressure encountered in break/clutch systems. Care must be taken that this fluid does not come in contact with painted surfaces or plastics. An opened container should always be resealed to prevent contamination by water or dirt.

- **Chain lubricants** are formulated especially for use on motorcycle final drive chains. A good chain lube should adhere well and have good penetrating qualities to be effective as a lubricant inside the chain and on the side plates, pins and rollers. Most chain lubes are either the foaming type or quick drying type and are usually marketed as sprays. Take care to use a lubricant marked as being suitable for O-ring chains.

- **Degreasers** are heavy duty solvents used to remove grease and grime that may accumulate on the engine and frame components. They can be sprayed or brushed on and, depending on the type, are rinsed with either water or solvent.

- **Solvents** are used alone or in combination with degreasers to clean parts and assemblies during repair and overhaul. The home mechanic should use only solvents that are non-flammable and that do not produce irritating fumes.

- **Gasket sealing compounds** may be used in conjunction with gaskets, to improve their sealing capabilities, or alone, to seal metal-to-metal joints. Many gasket sealers can withstand extreme heat, some are impervious to gasoline and lubricants, while others are capable of filling and sealing large cavities. Depending on the intended use, gasket sealers either dry hard or stay relatively soft and pliable. They are usually applied by hand, with a brush or are sprayed on the gasket sealing surfaces.

- **Thread locking compound** is an adhesive locking compound that prevents threaded fasteners from loosening because of vibration. It is available in a variety of types for different applications.

- **Moisture dispersants** are usually sprays that can be used to dry out electrical components such as the fuse block and wiring connectors. Some types an also be used as treatment for rubber and as a lubricant for hinges, cables and locks.

- **Waxes and polishes** are used to help protect painted and plated surfaces from the weather. Different types of pain may require the use of different types of wax polish. Some polishes utilize a chemical or abrasive cleaner to help remove the top layer of oxidized (dull) paint on older vehicles. In recent years, many non-wax polishes (that contain a wide variety of chemicals such as polymers and silicones) have been introduced. These non-wax polishes are usually easier to apply and last longer than conventional waxes and polishes.

REF•24 Storage

Preparing for storage

Before you start

If repairs or an overhaul is needed, see that this is carried out now rather than left until you want to ride the bike again.

Give the bike a good wash and scrub all dirt from its underside. Make sure the bike dries completely before preparing for storage.

Engine

● Remove the spark plug(s) and lubricate the cylinder bores with approximately a teaspoon of motor oil using a spout-type oil can **(see illustration 1)**. Reinstall the spark plug(s). Crank the engine over a couple of times to coat the piston rings and bores with oil. If the bike has a kickstart, use this to turn the engine over. If not, flick the kill switch to the OFF position and crank the engine over on the starter **(see illustration 2)**. If the nature of the ignition system prevents the starter operating with the kill switch in the OFF position, remove the spark plugs and fit them back in their caps; ensure that the plugs are grounded against the cylinder head when the starter is operated **(see illustration 3)**.

Warning: It is important that the plugs are grounded away from the spark plug holes otherwise there is a risk of atomized fuel from the cylinders igniting.

HAYNES HiNT On a single cylinder four-stroke engine, you can seal the combustion chamber completely by positioning the piston at TDC on the compression stroke.

● Drain the carburetor(s) otherwise there is a risk of jets becoming blocked by gum deposits from the fuel **(see illustration 4)**.

● If the bike is going into long-term storage, consider adding a fuel stabilizer to the fuel in the tank. If the tank is drained completely, corrosion of its internal surfaces may occur if left unprotected for a long period. The tank can be treated with a rust preventative especially for this purpose. Alternatively, remove the tank and pour half a liter of motor oil into it, install the filler cap and shake the tank to coat its internals with oil before draining off the excess. The same effect can also be achieved by spraying WD40 or a similar water-dispersant around the inside of the tank via its flexible nozzle.

● Make sure the cooling system contains the correct mix of antifreeze. Antifreeze also contains important corrosion inhibitors.

● The air intakes and exhaust can be sealed off by covering or plugging the openings. Ensure that you do not seal in any condensation; run the engine until it is hot,

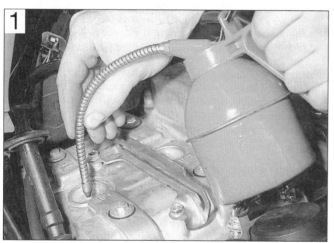

Squirt a drop of motor oil into each cylinder

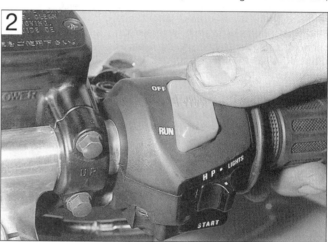

Flick the kill switch to OFF . . .

. . . and ensure that the metal bodies of the plugs (arrows) are grounded against the cylinder head

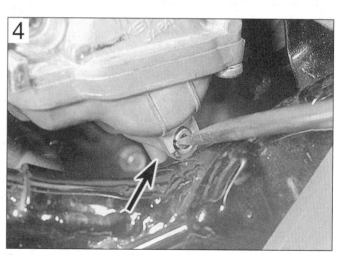

Connect a hose to the carburetor float chamber drain stub (arrow) and unscrew the drain screw

Storage REF•25

Exhausts can be sealed off with a plastic bag

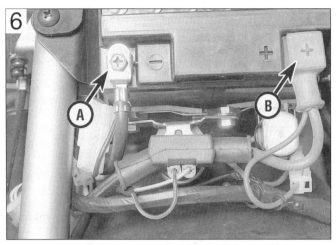

Disconnect the negative lead (A) first, followed by the positive lead (B)

then switch off and allow to cool. Tape a piece of thick plastic over the silencer end(s) **(see illustration 5)**. Note that some advocate pouring a tablespoon of motor oil into the silencer(s) before sealing them off.

Battery

- Remove it from the bike - in extreme cases of cold the battery may freeze and crack its case **(see illustration 6)**.
- Check the electrolyte level and top up if necessary (conventional refillable batteries). Clean the terminals.
- Store the battery off the motorcycle and away from any sources of fire. Position a wooden block under the battery if it is to sit on the ground.
- Give the battery a trickle charge for a few hours every month **(see illustration 7)**.

Tires

- Place the bike on its centerstand or an auxiliary stand which will support the motorcycle in an upright position. Position wood blocks under the tires to keep them off the ground and to provide insulation from damp. If the bike is being put into long-term

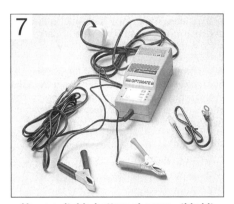

Use a suitable battery charger - this kit also assesses battery condition

storage, ideally both tires should be off the ground; not only will this protect the tires, but will also ensure that no load is placed on the steering head or wheel bearings.

- Deflate each tire by 5 to 10 psi, no more or the beads may unseat from the rim, making subsequent inflation difficult on tubeless tires.

Pivots and controls

- Lubricate all lever, pedal, stand and footrest pivot points. If grease nipples are fitted to the rear suspension components, apply lubricant to the pivots.
- Lubricate all control cables.

Cycle components

- Apply a wax protectant to all painted and plastic components. Wipe off any excess, but don't polish to a shine. Where fitted, clean the screen with soap and water.
- Coat metal parts with Vaseline (petroleum jelly). When applying this to the fork tubes, do not compress the forks otherwise the seals will rot from contact with the Vaseline.
- Apply a vinyl cleaner to the seat.

Storage conditions

- Aim to store the bike in a shed or garage which does not leak and is free from damp.
- Drape an old blanket or bedspread over the bike to protect it from dust and direct contact with sunlight (which will fade paint). Beware of tight-fitting plastic covers which may allow condensation to form and settle on the bike.

Getting back on the road

Engine and transmission

- Change the oil and replace the oil filter. If this was done prior to storage, check that the oil hasn't emulsified - a thick whitish substance which occurs through condensation.
- Remove the spark plugs. Using a spout-type oil can, squirt a few drops of oil into the cylinder(s). This will provide initial lubrication as the piston rings and bores comes back into contact. Service the spark plugs, or buy new ones, and install them in the engine.
- Check that the clutch isn't stuck on. The

plates can stick together if left standing for some time, preventing clutch operation. Engage a gear and try rocking the bike back and forth with the clutch lever held against the handlebar. If this doesn't work on cable-operated clutches, hold the clutch lever back against the handlebar with a strong rubber band or cable tie for a couple of hours **(see illustration 8)**.

- If the air intakes or silencer end(s) were blocked off, remove the plug or cover used.
- If the fuel tank was coated with a rust preventative, oil or a stabilizer added to the

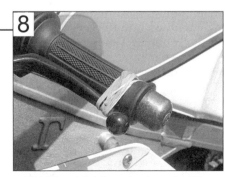

Hold the clutch lever back against the handlebar with rubber bands or a cable tie

Storage

fuel, drain and flush the tank and dispose of the fuel sensibly. If no action was taken with the fuel tank prior to storage, it is advised that the old fuel is disposed of since it will go bad over a period of time. Refill the fuel tank with fresh fuel.

Frame and running gear

● Oil all pivot points and cables.
● Check the tire pressures. They will definitely need inflating if pressures were reduced for storage.
● Lubricate the final drive chain (where applicable).
● Remove any protective coating applied to the fork tubes (stanchions) since this may well destroy the fork seals. If the fork tubes weren't protected and have picked up rust spots, remove them with very fine abrasive paper and refinish with metal polish.
● Check that both brakes operate correctly. Apply each brake hard and check that it's not possible to move the motorcycle forwards, then check that the brake frees off again once released. Brake caliper pistons can stick due to corrosion around the piston head, or on the sliding caliper types, due to corrosion of the slider pins. If the brake doesn't free after repeated operation, take the caliper off for examination. Similarly drum brakes can stick due to a seized operating cam, cable or rod linkage.
● If the motorcycle has been in long-term storage, replace the brake fluid and clutch fluid (where applicable).
● Depending on where the bike has been stored, the wiring, cables and hoses may have been nibbled by rodents. Make a visual check and investigate disturbed wiring loom tape.

Battery

● If the battery has been previously removed and given top up charges it can simply be reconnected. Remember to connect the positive cable first and the negative cable last.
● On conventional refillable batteries, if the battery has not received any attention, remove it from the motorcycle and check its electrolyte level. Top up if necessary then charge the battery. If the battery fails to hold a charge and a visual check show heavy white sulfation of the plates, the battery is probably defective and must be replaced. This is particularly likely if the battery is old. Confirm battery condition with a specific gravity check.
● On sealed (MF) batteries, if the battery has not received any attention, remove it from the motorcycle and charge it according to the information on the battery case - if the battery fails to hold a charge it must be replaced.

Starting procedure

● If a kickstart is fitted, turn the engine over a couple of times with the ignition OFF to distribute oil around the engine. If no kickstart is fitted, flick the engine kill switch OFF and the ignition ON and crank the engine over a couple of times to work oil around the upper cylinder components. If the nature of the ignition system is such that the starter won't work with the kill switch OFF, remove the spark plugs, fit them back into their caps and ground their bodies on the cylinder head. Reinstall the spark plugs afterwards.
● Switch the kill switch to RUN, operate the choke and start the engine. If the engine won't start don't continue cranking the engine - not only will this flatten the battery, but the starter motor will overheat. Switch the ignition off and try again later. If the engine refuses to start, go through the troubleshooting procedures in this manual. **Note:** *If the bike has been in storage for a long time, old fuel or a carburetor blockage may be the problem. Gum deposits in carburetors can block jets - if a carburetor cleaner doesn't prove successful the carburetors must be dismantled for cleaning.*
● Once the engine has started, check that the lights, turn signals and horn work properly.
● Treat the bike gently for the first ride and check all fluid levels on completion. Settle the bike back into the maintenance schedule.

Troubleshooting

This Section provides an easy reference-guide to the more common faults that are likely to afflict your machine. Obviously, the opportunities are almost limitless for faults to occur as a result of obscure failures, and to try and cover all eventualities would require a book. Indeed, a number have been written on the subject.

Successful troubleshooting is not a mysterious 'black art' but the application of a bit of knowledge combined with a systematic and logical approach to the problem. Approach any troubleshooting by first accurately identifying the symptom and then checking through the list of possible causes, starting with the simplest or most obvious and progressing in stages to the most complex. Take nothing for granted, but above all apply liberal quantities of common sense.

The main symptom of a fault is given in the text as a major heading below which are listed the various systems or areas which may contain the fault. Details of each possible cause for a fault and the remedial action to be taken are given. Further information should be sought in the relevant Chapter.

1 Engine doesn't start or is difficult to start
- [ ] Starter motor doesn't rotate
- [ ] Starter motor rotates but engine does not turn over
- [ ] Starter works but engine won't turn over (seized)
- [ ] No fuel flow
- [ ] Engine flooded
- [ ] No spark or weak spark
- [ ] Compression low
- [ ] Stalls after starting
- [ ] Rough idle

2 Poor running at low speed
- [ ] Spark weak
- [ ] Fuel/air mixture incorrect
- [ ] Compression low
- [ ] Poor acceleration

3 Poor running or no power at high speed
- [ ] Firing incorrect
- [ ] Fuel/air mixture incorrect
- [ ] Compression low
- [ ] Knocking or pinging
- [ ] Miscellaneous causes

4 Overheating
- [ ] Engine overheats
- [ ] Firing incorrect
- [ ] Fuel/air mixture incorrect
- [ ] Compression too high
- [ ] Engine load excessive
- [ ] Lubrication inadequate
- [ ] Miscellaneous causes

5 Clutch problems
- [ ] Clutch slipping
- [ ] Clutch not disengaging completely

6 Gearchanging problems
- [ ] Doesn't go into gear, or lever doesn't return
- [ ] Jumps out of gear
- [ ] Overselects

7 Abnormal engine noise
- [ ] Knocking or pinging
- [ ] Piston slap or rattling
- [ ] Valve noise
- [ ] Other noise

8 Abnormal driveline noise
- [ ] Clutch noise
- [ ] Transmission noise
- [ ] Final drive noise

9 Abnormal frame and suspension noise
- [ ] Front end noise
- [ ] Shock absorber noise
- [ ] Brake noise

10 Oil pressure warning light comes on
- [ ] Engine lubrication system
- [ ] Electrical system

11 Excessive exhaust smoke
- [ ] White smoke
- [ ] Black smoke

12 Poor handling or stability
- [ ] Handlebar hard to turn
- [ ] Handlebar shakes or vibrates excessively
- [ ] Handlebar pulls to one side
- [ ] Poor shock absorbing qualities

13 Braking problems
- [ ] Brakes are spongy, don't hold
- [ ] Brake lever or pedal pulsates
- [ ] Brakes drag

14 Electrical problems
- [ ] Battery dead or weak
- [ ] Battery overcharged

Troubleshooting

1 Engine doesn't start or is difficult to start

Starter motor doesn't rotate

- [ ] Engine kill switch OFF.
- [ ] Fuse blown. Check main fuse and starter circuit fuse (Chapter 9).
- [ ] Battery voltage low. Check and recharge battery (Chapter 9).
- [ ] Starter motor defective. Make sure the wiring to the starter is secure. Make sure the starter relay clicks when the start button is pushed. If the relay clicks, then the fault is in the wiring or motor.
- [ ] Starter relay faulty. Check it according to the procedure in Chapter 9.
- [ ] Starter switch not contacting. The contacts could be wet, corroded or dirty. Disassemble and clean the switch (Chapter 9).
- [ ] Wiring open or shorted. Check all wiring connections and harnesses to make sure that they are dry, tight and not corroded. Also check for broken or frayed wires that can cause a short to ground (see wiring diagram, Chapter 9).
- [ ] Ignition (main) switch defective. Check the switch according to the procedure in Chapter 9. Replace the switch with a new one if it is defective.
- [ ] Engine kill switch defective. Check for wet, dirty or corroded contacts. Clean or replace the switch as necessary (Chapter 9).
- [ ] Faulty neutral, side stand or clutch switch. Check the wiring to each switch and the switch itself according to the procedures in Chapter 9.

Starter motor rotates but engine does not turn over

- [ ] Starter motor clutch defective. Inspect and repair or replace (Chapter 2).
- [ ] Damaged idler or starter gears. Inspect and replace the damaged parts (Chapter 2).

Starter works but engine won't turn over (seized)

- [ ] Seized engine caused by one or more internally damaged components. Failure due to wear, abuse or lack of lubrication. Damage can include seized valves, followers/rocker arms, camshafts, pistons, crankshaft, connecting rod bearings, or transmission gears or bearings. Refer to Chapter 2 for engine disassembly.

No fuel flow

- [ ] No fuel in tank.
- [ ] Fuel tank breather hose obstructed.
- [ ] Fuel filter is blocked (see Chapter 1).

Engine flooded

- [ ] Starting technique incorrect. Under normal circumstances the machine should start with little or no throttle. When the engine is cold, the choke should be operated and the engine started without opening the throttle. When the engine is at operating temperature, only a very slight amount of throttle should be necessary.

No spark or weak spark

- [ ] Ignition switch OFF.
- [ ] Engine kill switch turned to the OFF position.
- [ ] Battery voltage low. Check and recharge the battery as necessary (Chapter 9).
- [ ] Spark plugs dirty, defective or worn out. Locate reason for fouled plugs using spark plug condition chart and follow the plug maintenance procedures (Chapter 1).
- [ ] Spark plug caps or secondary (HT) wiring faulty. Check condition. Replace either or both components if cracks or deterioration are evident (Chapter 5).
- [ ] Spark plug caps not making good contact. Make sure that the plug caps fit snugly over the plug ends.
- [ ] Ignition HT coils defective. Check the coils, referring to Chapter 5.
- [ ] IC igniter unit defective. Refer to Chapter 5 for details.
- [ ] Pick-up coil defective. Check the unit, referring to Chapter 5 for details.
- [ ] Ignition or kill switch shorted. This is usually caused by water, corrosion, damage or excessive wear. The switches can be disassembled and cleaned with electrical contact cleaner. If cleaning does not help, replace the switches (Chapter 9).
- [ ] Wiring shorted or broken between:

    a) Ignition (main) switch and engine kill switch (or blown fuse)
    b) IC igniter unit and engine kill switch
    c) IC igniter unit and ignition HT coils
    d) Ignition HT coils and spark plugs
    e) IC igniter unit and ignition pick-up coil.

- [ ] Make sure that all wiring connections are clean, dry and tight. Look for chafed and broken wires (Chapters 5 and 9).

Compression low

- [ ] Spark plugs loose. Remove the plugs and inspect their threads. Reinstall and tighten to the specified torque (Chapter 1).
- [ ] Cylinder head not sufficiently tightened down. If the cylinder head is suspected of being loose, then there's a chance that the gasket or head is damaged if the problem has persisted for any length of time. The head bolts should be tightened to the proper torque in the correct sequence (Chapter 2).
- [ ] Improper valve clearance. This means that the valve is not closing completely and compression pressure is leaking past the valve. Check and adjust the valve clearances (Chapter 1).
- [ ] Cylinder and/or piston worn. Excessive wear will cause compression pressure to leak past the rings. This is usually accompanied by worn rings as well. A top-end overhaul is necessary (Chapter 2).
- [ ] Piston rings worn, weak, broken, or sticking. Broken or sticking piston rings usually indicate a lubrication or fuelling problem that causes excess carbon deposits or seizures to form on the pistons and rings. Top-end overhaul is necessary (Chapter 2).
- [ ] Piston ring-to-groove clearance excessive. This is caused by excessive wear of the piston ring lands. Piston replacement is necessary (Chapter 2).
- [ ] Cylinder head gasket damaged. If a head is allowed to become loose, or if excessive carbon build-up on the piston crown and combustion chamber causes extremely high compression, the head gasket may leak. Retorquing the head is not always sufficient to restore the seal, so gasket replacement is necessary (Chapter 2).
- [ ] Cylinder head warped. This is caused by overheating or improperly tightened head bolts. Machine shop resurfacing or head replacement is necessary (Chapter 2).
- [ ] Valve spring broken or weak. Caused by component failure or wear; the springs must be replaced (Chapter 2).
- [ ] Valve not seating properly. This is caused by a bent valve (from over-revving or improper valve adjustment), burned valve or seat (improper fuelling) or an accumulation of carbon deposits on the seat (from fuelling or lubrication problems). The valves must be cleaned and/or replaced and the seats serviced if possible (Chapter 2).

Troubleshooting REF•29

1 Engine doesn't start or is difficult to start (continued)

Stalls after starting

- [ ] Improper choke action (carbureted models). Make sure the choke linkage shaft is getting a full stroke and staying in the out position (Chapter 4).
- [ ] Ignition malfunction. See Chapter 5.
- [ ] Carburetor or fuel injection malfunction. See Chapter 4.
- [ ] Fuel contaminated. The fuel can be contaminated with either dirt or water, or can change chemically if the machine is allowed to sit for several months or more. Drain the tank (Chapter 4).
- [ ] Intake air leak. Check for loose intake manifold retaining clips and damaged/disconnected vacuum hoses (Chapter 4).
- [ ] Engine idle speed incorrect. Turn idle adjusting screw until the engine idles at the specified rpm (Chapter 1).

Rough idle

- [ ] Ignition malfunction. See Chapter 5.
- [ ] Idle speed incorrect. See Chapter 1.
- [ ] Carburetors not synchronized (twin carburetor models). Adjust them with vacuum gauge or manometer set as described in Chapter 4.
- [ ] Carburetor or fuel injection malfunction. See Chapter 4.
- [ ] Fuel contaminated. The fuel can be contaminated with either dirt or water, or can change chemically if the machine is allowed to sit for several months or more. Drain the tank (Chapter 4).
- [ ] Intake air leak. Check for loose intake manifold retaining clips and damaged/disconnected vacuum hoses. Replace the intake ducts if they are split or deteriorated (Chapter 4).
- [ ] Air filter clogged. Replace the air filter element (Chapter 1).

2 Poor running at low speeds

Spark weak

- [ ] Battery voltage low. Check and recharge battery (Chapter 9).
- [ ] Spark plugs fouled, defective or worn out. Refer to Chapter 1 for spark plug maintenance.
- [ ] Spark plug cap or HT wiring defective. Refer to Chapters 1 and 5 for details on the ignition system.
- [ ] Spark plug caps not making contact.
- [ ] Incorrect spark plugs. Wrong type, heat range or cap configuration. Check and install correct plugs listed in Chapter 1.
- [ ] IC igniter unit or ECM faulty. See Chapter 4.
- [ ] Pick-up coil defective. See Chapter 4.
- [ ] Ignition coils defective. See Chapter 5.

Fuel/air mixture incorrect

- [ ] Pilot screws incorrectly set (Chapter 4)
- [ ] Pilot jet or air passage blocked. Remove and overhaul the carburetors (Chapter 4).
- [ ] Air filter clogged, poorly sealed or missing (Chapter 1).
- [ ] Air filter housing poorly sealed. Look for cracks, holes or loose clamps and replace or repair defective parts.
- [ ] Fuel tank breather hose obstructed.
- [ ] Intake air leak. Check for loose intake manifold retaining clips and damaged/disconnected vacuum hoses. Replace the intake ducts if they are split or deteriorated (Chapter 4).

Compression low

- [ ] Spark plugs loose. Remove the plugs and inspect their threads. Reinstall and tighten to the specified torque (Chapter 1).
- [ ] Cylinder head not sufficiently tightened down. If the cylinder head is suspected of being loose, then there's a chance that the gasket and head are damaged if the problem has persisted for any length of time. The head bolts should be tightened to the proper torque in the correct sequence (Chapter 2).
- [ ] Improper valve clearance. This means that the valve is not closing completely and compression pressure is leaking past the valve. Check and adjust the valve clearances (Chapter 1).
- [ ] Cylinder and/or piston worn. Excessive wear will cause compression pressure to leak past the rings. This is usually accompanied by worn rings as well. A top-end overhaul is necessary (Chapter 2).
- [ ] Piston rings worn, weak, broken, or sticking. Broken or sticking piston rings usually indicate a lubrication or fuelling problem that causes excess carbon deposits or seizures to form on the pistons and rings. Top-end overhaul is necessary (Chapter 2).
- [ ] Piston ring-to-groove clearance excessive. This is caused by excessive wear of the piston ring lands. Piston replacement is necessary (Chapter 2).
- [ ] Cylinder head gasket damaged. If a head is allowed to become loose, or if excessive carbon build-up on the piston crown and combustion chamber causes extremely high compression, the head gasket may leak. Retorquing the head is not always sufficient to restore the seal, so gasket replacement is necessary (Chapter 2).
- [ ] Cylinder head warped. This is caused by overheating or improperly tightened head bolts. Machine shop resurfacing or head replacement is necessary (Chapter 2).
- [ ] Valve spring broken or weak. Caused by component failure or wear; the springs must be replaced (Chapter 2).
- [ ] Valve not seating properly. This is caused by a bent valve (from over-revving or improper valve adjustment), burned valve or seat (improper fuelling) or an accumulation of carbon deposits on the seat (from fuelling, lubrication problems). The valves must be cleaned and/or replaced and the seats serviced if possible (Chapter 2).

Poor acceleration

- [ ] Fuel system fault. Remove and overhaul the carburetors or check the fuel injection system (Chapter 4).
- [ ] Engine oil viscosity too high. Using a heavier oil than that recommended in Chapter 1 can damage the oil pump or lubrication system and cause drag on the engine.
- [ ] Brakes dragging. Usually caused by debris which has entered the brake piston seals, or from a warped disc or drum or bent axle. Repair as necessary (Chapter 7).

3 Poor running or no power at high speed

Firing incorrect

- [ ] Air filter restricted. Clean or replace filter (Chapter 1).
- [ ] Spark plugs fouled, defective or worn out. See Chapter 1 for spark plug maintenance.
- [ ] Spark plug caps or HT wiring defective. See Chapters 1 and 5 for details of the ignition system.
- [ ] Spark plug caps not in good contact. See Chapter 5.
- [ ] Incorrect spark plugs. Wrong type, heat range or cap configuration. Check and install correct plugs listed in Chapter 1.
- [ ] IC igniter unit or ECM defective. See Chapter 5.
- [ ] Pick-up coil defective. See Chapter 5.
- [ ] Ignition coils defective. See Chapter 5.

Fuel/air mixture incorrect

- [ ] Fuel system fault. Remove and overhaul the carburetors or check the fuel injection system (Chapter 4).
- [ ] Air filter clogged, poorly sealed, or missing (Chapter 1).
- [ ] Air filter housing poorly sealed. Look for cracks, holes or loose clamps, and replace or repair defective parts.
- [ ] Fuel tank breather hose obstructed.
- [ ] Intake air leak. Check for loose intake manifold retaining clips and damaged/disconnected vacuum hoses. Replace the intake ducts if they are split or deteriorated (Chapter 4).

Compression low

- [ ] Spark plugs loose. Remove the plugs and inspect their threads. Reinstall and tighten to the specified torque (Chapter 1).
- [ ] Cylinder head not sufficiently tightened down. If the cylinder head is suspected of being loose, then there's a chance that the gasket and head are damaged if the problem has persisted for any length of time. The head bolts should be tightened to the proper torque in the correct sequence (Chapter 2).
- [ ] Improper valve clearance. This means that the valve is not closing completely and compression pressure is leaking past the valve. Check and adjust the valve clearances (Chapter 1).
- [ ] Cylinder and/or piston worn. Excessive wear will cause compression pressure to leak past the rings. This is usually accompanied by worn rings as well. A top-end overhaul is necessary (Chapter 2).
- [ ] Piston rings worn, weak, broken, or sticking. Broken or sticking piston rings usually indicate a lubrication or fueling problem that causes excess carbon deposits or seizures to form on the pistons and rings. Top-end overhaul is necessary (Chapter 2).
- [ ] Piston ring-to-groove clearance excessive. This is caused by excessive wear of the piston ring lands. Piston replacement is necessary (Chapter 2).
- [ ] Cylinder head gasket damaged. If a head is allowed to become loose, or if excessive carbon build-up on the piston crown and combustion chamber causes extremely high compression, the head gasket may leak. Retorquing the head is not always sufficient to restore the seal, so gasket replacement is necessary (Chapter 2).
- [ ] Cylinder head warped. This is caused by overheating or improperly tightened head bolts. Machine shop resurfacing or head replacement is necessary (Chapter 2).
- [ ] Valve spring broken or weak. Caused by component failure or wear; the springs must be replaced (Chapter 2).
- [ ] Valve not seating properly. This is caused by a bent valve (from over-revving or improper valve adjustment), burned valve or seat (improper fuelling) or an accumulation of carbon deposits on the seat (from fuelling or lubrication problems). The valves must be cleaned and/or replaced and the seats serviced if possible (Chapter 2).

Knocking or pinging

- [ ] Carbon build-up in combustion chamber. Use of a fuel additive that will dissolve the adhesive bonding the carbon particles to the crown and chamber is the easiest way to remove the build-up. Otherwise, the cylinder head will have to be removed and decarbonized (Chapter 2).
- [ ] Incorrect or poor quality fuel. Old or improper grades of fuel can cause detonation. This causes the piston to rattle, thus the knocking or pinging sound. Drain old fuel and always use the recommended fuel grade.
- [ ] Spark plug heat range incorrect. Uncontrolled detonation indicates the plug heat range is too hot. The plug in effect becomes a glow plug, raising cylinder temperatures. Install the proper heat range plug (Chapter 1).
- [ ] Improper air/fuel mixture. This will cause the cylinders to run hot, which leads to detonation. An intake air leak can cause this imbalance. See Chapter 4.

Miscellaneous causes

- [ ] Throttle valve doesn't open fully. Adjust the throttle grip freeplay (Chapter 1).
- [ ] Clutch slipping. May be caused by loose or worn clutch components. Refer to Chapter 2 for clutch overhaul procedures.
- [ ] Engine oil viscosity too high. Using a heavier oil than the one recommended in Chapter 1 can damage the oil pump or lubrication system and cause drag on the engine.
- [ ] Brakes dragging. Usually caused by debris which has entered the brake piston seals, or from a warped disc, out-of-round drum or bent axle. Repair as necessary.

Troubleshooting REF•31

4 Overheating

Engine overheats
- ☐ Coolant level low. Check and add coolant (Chapter 1).
- ☐ Leak in cooling system. Check cooling system hoses and radiator for leaks and other damage. Repair or replace parts as necessary (Chapter 3).
- ☐ Thermostat sticking open or closed. Check and replace as described in Chapter 3.
- ☐ Faulty pressure cap. Remove the cap and have it pressure tested (Chapter 3).
- ☐ Coolant passages clogged. Have the entire system drained and flushed, then refill with fresh coolant.
- ☐ Water pump defective. Remove the pump and check the components (Chapter 3).
- ☐ Clogged radiator fins. Clean them by blowing compressed air through the fins from the backside.
- ☐ Cooling fan or fan switch fault (Chapter 3).

Firing incorrect
- ☐ Spark plugs fouled, defective or worn out. See Chapter 1 for spark plug maintenance.
- ☐ Incorrect spark plugs.
- ☐ IC igniter unit or ECM defective. See Chapter 5.
- ☐ Pick-up coil faulty. See Chapter 5.
- ☐ Faulty ignition coils. See Chapter 5.

Fuel/air mixture incorrect
- ☐ Fuel system fault. Remove and overhaul the carburetors or check the fuel injection system (Chapter 4).
- ☐ Air filter clogged, poorly sealed, or missing (Chapter 1).
- ☐ Air filter housing poorly sealed. Look for cracks, holes or loose clamps, and replace or repair defective parts.
- ☐ Fuel tank breather hose obstructed.
- ☐ Intake air leak. Check for loose intake manifold retaining clips and damaged/disconnected vacuum hoses. Replace the intake manifold(s) if they are split or deteriorated (Chapter 4).

Compression too high
- ☐ Carbon build-up in combustion chamber. Use of a fuel additive that will dissolve the adhesive bonding the carbon particles to the piston crown and chamber is the easiest way to remove the build-up. Otherwise, the cylinder head will have to be removed and decarbonized (Chapter 2).
- ☐ Improperly machined head surface or installation of incorrect gasket during engine assembly.

Engine load excessive
- ☐ Clutch slipping. Can be caused by damaged, loose or worn clutch components. Refer to Chapter 2 for overhaul procedures.
- ☐ Engine oil level too high. The addition of too much oil will cause pressurization of the crankcase and inefficient engine operation. Check Specifications and drain to proper level (Chapter 1).
- ☐ Engine oil viscosity too high. Using a heavier oil than the one recommended in Chapter 1 can damage the oil pump or lubrication system as well as cause drag on the engine.
- ☐ Brakes dragging. Usually caused by debris which has entered the brake piston seals, or from a warped disc or drum or bent axle. Repair as necessary.

Lubrication inadequate
- ☐ Engine oil level too low. Friction caused by intermittent lack of lubrication or from oil that is overworked can cause overheating. The oil provides a definite cooling function in the engine. Check the oil level (Chapter 1).
- ☐ Poor quality engine oil or incorrect viscosity or type. Oil is rated not only according to viscosity but also according to type. Some oils are not rated high enough for use in this engine. Check the Specifications section and change to the correct oil (Chapter 1).

Miscellaneous causes
- ☐ Modification to exhaust system. Most aftermarket exhaust systems cause the engine to run leaner, which makes it run hotter.

5 Clutch problems

Clutch slipping
- ☐ Clutch cable freeplay incorrectly adjusted (cable clutch models) (Chapter 1).
- ☐ Friction plates worn or warped. Overhaul the clutch assembly (Chapter 2).
- ☐ Plain plates warped (Chapter 2).
- ☐ Clutch springs broken or weak. Old or heat-damaged (from slipping clutch) springs should be replaced with new ones (Chapter 2).
- ☐ Clutch pushrod bent. Check and, if necessary, replace (Chapter 2).
- ☐ Clutch center or housing unevenly worn. This causes improper engagement of the plates. Replace the damaged or worn parts (Chapter 2).

Clutch not disengaging completely
- ☐ Clutch cable freeplay incorrectly adjusted (Chapter 1).
- ☐ Air in clutch hydraulic system (hydraulic clutch models). Bleed the system (Chapter 2).
- ☐ Worn master or slave cylinder (hydraulic clutch models). Inspect and repair or replace as necessary (Chapter 2).
- ☐ Clutch plates warped or damaged. This will cause clutch drag, which in turn will cause the machine to creep. Overhaul the clutch assembly (Chapter 2).
- ☐ Clutch spring tension uneven. Usually caused by a sagged or broken spring. Check and replace the springs as a set (Chapter 2).
- ☐ Engine oil deteriorated. Old, thin, worn out oil will not provide proper lubrication for the plates, causing the clutch to drag. Replace the oil and filter (Chapter 1).
- ☐ Engine oil viscosity too high. Using a heavier oil than recommended in Chapter 1 can cause the plates to stick together, putting a drag on the engine. Change to the correct weight oil (Chapter 1).
- ☐ Clutch housing bearing seized. Lack of lubrication, severe wear or damage can cause the bearing to seize on the input shaft. Overhaul of the clutch, and perhaps transmission, may be necessary to repair the damage (Chapter 2).
- ☐ Loose clutch center nut. Causes housing and center misalignment putting a drag on the engine. Engagement adjustment continually varies. Overhaul the clutch assembly (Chapter 2).

REF•32 Troubleshooting

6 Gearchanging problems

Doesn't go into gear or lever doesn't return
- [ ] Clutch not disengaging. See above.
- [ ] Shift fork(s) bent or seized. Often caused by dropping the machine or from lack of lubrication. Overhaul the transmission (Chapter 2).
- [ ] Gear(s) stuck on shaft. Most often caused by a lack of lubrication or excessive wear in transmission bearings and bushings. Overhaul the transmission (Chapter 2).
- [ ] Gear shift drum binding. Caused by lubrication failure or excessive wear. Replace the drum and bearing (Chapter 2).
- [ ] Gear shift lever pawl spring weak or broken (Chapter 2).
- [ ] Gear shift lever broken. Splines stripped out of lever or shaft, caused by allowing the lever to get loose or from dropping the machine. Replace necessary parts (Chapter 2).
- [ ] Gear shift mechanism stopper arm broken or worn. Full engagement and rotary movement of shift drum results. Replace the arm (Chapter 2).
- [ ] Stopper arm spring broken. Allows arm to float, causing sporadic shift operation. Replace spring (Chapter 2).

Jumps out of gear
- [ ] Shift fork(s) worn. Overhaul the transmission (Chapter 2).
- [ ] Gear groove(s) worn. Overhaul the transmission (Chapter 2).
- [ ] Gear dogs or dog slots worn or damaged. The gears should be inspected and replaced. No attempt should be made to service the worn parts.

Overselects
- [ ] Stopper arm spring weak or broken (Chapter 2).
- [ ] Return spring post broken or distorted (Chapter 2).

7 Abnormal engine noise

Knocking or pinging
- [ ] Carbon build-up in combustion chamber. Use of a fuel additive that will dissolve the adhesive bonding the carbon particles to the piston crown and chamber is the easiest way to remove the build-up. Otherwise, the cylinder head will have to be removed and decarbonized (Chapter 2).
- [ ] Incorrect or poor quality fuel. Old or improper fuel can cause detonation. This causes the pistons to rattle, thus the knocking or pinging sound. Drain the old fuel and always use the recommended grade fuel (Chapter 4).
- [ ] Spark plug heat range incorrect. Uncontrolled detonation indicates that the plug heat range is too hot. The plug in effect becomes a glow plug, raising cylinder temperatures. Install the proper heat range plug (Chapter 1).
- [ ] Improper air/fuel mixture. This will cause the cylinders to run hot and lead to detonation. Blocked carburetor jets or an air leak can cause this imbalance. See Chapter 4.

Piston slap or rattling
- [ ] Cylinder-to-piston clearance excessive. Caused by improper assembly. Inspect and overhaul top-end parts (Chapter 2).
- [ ] Connecting rod bent. Caused by over-revving, trying to start a badly flooded engine or from ingesting a foreign object into the combustion chamber. Replace the damaged parts (Chapter 2).
- [ ] Piston pin or piston pin bore worn or seized from wear or lack of lubrication. Replace damaged parts (Chapter 2).
- [ ] Piston ring(s) worn, broken or sticking. Overhaul the top-end (Chapter 2).
- [ ] Piston seizure damage. Usually from lack of lubrication or overheating. Replace the pistons and cylinders, as necessary (Chapter 2).
- [ ] Connecting rod bearing clearance excessive. Caused by excessive wear or lack of lubrication. Replace worn parts.

Valve noise
- [ ] Incorrect valve clearances. Adjust the clearances by referring to Chapter 1.
- [ ] Valve spring broken or weak. Check and replace weak valve springs (Chapter 2).
- [ ] Camshaft or cylinder head worn or damaged. Lack of lubrication at high rpm is usually the cause of damage. Insufficient oil or failure to change the oil at the recommended intervals are the chief causes. Since there are no replaceable bearings in the head, the head itself will have to be replaced if there is excessive wear or damage (Chapter 2).

Other noise
- [ ] Cylinder head gasket leaking.
- [ ] Exhaust pipe leaking at cylinder head connection. Caused by improper fit of pipe(s) or loose exhaust nuts. All exhaust fasteners should be tightened evenly and carefully. Failure to do this will lead to a leak.
- [ ] Crankshaft runout excessive. Caused by a bent crankshaft (from over-revving) or damage from an upper cylinder component failure. Can also be attributed to dropping the machine on either of the crankshaft ends.
- [ ] Engine mounting bolts loose. Tighten all engine mount bolts (Chapter 2).
- [ ] Crankshaft bearings worn (Chapter 2).
- [ ] Cam chain, tensioner or guides worn. Replace according to the procedure in Chapter 2.

Troubleshooting REF•33

8 Abnormal driveline noise

Clutch noise
- [ ] Clutch outer drum/friction plate clearance excessive (Chapter 2).
- [ ] Loose or damaged clutch pressure plate and/or bolts (Chapter 2).

Transmission noise
- [ ] Bearings worn. Also includes the possibility that the shafts are worn. Overhaul the transmission (Chapter 2).
- [ ] Gears worn or chipped (Chapter 2).
- [ ] Metal chips jammed in gear teeth. Probably pieces from a broken clutch, gear or shift mechanism that were picked up by the gears. This will cause early bearing failure (Chapter 2).
- [ ] Engine oil level too low. Causes a howl from transmission. Also affects engine power and clutch operation (Chapter 1).

Final drive noise
- [ ] Chain not adjusted properly (Vulcan 800 models) (Chapter 1).
- [ ] Front or rear sprocket loose. Tighten fasteners (Chapter 6).
- [ ] Sprockets worn. Replace sprockets (Chapter 6).
- [ ] Rear sprocket warped. Replace sprockets (Chapter 6).
- [ ] Differential oil level low (Vulcan 700/750 models). Top up with the correct oil (Chapter 1).
- [ ] Differential worn or damaged. Have it repaired or replace it (Chapter 7).

9 Abnormal frame and suspension noise

Front end noise
- [ ] Low fluid level or improper viscosity oil in forks. This can sound like spurting and is usually accompanied by irregular fork action (Chapter 6).
- [ ] Spring weak or broken. Makes a clicking or scraping sound. Fork oil, when drained, will have a lot of metal particles in it (Chapter 6).
- [ ] Steering head bearings loose or damaged. Clicks when braking. Check and adjust or replace as necessary (Chapters 1 and 6).
- [ ] Triple clamps loose. Make sure all clamp bolts are tightened to the specified torque (Chapter 6).
- [ ] Fork tube bent. Good possibility if machine has been dropped. Replace tube with a new one (Chapter 6).
- [ ] Front axle bolt or axle pinch bolts loose. Tighten them to the specified torque (Chapter 7).
- [ ] Loose or worn wheel bearings. Check and replace as needed (Chapter 7).

Shock absorber noise
- [ ] Fluid level incorrect. Indicates a leak caused by defective seal. Shock will be covered with oil. Replace shock or seek advice on repair from a Suzuki dealer (Chapter 6).
- [ ] Defective shock absorber with internal damage. This is in the body of the shock and can't be remedied. The shock must be replaced with a new one (Chapter 6).
- [ ] Bent or damaged shock body. Replace the shock with a new one (Chapter 6).
- [ ] Loose or worn suspension linkage components (single-shock). Check and replace as necessary (Chapter 6).

Brake noise
- [ ] Squeal caused by dust on brake pads. Usually found in combination with glazed pads. Clean using brake cleaning solvent (Chapter 7).
- [ ] Contamination of brake pads. Oil, brake fluid or dirt causing brake to chatter or squeal. Clean or replace pads (Chapter 7).
- [ ] Pads glazed. Caused by excessive heat from prolonged use or from contamination. Do not use sandpaper/emery cloth or any other abrasive to roughen the pad surfaces as abrasives will stay in the pad material and damage the disc. A very fine flat file can be used, but pad replacement is suggested as a cure (Chapter 7).
- [ ] Disc warped. Can cause a chattering, clicking or intermittent squeal. Usually accompanied by a pulsating lever and uneven braking. Replace the disc (Chapter 7).
- [ ] Loose or worn wheel bearings. Check and replace as needed (Chapter 7).

10 Oil pressure warning light comes on

Engine lubrication system
- [ ] Engine oil pump defective, blocked oil strainer screen or failed relief valve. Carry out oil pressure check (Chapter 1).
- [ ] Engine oil level low. Inspect for leak or other problem causing low oil level and add recommended oil (Chapter 1).
- [ ] Engine oil viscosity too low. Very old, thin oil or an improper weight of oil used in the engine. Change to correct oil (Chapter 1).
- [ ] Camshaft or journals worn. Excessive wear causing drop in oil pressure. Replace cam and/or cylinder head. Abnormal wear could be caused by oil starvation at high rpm from low oil level or improper weight or type of oil (Chapter 1).
- [ ] Crankshaft and/or bearings worn. Same problems as above. Check and replace crankshaft and/or bearings (Chapter 2).

Electrical system
- [ ] Oil pressure switch defective. Check the switch according to the procedure in Chapter 9. Replace it if it is defective.
- [ ] Oil pressure indicator light circuit defective. Check for pinched, shorted, disconnected or damaged wiring (Chapter 9).

Troubleshooting

11 Excessive exhaust smoke

White smoke
- [ ] Piston oil ring worn. The ring may be broken or damaged, causing oil from the crankcase to be pulled past the piston into the combustion chamber. Replace the rings with new ones (Chapter 2).
- [ ] Cylinders worn, cracked, or scored. Caused by overheating or oil starvation. Install a new cylinder block (Chapter 2).
- [ ] Valve oil seal damaged or worn. Replace oil seals with new ones (Chapter 2).
- [ ] Valve guide worn. Perform a complete valve job (Chapter 2).
- [ ] Engine oil level too high, which causes the oil to be forced past the rings. Drain oil to the proper level (Chapter 1).
- [ ] Head gasket broken between oil return and cylinder. Causes oil to be pulled into the combustion chamber. Replace the head gasket and check the head for warpage (Chapter 2).
- [ ] Abnormal crankcase pressurization, which forces oil past the rings. Clogged breather is usually the cause.

Black smoke
- [ ] Air filter clogged. Clean or replace the element (Chapter 1).
- [ ] Carburetor flooding. Remove and overhaul the carburetor(s) (Chapter 4).
- [ ] Main jet too large. Remove and overhaul the carburetor(s) (Chapter 4).
- [ ] Choke cable stuck (Chapter 4).
- [ ] Fuel level too high. Check the fuel level (Chapter 4).
- [ ] Fuel injector problem (Chapter 4).

12 Poor handling or stability

Handlebar hard to turn
- [ ] Steering head bearing adjuster nut too tight. Check adjustment as described in Chapter 1.
- [ ] Bearings damaged. Roughness can be felt as the bars are turned from side-to-side. Replace bearings and races (Chapter 6).
- [ ] Races dented or worn. Denting results from wear in only one position (e.g., straight ahead), from a collision or hitting a pothole or from dropping the machine. Replace races and bearings (Chapter 6).
- [ ] Steering stem lubrication inadequate. Causes are grease getting hard from age or being washed out by high pressure car washes. Disassemble steering head and repack bearings (Chapter 6).
- [ ] Steering stem bent. Caused by a collision, hitting a pothole or by dropping the machine. Replace damaged part. Don't try to straighten the steering stem (Chapter 6).
- [ ] Front tire air pressure too low (Chapter 1).

Handlebar shakes or vibrates excessively
- [ ] Tires worn or out of balance (Chapter 7).
- [ ] Swingarm bearings worn. Replace worn bearings (Chapter 6).
- [ ] Wheel rim(s) warped or damaged. Inspect wheels for runout (Chapter 7).
- [ ] Wheel bearings worn. Worn front or rear wheel bearings can cause poor tracking. Worn front bearings will cause wobble (Chapter 7).
- [ ] Handlebar clamp bolts loose (Chapter 6).
- [ ] Fork yoke bolts loose. Tighten them to the specified torque (Chapter 6).
- [ ] Engine mounting bolts loose. Will cause excessive vibration with increased engine rpm (Chapter 2).

Handlebar pulls to one side
- [ ] Frame bent. Definitely suspect this if the machine has been dropped. May or may not be accompanied by cracking near the bend. Replace the frame (Chapter 8).
- [ ] Wheels out of alignment. Caused by improper location of axle spacers or from bent steering stem or frame (Chapters 6 and 8).
- [ ] Swingarm bent or twisted. Caused by age (metal fatigue) or impact damage. Replace the arm (Chapter 6).
- [ ] Steering stem bent. Caused by impact damage or by dropping the motorcycle. Replace the steering stem (Chapter 6).
- [ ] Fork tube bent. Disassemble the forks and replace the damaged parts (Chapter 6).
- [ ] Fork oil level uneven. Check and add or drain as necessary (Chapter 1).

Poor shock absorbing qualities
Too hard:
 a) Fork oil level excessive (Chapter 1).
 b) Fork oil viscosity too high. Use a lighter oil (see the Specifications in Chapter 1).
 c) Fork tube bent. Causes a harsh, sticking feeling (Chapter 6).
 d) Shock shaft or body bent or damaged (Chapter 6).
 e) Fork internal damage (Chapter 6).
 f) Shock internal damage.
 g) Tire pressure too high (Chapter 1).
Too soft:
 a) Fork or shock oil insufficient and/or leaking (Chapter 1).
 b) Fork oil level too low (Chapter 6).
 c) Fork oil viscosity too light (Chapter 6).
 d) Fork springs weak or broken (Chapter 6).
 e) Shock internal damage or leakage (Chapter 6).

Troubleshooting REF•35

13 Braking problems

Brakes are spongy, don't hold
- ☐ Air in brake line. Caused by inattention to master cylinder fluid level or by leakage. Locate problem and bleed brakes (Chapter 7).
- ☐ Pad or disc worn (Chapters 1 and 7).
- ☐ Brake fluid leak. See paragraph 1.
- ☐ Contaminated pads. Caused by contamination with oil, grease, brake fluid, etc. Clean or replace pads. Clean disc thoroughly with brake cleaner (Chapter 7).
- ☐ Brake fluid deteriorated. Fluid is old or contaminated. Drain system, replenish with new fluid and bleed the system (Chapter 7).
- ☐ Master cylinder internal parts worn or damaged causing fluid to bypass (Chapter 7).
- ☐ Master cylinder bore scratched by foreign material or broken spring. Repair or replace master cylinder (Chapter 7).
- ☐ Disc warped. Replace disc (Chapter 7).

Brake lever or pedal pulsates
- ☐ Disc warped. Replace disc (Chapter 7).
- ☐ Axle bent. Replace axle (Chapter 7).
- ☐ Brake caliper bolts loose (Chapter 7).
- ☐ Wheel warped or otherwise damaged (Chapter 7).
- ☐ Wheel bearings damaged or worn (Chapter 7).
- ☐ Brake drum out of round. Replace brake drum.

Brakes drag
- ☐ Master cylinder piston seized. Caused by wear or damage to piston or cylinder bore (Chapter 7).
- ☐ Lever binding. Check pivot and lubricate (Chapter 7).
- ☐ Brake caliper piston seized in bore. Caused by wear or ingestion of dirt past deteriorated seal (Chapter 7).
- ☐ Brake caliper mounting bracket pins corroded. Clean off corrosion and lubricate (Chapter 7).
- ☐ Brake pad or shoe damaged. Material separated from backing plate. Usually caused by faulty manufacturing process or from contact with chemicals. Replace pads or shoes (Chapter 7).
- ☐ Pads improperly installed (Chapter 7).
- ☐ Drum brake springs weak. Replace springs

14 Electrical problems

Battery dead or weak
- ☐ Battery faulty. Caused by sulfated plates which are shorted through sedimentation. Also, broken battery terminal making only occasional contact (Chapter 9).
- ☐ Battery cables making poor contact (Chapter 9).
- ☐ Load excessive. Caused by addition of high wattage lights or other electrical accessories.
- ☐ Ignition (main) switch defective. Switch either grounds internally or fails to shut off system. Replace the switch (Chapter 9).
- ☐ Regulator/rectifier defective (Chapter 9).
- ☐ Alternator stator coil open or shorted (Chapter 9).
- ☐ Wiring faulty. Wiring grounded or connections loose in ignition, charging or lighting circuits (Chapter 9).

Battery overcharged
- ☐ Regulator/rectifier defective. Overcharging is noticed when battery gets excessively warm (Chapter 9).
- ☐ Battery defective. Replace battery with a new one (Chapter 9).
- ☐ Battery amperage too low, wrong type or size. Install manufacturer's specified amp-hour battery to handle charging load (Chapter 9).

REF•36 Troubleshooting Equipment

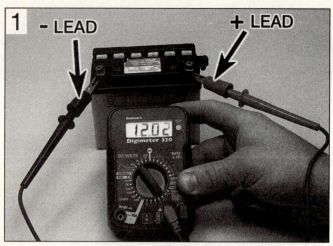

Measuring open-circuit battery voltage

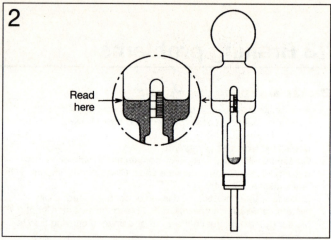

Float-type hydrometer for measuring battery specific gravity

Checking engine compression

● Low compression will result in exhaust smoke, heavy oil consumption, poor starting and poor performance. A compression test will provide useful information about an engine's condition and if performed regularly, can give warning of trouble before any other symptoms become apparent.
● A compression gauge will be required, along with an adapter to suit the spark plug hole thread size. Note that the screw-in type gauge/adapter set up is preferable to the rubber cone type.
● Before carrying out the test, first check the valve clearances as described in Chapter 1 (Vulcan 800 models).
● Compression testing procedures for the motorcycles covered in this manual are described in Chapter 2).

Checking battery open-circuit voltage

⚠ **Warning: The gases produced by the battery are explosive - never smoke or create any sparks in the vicinity of the battery. Never allow the electrolyte to contact your skin or clothing - if it does, wash it off and seek immediate medical attention.**

● Before any electrical fault is investigated the battery should be checked.
● You'll need a dc voltmeter or multimeter to check battery voltage. Check that the leads are inserted in the correct terminals on the meter, red lead to positive (+), black lead to negative (-). Incorrect connections can damage the meter.
● A sound, fully-charged 12 volt battery should produce between 12.3 and 12.6 volts across its terminals (12.8 volts for a maintenance-free battery). On machines with a 6 volt battery, voltage should be between 6.1 and 6.3 volts.
1 Set a multimeter to the 0 to 20 volts dc range and connect its probes across the battery terminals. Connect the meter's positive (+) probe, usually red, to the battery positive (+) terminal, followed by the meter's negative (-) probe, usually black, to the battery negative terminal (-) **(see illustration 1)**.
2 If battery voltage is low (below 10 volts on a 12 volt battery or below 4 volts on a six volt battery), charge the battery and test the voltage again. If the battery repeatedly goes flat, investigate the motorcycle's charging system.

Checking battery specific gravity (SG)

⚠ **Warning: The gases produced by the battery are explosive - never smoke or create any sparks in the vicinity of the battery. Never allow the electrolyte to contact your skin or clothing - if it does, wash it off and seek immediate medical attention.**

● The specific gravity check gives an indication of a battery's state of charge.
● A hydrometer is used for measuring specific gravity. Make sure you purchase one which has a small enough hose to insert in the aperture of a motorcycle battery.
● Specific gravity is simply a measure of the electrolyte's density compared with that of water. Water has an SG of 1.000 and fully-charged battery electrolyte is about 26% heavier, at 1.260.
● Specific gravity checks are not possible on maintenance-free batteries. Testing the open-circuit voltage is the only means of determining their state of charge.
1 To measure SG, remove the battery from the motorcycle and remove the first cell cap. Draw some electrolyte into the hydrometer and note the reading **(see illustration 2)**. Return the electrolyte to the cell and install the cap.
2 The reading should be in the region of 1.260 to 1.280. If SG is below 1.200 the battery needs charging. Note that SG will vary with temperature; it should be measured at 20°C (68°F). Add 0.007 to the reading for every 10°C above 20°C, and subtract 0.007 from the reading for every 10°C below 20°C. Add 0.004 to the reading for every 10°F above 68°F, and subtract 0.004 from the reading for every 10°F below 68°F.
3 When the check is complete, rinse the hydrometer thoroughly with clean water.

Checking for continuity

● The term continuity describes the uninterrupted flow of electricity through an electrical circuit. A continuity check will determine whether an **open-circuit** situation exists.
● Continuity can be checked with an ohmmeter, multimeter, continuity tester or battery and bulb test circuit **(see illustrations 3, 4 and 5)**.
● All of these instruments are self-powered by a battery, therefore the checks are made with the ignition OFF.
● As a safety precaution, always disconnect the battery negative (-) lead before making checks, particularly if ignition switch checks are being made.
● If using a meter, select the appropriate

Troubleshooting Equipment REF•37

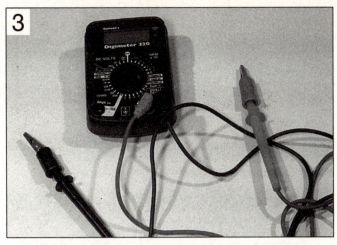

Digital multimeter can be used for all electrical tests

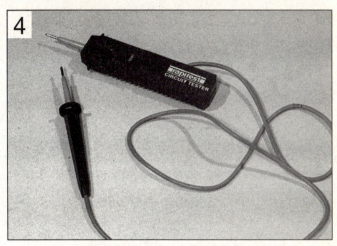

Battery-powered continuity tester

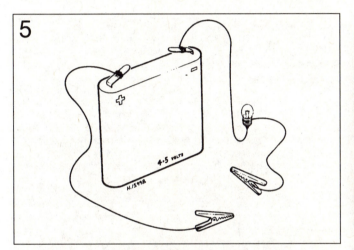

Battery and bulb test circuit

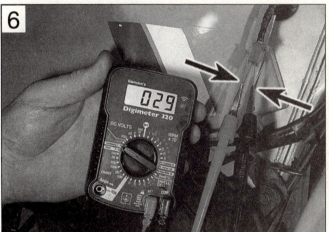

Continuity check of front brake light switch using a meter - note cotter pins used to access connector terminals

ohms scale and check that the meter reads infinity (∞). Touch the meter probes together and check that meter reads zero; where necessary adjust the meter so that it reads zero.
● After using a meter, always switch it OFF to conserve its battery.

Switch checks

1 If a switch is at fault, trace its wiring up to the wiring connectors. Separate the wire connectors and inspect them for security and condition. A build-up of dirt or corrosion here will most likely be the cause of the problem - clean up and apply a water dispersant such as WD40.
2 If using a test meter, set the meter to the ohms x 10 scale and connect its probes across the wires from the switch **(see illustration 6)**. Simple ON/OFF type switches, such as brake light switches, only have two wires whereas combination switches, like the ignition switch, have many internal links. Study the wiring diagram to ensure that you are connecting across the correct pair of wires. Continuity (low or no measurable resistance - 0 ohms) should be indicated with the switch ON and no continuity (high resistance) with it OFF.
3 Note that the polarity of the test probes doesn't matter for continuity checks, although care should be taken to follow specific test procedures if a diode or solid-state component is being checked.
4 A continuity tester or battery and bulb circuit can be used in the same way. Connect its probes as described above **(see illustration 7)**. The light should come on to indicate continuity in the ON switch position, but should extinguish in the OFF position.

Wiring checks

● Many electrical faults are caused by damaged wiring, often due to incorrect routing or chaffing on frame components.
● Loose, wet or corroded wire connectors

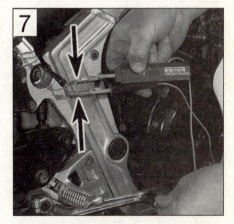

Continuity check of rear brake light switch using a continuity tester

can also be the cause of electrical problems, especially in exposed locations.

REF•38 Troubleshooting Equipment

Continuity check of front brake light switch sub-harness

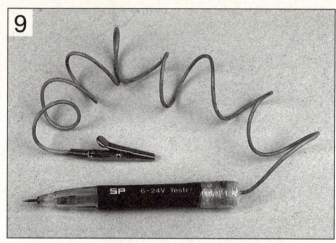

A simple test light can be used for voltage checks

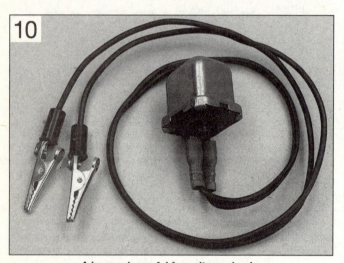

A buzzer is useful for voltage checks

Checking for voltage at the rear brake light power supply wire using a meter . . .

1 A continuity check can be made on a single length of wire by disconnecting it at each end and connecting a meter or continuity tester across both ends of the wire **(see illustration 8)**.

2 Continuity (low or no resistance - 0 ohms) should be indicated if the wire is good. If no continuity (high resistance) is shown, suspect a broken wire.

Checking for voltage

● A voltage check can determine whether current is reaching a component.
● Voltage can be checked with a dc voltmeter, multimeter set on the dc volts scale, test light or buzzer **(see illustrations 9 and 10)**. A meter has the advantage of being able to measure actual voltage.
● When using a meter, check that its leads are inserted in the correct terminals on the meter, red to positive (+), black to negative (-). Incorrect connections can damage the meter.
● A voltmeter (or multimeter set to the dc volts scale) should always be connected in parallel (across the load). Connecting it in series will destroy the meter.
● Voltage checks are made with the ignition ON.

1 First identify the relevant wiring circuit by referring to the wiring diagram at the end of this manual. If other electrical components share the same power supply (ie are fed from the same fuse), take note whether they are working correctly - this is useful information in deciding where to start checking the circuit.

2 If using a meter, check first that the meter leads are plugged into the correct terminals on the meter (see above). Set the meter to the dc volts function, at a range suitable for the battery voltage. Connect the meter red probe (+) to the power supply wire and the black probe to a good metal ground on the motor-cycle's frame or directly to the battery negative (-) terminal **(see illustration 11)**. Battery voltage should be shown on the meter with the ignition switched ON.

3 If using a test light or buzzer, connect its positive (+) probe to the power supply terminal and its negative (-) probe to a good ground on the motorcycle's frame or directly to the battery negative (-) terminal **(see illustration 12)**. With the ignition ON, the test light should illuminate or the buzzer sound.

4 If no voltage is indicated, work back towards the fuse continuing to check for voltage. When you reach a point where there is voltage, you know the problem lies between that point and your last check point.

Checking the ground

● Ground connections are made either

Troubleshooting Equipment REF•39

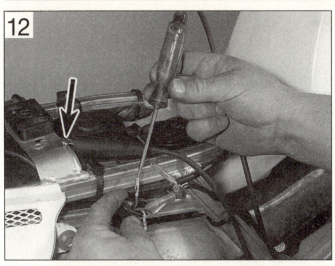

. . . or a test light - note the ground connection to the frame (arrow)

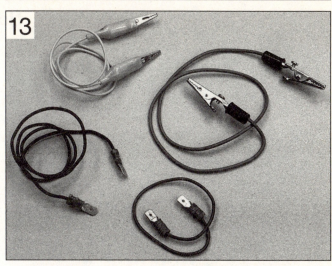

A selection of jumper wires for making ground checks

directly to the engine or frame (such as sensors, neutral switch etc. which only have a positive feed) or by a separate wire into the ground circuit of the wiring harness. Alternatively a short ground wire is sometimes run directly from the component to the motorcycle's frame.

● Corrosion is often the cause of a poor ground connection.

● If total failure is experienced, check the security of the main ground lead from the negative (-) terminal of the battery and also the main ground point on the wiring harness. If corroded, dismantle the connection and clean all surfaces back to bare metal.

1 To check the ground on a component, use an insulated jumper wire to temporarily bypass its ground connection **(see illustration 13)**. Connect one end of the jumper wire between the ground terminal or metal body of the component and the other end to the motorcycle's frame.

2 If the circuit works with the jumper wire installed, the original ground circuit is faulty. Check the wiring for open-circuits or poor connections. Clean up direct ground connections, removing all traces of corrosion and remake the joint. Apply petroleum jelly to the joint to prevent future corrosion.

Tracing a short-circuit

● A short-circuit occurs where current shorts to ground bypassing the circuit components. This usually results in a blown fuse.

● A short-circuit is most likely to occur where the insulation has worn through due to wiring chafing on a component, allowing a direct path to ground on the frame.

1 Remove any body panels necessary to access the circuit wiring.

2 Check that all electrical switches in the circuit are OFF, then remove the circuit fuse and connect a test light, buzzer or voltmeter (set to the dc scale) across the fuse terminals. No voltage should be shown.

3 Move the wiring from side to side while observing the test light or meter. When the test light comes on, buzzer sounds or meter shows voltage, you have found the cause of the short. It will usually shown up as damaged or burned insulation.

4 Note that the same test can be performed on each component in the circuit, even the switch.

Notes

Technical Terms Explained

A

ABS (Anti-lock braking system) A system, usually electronically controlled, that senses incipient wheel lockup during braking and relieves hydraulic pressure at wheel which is about to skid.

Aftermarket Components suitable for the motorcycle, but not produced by the motorcycle manufacturer.

Allen key A hexagonal wrench which fits into a recessed hexagonal hole.

Alternating current (ac) Current produced by an alternator. Requires converting to direct current by a rectifier for charging purposes.

Alternator Converts mechanical energy from the engine into electrical energy to charge the battery and power the electrical system.

Ampere (amp) A unit of measurement for the flow of electrical current. Current = Volts ÷ Ohms.

Ampere-hour (Ah) Measure of battery capacity.

Angle-tightening A torque expressed in degrees. Often follows a conventional tightening torque for cylinder head or main bearing fasteners **(see illustration)**.

Angle-tightening cylinder head bolts

Antifreeze A substance (usually ethylene glycol) mixed with water, and added to the cooling system, to prevent freezing of the coolant in winter. Antifreeze also contains chemicals to inhibit corrosion and the formation of rust and other deposits that would tend to clog the radiator and coolant passages and reduce cooling efficiency.

Anti-dive System attached to the fork lower leg (slider) to prevent fork dive when braking hard.

Anti-seize compound A coating that reduces the risk of seizing on fasteners that are subjected to high temperatures, such as exhaust clamp bolts and nuts.

API American Petroleum Institute. A quality standard for 4-stroke motor oils.

Asbestos A natural fibrous mineral with great heat resistance, commonly used in the composition of brake friction materials. Asbestos is a health hazard and the dust created by brake systems should never be inhaled or ingested.

ATF Automatic Transmission Fluid. Often used in front forks.

ATU Automatic Timing Unit. Mechanical device for advancing the ignition timing on early engines.

ATV All Terrain Vehicle. Often called a Quad.

Axial play Side-to-side movement.

Axle A shaft on which a wheel revolves. Also known as a spindle.

B

Backlash The amount of movement between meshed components when one component is held still. Usually applies to gear teeth.

Ball bearing A bearing consisting of a hardened inner and outer race with hardened steel balls between the two races.

Bearings Used between two working surfaces to prevent wear of the components and a build-up of heat. Four types of bearing are commonly used on motorcycles: plain shell bearings, ball bearings, tapered roller bearings and needle roller bearings.

Bevel gears Used to turn the drive through 90°. Typical applications are shaft final drive and camshaft drive **(see illustration)**.

BHP Brake Horsepower. The British measure-ment for engine power output. Power output is now usually expressed in kilowatts (kW).

Bevel gears are used to turn the drive through 90°

Bias-belted tire Similar construction to radial tire, but with outer belt running at an angle to the wheel rim.

Big-end bearing The bearing in the end of the connecting rod that's attached to the crankshaft.

Bleeding The process of removing air from a hydraulic system via a bleed nipple or bleed screw.

Bottom-end A description of an engine's crankcase components and all components contained therein.

BTDC Before Top Dead Center in terms of piston position. Ignition timing is often expressed in terms of degrees or millimeters BTDC.

Bush A cylindrical metal or rubber component used between two moving parts.

Burr Rough edge left on a component after machining or as a result of excessive wear.

C

Cam chain The chain which takes drive from the crankshaft to the camshaft(s).

Canister The main component in an evap-orative emission control system (California market only); contains activated charcoal granules to trap vapors from the fuel system rather than allowing them to vent to the atmosphere.

Castellated Resembling the parapets along the top of a castle wall. For example, a castellated wheel axle or spindle nut.

Catalytic converter A device in the exhaust system of some machines which

Technical Terms Explained

Cush drive rubber segments dampen out transmission shocks

converts certain pollutants in the exhaust gases into less harmful substances.

Charging system Description of the components which charge the battery, ie the alternator, rectifier and regulator.

Clearance The amount of space between two parts. For example, between a piston and a cylinder, between a bearing and a journal, etc.

Coil spring A spiral of elastic steel found in various sizes throughout a vehicle, for example as a springing medium in the suspension and in the valve train.

Compression Reduction in volume, and increase in pressure and temperature, of a gas, caused by squeezing it into a smaller space.

Compression damping Controls the speed the suspension compresses when hitting a bump.

Compression ratio The relationship between cylinder volume when the piston is at top dead center and cylinder volume when the piston is at bottom dead center.

Continuity The uninterrupted path in the flow of electricity. Little or no measurable resistance.

Continuity tester Self-powered bleeper or test light which indicates continuity.

Cp Candlepower. Bulb rating commonly found on US motorcycles.

Crossply tire Tire plies arranged in a criss-cross pattern. Usually four or six plies used, hence 4PR or 6PR in tire size codes.

Cush drive Rubber damper segments fitted between the rear wheel and final drive sprocket to absorb transmission shocks **(see illustration)**.

D

Degree disc Calibrated disc for measuring piston position. Expressed in degrees.

Dial gauge Clock-type gauge with adapters for measuring runout and piston position. Expressed in mm or inches.

Diaphragm The rubber membrane in a master cylinder or carburetor which seals the upper chamber.

Diaphragm spring A single sprung plate often used in clutches.

Direct current (dc) Current produced by a dc generator.

Decarbonization The process of removing carbon deposits - typically from the combustion chamber, valves and exhaust port/system.

Detonation Destructive and damaging explosion of fuel/air mixture in combustion chamber instead of controlled burning.

Diode An electrical valve which only allows current to flow in one direction. Commonly used in rectifiers and starter interlock systems.

Disc valve (or rotary valve) An induction system used on some two-stroke engines.

Double-overhead camshaft (DOHC) An engine that uses two overhead camshafts, one for the intake valves and one for the exhaust valves.

Drivebelt A toothed belt used to transmit drive to the rear wheel on some motorcycles. A drivebelt has also been used to drive the camshafts. Drivebelts are usually made of Kevlar.

Driveshaft Any shaft used to transmit motion. Commonly used when referring to the final driveshaft on shaft drive motorcycles.

E

ECU (Electronic Control Unit) A computer which controls (for instance) an ignition system, or an anti-lock braking system.

EGO Exhaust Gas Oxygen sensor. Some-times called a Lambda sensor.

Electrolyte The fluid in a lead-acid battery.

EMS (Engine Management System) A computer controlled system which manages the fuel injection and the ignition systems in an integrated fashion.

Endfloat The amount of lengthways movement between two parts. As applied to a crankshaft, the distance that the crankshaft can move side-to-side in the crankcase.

Endless chain A chain having no joining link. Common use for cam chains and final drive chains.

EP (Extreme Pressure) Oil type used in locations where high loads are applied, such as between gear teeth.

Evaporative emission control system Describes a charcoal filled canister which stores fuel vapors from the tank rather than allowing them to vent to the atmosphere. Usually only fitted to California models and referred to as an EVAP system.

Expansion chamber Section of two-stroke engine exhaust system so designed to improve engine efficiency and boost power.

F

Feeler blade or gauge A thin strip or blade of hardened steel, ground to an exact thickness, used to check or measure clearances between parts.

Final drive Description of the drive from the transmission to the rear wheel. Usually by chain or shaft, but sometimes by belt.

Firing order The order in which the engine cylinders fire, or deliver their power strokes, beginning with the number one cylinder.

Flooding Term used to describe a high fuel level in the carburetor float chambers, leading to fuel overflow. Also refers to excess fuel in the combustion chamber due to incorrect starting technique.

Free length The no-load state of a component when measured. Clutch, valve and fork spring lengths are measured at rest, without any preload.

Freeplay The amount of travel before any action takes place. The looseness in a linkage, or an assembly of parts, between the initial application of force and actual movement. For example, the distance the rear brake pedal moves before the rear brake is actuated.

Fuel injection The fuel/air mixture is metered electronically and directed into the engine intake ports (indirect injection) or into the cylinders (direct injection). Sensors supply information on engine speed and conditions.

Fuel/air mixture The charge of fuel and air going into the engine. See Stoichiometric ratio.

Fuse An electrical device which protects a circuit against accidental overload. The typical fuse contains a soft piece of metal which is calibrated to melt at a predetermined current flow (expressed as amps) and break the circuit.

G

Gap The distance the spark must travel in jumping from the center electrode to the side electrode in a spark plug. Also refers to the distance between the ignition rotor and the pickup coil in an electronic ignition system.

Gasket Any thin, soft material - usually cork, cardboard, asbestos or soft metal - installed between two metal surfaces to ensure a good seal. For instance, the cylinder head gasket seals the joint between the block and the cylinder head.

Gauge An instrument panel display used to monitor engine conditions. A gauge with a movable pointer on a dial or a fixed scale is an analog gauge. A gauge with a numerical readout is called a digital gauge.

Gear ratios The drive ratio of a pair of gears in a gearbox, calculated on their number of teeth.

Glaze-busting see **Honing**

Grinding Process for renovating the valve face and valve seat contact area in the cylinder head.

Ground return The return path of an electrical circuit, utilizing the motorcycle's frame.

Gudgeon pin The shaft which connects the connecting rod small-end with the piston. Often called a piston pin or wrist pin.

H

Helical gears Gear teeth are slightly curved and produce less gear noise that straight-cut gears. Often used for primary drives.

Helicoil A thread insert repair system. Commonly used as a repair for stripped spark plug threads (see illustration).

Installing a Helicoil thread insert in a cylinder head

Honing A process used to break down the glaze on a cylinder bore (also called glaze-busting). Can also be carried out to roughen a rebored cylinder to aid ring bedding-in.

HT (High Tension) Description of the electrical circuit from the secondary winding of the ignition coil to the spark plug.

Hydraulic A liquid filled system used to transmit pressure from one component to another. Common uses on motorcycles are brakes and clutches.

Hydrometer An instrument for measuring the specific gravity of a lead-acid battery.

Hygroscopic Water absorbing. In motorcycle applications, braking efficiency will be reduced if DOT 3 or 4 hydraulic fluid absorbs water from the air - care must be taken to keep new brake fluid in tightly sealed containers.

I

lbf ft Pounds-force feet. A unit of torque. Sometimes written as ft-lbs.

lbf in Pound-force inch. A unit of torque, applied to components where a very low torque is required. Sometimes written as inch-lbs.

IC Abbreviation for Integrated Circuit.

Ignition advance Means of increasing the timing of the spark at higher engine speeds. Done by mechanical means (ATU) on early engines or electronically by the ignition control unit on later engines.

Ignition timing The moment at which the spark plug fires, expressed in the number of crankshaft degrees before the piston reaches the top of its stroke, or in the number of millimeters before the piston reaches the top of its stroke.

Infinity (∞) Description of an open-circuit electrical state, where no continuity exists.

Inverted forks (upside down forks) The sliders or lower legs are held in the yokes and the fork tubes or stanchions are connected to the wheel axle (spindle). Less unsprung weight and stiffer construction than conventional forks.

J

JASO Japan Automobile Standards Organization. JASO MA is a standard for motorcycle oil equivalent to API SJ, but designed to prevent problems with wet-type motorcycle clutches.

Joule The unit of electrical energy.

Journal The bearing surface of a shaft.

K

Kickstart Mechanical means of turning the engine over for starting purposes.

Technical Terms Explained

Only usually fitted to mopeds, small capacity motorcycles and off-road motorcycles.

Kill switch Handebar-mounted switch for emergency ignition cut-out. Cuts the ignition circuit on all models, and additionally prevent starter motor operation on others.

km Symbol for kilometer.

kmh Abbreviation for kilometers per hour.

L

Lambda sensor A sensor fitted in the exhaust system to measure the exhaust gas oxygen content (excess air factor). Also called oxygen sensor.

Lapping see **Grinding**.

LCD Abbreviation for Liquid Crystal Display.

LED Abbreviation for Light Emitting Diode.

Liner A steel cylinder liner inserted in an aluminum alloy cylinder block.

Locknut A nut used to lock an adjustment nut, or other threaded component, in place.

Lockstops The lugs on the lower triple clamp (yoke) which abut those on the frame, preventing handlebar-to-fuel tank contact.

Lockwasher A form of washer designed to prevent an attaching nut from working loose.

LT Low Tension Description of the electrical circuit from the power supply to the primary winding of the ignition coil.

M

Main bearings The bearings between the crankshaft and crankcase.

Maintenance-free (MF) battery A sealed battery which cannot be topped up.

Manometer Mercury-filled calibrated tubes used to measure intake tract vacuum. Used to synchronize carburetors on multi-cylinder engines.

Tappet shims are measured with a micrometer

Micrometer A precision measuring instru-ment that measures component outside diameters **(see illustration)**.

MON (Motor Octane Number) A measure of a fuel's resistance to knock.

Monograde oil An oil with a single viscosity, eg SAE80W.

Monoshock A single suspension unit linking the swingarm or suspension linkage to the frame.

mph Abbreviation for miles per hour.

Multigrade oil Having a wide viscosity range (eg 10W40). The W stands for Winter, thus the viscosity ranges from SAE10 when cold to SAE40 when hot.

Multimeter An electrical test instrument with the capability to measure voltage, current and resistance. Some meters also incorporate a continuity tester and buzzer.

N

Needle roller bearing Inner race of caged needle rollers and hardened outer race. Examples of uncaged needle rollers can be found on some engines. Commonly used in rear suspension applications and in two-stroke engines.

Nm Newton meters.

NOx Oxides of Nitrogen. A common toxic pollutant emitted by gasoline engines at higher temperatures.

O

Octane The measure of a fuel's resistance to knock.

OE (Original Equipment) Relates to components fitted to a motorcycle as standard or replacement parts supplied by the motorcycle manufacturer.

Ohms The unit of electrical resistance. Ohms = Volts ÷ Current.

Ohmmeter An instrument for measuring electrical resistance.

Oil cooler System for diverting engine oil outside of the engine to a radiator for cooling purposes.

Oil injection A system of two-stroke engine lubrication where oil is pump-fed to the engine in accordance with throttle position.

Open-circuit An electrical condition where there is a break in the flow of electricity - no continuity (high resistance).

O-ring A type of sealing ring made of a special rubber-like material; in use, the O-ring is compressed into a groove to provide the sealing action.

Oversize (OS) Term used for piston and ring size options fitted to a rebored cylinder.

Overhead cam (sohc) engine An engine with single camshaft located on top of the cylinder head.

Overhead valve (ohv) engine An engine with the valves located in the cylinder head, but with the camshaft located in the engine block or crankcase.

Oxygen sensor A device installed in the exhaust system which senses the oxygen content in the exhaust and converts this information into an electric current. Also called a Lambda sensor.

P

Plastigage A thin strip of plastic thread, available in different sizes, used for measuring clearances. For example, a strip of Plastigage is laid across a bearing journal. The parts are assembled and dismantled; the width of the crushed strip indicates the clearance between journal and bearing.

Polarity Either negative or positive ground, determined by which battery lead is connected to the frame (ground return). Modern motorcycles are usually negative ground.

Technical Terms Explained REF•45

Pre-ignition A situation where the fuel/air mixture ignites before the spark plug fires. Often due to a hot spot in the combustion chamber caused by carbon build-up. Engine has a tendency to 'run-on'.

Pre-load (suspension) The amount a spring is compressed when in the unloaded state. Preload can be applied by gas, spacer or mechanical adjuster.

Premix The method of engine lubrication on some gasoline two-stroke engines. Engine oil is mixed with the gasoline in the fuel tank in a specific ratio. The fuel/oil mix is sometimes referred to as "petrol".

Primary drive Description of the drive from the crankshaft to the clutch. Usually by gear or chain.

PS Pferdestärke - a German interpretation of BHP.

PSI Pounds-force per square inch. Imperial measurement of tire pressure and cylinder pressure measurement.

PTFE Polytetrafluroethylene. A low friction substance.

Pulse secondary air injection system A process of promoting the burning of excess fuel present in the exhaust gases by routing fresh air into the exhaust ports.

Q

Quartz halogen bulb Tungsten filament surrounded by a halogen gas. Typically used for the headlight (see illustration).

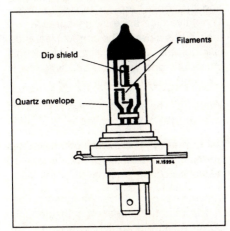

Quartz halogen headlight bulb construction

R

Rack-and-pinion A pinion gear on the end of a shaft that mates with a rack (think of a geared wheel opened up and laid flat). Sometimes used in clutch operating systems.

Radial play Up and down movement about a shaft.

Radial ply tires Tire plies run across the tire (from bead to bead) and around the circumference of the tire. Less resistant to tread distortion than other tire types.

Radiator A liquid-to-air heat transfer device designed to reduce the temperature of the coolant in a liquid cooled engine.

Rake A feature of steering geometry - the angle of the steering head in relation to the vertical (see illustration).

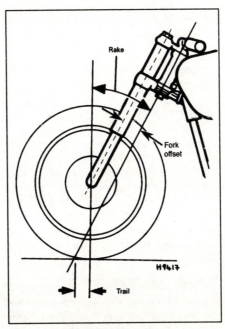

Steering geometry

Rebore Providing a new working surface to the cylinder bore by boring out the old surface. Necessitates the use of oversize piston and rings.

Rebound damping A means of controlling the oscillation of a suspension unit spring after it has been compressed. Resists the spring's natural tendency to bounce back after being compressed.

Rectifier Device for converting the ac output of an alternator into dc for battery charging.

Reed valve An induction system commonly used on two-stroke engines.

Regulator Device for maintaining the charging voltage from the generator or alternator within a specified range.

Relay A electrical device used to switch heavy current on and off by using a low current auxiliary circuit.

Resistance Measured in ohms. An electrical component's ability to pass electrical current.

RON (Research Octane Number) A measure of a fuel's resistance to knock.

rpm revolutions per minute.

Runout The amount of wobble (in-and-out movement) of a wheel or shaft as it's rotated. The amount a shaft rotates out-of-true. The out-of-round condition of a rotating part.

S

SAE (Society of Automotive Engineers) A standard for the viscosity of a fluid.

Sealant A liquid or paste used to prevent leakage at a joint. Sometimes used in conjunction with a gasket.

Service limit Term for the point where a component is no longer useable and must be replaced.

Shaft drive A method of transmitting drive from the transmission to the rear wheel.

Shell bearings Plain bearings consisting of two shell halves. Most often used as big-end and main bearings in a four-stroke engine. Often called bearing inserts.

Shim Thin spacer, commonly used to adjust the clearance or relative positions between two parts. For example, shims inserted into or under tappets or followers to control valve clearances. Clearance is adjusted by changing the thickness of the shim.

Short-circuit An electrical condition where current shorts to ground bypassing the circuit components.

Technical Terms Explained

Skimming Process to correct warpage or repair a damaged surface, eg on brake discs or drums.

Slide-hammer A special puller that screws into or hooks onto a component such as a shaft or bearing; a heavy sliding handle on the shaft bottoms against the end of the shaft to knock the component free.

Small-end bearing The bearing in the upper end of the connecting rod at its joint with the gudgeon pin.

Snap-ring A ring-shaped clip used to prevent endwise movement of cylindrical parts and shafts. An internal snap-ring is installed in a groove in a housing; an external snap-ring fits into a groove on the outside of a cylindrical piece such as a shaft. Also known as a circlip.

Spalling Damage to camshaft lobes or bearing journals shown as pitting of the working surface.

Specific gravity (SG) The state of charge of the electrolyte in a lead-acid battery. A measure of the electrolyte's density compared with water.

Straight-cut gears Common type gear used on gearbox shafts and for oil pump and water pump drives.

Stanchion The inner sliding part of the front forks, held by the yokes. Often called a fork tube.

Stoichiometric ratio The optimum chemical air/fuel ratio for a gasoline engine, said to be 14.7 parts of air to 1 part of fuel.

Sulphuric acid The liquid (electrolyte) used in a lead-acid battery. Poisonous and extremely corrosive.

Surface grinding (lapping) Process to correct a warped gasket face, commonly used on cylinder heads.

T

Tapered-roller bearing Tapered inner race of caged needle rollers and separate tapered outer race. Examples of taper roller bearings can be found on steering heads.

Tappet A cylindrical component which transmits motion from the cam to the valve stem, either directly or via a pushrod and rocker arm. Also called a cam follower.

TCS Traction Control System. An electron-ically-controlled system which senses wheel spin and reduces engine speed accordingly.

TDC Top Dead Center denotes that the piston is at its highest point in the cylinder.

Thread-locking compound Solution applied to fastener threads to prevent loosening. Select type to suit application.

Thrust washer A washer positioned between two moving components on a shaft. For example, between gear pinions on gearshaft.

Timing chain See **Cam Chain**.

Timing light Stroboscopic lamp for carrying out ignition timing checks with the engine running.

Top-end A description of an engine's cylinder block, head and valve gear components.

Torque Turning or twisting force about a shaft.

Torque setting A prescribed tightness specified by the motorcycle manufacturer to ensure that the bolt or nut is secured correctly. Undertightening can result in the bolt or nut coming loose or a surface not being sealed. Overtightening can result in stripped threads, distortion or damage to the component being retained.

Torx key A six-point wrench.

Tracer A stripe of a second color applied to a wire insulator to distinguish that wire from another one with the same color insulator. For example, Br/W is often used to denote a brown insulator with a white tracer.

Trail A feature of steering geometry. Distance from the steering head axis to the tire's central contact point.

Triple clamps The cast components which extend from the steering head and support the fork stanchions or tubes. Often called fork yokes.

Turbocharger A centrifugal device, driven by exhaust gases, that pressurizes the intake air. Normally used to increase the power output from a given engine displacement.

TWI Abbreviation for Tire Wear Indicator. Indicates the location of the tread depth indicator bars on tires.

U

Universal joint or U-joint (UJ) A double-pivoted connection for transmitting power from a driving to a driven shaft through an angle. Typically found in shaft drive assemblies.

Unsprung weight Anything not supported by the bike's suspension (ie the wheel, tires, brakes, final drive and bottom (moving) part of the suspension).

V

Vacuum gauges Clock-type gauges for measuring intake tract vacuum. Used for carburetor synchronization on multi-cylinder engines.

Valve A device through which the flow of liquid, gas or vacuum may be stopped, started or regulated by a moveable part that opens, shuts or partially obstructs one or more ports or passageways. The intake and exhaust valves in the cylinder head are of the poppet type.

Valve clearance The clearance between the valve tip (the end of the valve stem) and the rocker arm or tappet/follower. The valve clearance is measured when the valve is closed. The correct clearance is important - if too small the valve won't close fully and will burn out, whereas if too large noisy operation will result.

Valve lift The amount a valve is lifted off its seat by the camshaft lobe.

Valve timing The exact setting for the opening and closing of the valves in relation to piston position.

Vernier caliper A precision measuring instrument that measures inside and outside dimensions. Not quite as accurate as a micrometer, but more convenient.

Technical Terms Explained REF•47

VIN Vehicle Identification Number. Term for the bike's engine and frame numbers.

Viscosity The thickness of a liquid or its resistance to flow.

Volt A unit for expressing electrical "pressure" in a circuit. Volts = current x ohms.

W

Water pump A mechanically-driven device for moving coolant around the engine.

Watt A unit for expressing electrical power. Watts = volts x current.

Wet liner arrangement

Wear limit see **Service limit**

Wet liner A liquid-cooled engine design where the pistons run in liners which are directly surrounded by coolant **(see illustration)**.

Wheelbase Distance from the center of the front wheel to the center of the rear wheel.

Wiring harness or loom Describes the electrical wires running the length of the motorcycle and enclosed in tape or plastic sheathing. Wiring coming off the main harness is usually referred to as a sub harness.

Woodruff key A key of semi-circular or square section used to locate a gear to a shaft. Often used to locate the alternator rotor on the crankshaft.

Wrist pin Another name for gudgeon or piston pin.

Notes

Index

Note: *References throughout this index are in the form – "Chapter number"•"Page number"*

A

About this manual - 0•8
Acknowledgements - 0•8
Air filter
   element, servicing - 1•17
   housing and intake duct, removal and installation - 4B•8
   housing, removal and installation - 4A•16
Alternator
   rotor and starter clutch, removal and installation - 9•21
   coil replacement - 9•22
   testing - 9•20

B

Battery
   charging - 9•6
   electrolyte level/specific gravity, check - 1•11
   inspection and maintenance - 9•4
Brake
   caliper, removal, overhaul and installation - 7•5
   disc, inspection, removal and installation - 7•6
   fluid level check - 0•14
   hoses and lines, inspection and replacement - 7•9
   light switches, check and replacement - 9•11
   master cylinder, removal, overhaul and installation - 7•7
   pads and linings, wear check - 1•8
   pads, replacement - 7•3
   pedal and linkage, removal and installation - 7•9
   pedal position and play, check and adjustment - 1•9
   rear drum brake, removal, inspection and installation, 7•8
   system bleeding, 7•9
   system, general check, 1•8
Brakes, wheels and tires - 7•1 through 7•18
Buying spare parts - 0•10

C

Caliper, brake, removal, overhaul and installation - 7•5
Cam chain tensioners, locking, removal and installation - 2•14
Camshaft chains and guides, removal, inspection and installation - 2•31
Camshafts, removal, inspection and installation - 2•10
Carburetor
   disassembly, cleaning and inspection - 4A•10
   reassembly and fuel level adjustment - 4A•14
   removal and installation
      single-carb models - 4A•10
      twin-carb models - 4A•9
Carburetor overhaul, general information - 4A•8
Carburetor synchronization, check and adjustment - 1•16
Carburetors, separation and reconnection (twin carb models) - 4A•10
Catalytic converter - 4B•18
Chain and sprockets, check, adjustment and lubrication - 1•7
Chain, removal, cleaning, inspection and installation - 6•16
Charging system
   alternator
      coil replacement - 9•22
      rotor and starter clutch, removal and installation - 9•21
      testing - 9•20
   running voltage test - 9•19
   testing, general information and precautions - 9•19
   voltage regulator/rectifier, check and replacement - 9•20
Chemicals and lubricants - REF•23
Choke and throttle cables, removal and installation - 4A•14
Choke and throttle operation/grip freeplay, check and adjustment - 1•14
Clutch
   cable, replacement - 2•24
   check and adjustment - 1•10
   hydraulic system, bleeding, removal, inspection and installation - 2•21
   release mechanism (cable clutch), removal, inspection and installation - 2•24
   removal, inspection and installation - 2•24
Clutch fluid level check - 0•14
Clutch, removal, inspection and installation - 2•24
Coils, ignition, check, removal and installation - 5•2
Connecting rod bearings, general note - 2•34
Connecting rods and bearings, removal, inspection, bearing selection and installation - 2•35
Conversion factors - REF•22
Coolant level check - 0•13

Index

Coolant reservoir or catch bottle, removal and installation - 3•2
Coolant temperature sender, check and replacement - 3•3
Cooling fan and thermostatic switch, check and replacement - 3•2
Cooling system - 3•1 through 3•6
Cooling system, check - 1•18
Cooling system, draining, flushing and refilling - 1•21
Crankcase components, inspection and servicing - 2•33
Crankcase, disassembly and reassembly - 2•32
Crankshaft and main bearings, removal, inspection and installation - 2•34
Cylinder compression, check - 2•6
Cylinder head and valves, disassembly, inspection and reassembly - 2•16
Cylinder heads and cylinders, removal, separation and installation - 2•12
Cylinders, inspection - 2•18

D

Diagnosis - REF•27
Dimensions and weights - REF•1
Disc, brake, inspection, removal and installation - 7•6
Drive chain and sprockets, check, adjustment and lubrication - 1•7
Drive chain, removal, cleaning, inspection and installation - 6•16
Drum brake, removal, inspection and installation - 7•8

E

ECM, removal, check and installation - 5•3
Electrical system - 9•1 through 9•26
Electrical troubleshooting - 9•4
Engine
    cam chain tensioners, locking, removal and installation - 2•14
    camshaft chains and guides, removal, inspection and installation - 2•31
    camshafts, removal, inspection and installation - 2•10
    connecting rod bearings, general note - 2•34
    connecting rods and bearings, removal, inspection, bearing selection and installation - 2•35
    crankcase components, inspection and servicing - 2•33
    crankcase, disassembly and reassembly - 2•32
    crankshaft and main bearings, removal, inspection and installation - 2•34
    cylinder compression, check - 2•6
    cylinder head and valves, disassembly, inspection and reassembly - 2•16
    cylinder heads and cylinders, removal, separation and installation - 2•12
    cylinders, inspection - 2•18
    disassembly and reassembly, general information - 2•8
    initial start-up after overhaul - 2•41
    major engine repair, general note - 2•6
    oil pump, removal and installation - 2•37
    operations possible with the engine in the frame - 2•6
    operations requiring engine removal - 2•6
    piston rings, installation - 2•20
    pistons, removal, inspection and installation - 2•18
    recommended break-in procedure - 2•41
    removal and installation - 2•7
    rocker assemblies, removal and installation - 2•9
    valves/valve seats/valve guides, servicing - 2•16
Engine oil and filter, change - 1•20
Engine, clutch and transmission - 2•1 through 2•42
Engine/transmission oil level check - 0•12
Evaporative emission control system
    carbureted models - 4A•18
    fuel-injected models - 4B•18
Evaporative emission control system, check - 1•19
Exhaust system
    check - 1•19
    removal and installation
        carbureted models - 4A•17
        fuel-injected models - 4B•17
External shift mechanism, removal, inspection and installation - 2•28

F

Fast idle speed, fuel-injected models, check and adjustment - 4B•17
Fasteners, check - 1•18
Fault finding - REF•27
Fender, removal and installation
    front - 8•4
    rear - 8•5
Final drive oil level (shaft drive models), check - 1•8
Final drive unit and driveshaft, removal, inspection and installation - 6•14
Fluid levels, check - 1•8
Footpegs, floorboards and brackets, removal and installation - 8•1
Forks
    disassembly, inspection and reassembly - 6•5
    removal and installation - 6•4
Frame and bodywork - 8•1 through 8•6
Frame, inspection and repair - 8•1
Front bevel gears, removal, inspection and installation - 6•15
Front wheel, removal, inspection and installation - 7•11
Fuel
    carburetor
        disassembly, cleaning and inspection - 4A•10
        overhaul, general information - 4A•8
        reassembly and fuel level adjustment - 4A•14
        removal and installation
            single-carb models - 4A•10
            twin-carb models - 4A•9
    idle fuel/air mixture adjustment, general information - 4A•8
    injection system
        components, check, removal and installation - 4B•11
        description - 4B•9
        troubleshooting - 4B•9
    pressure check (fuel-injected models) - 4B•4

pressure regulator, removal and installation - 4B•8
pump relay, check, removal and installation - 4B•5
pump, removal, disassembly and installation - 4B•5
pump, testing and replacement - 4A•18
rails and injectors, removal and installation - 4B•15
strainer and filter, removal and installation - 4B•6
system, check and filter cleaning - 1•19

tank
   cleaning and repair - 4A•8
   removal and installation
      carbureted models - 4A•7
      fuel-injected models - 4B•3

Fuel and exhaust systems, carbureted models - 4A•1 through 4A•20
Fuel, engine management and exhaust systems, fuel injected models - 4B•1 through 4B•18
Fuses, check and replacement - 9•7

G

Glossary - REF•41

H

Handlebar switches
   check - 9•15
   removal and installation - 9•16
Handlebars, removal and installation - 6•3
Headlight
   aim, check and adjustment - 9•10
   assembly, removal and installation - 9•9
   bulb, replacement - 9•9
Horn, check and replacement - 9•16

I

IC igniter or ECM, removal, check and installation - 5•3
Identification numbers - 0•10
Idle fuel/air mixture adjustment, general information - 4A•8
Idle speed, check and adjustment - 1•16
Ignition system - 5•1 through 5•4
   coils, check, removal and installation - 5•2
   IC igniter or ECM, removal, check and installation - 5•3
   main (key) switch, check and replacement - 9•15
   pickup coil(s), check and replacement - 5•3
   system, check - 5•2
Initial start-up after overhaul - 2•41
Instrument and warning light
   bulbs, replacement - 9•14
   housings, removal and installation - 9•12
Introduction to tune-up and routine maintenance - 1•7

K

Kickstand, maintenance - 8•2

L

Lighting system, check - 9•8
Lubricants and chemicals - REF•23
Lubrication, general - 1•10

M

Maintenance intervals - 1•6
Major engine repair, general note - 2•6
Master cylinder, brake, removal, overhaul and installation - 7•7
Meters and gauges, check and replacement - 9•14
Mirrors, removal and installation - 8•2
Motorcycle chemicals and lubricants - REF•23

N

Neutral switch, check and replacement - 9•16

O

Oil and filter, engine, change - 1•20
Oil level check, engine/transmission - 0•12
Oil pressure switch, check and replacement - 9•15
Oil pump, removal and installation - 2•37
Operations possible with the engine in the frame - 2•6
Operations requiring engine removal - 2•6

P

Pads, brake, replacement - 7•3
PAIR system
   carbureted models - 4A•17
   check - 1•19
   fuel-injected models - 4B•17
Pedal and linkage, brake, removal and installation - 7•9
Pickup coil(s), check and replacement - 5•3
Piston rings, installation - 2•20
Pistons, removal, inspection and installation - 2•18
Primary drive gear, removal, inspection and installation - 2•30

R

Radiator cap, check - 3•2
Radiator, removal and installation - 3•5
Rear drum brake, removal, inspection and installation - 7•8
Rear shock absorbers, removal and installation - 6•11
Rear suspension linkage, removal, inspection and installation - 6•12
Rear view mirrors, removal and installation - 8•2
Rear wheel coupling/rubber damper, check and replacement - 6•17

Index

Rear wheel, removal, inspection and installation - 7•12
Recommended break-in procedure - 2•41
Reference - REF•1 through REF•48
Rocker assemblies, removal and installation - 2•9
Rotor, brake, inspection, removal and installation - 7•6
Routine maintenance intervals - 1•6

S

Saddlebags, removal and installation - 8•5
Safety first! - 0•11
Seat, removal and installation - 8•2
Secondary drive gear, removal, inspection and installation - 2•40
Shift drum and forks, removal, inspection and installation - 2•38
Side covers, removal and installation - 8•3
Sidestand switch, check and replacement - 9•16
Sidestand, maintenance - 8•2
Single carburetor, removal and installation - 4A•10
Spark plug
    replacement - 1•11
    torque - 1•2
    type and gap - 1•1
Sprockets and drive chain, check, adjustment and lubrication - 1•7
Sprockets, check and replacement - 6•16
Starter
    motor
        disassembly, inspection and reassembly - 9•17
        removal and installation - 9•17
    reduction gears, removal, inspection and installation - 9•19
    relay, check and replacement - 9•16
Steering head
    bearings
        check - 1•11
        replacement and adjustment - 6•9
    covers, removal and installation - 8•4
Steering, suspension and final drive - 6•1 through 6•18
Storage - REF•24
Suspension, check - 1•19
Suzuki, Every Which Way - 0•4
Swingarm
    bearings
        check - 6•12
        replacement - 6•14
    removal and installation - 6•12

T

Technical terms explained - REF•41
Thermostat, removal, check and installation - 3•4
Throttle and choke cables, carbureted models, removal and installation - 4A•14
Throttle and choke operation/grip freeplay, check and adjustment - 1•14
Throttle body, removal, inspection, installation and synchronization - 4B•14
Throttle cables, fuel-injected models, removal and installation - 4B•16
Tire checks - 0•15
Tires/wheels, general check - 1•9
Tools and workshop tips - REF•4
Transmission
    external shift mechanism, removal, inspection and installation - 2•28
    primary drive gear, removal, inspection and installation - 2•30
    secondary drive gear, removal, inspection and installation - 2•40
    shafts
        disassembly, inspection and reassembly - 2•39
        removal and installation - 2•39
    shift drum and forks, removal, inspection and installation - 2•38
Transmission oil level check - 0•12
Troubleshooting - REF•27
Troubleshooting equipment - REF•36
Tube tires, removal and installation - 7•14
Tubeless tires, general information - 7•14
Tubes, repair - 7•15
Tune-up and routine maintenance - 1•1 through 1•22
Turn signal circuit, check - 9•11
Turn signal, tail/brake light and license plate light bulbs, replacement - 9•10
Twin carburetors
    removal and installation - 4A•9
    separation and reconnection - 4A•10

V

Valve clearances, check and adjustment - 1•12
Valves/valve seats/valve guides, servicing - 2•16
Voltage regulator/rectifier, check and replacement - 9•20

W

Water pump, check, removal, inspection and installation - 3•5
Wheel
    bearings, inspection and maintenance - 7•13
    removal, inspection and installation
        front - 7•11
        rear - 7•12
    tube tires, removal and installation - 7•14
    tubeless tires, general information - 7•14
    ubes, repair - 7•15
Wheels, inspection, repair and alignment check - 7•11
Wiring diagrams - 9•22
Workshop tips and tools - REF•4